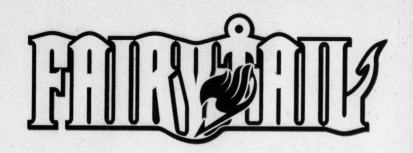

13

Hiro Mashima

Translated and adapted by William Flanagan
Lettered by North Market Street Graphics

KODANSHA COMICS

Fairy Tail volume 13 is a work of fiction. Names, characters, places, and incidents are the products of the author's imagination or are used fictitiously. Any resemblance to actual events, locales, or persons, living or dead, is entirely coincidental.

A Kodansha Comics Trade Paperback Original.

Published in the United States by Kodansha Comics, an imprint of Kodansha USA Publishing, LLC., New York.

Publication rights for this English edition arranged through Kodansha Ltd., Tokyo.

First published in Japan in 2008 by Kodansha Ltd., Tokyo.

ISBN 978-1-935-42932-6

Printed in the United States of America.

www.kodanshacomics.com

9 8 7 6 5 4 3 2 1

Translator/Adapter: William Flanagan
Lettering: North Market Street Graphics

Contents

Honorifics Explained

Throughout the Kodansha Comics books, you will find Japanese honorifics left intact in the translations. For those not familiar with how the Japanese use honorifics and, more important, how they differ from American honorifics, we present this brief overview.

Politeness has always been a critical facet of Japanese culture. Ever since the feudal era, when Japan was a highly stratified society, use of honorifics—which can be defined as polite speech that indicates relationship or status—has played an essential role in the Japanese language. When addressing someone in Japanese, an honorific usually takes the form of a suffix attached to one's name (example: "Asuna-san"), is used as a title at the end of one's name, or appears in place of the name itself (example: "Negi-sensei," or simply "Sensei!").

Honorifics can be expressions of respect or endearment. In the context of manga and anime, honorifics give insight into the nature of the relationship between characters. Many English translations leave out these important honorifics and therefore distort the feel of the original Japanese. Because Japanese honorifics contain nuances that English honorifics lack, it is our policy at Kodansha Comics not to translate them. Here, instead, is a guide to some of the honorifics you may encounter in Kodansha Comics Manga.

-san: This is the most common honorific and is equivalent to Mr., Miss, Ms., or Mrs. It is the all-purpose honorific and can be used in any situation where politeness is required.

-sama: This is one level higher than "-san" and is used to confer great respect.

-dono: This comes from the word "tono," which means "lord." It is an even higher level than "-sama" and confers utmost respect.

-kun: This suffix is used at the end of boys' names to express familiarity or endearment. It is also sometimes used by men among friends, or when addressing someone younger or of a lower station.

-chan: This is used to express endearment, mostly toward girls. It is also used for little boys, pets, and even among lovers. It gives a sense of childish cuteness.

Bozu: This is an informal way to refer to a boy, similar to the English terms "kid" and "squirt."

Sempai/
Senpai: This title suggests that the addressee is one's senior in a group or organization. It is most often used in a school setting, where underclassmen refer to their upperclassmen as "sempai." It can also be used in the workplace, such as when a newer employee addresses an employee who has seniority in the company.

Kohai: This is the opposite of "sempai" and is used toward underclassmen in school or newcomers in the workplace. It connotes that the addressee is of a lower station.

Sensei: Literally meaning "one who has come before," this title is used for teachers, doctors, or masters of any profession or art.

-[blank]: This is usually forgotten in these lists, but it is perhaps the most significant difference between Japanese and English. The lack of honorific means that the speaker has permission to address the person in a very intimate way. Usually, only family, spouses, or very close friends have this kind of permission. Known as *yobisute*, it can be gratifying when someone who has earned the intimacy starts to call one by one's name without an honorific. But when that intimacy hasn't been earned, it can be very insulting.

FAIRY TAIL

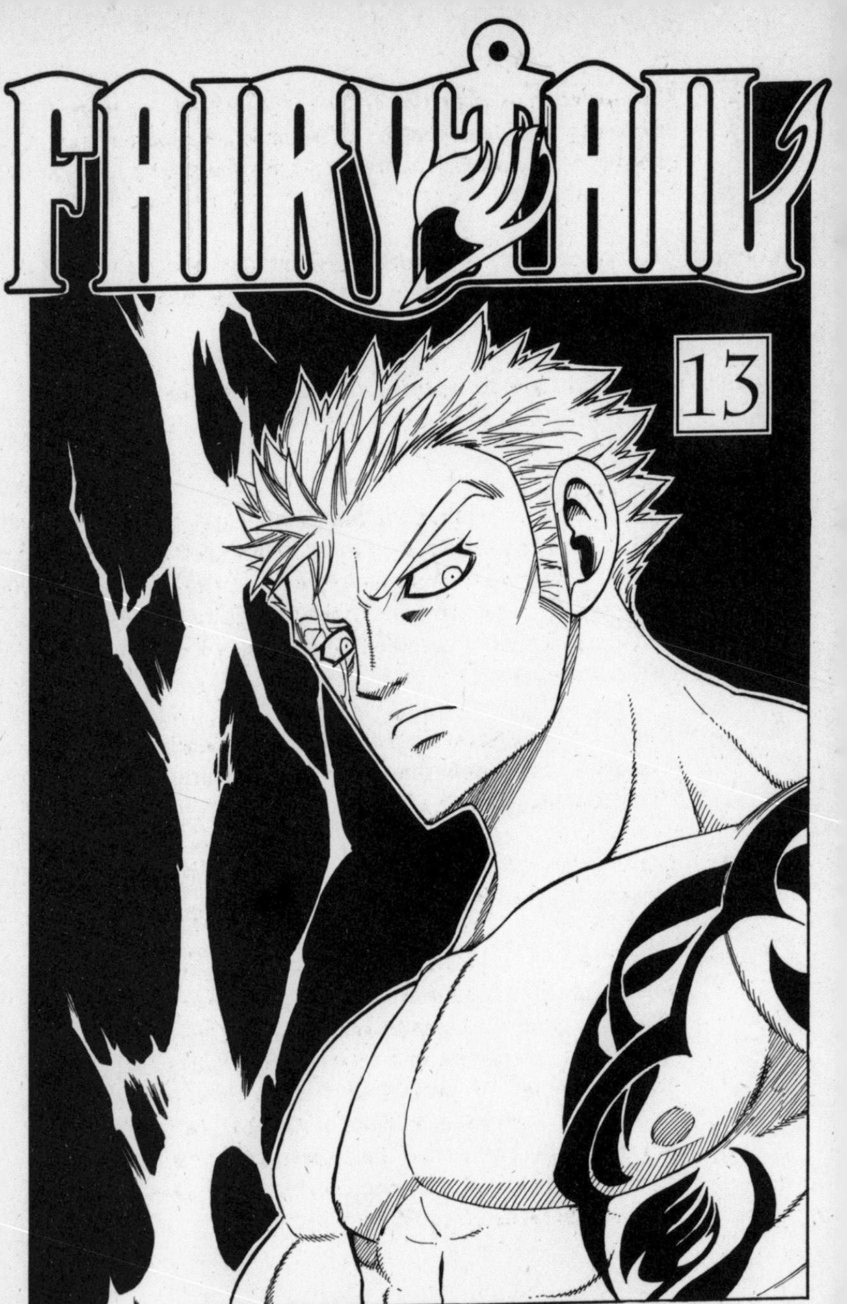
13

HIRO MASHIMA

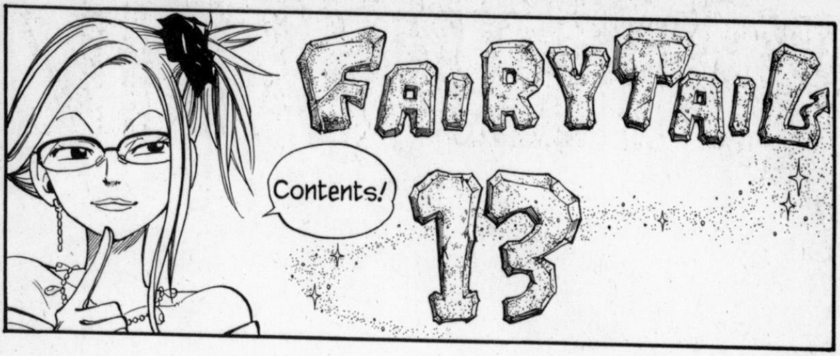
FAIRY TAIL
13
Contents!

FAIRY TAIL

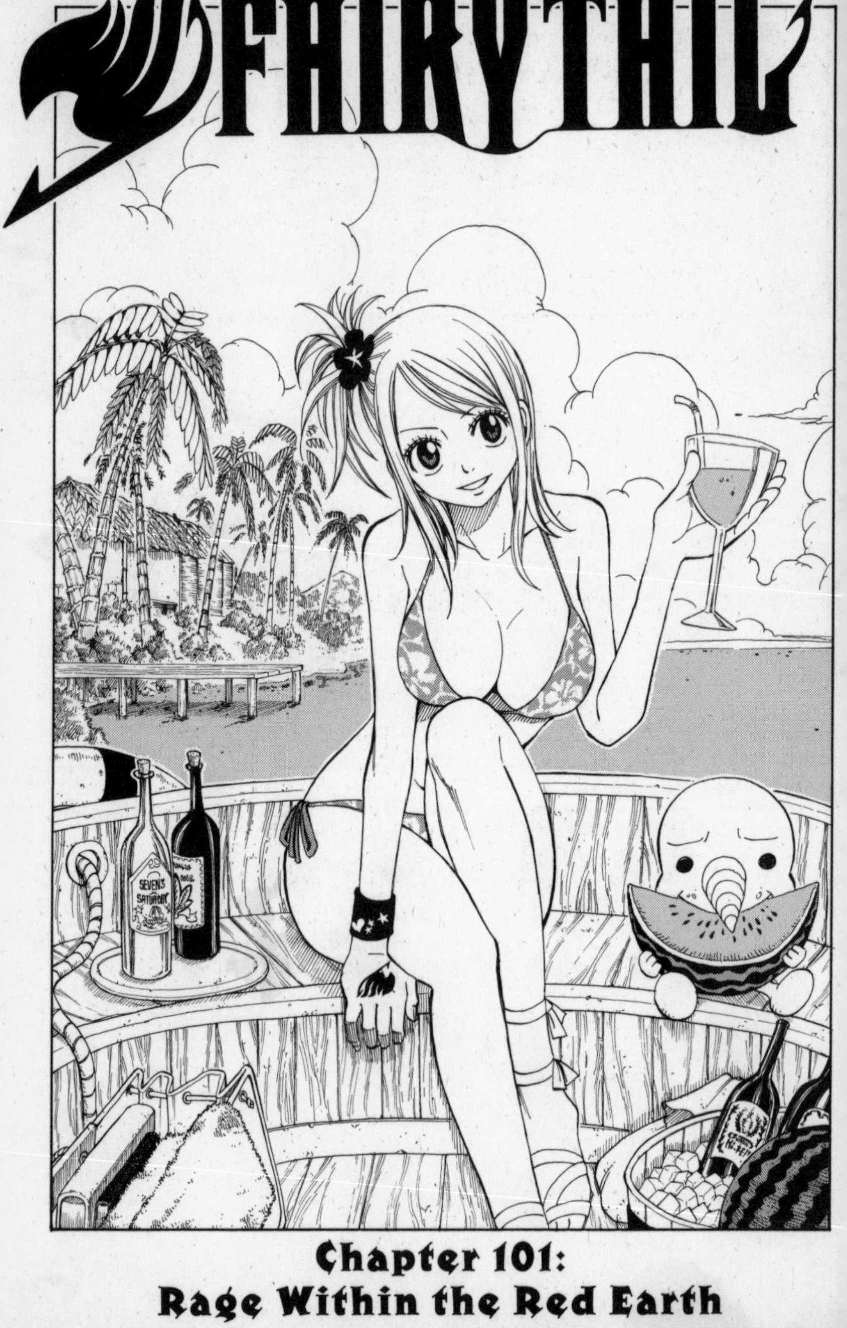
SEVEN'S SATURDAY

Chapter 101:
Rage Within the Red Earth

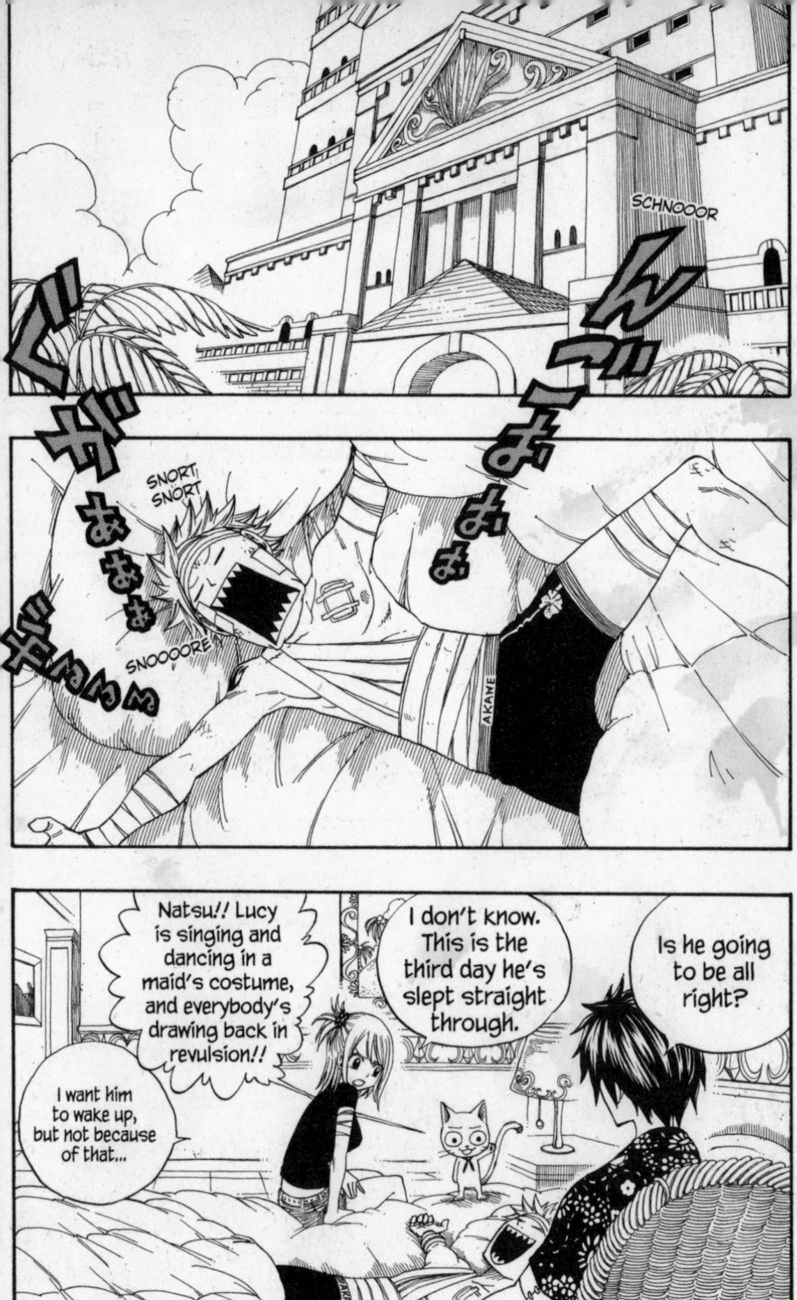
SCHNOOOR
SNORT SNORT
SNOOOORE
Is he going to be all right?
I don't know. This is the third day he's slept straight through.
Natsu!! Lucy is singing and dancing in a maid's costume, and everybody's drawing back in revulsion!!
I want him to wake up, but not because of that...

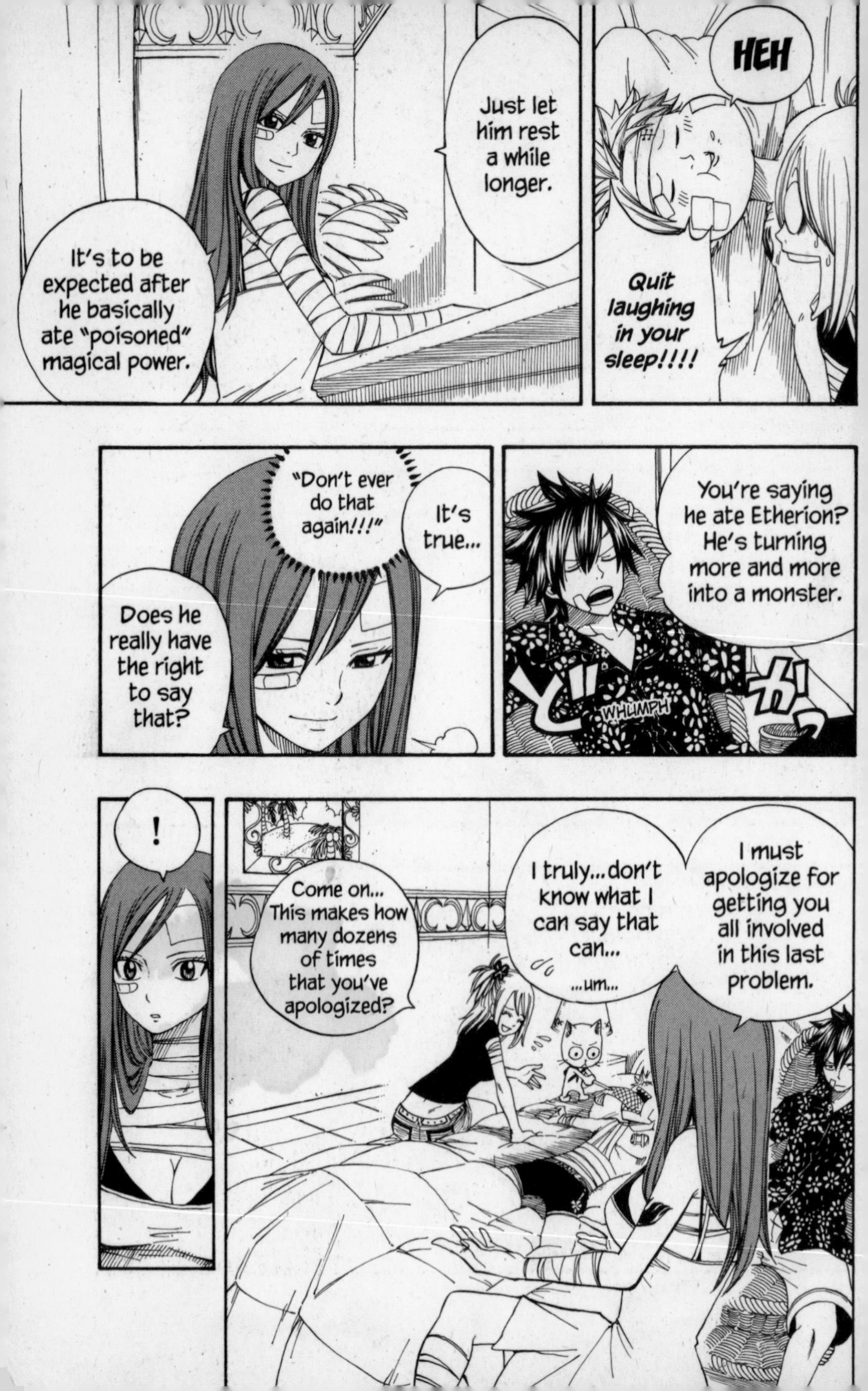
HEH
Quit laughing in your sleep!!!!
Just let him rest a while longer.
It's to be expected after he basically ate "poisoned" magical power.
You're saying he ate Etherion? He's turning more and more into a monster.
WHUMPH
It's true...
"Don't ever do that again!!!"
Does he really have the right to say that?
I must apologize for getting you all involved in this last problem.
I truly...don't know what I can say that can...
...um...
Come on... This makes how many dozens of times that you've apologized?
!

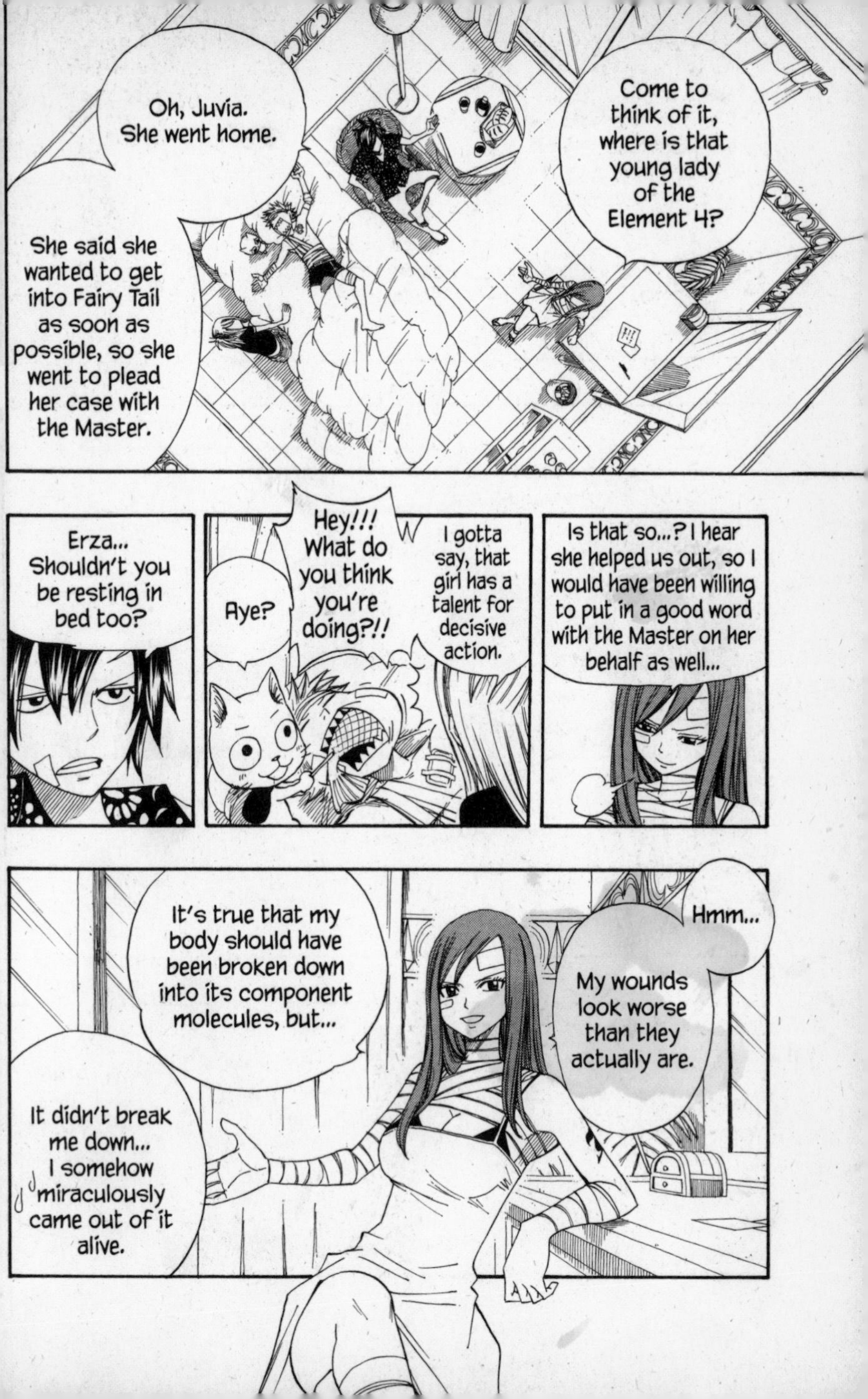
Come to think of it, where is that young lady of the Element 4?
Oh, Juvia. She went home.
She said she wanted to get into Fairy Tail as soon as possible, so she went to plead her case with the Master.
Is that so...? I hear she helped us out, so I would have been willing to put in a good word with the Master on her behalf as well...
I gotta say, that girl has a talent for decisive action.
Hey!!! What do you think you're doing?!!
Aye?
Erza... Shouldn't you be resting in bed too?
Hmm...
My wounds look worse than they actually are.
It's true that my body should have been broken down into its component molecules, but...
It didn't break me down... I somehow miraculously came out of it alive.

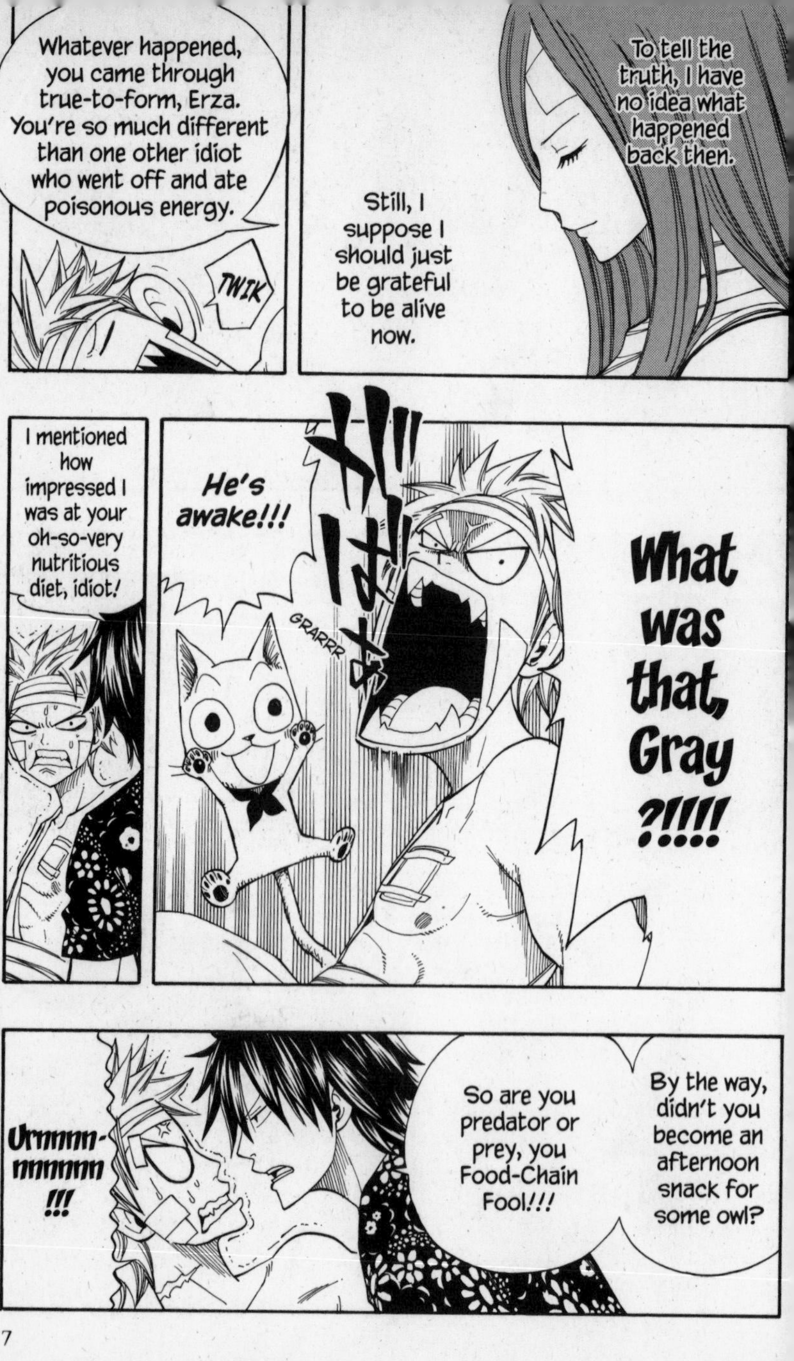

To tell the truth, I have no idea what happened back then.
Still, I suppose I should just be grateful to be alive now.
Whatever happened, you came through true-to-form, Erza. You're so much different than one other idiot who went off and ate poisonous energy.
TWIK
What was that, Gray ?!!!!
He's awake!!!
GRARRR
I mentioned how impressed I was at your oh-so-very nutritious diet, idiot!
By the way, didn't you become an afternoon snack for some owl?
So are you predator or prey, you Food-Chain Fool!!!
Urnnnn-nnnnnn !!!

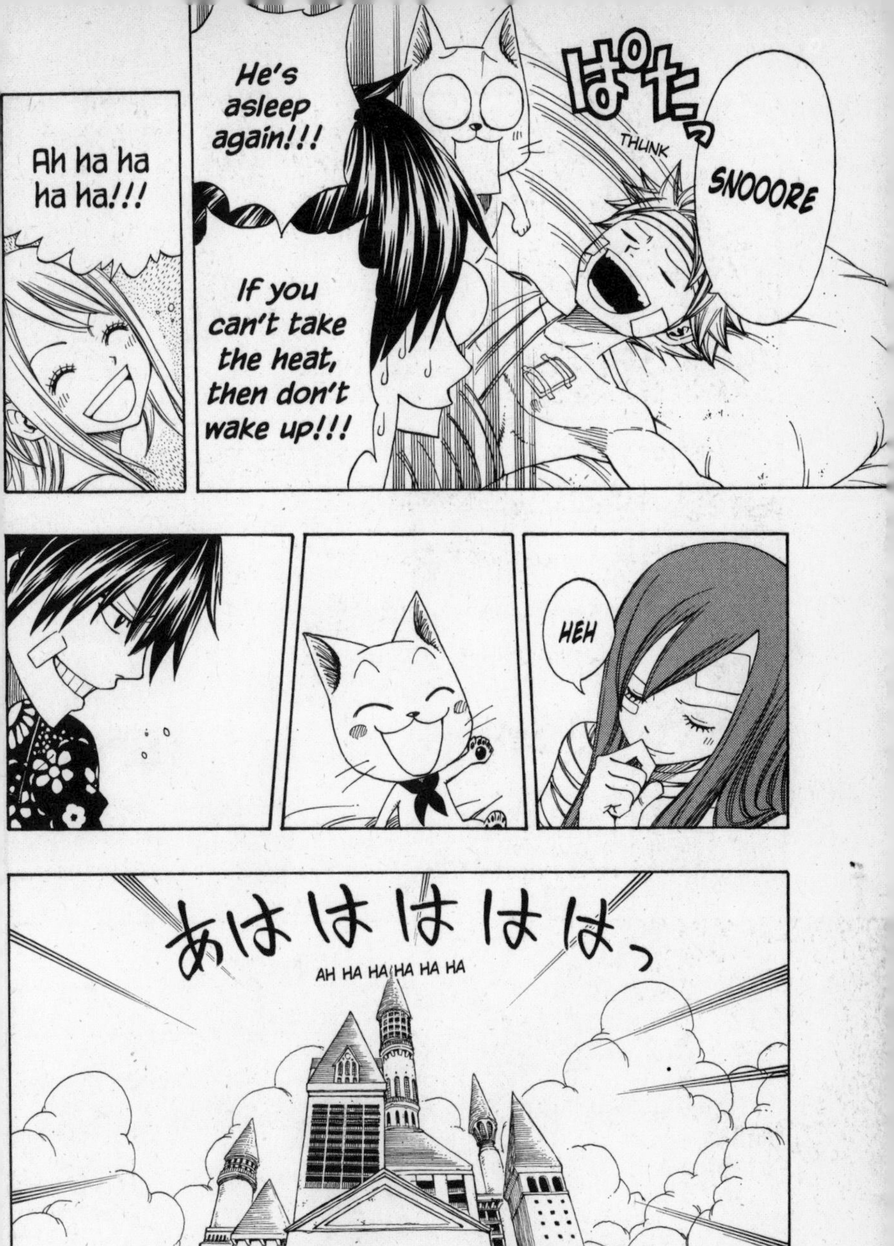
ぱたっ
THUNK
SNOOORE
He's asleep again!!!
If you can't take the heat, then don't wake up!!!
Ah ha ha ha ha!!!
HEH
あははははは っ
AH HA HA HA HA HA

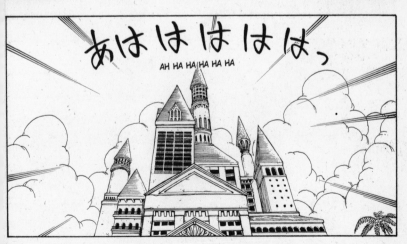

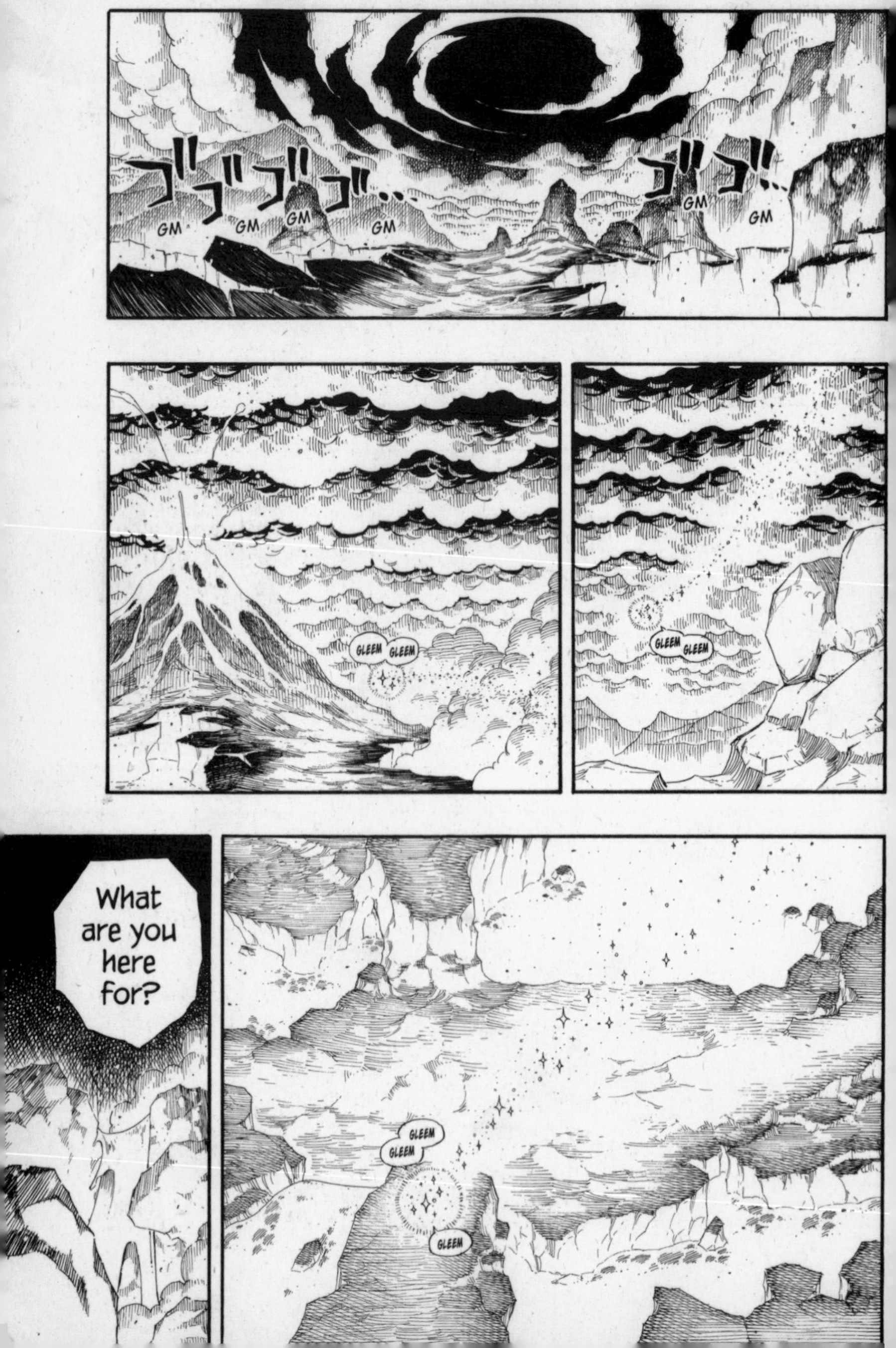
ゴゴ!!…
GM
GM
ゴゴゴゴ…
GM
GM
GM
GM
GLEEM
GLEEM
GLEEM
GLEEM
GLEEM
GLEEM
GLEEM
What are you here for?

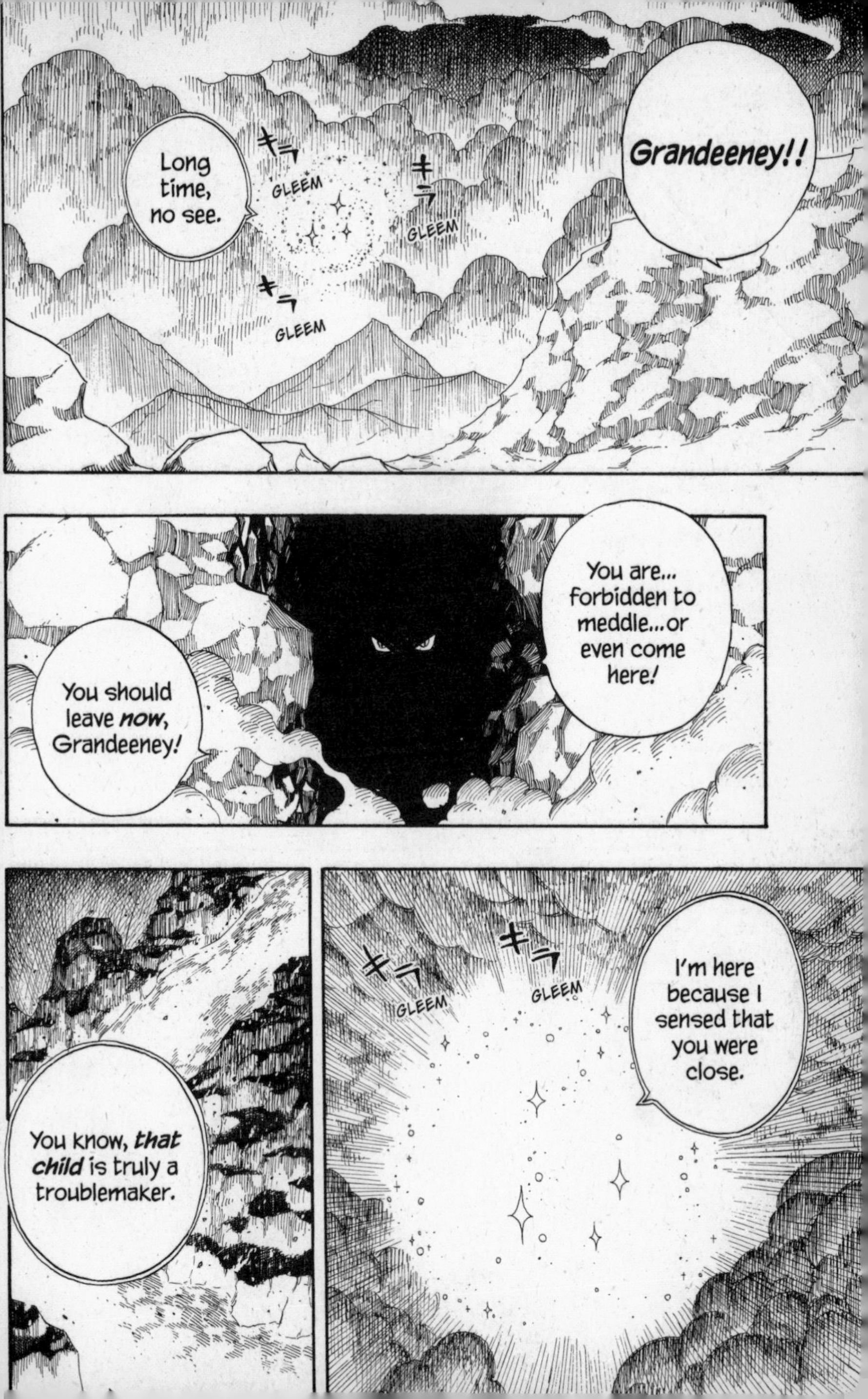
Grandeeney!!
キラ
GLEEM
キラ
GLEEM
Long time, no see.
キラ
GLEEM
You are... forbidden to meddle...or even come here!
You should leave *now*, Grandeeney!
I'm here because I sensed that you were close.
キラ
GLEEM
キラ
GLEEM
You know, ***that child*** is truly a troublemaker.

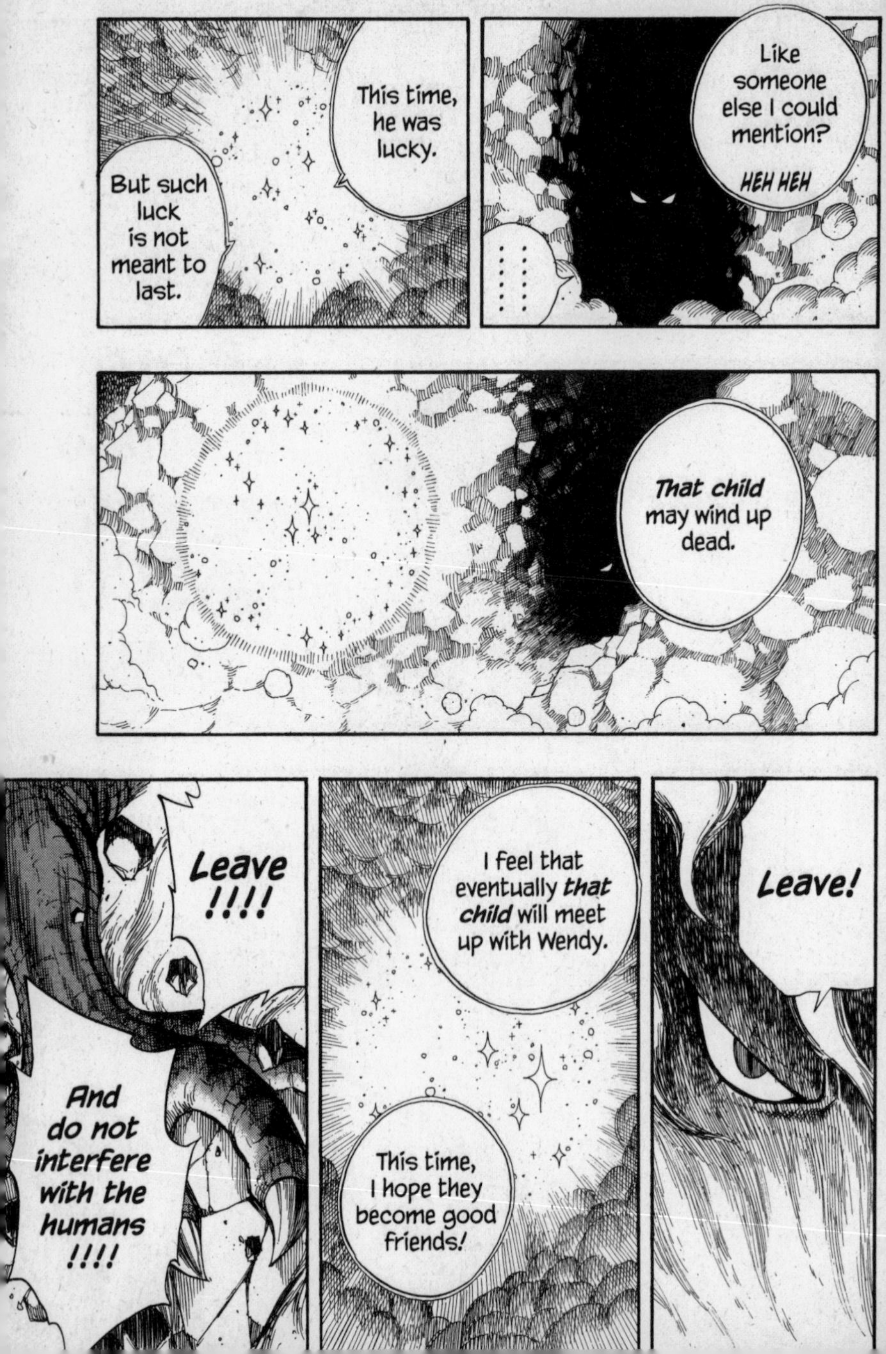

Like someone else I could mention?
HEH HEH
......
This time, he was lucky.
But such luck is not meant to last.
That child may wind up dead.
Leave!
I feel that eventually *that child* will meet up with Wendy.
This time, I hope they become good friends!
Leave!!!!
And do not interfere with the humans!!!!

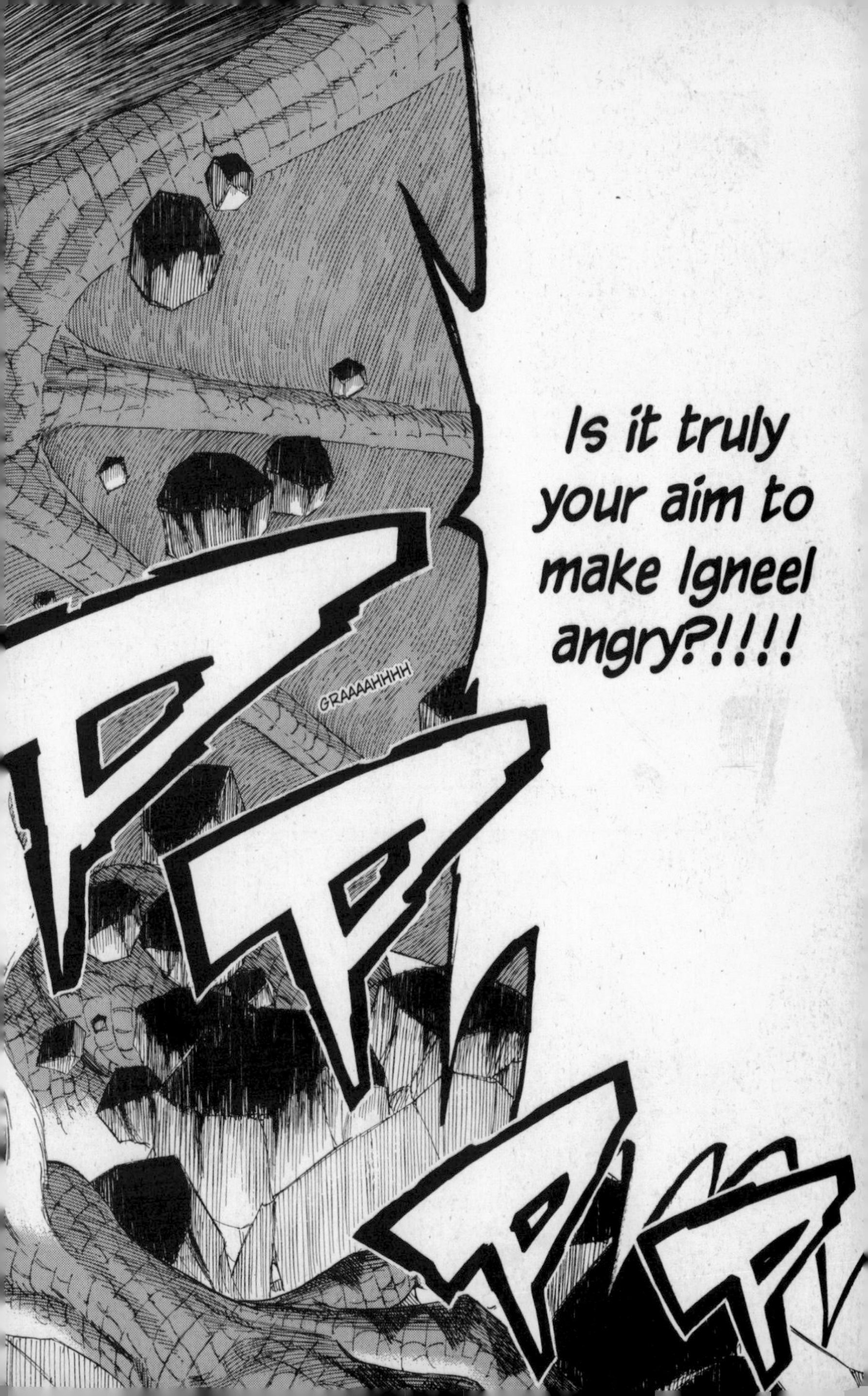
Is it truly your aim to make Igneel angry?!!!!
GRAAAAHHHH

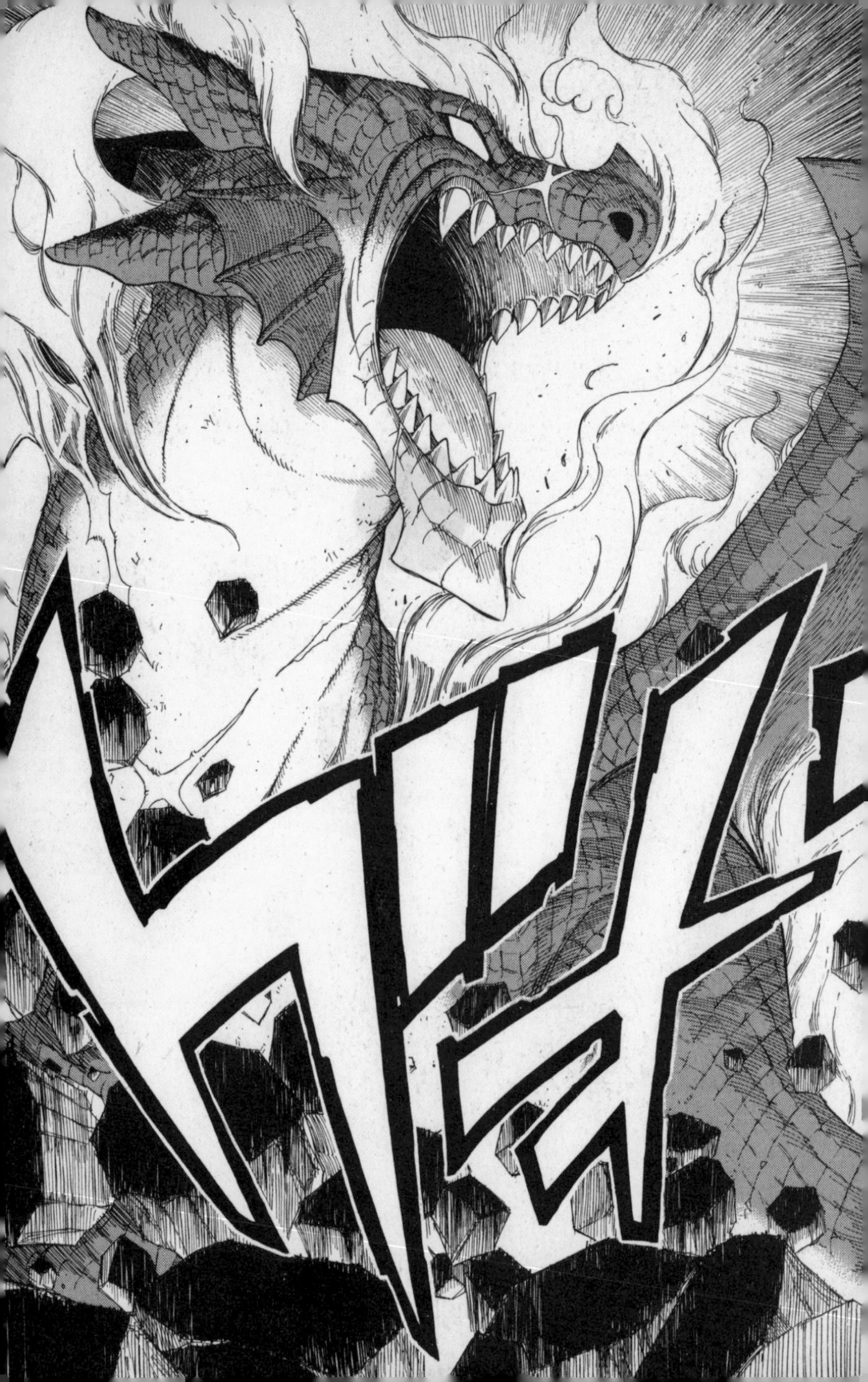

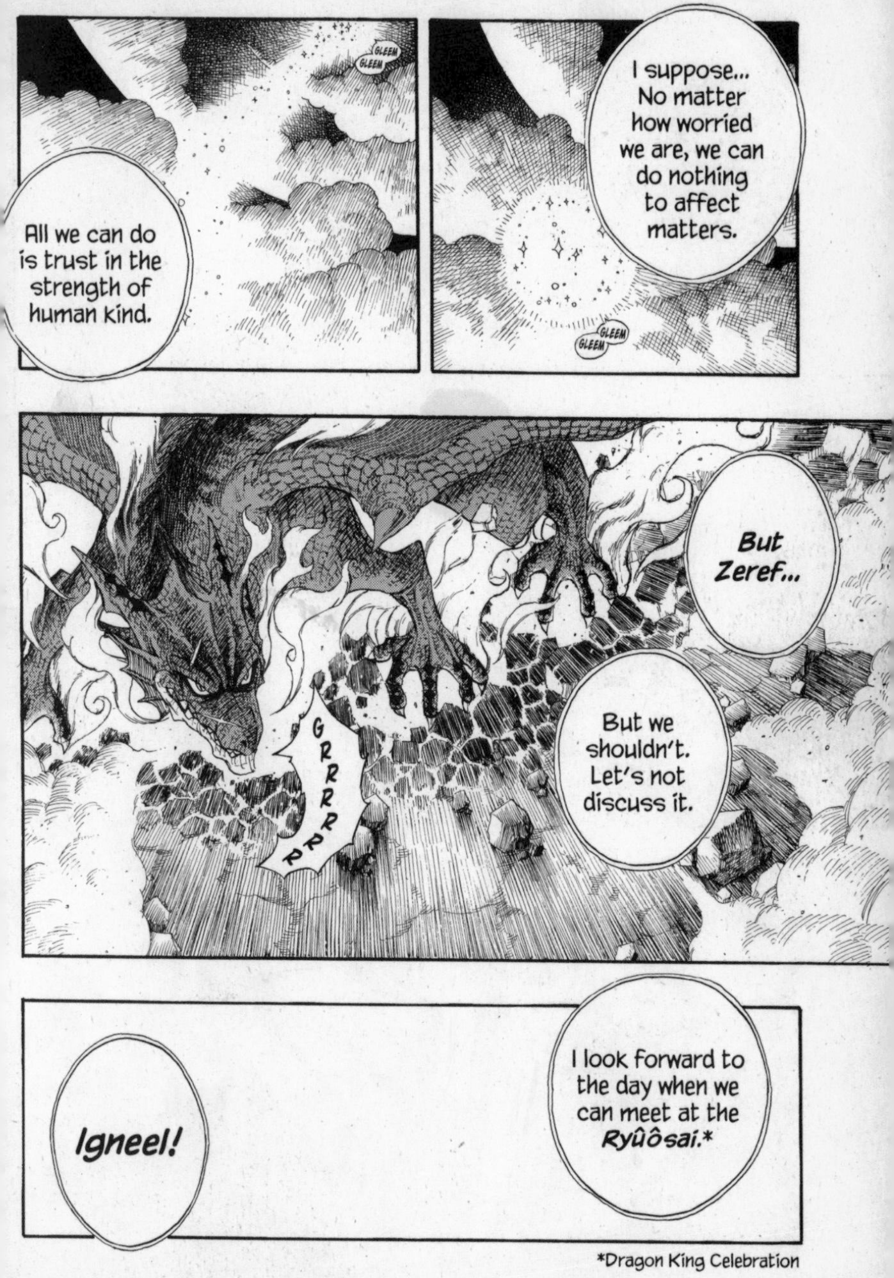
GLEEM GLEEM
I suppose... No matter how worried we are, we can do nothing to affect matters.
GLEEM GLEEM
All we can do is trust in the strength of human kind.
But Zeref...
But we shouldn't. Let's not discuss it.
GRRRRRR
I look forward to the day when we can meet at the *Ryûôsai.**
Igneel!

*Dragon King Celebration

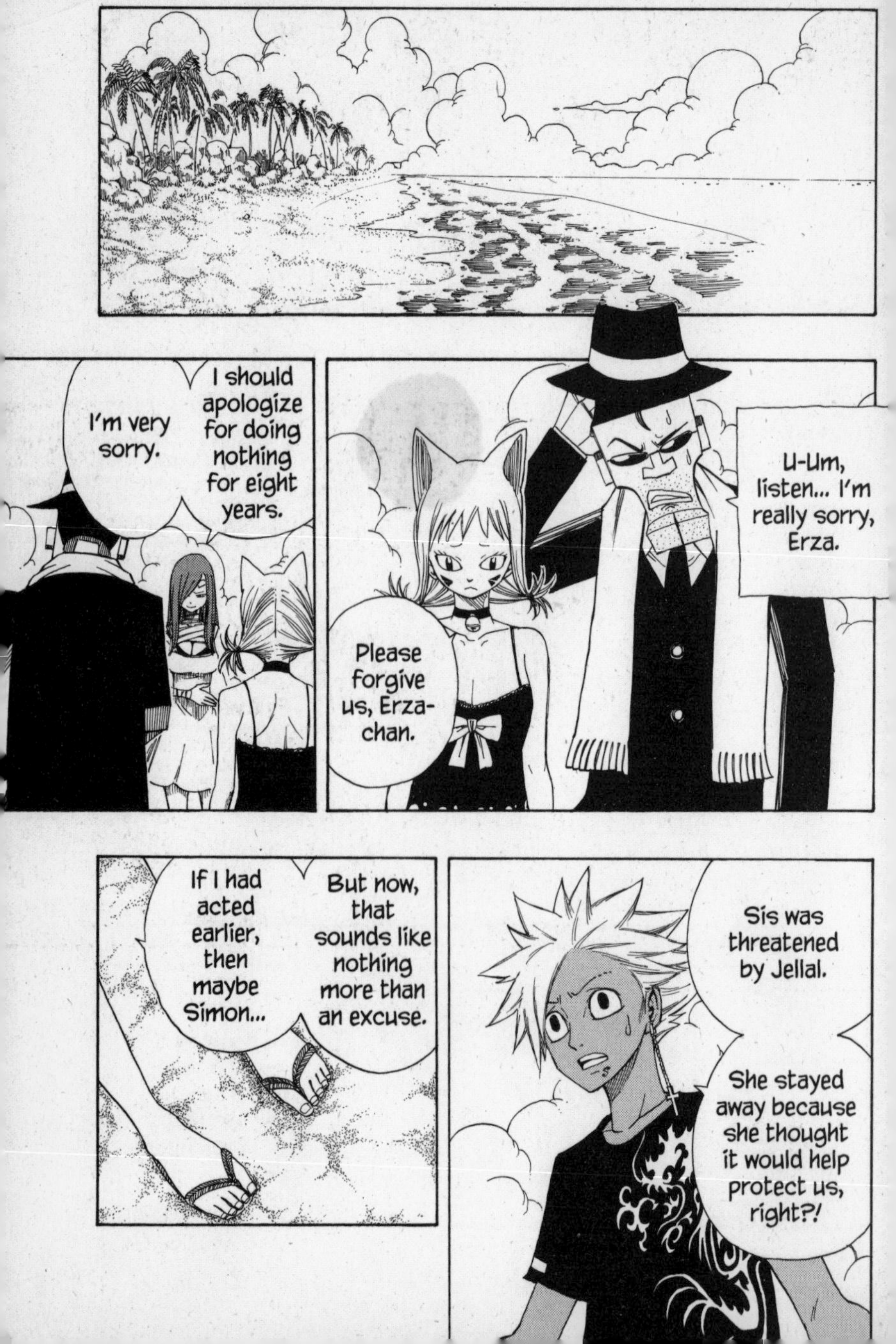
U-Um, listen... I'm really sorry, Erza.
Please forgive us, Erza-chan.
I should apologize for doing nothing for eight years.
I'm very sorry.
Sis was threatened by Jellal.
She stayed away because she thought it would help protect us, right?!
But now, that sounds like nothing more than an excuse.
If I had acted earlier, then maybe Simon...

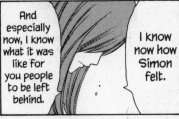

And especially now, I know what it was like for you people to be left behind.

I know now how Simon felt.

Simon was a true man!! H-He wanted to be the man to protect you, Erza, for so long...

Wally!!!

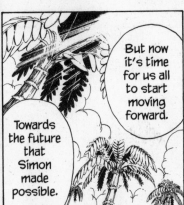

But now it's time for us all to start moving forward.

Towards the future that Simon made possible.

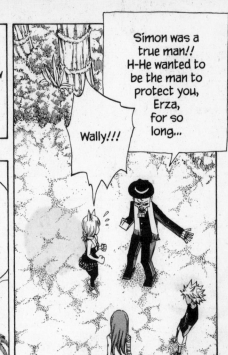

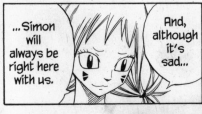

...Simon will always be right here with us.

And, although it's sad...

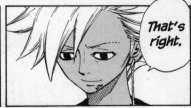

That's right.

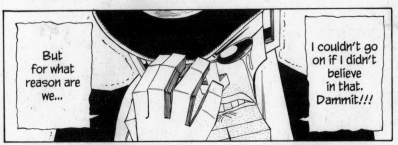

But for what reason are we...

I couldn't go on if I didn't believe in that. Dammit!!!

16

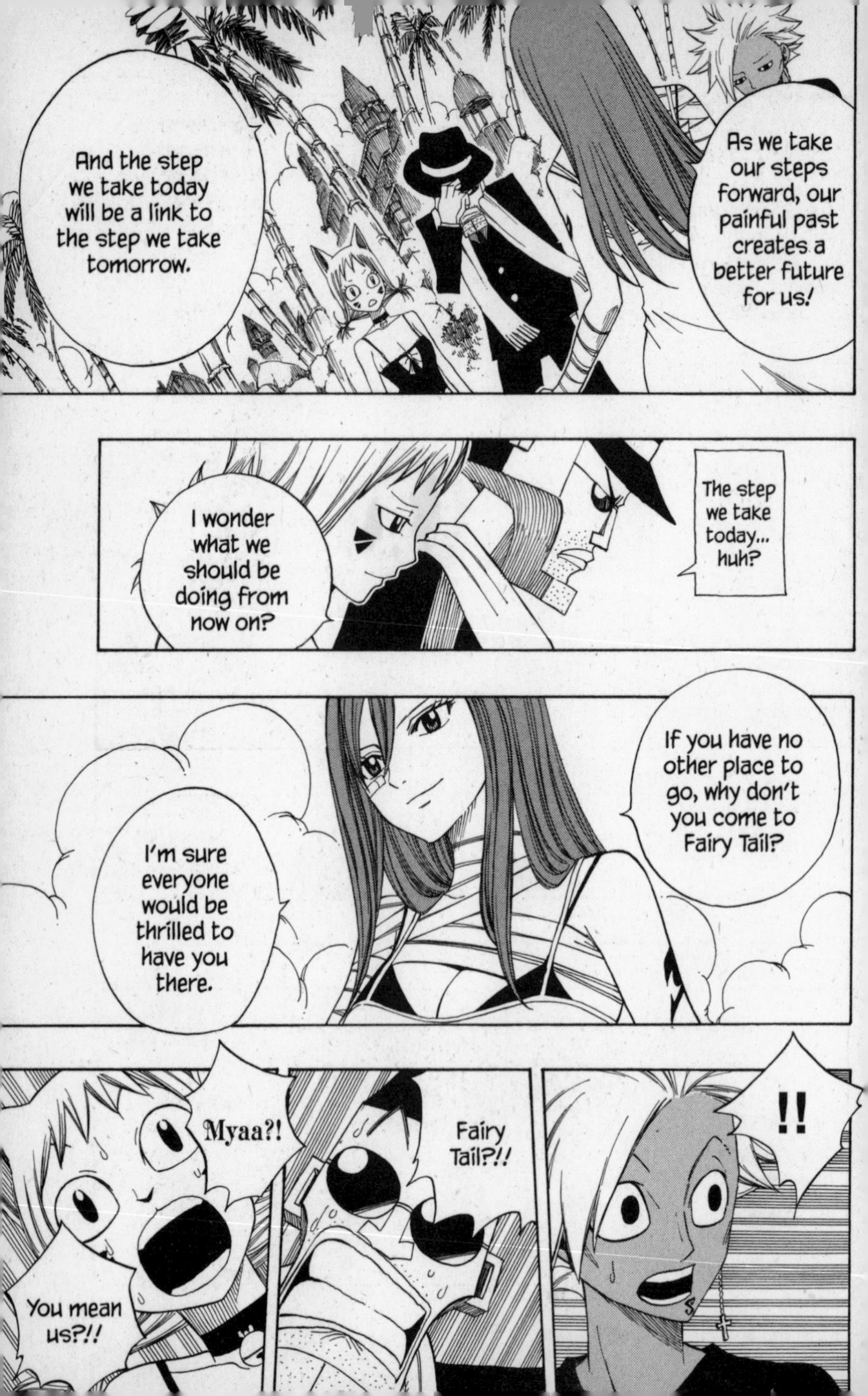
As we take our steps forward, our painful past creates a better future for us!
And the step we take today will be a link to the step we take tomorrow.
The step we take today... huh?
I wonder what we should be doing from now on?
If you have no other place to go, why don't you come to Fairy Tail?
I'm sure everyone would be thrilled to have you there.
!!
Fairy Tail?!!
Myaa?!
You mean us?!!

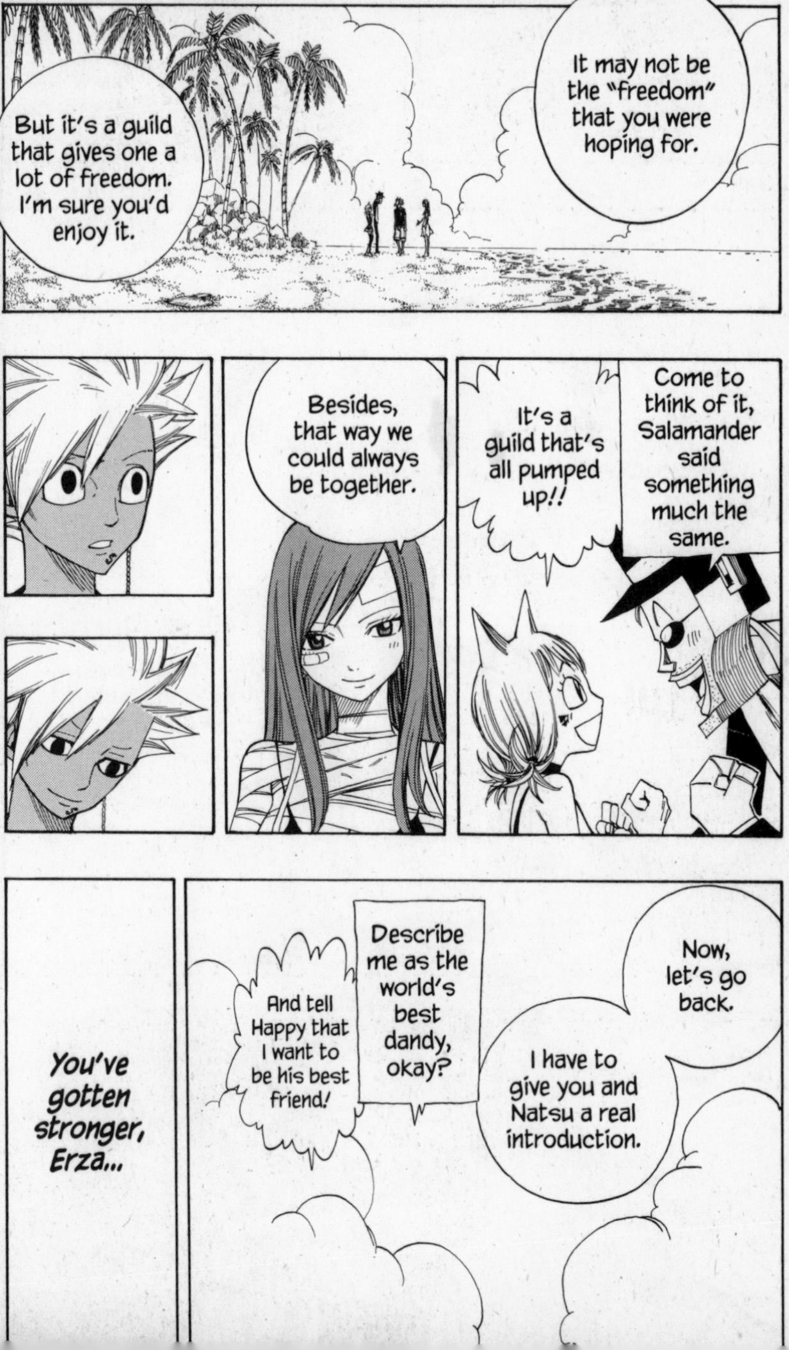
It may not be the "freedom" that you were hoping for.
But it's a guild that gives one a lot of freedom. I'm sure you'd enjoy it.
Come to think of it, Salamander said something much the same.
It's a guild that's all pumped up!!
Besides, that way we could always be together.
Now, let's go back.
I have to give you and Natsu a real introduction.
Describe me as the world's best dandy, okay?
And tell Happy that I want to be his best friend!
You've gotten stronger, Erza...

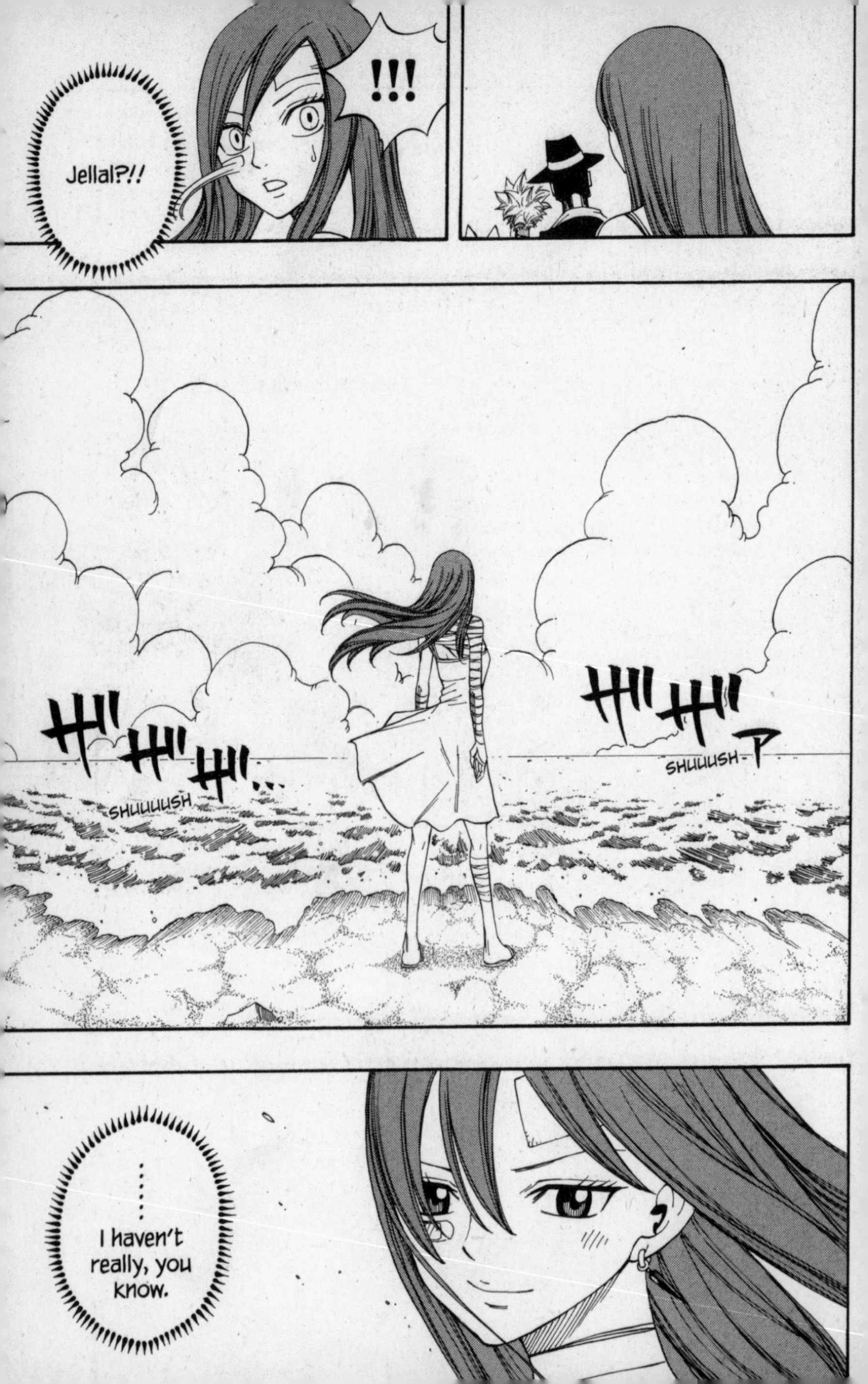
!!!
Jellal?!!
ザザァ
SHUUUSH-
ザザザ…
SHUUUUSH
……
I haven't really, you know.

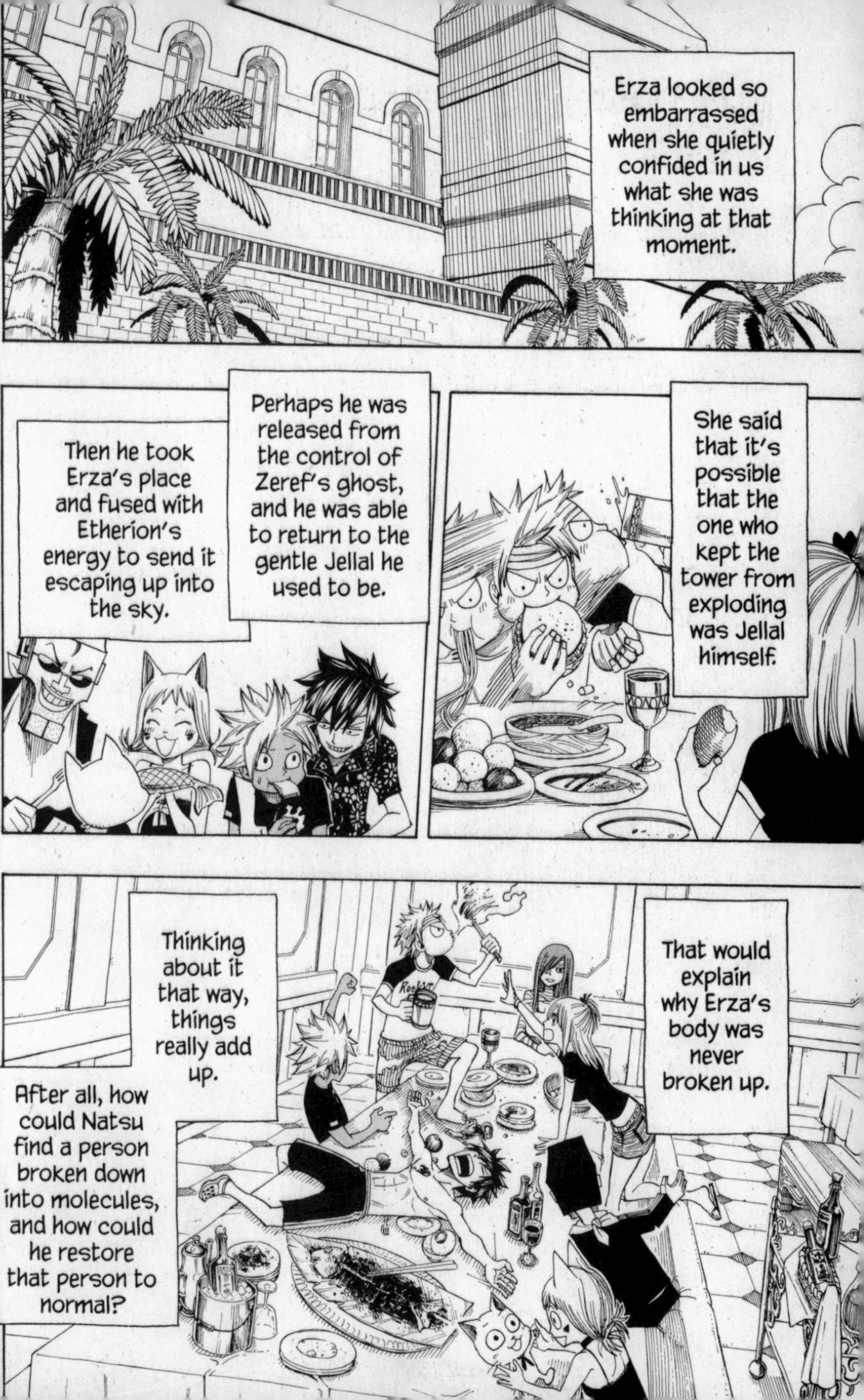
Erza looked so embarrassed when she quietly confided in us what she was thinking at that moment.
She said that it's possible that the one who kept the tower from exploding was Jellal himself.
Perhaps he was released from the control of Zeref's ghost, and he was able to return to the gentle Jellal he used to be.
Then he took Erza's place and fused with Etherion's energy to send it escaping up into the sky.
That would explain why Erza's body was never broken up.
Thinking about it that way, things really add up.
After all, how could Natsu find a person broken down into molecules, and how could he restore that person to normal?

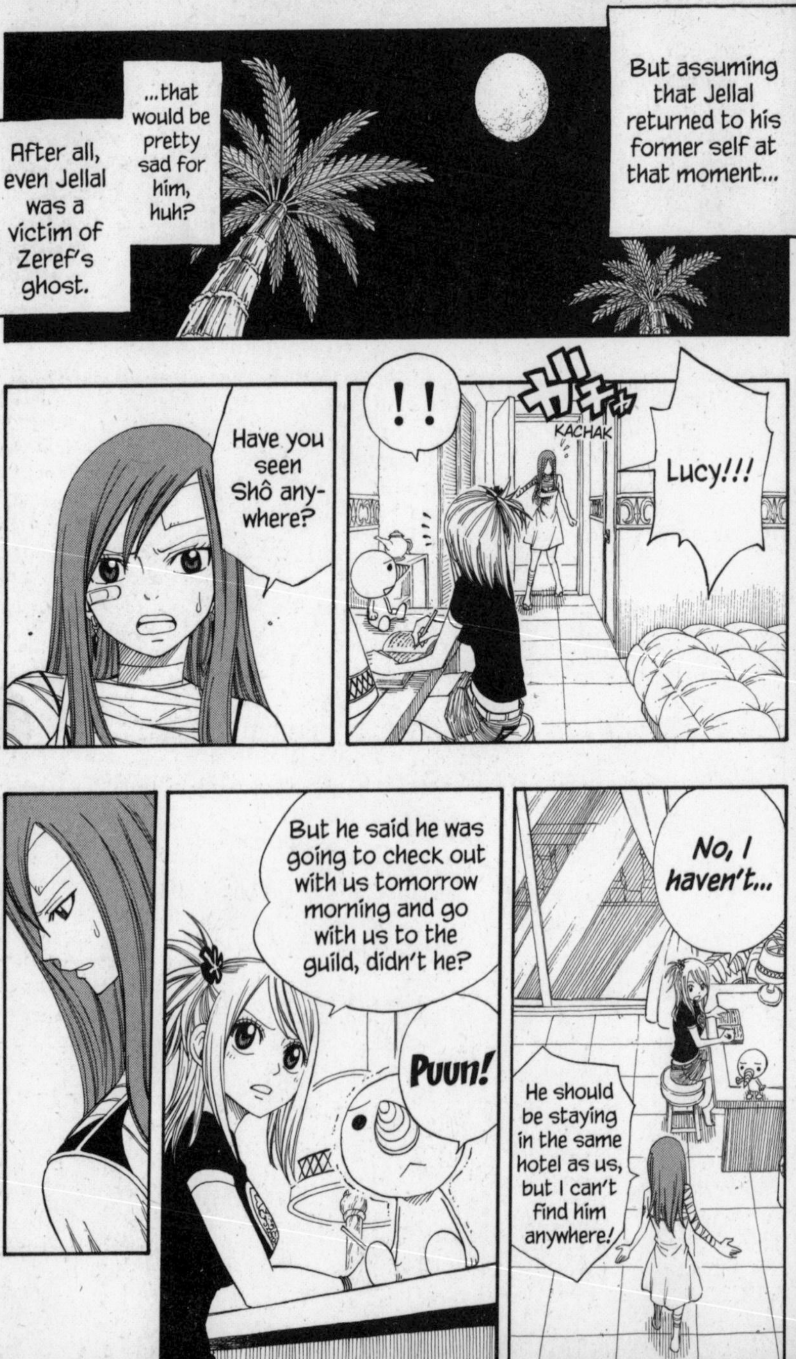
But assuming that Jellal returned to his former self at that moment...
...that would be pretty sad for him, huh?
After all, even Jellal was a victim of Zeref's ghost.
Lucy!!!
KACHAK
!!
Have you seen Shô any-where?
No, I haven't...
He should be staying in the same hotel as us, but I can't find him anywhere!
But he said he was going to check out with us tomorrow morning and go with us to the guild, didn't he?
Puun!

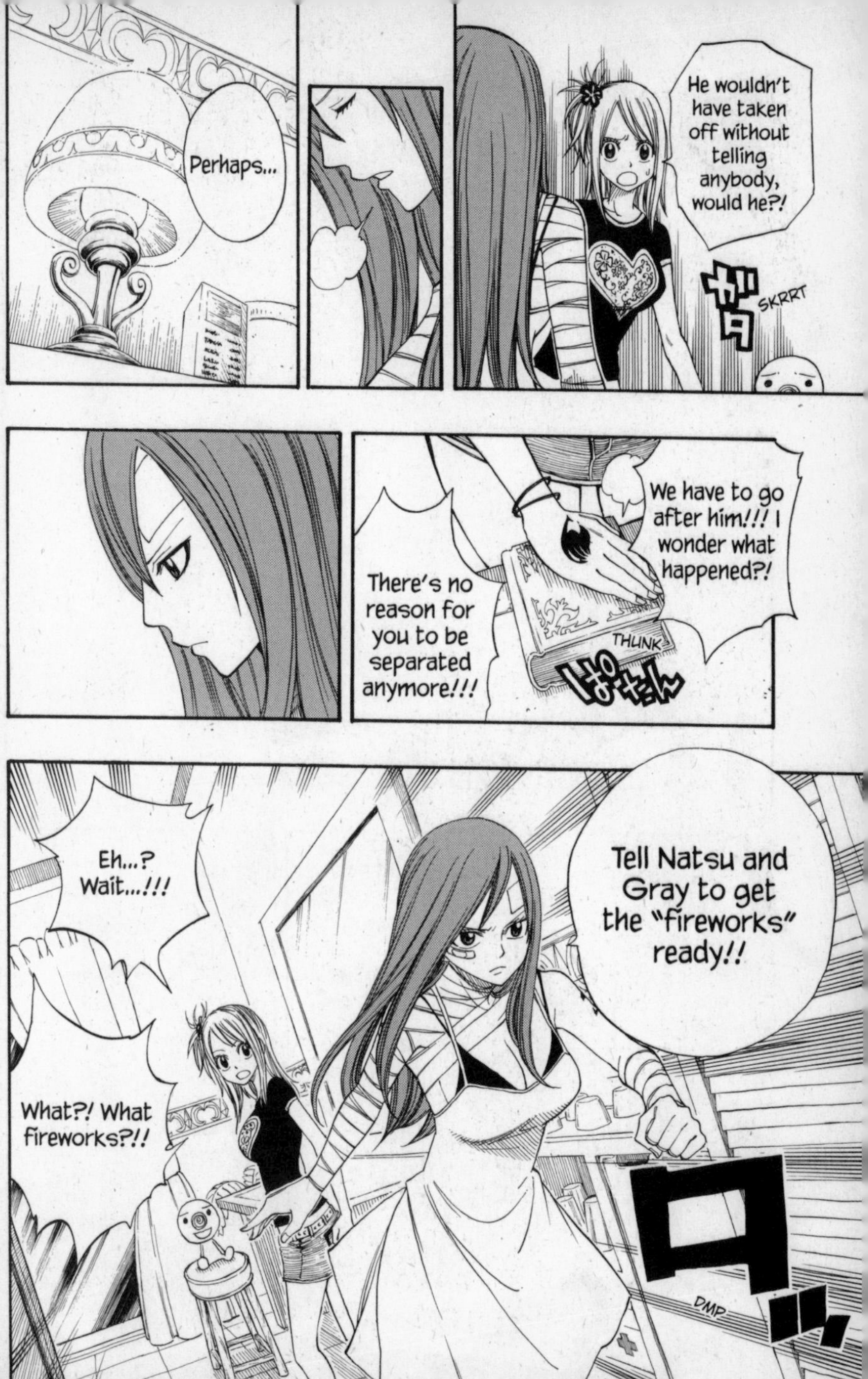
He wouldn't have taken off without telling anybody, would he?!
SKRRT
Perhaps...
We have to go after him!!! I wonder what happened?!
There's no reason for you to be separated anymore!!!
THUNK
Tell Natsu and Gray to get the "fireworks" ready!!
Eh...? Wait...!!!
What?! What fireworks?!!
DMP

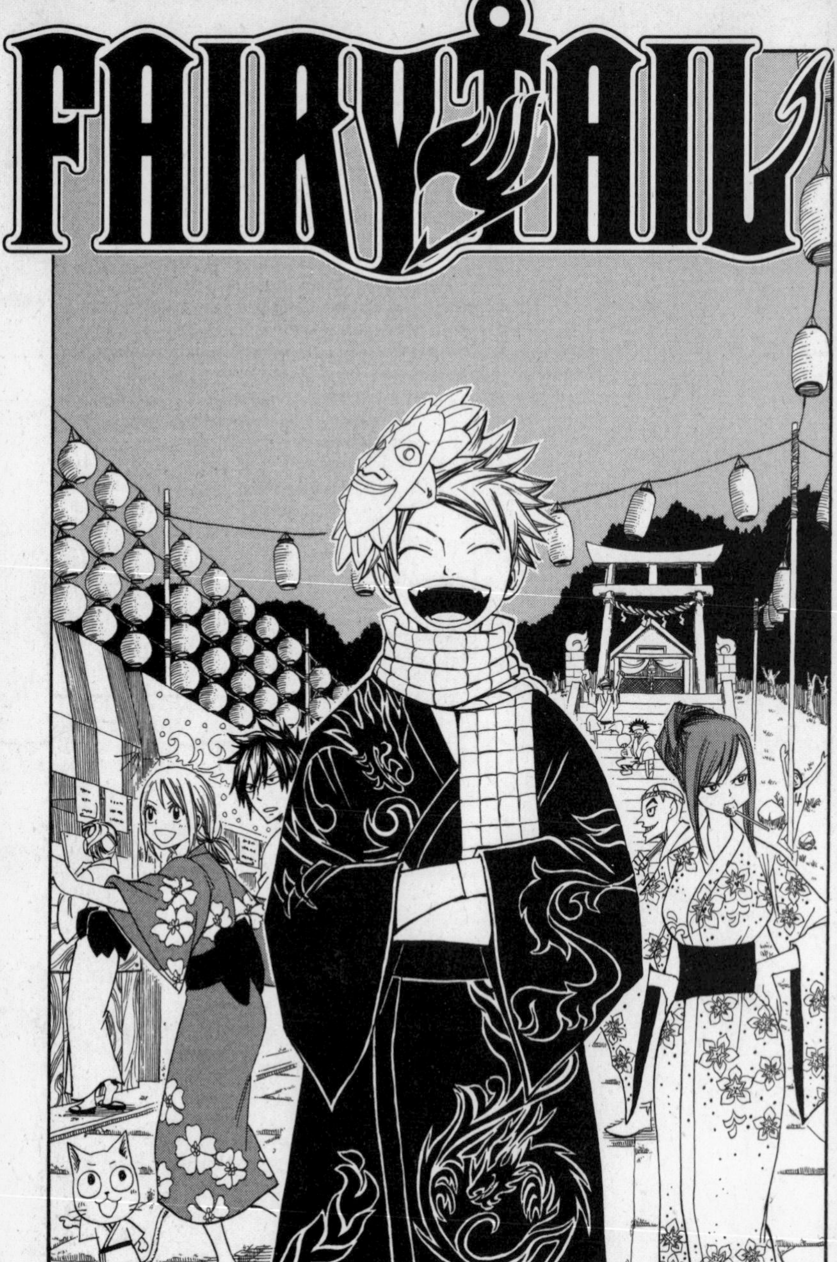
FAIRY TAIL

Chapter 102: Walk Strong

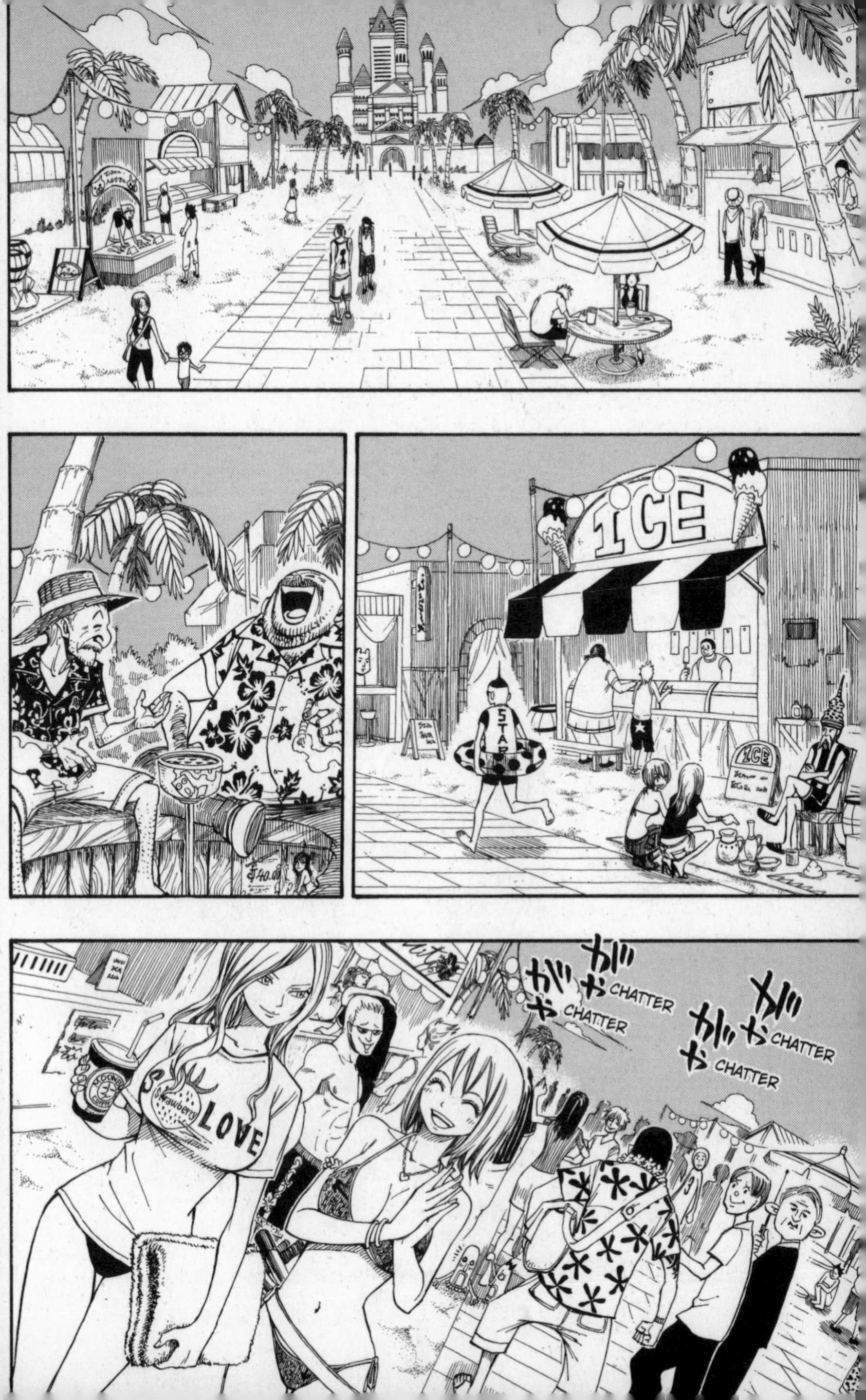
ICE
ICE
STAR
$40.00
Strawberry
LOVE
ガヤ CHATTER
ガヤ CHATTER
ガヤ CHATTER
ガヤ CHATTER

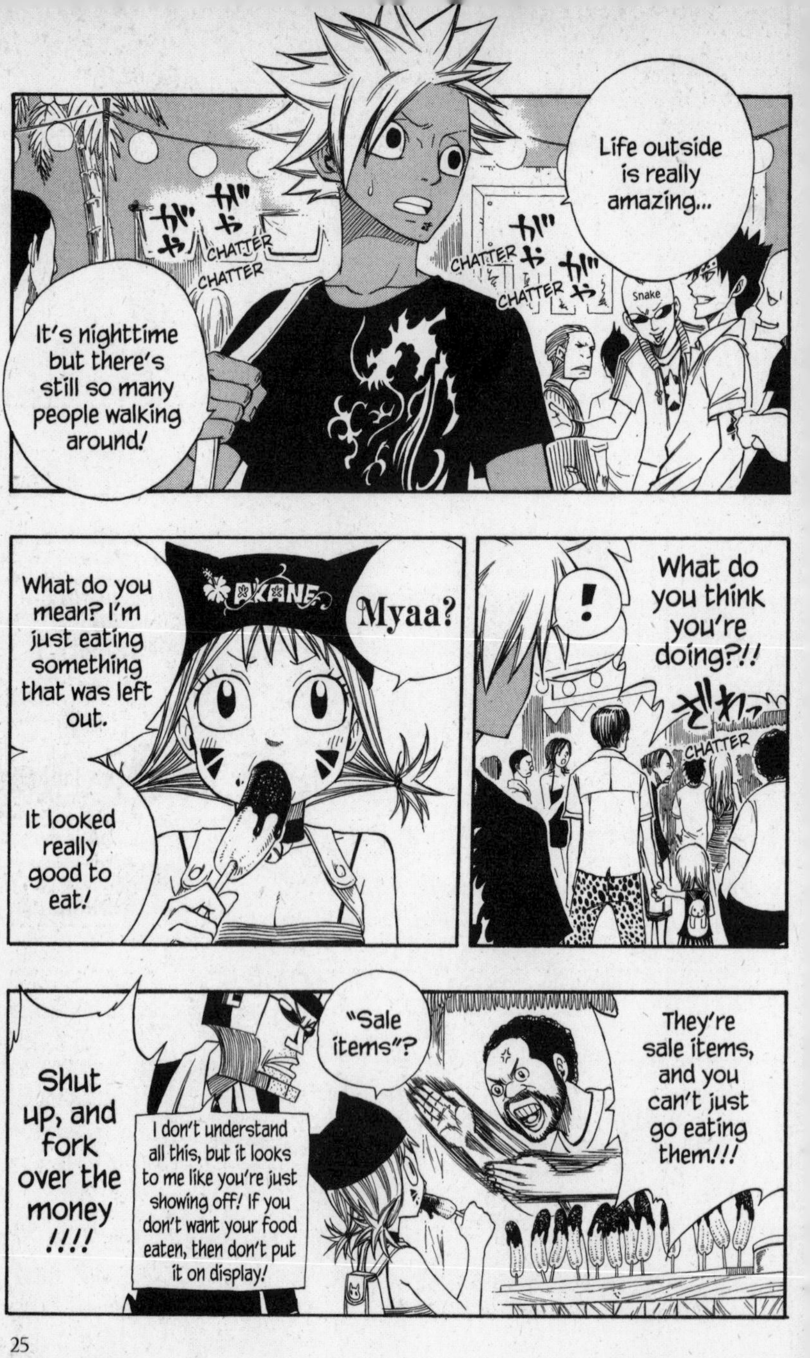
Life outside is really amazing...
ガヤ
CHATTER
ガヤ
CHATTER
ガヤ
CHATTER
ガヤ
CHATTER
Snake
It's nighttime but there's still so many people walking around!
!
What do you think you're doing?!!
ざわっ
CHATTER
Myaa?
What do you mean? I'm just eating something that was left out.
It looked really good to eat!
AKANE
They're sale items, and you can't just go eating them!!!
"Sale items"?
I don't understand all this, but it looks to me like you're just showing off! If you don't want your food eaten, then don't put it on display!
Shut up, and fork over the money !!!!

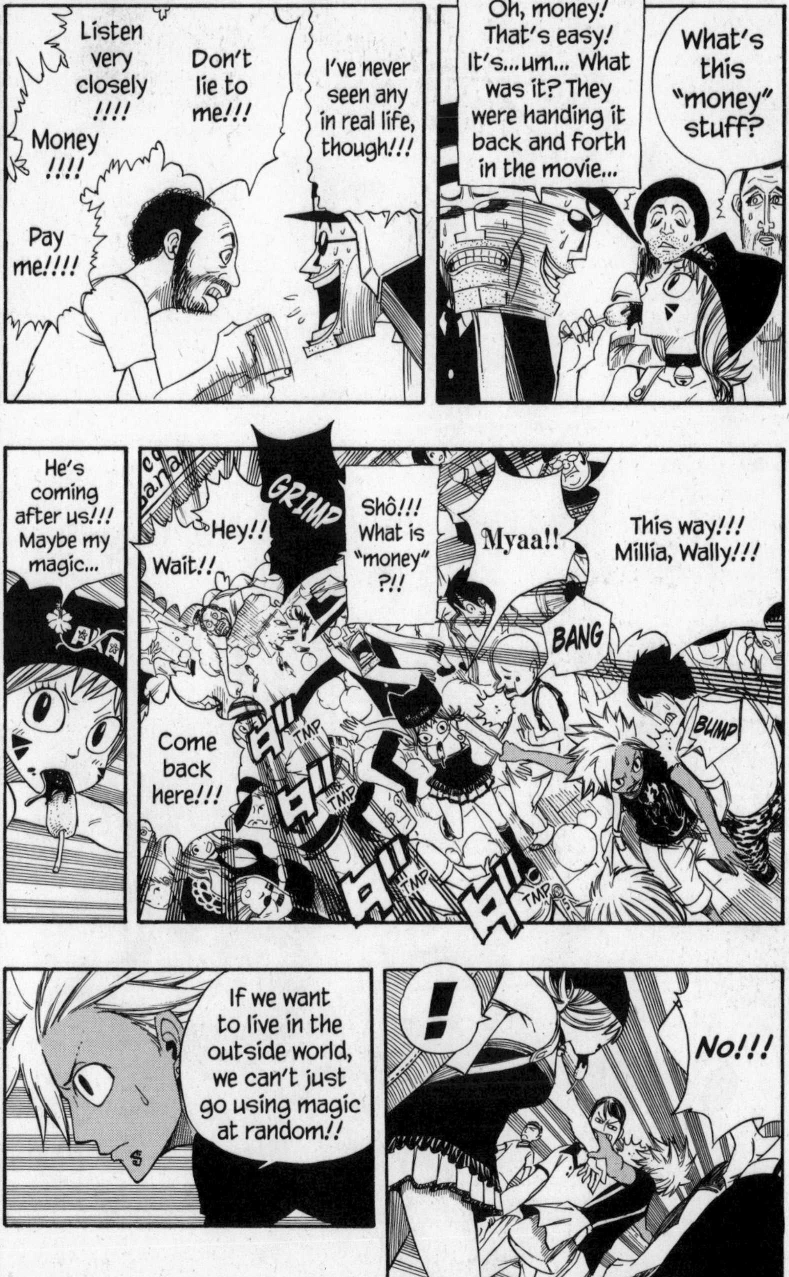
What's this "money" stuff?
Oh, money! That's easy! It's...um... What was it? They were handing it back and forth in the movie...
I've never seen any in real life, though!!!
Don't lie to me!!!
Listen very closely !!!!
Money !!!!
Pay me!!!!
This way!!! Millia, Wally!!!
BANG
BUMP
Myaa!!
Shô!!! What is "money" ?!!
GRIMP
Hey!!
Wait!!
Come back here!!!
TMP
TMP
TMP
TMP
He's coming after us!!! Maybe my magic...
No!!!
!
If we want to live in the outside world, we can't just go using magic at random!!

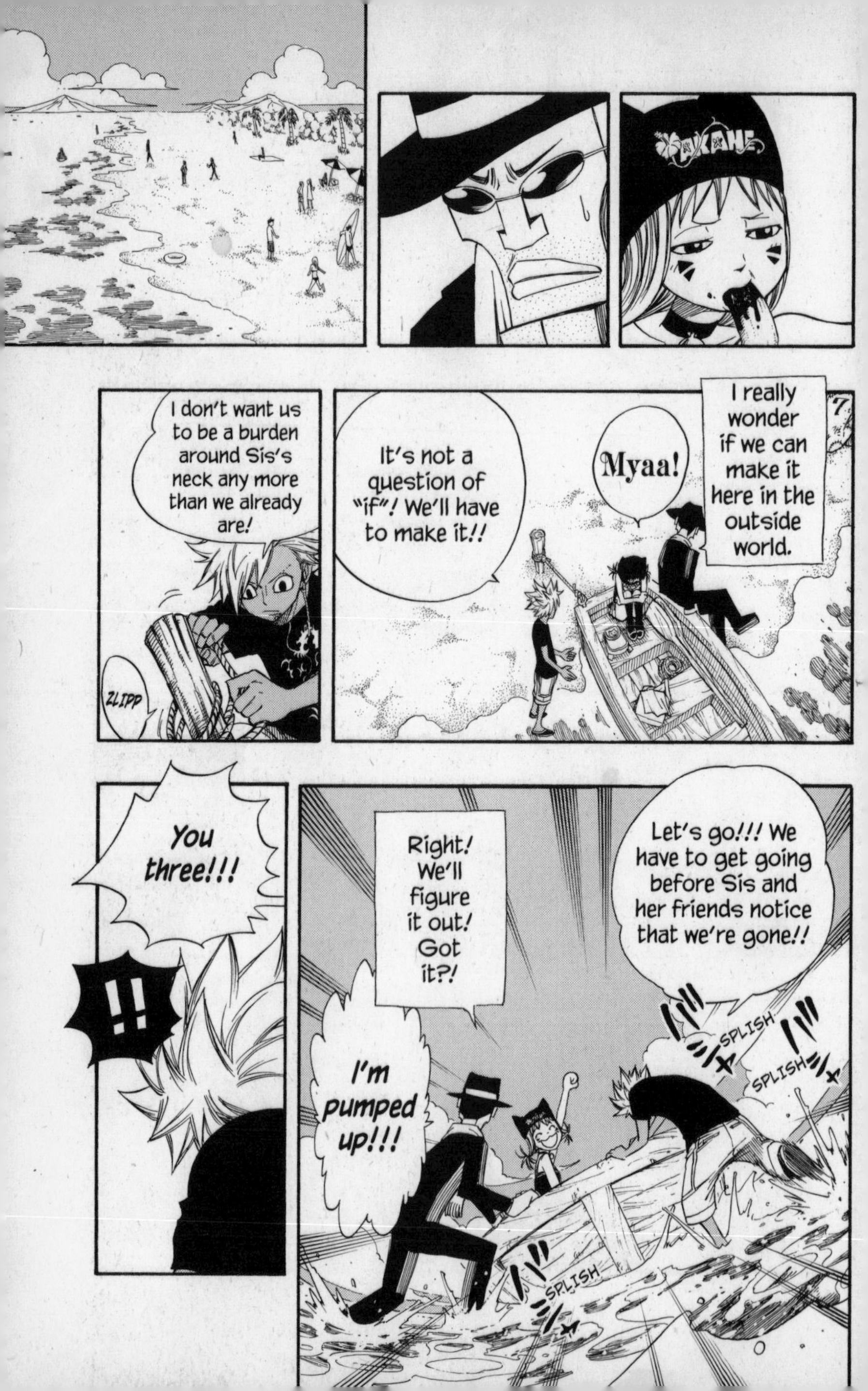

I really wonder if we can make it here in the outside world.
Myaa!
It's not a question of "if"! We'll have to make it!!
I don't want us to be a burden around Sis's neck any more than we already are!
ZLIPP
Let's go!!! We have to get going before Sis and her friends notice that we're gone!!
Right! We'll figure it out! Got it?!
SPLISH
SPLISH
I'm pumped up!!!
SPLISH
You three!!!
!!

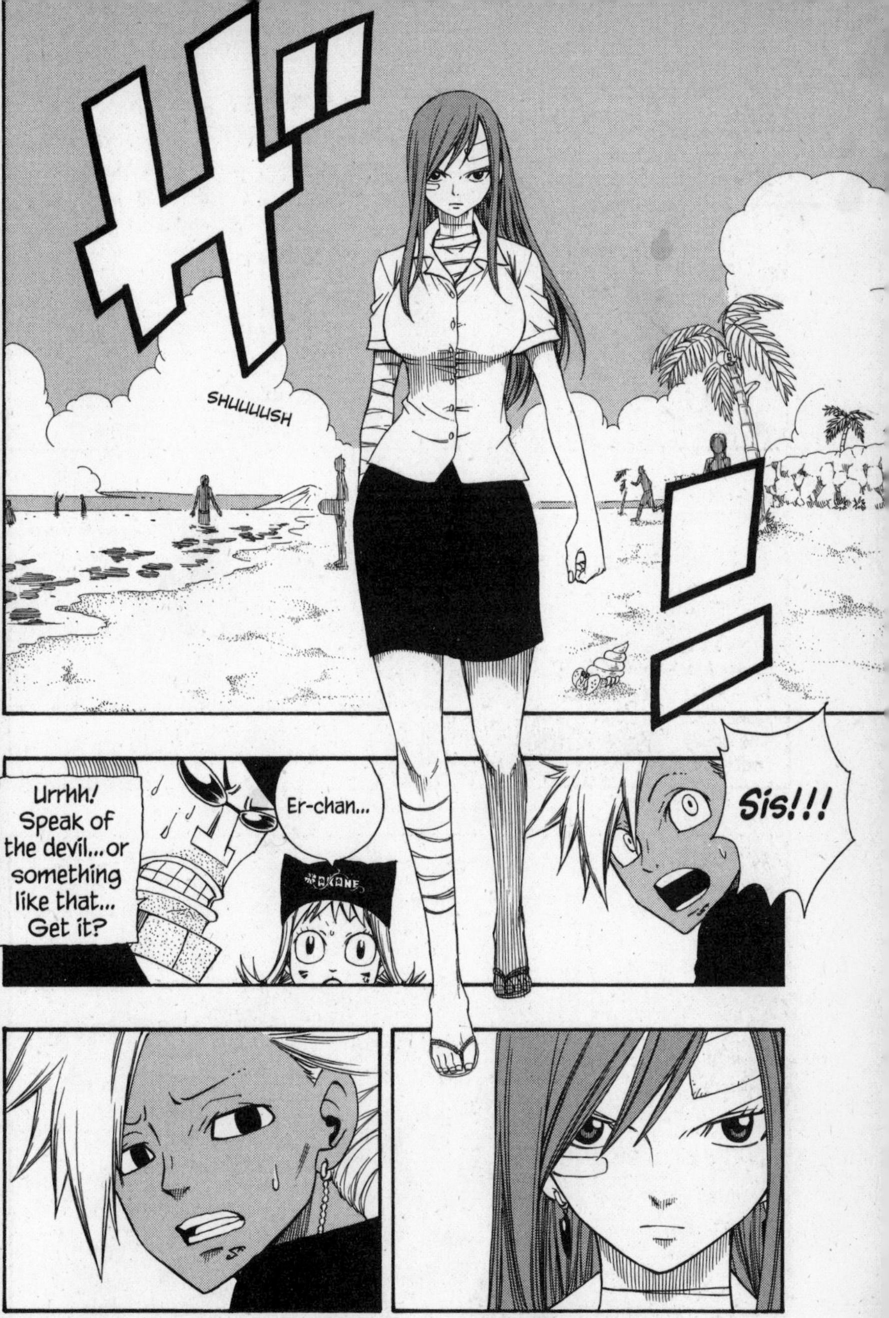
SHUUUUSH
Sis!!!
Er-chan...
Urrhh! Speak of the devil...or something like that... Get it?

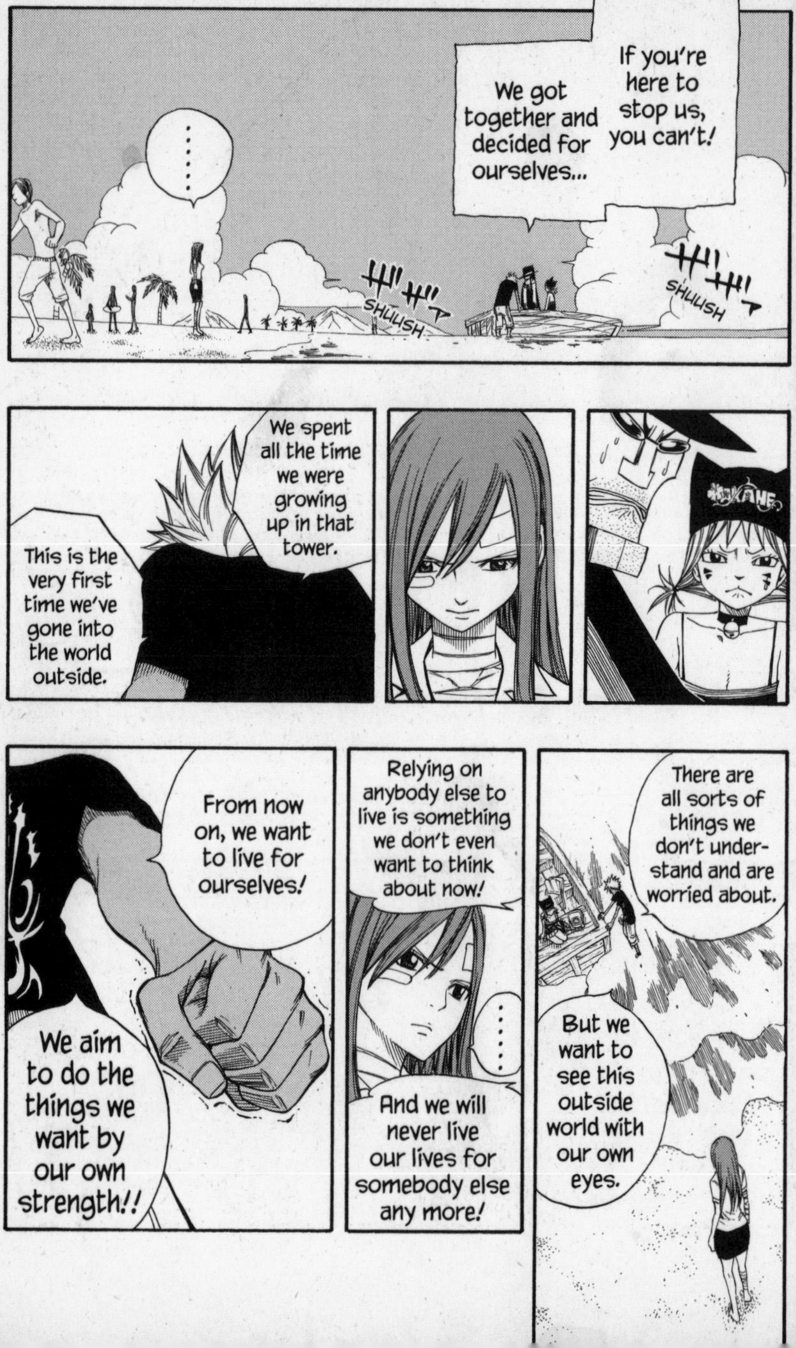
If you're here to stop us, you can't!
We got together and decided for ourselves...
SHUUSH
SHUUSH
......
We spent all the time we were growing up in that tower.
This is the very first time we've gone into the world outside.
There are all sorts of things we don't under-stand and are worried about.
But we want to see this outside world with our own eyes.
Relying on anybody else to live is something we don't even want to think about now!
......
And we will never live our lives for somebody else any more!
From now on, we want to live for ourselves!
We aim to do the things we want by our own strength!!

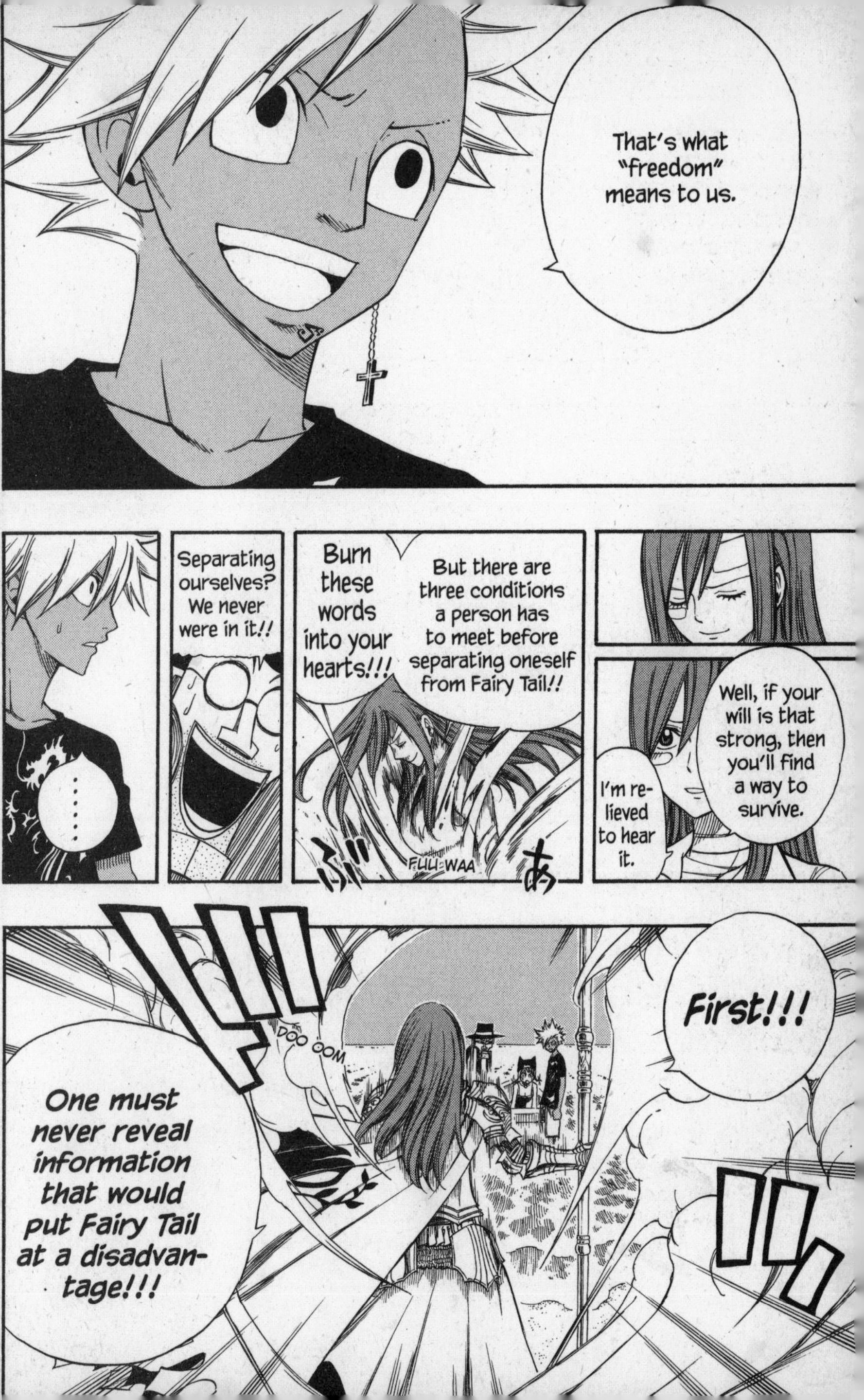
That's what "freedom" means to us.
Well, if your will is that strong, then you'll find a way to survive.
I'm relieved to hear it.
But there are three conditions a person has to meet before separating oneself from Fairy Tail!!
Burn these words into your hearts!!!
あ
FUU WAA
ぶ
Separating ourselves? We never were in it!!
......
First!!!
DOO OOM
One must never reveal information that would put Fairy Tail at a disadvantage!!!

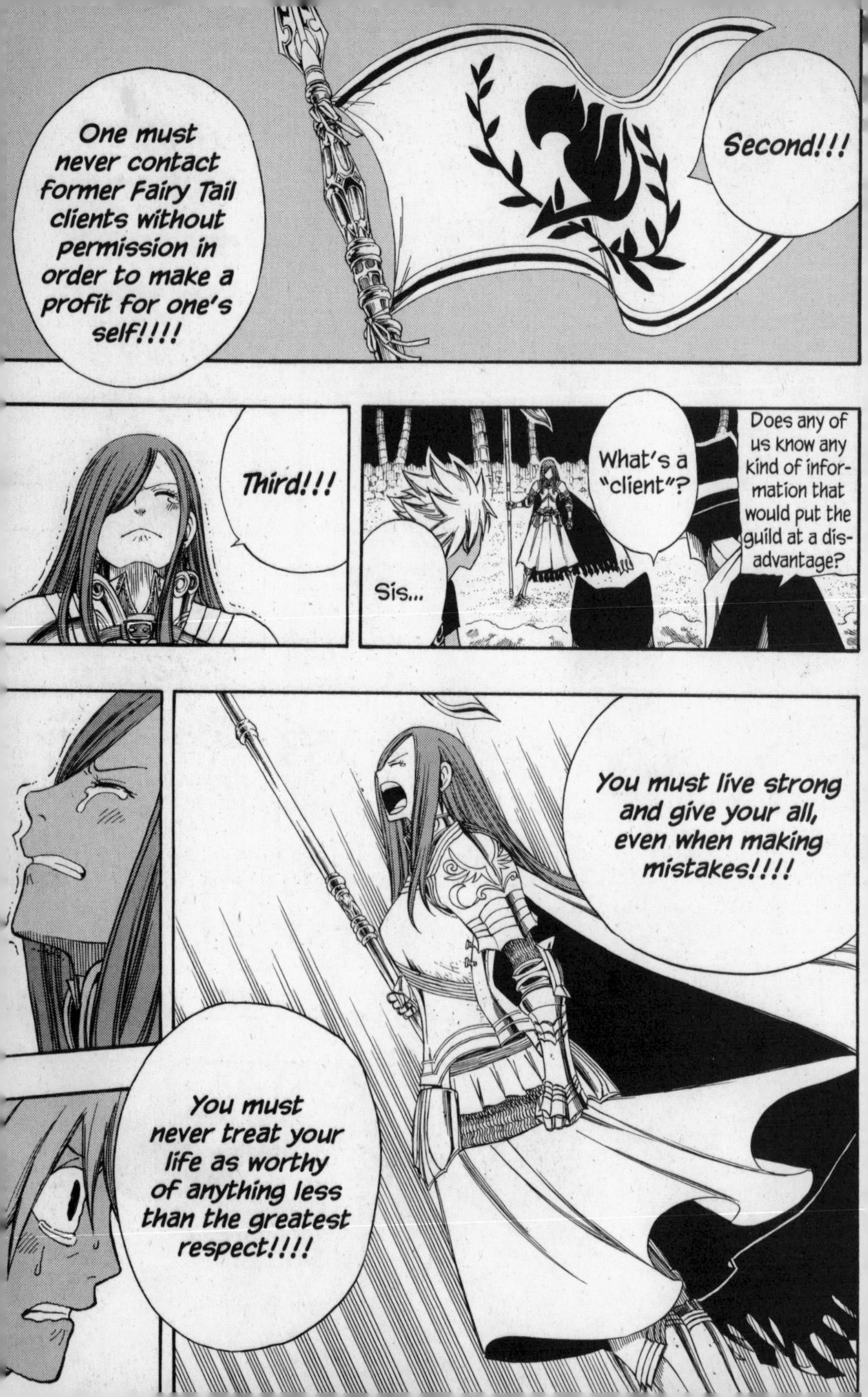
Second!!!
One must never contact former Fairy Tail clients without permission in order to make a profit for one's self!!!!
Does any of us know any kind of information that would put the guild at a disadvantage?
What's a "client"?
Sis...
Third!!!
You must live strong and give your all, even when making mistakes!!!!
You must never treat your life as worthy of anything less than the greatest respect!!!!

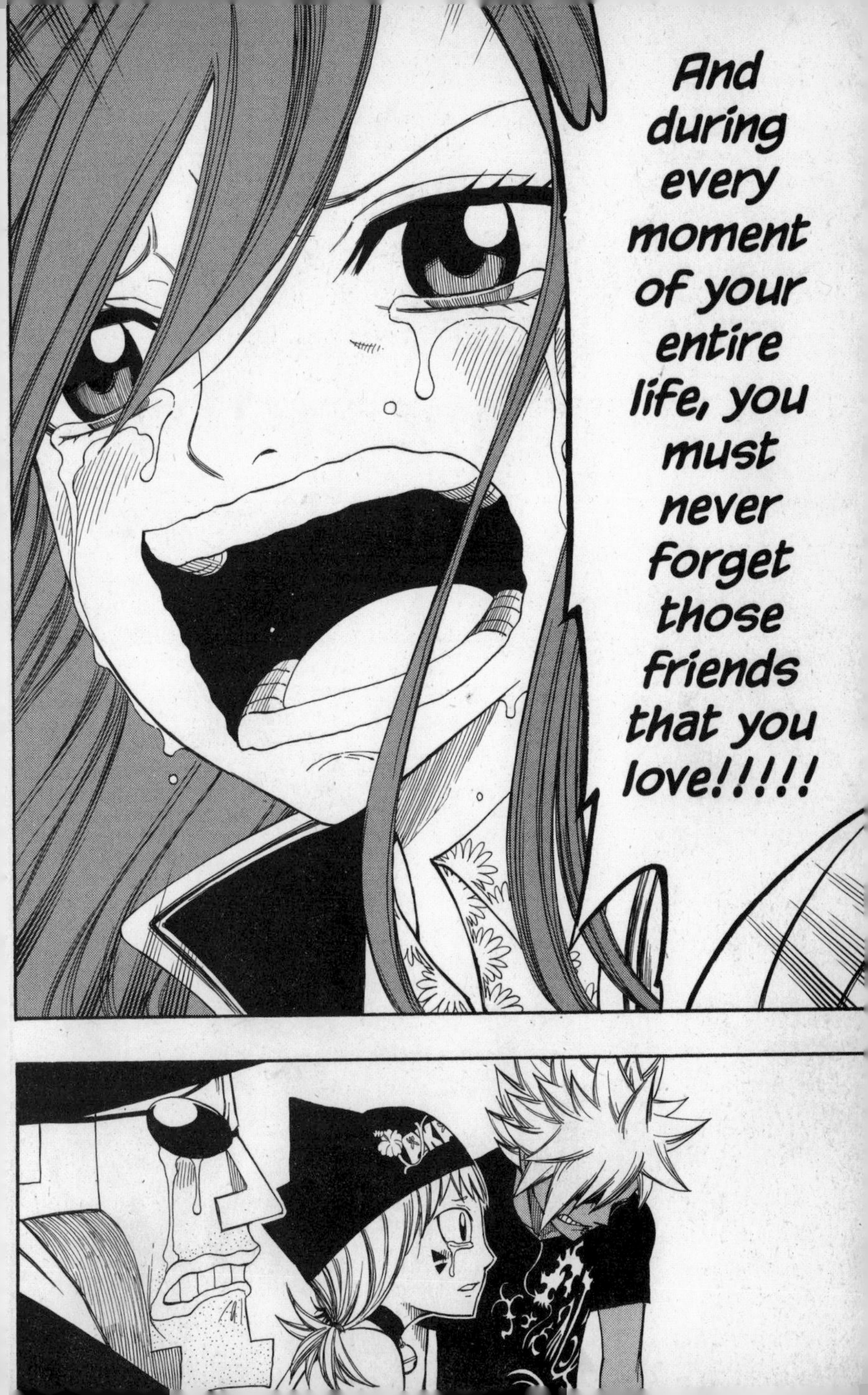
And during every moment of your entire life, you must never forget those friends that you love!!!!!

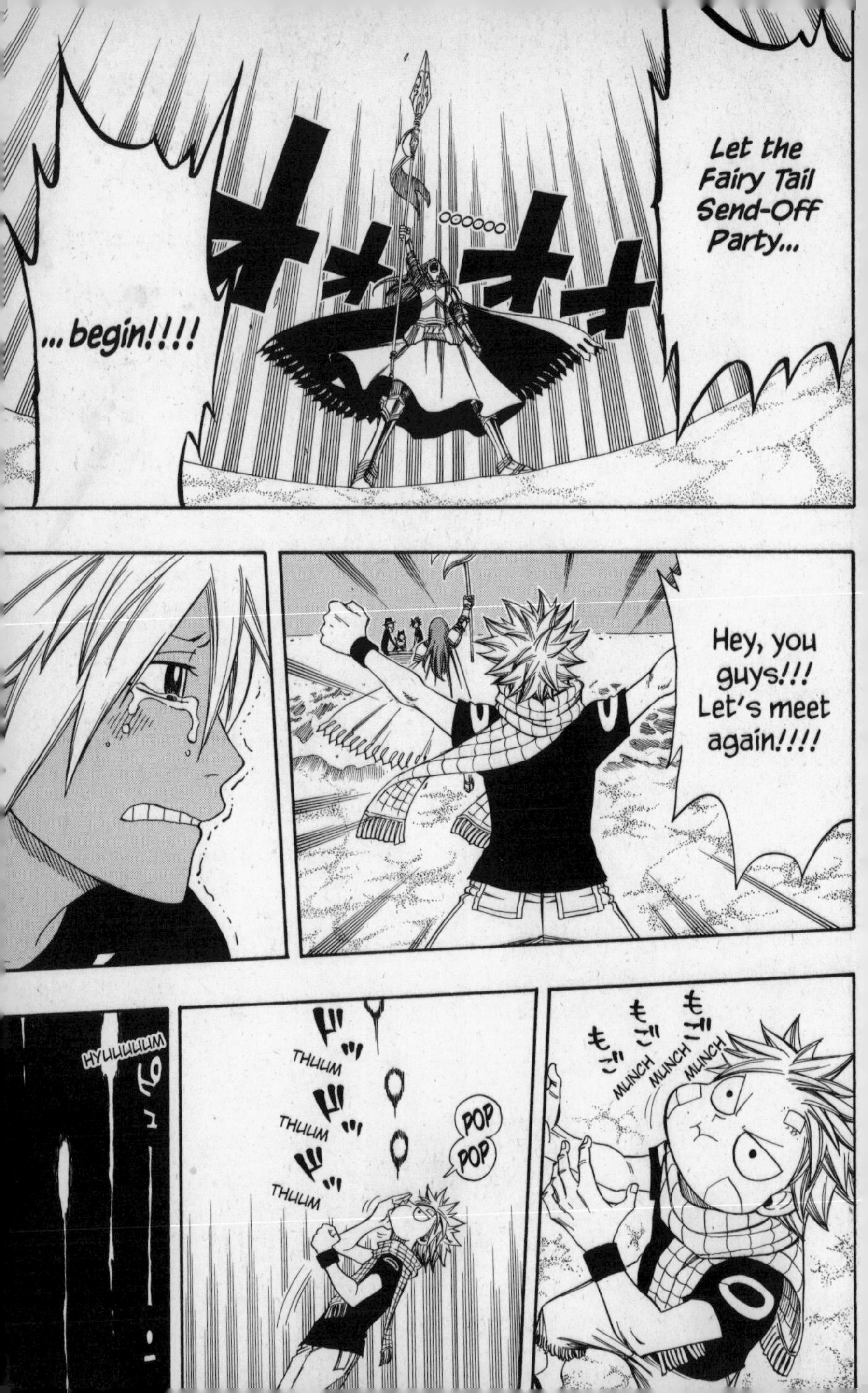
Let the Fairy Tail Send-Off Party...
OOOOOO
...begin!!!!
Hey, you guys!!! Let's meet again!!!!
もご もご もご
MUNCH MUNCH MUNCH
THUUM THUUM THUUM
POP POP
HYUUUUUM

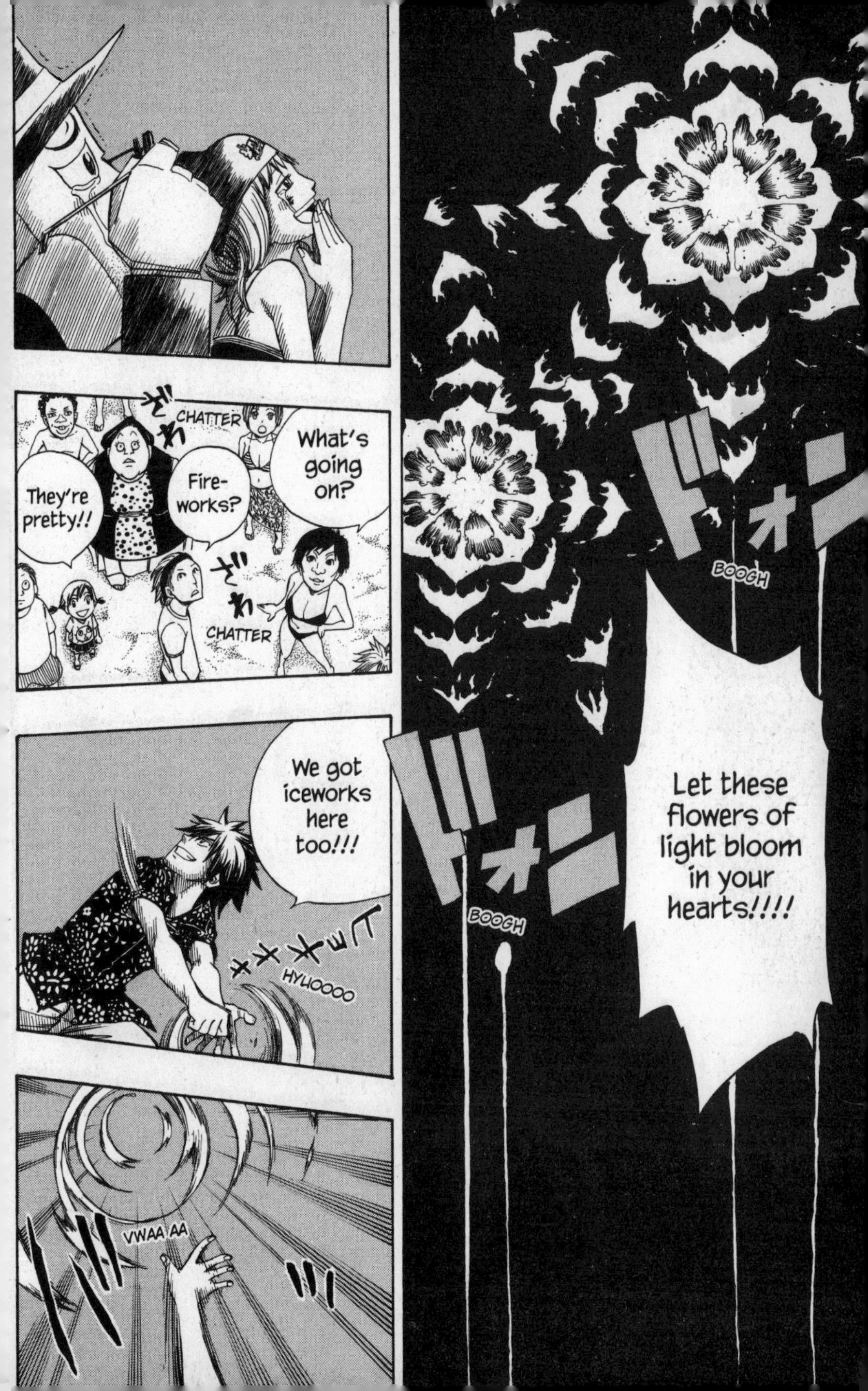
ドォン
BOOGH
ドォン
BOOGH
Let these flowers of light bloom in your hearts!!!!
What's going on?
ざわ
CHATTER
Fire-works?
They're pretty!!
ざわ
CHATTER
We got iceworks here too!!!
HYUOOOO
VWAA AA

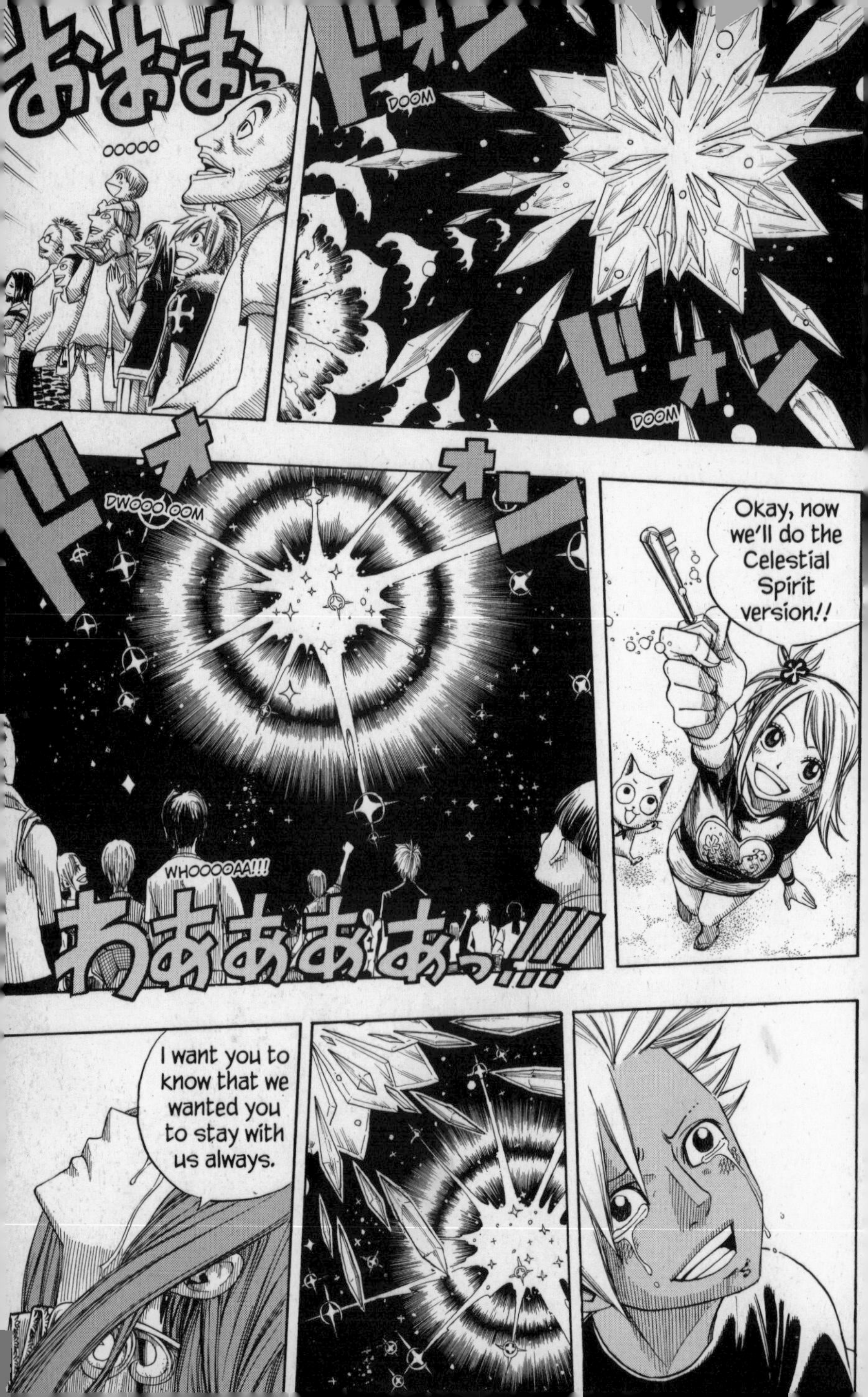
ドォン
DOOM
ドォン
DOOM
おおおっ
OOOOO
Okay, now we'll do the Celestial Spirit version!!
ドォォン
DWOOO OOM
WHOOOOAA!!!
わあああああっ!!!
I want you to know that we wanted you to stay with us always.

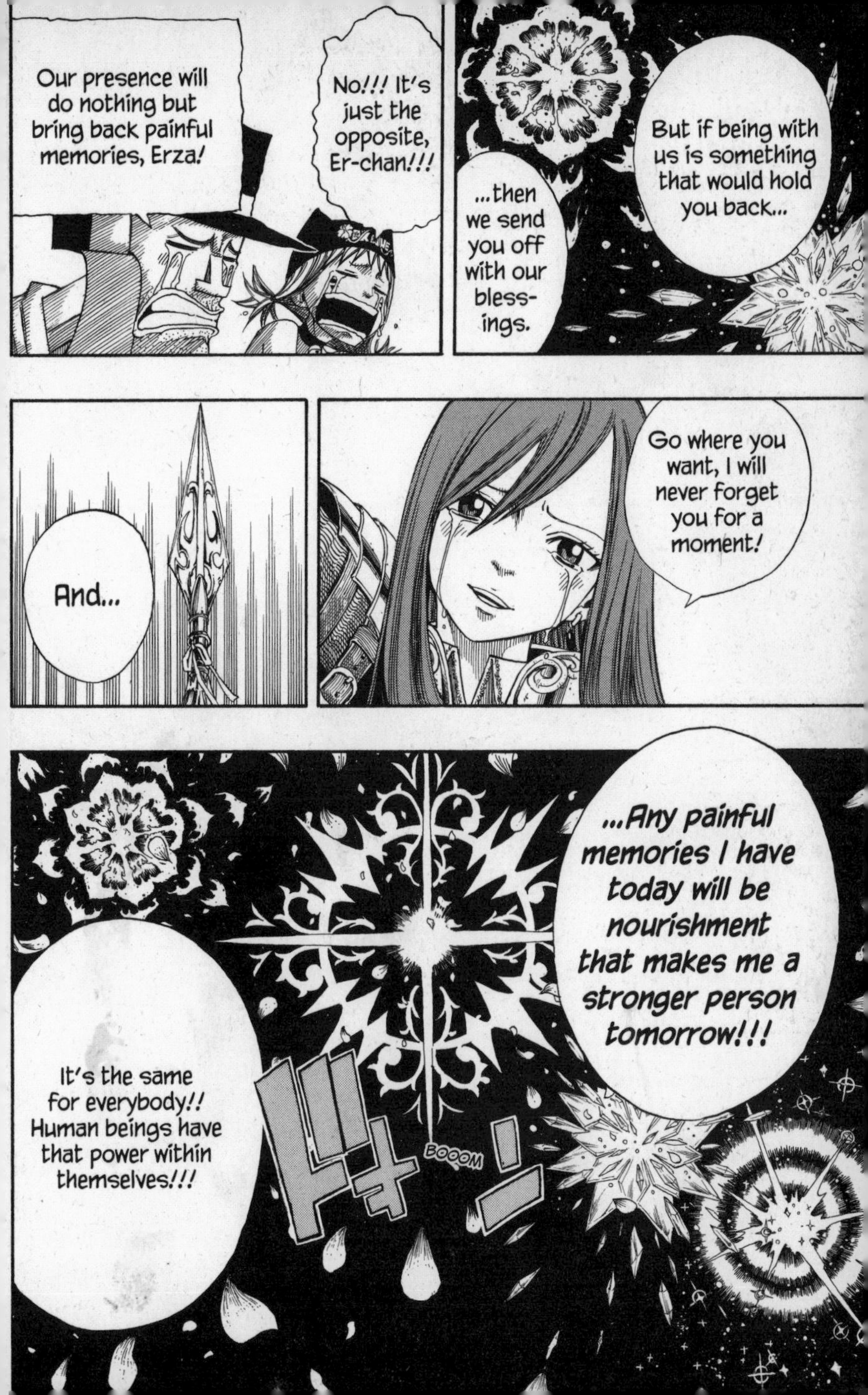
But if being with us is something that would hold you back...
...then we send you off with our bless-ings.
No!!! It's just the opposite, Er-chan!!!
Our presence will do nothing but bring back painful memories, Erza!
Go where you want, I will never forget you for a moment!
And...
...Any painful memories I have today will be nourishment that makes me a stronger person tomorrow!!!
BOOOM
It's the same for everybody!! Human beings have that power within themselves!!!

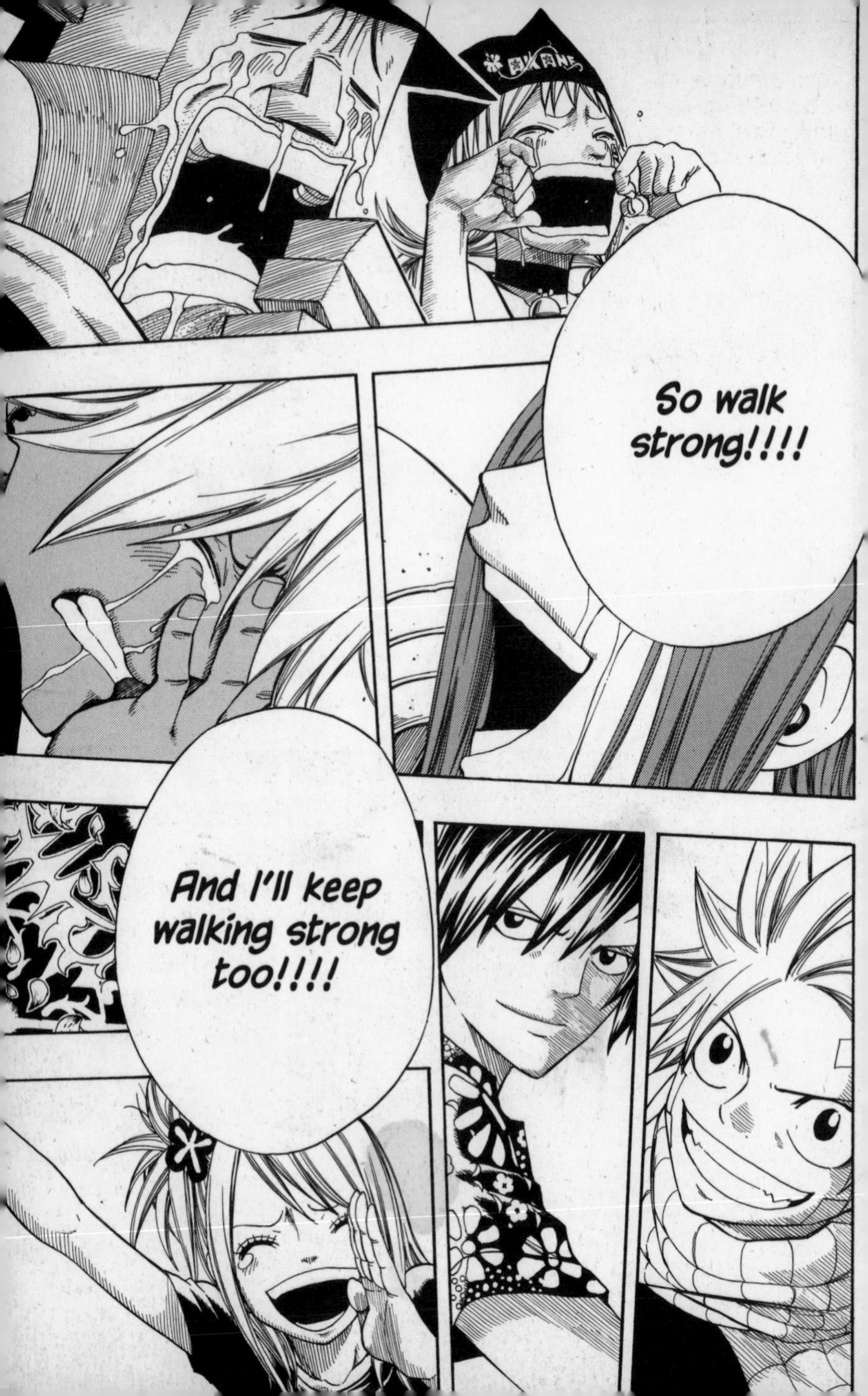
So walk strong!!!!
And I'll keep walking strong too!!!!

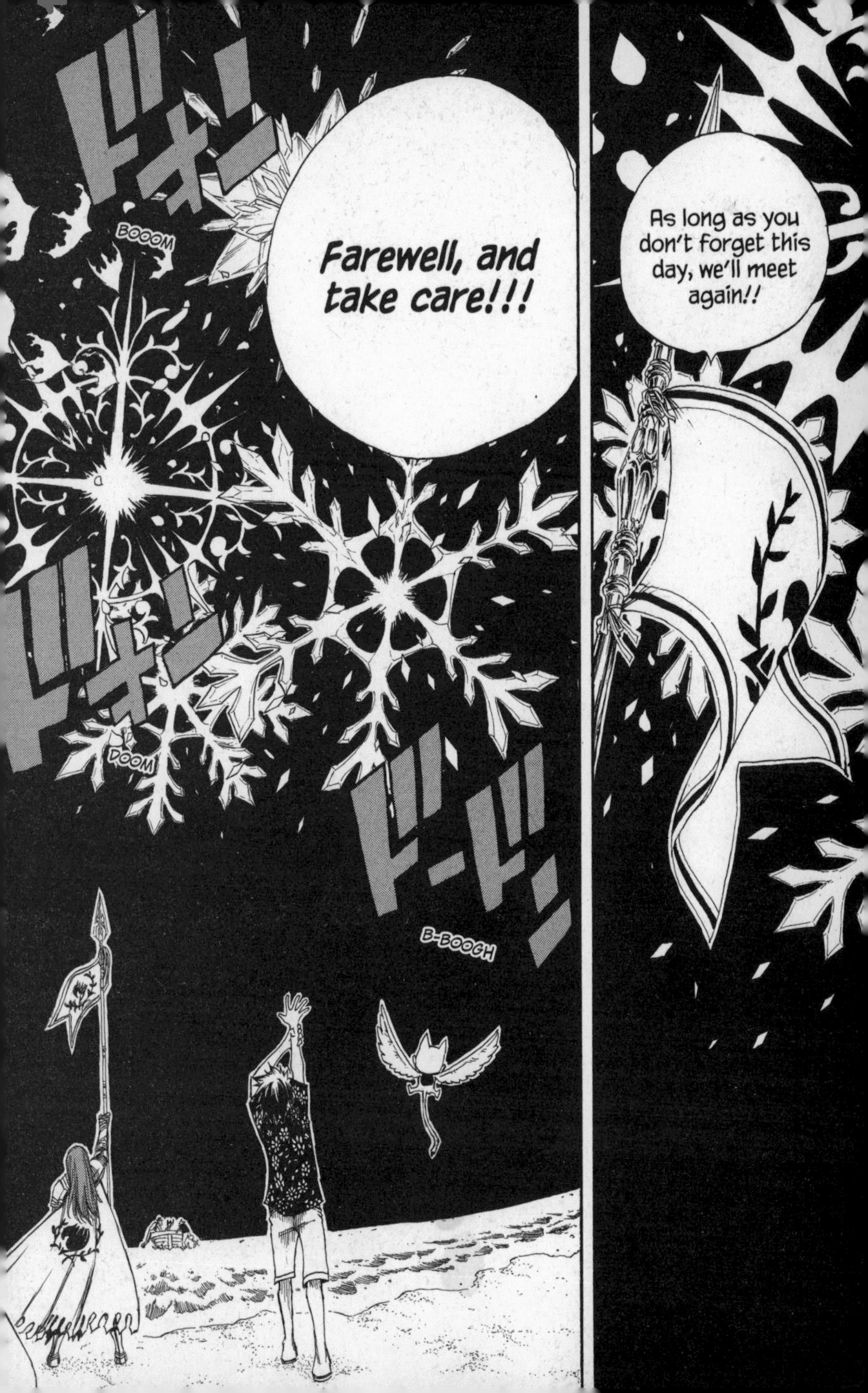
As long as you don't forget this day, we'll meet again!!
Farewell, and take care!!!
BOOOM
DOOM
B-BOOGH

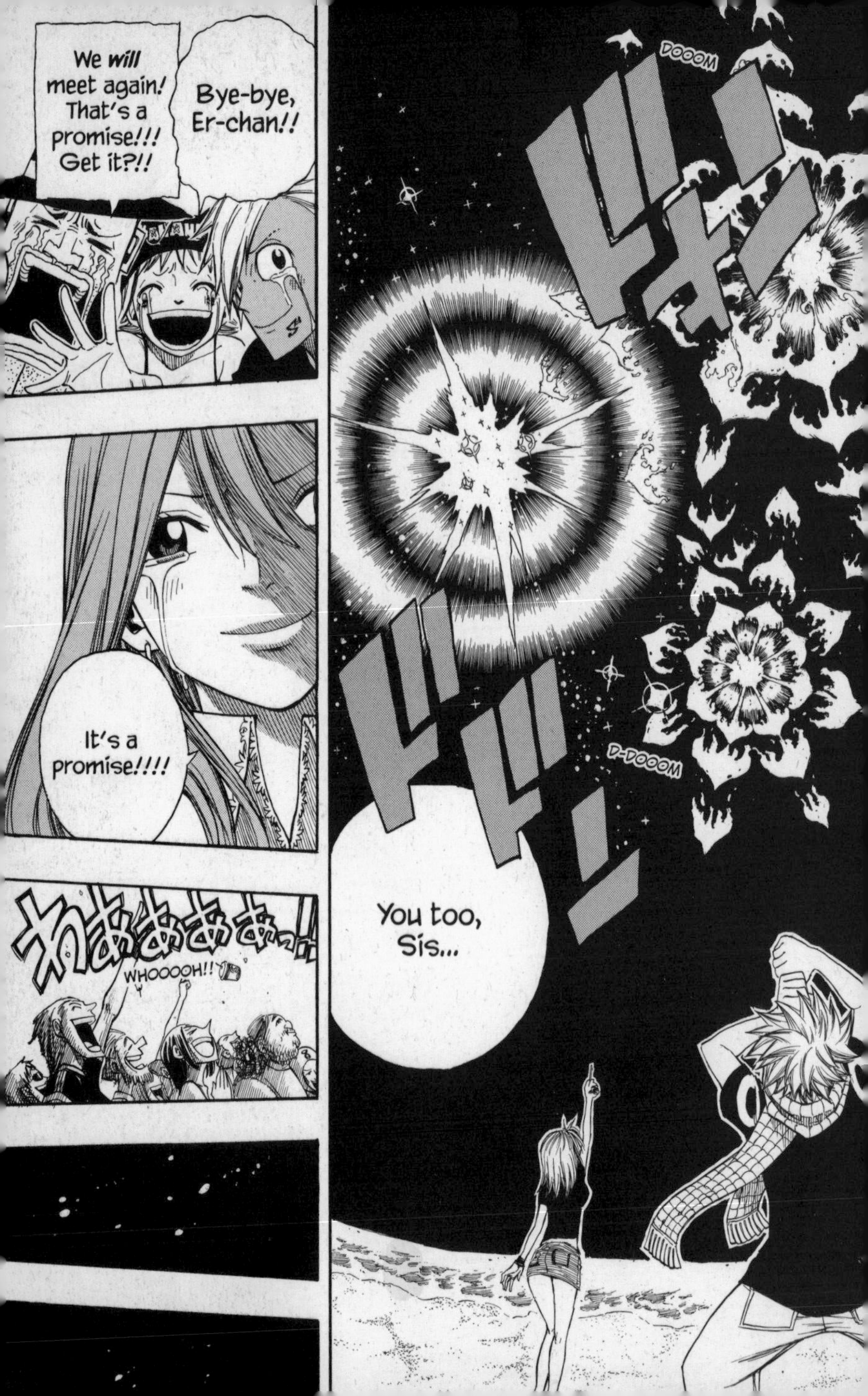
DOOOM
D-DOOOM
You too, Sis...
Bye-bye, Er-chan!!
We **will** meet again! That's a promise!!! Get it?!!
It's a promise!!!!
WHOOOOH!!

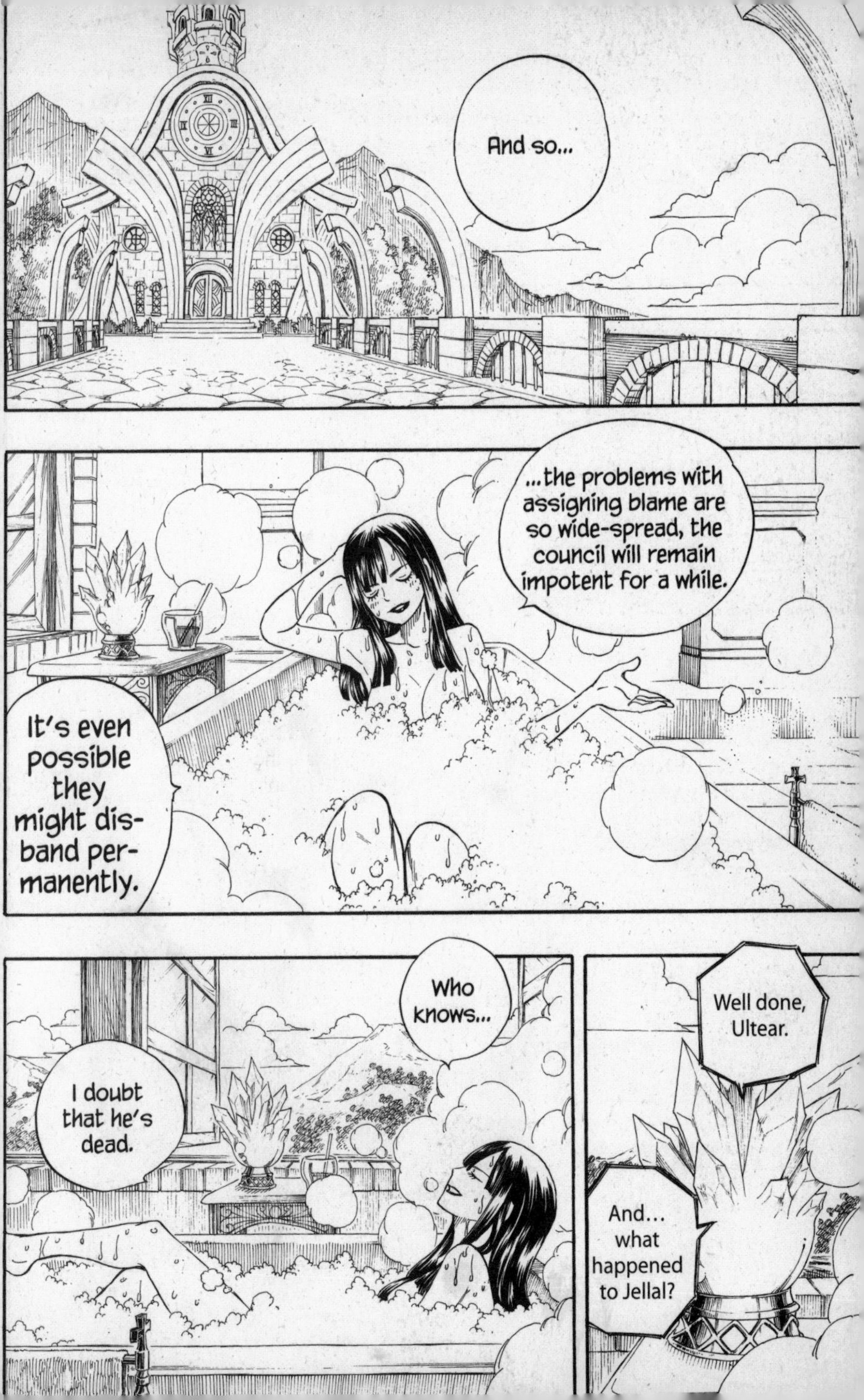
And so...
...the problems with assigning blame are so wide-spread, the council will remain impotent for a while.
It's even possible they might dis-band per-manently.
Well done, Ultear.
And... what happened to Jellal?
Who knows...
I doubt that he's dead.

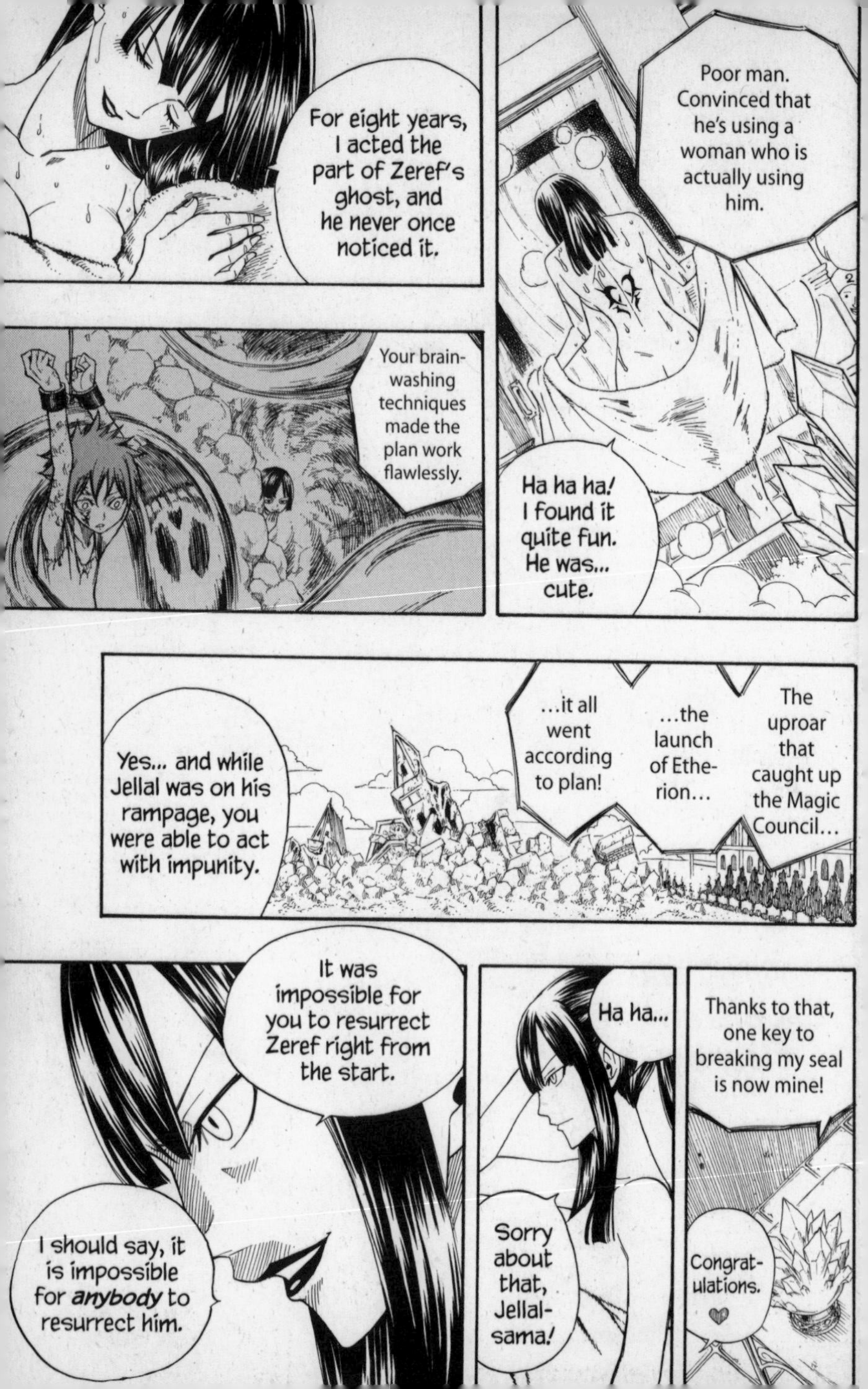
Poor man. Convinced that he's using a woman who is actually using him.
Ha ha ha! I found it quite fun. He was... cute.
For eight years, I acted the part of Zeref's ghost, and he never once noticed it.
Your brain-washing techniques made the plan work flawlessly.
The uproar that caught up the Magic Council…
…the launch of Ethe-rion…
…it all went according to plan!
Yes... and while Jellal was on his rampage, you were able to act with impunity.
Thanks to that, one key to breaking my seal is now mine!
Congrat-ulations. ♥
Ha ha...
Sorry about that, Jellal-sama!
It was impossible for you to resurrect Zeref right from the start.
I should say, it is impossible for ***anybody*** to resurrect him.

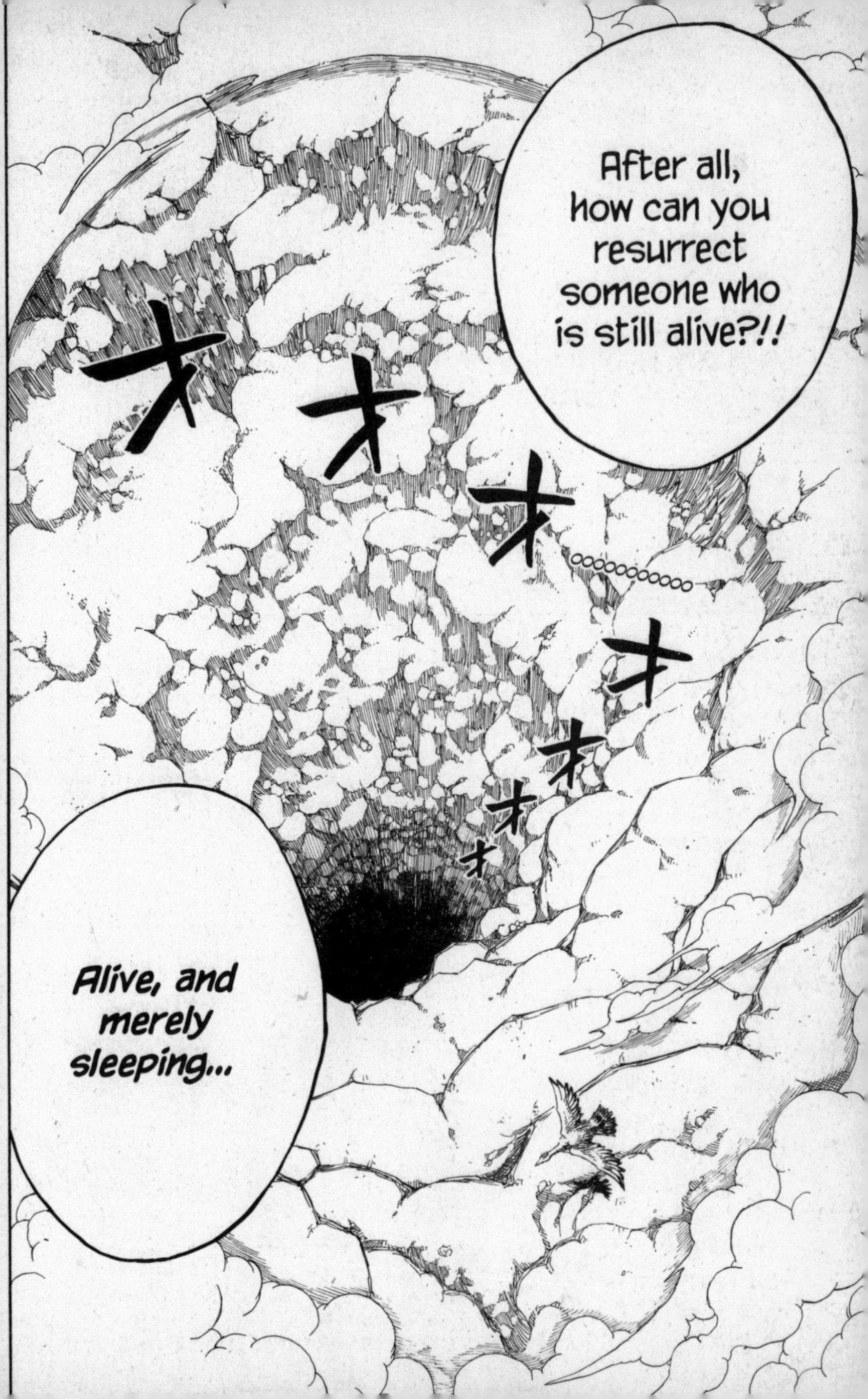
After all, how can you resurrect someone who is still alive?!!
オオオ
OOOOOOOOOOO
オオオオ
Alive, and merely sleeping...

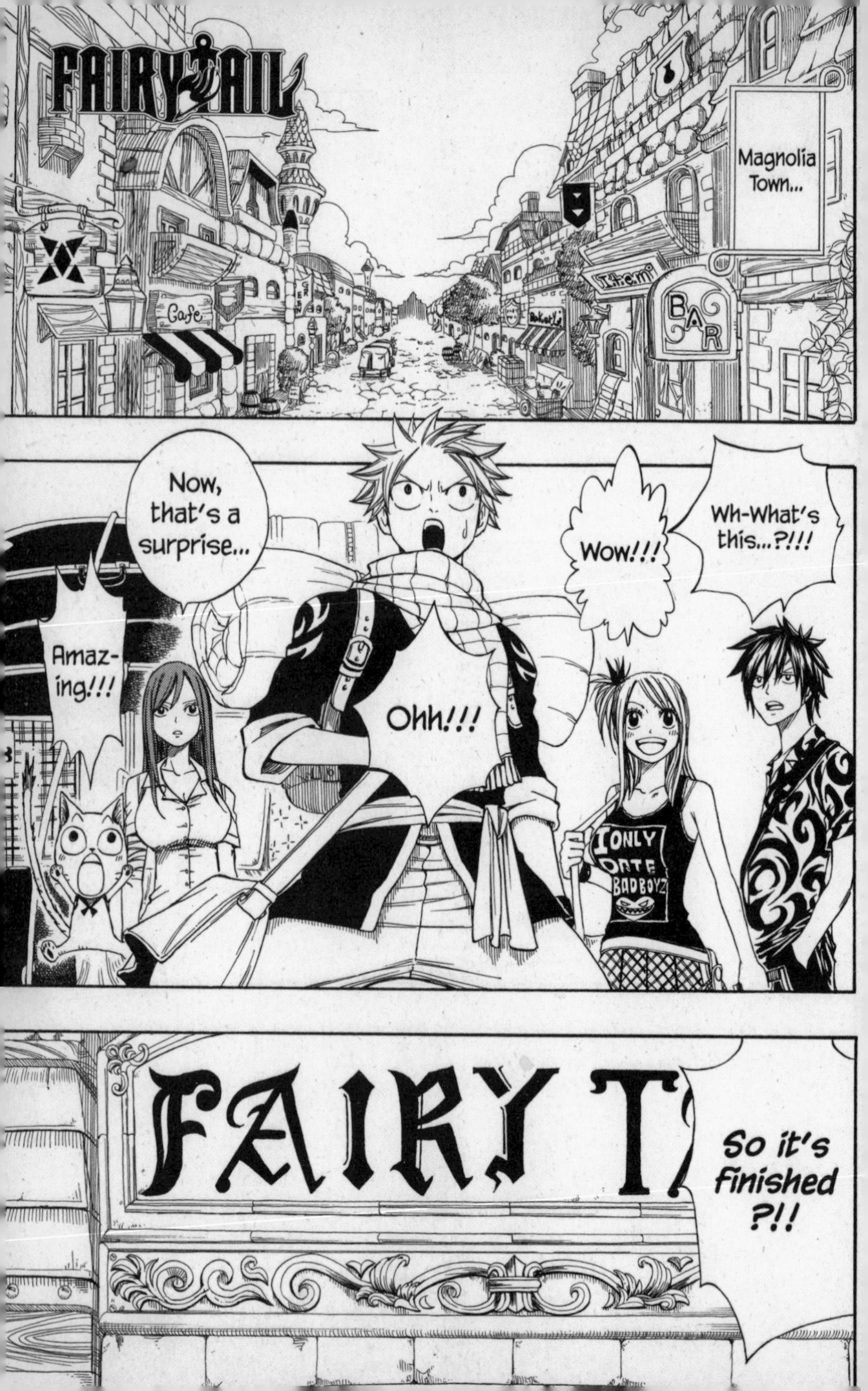
FAIRY TAIL
Magnolia Town...
Wh-What's this...?!!!
Wow!!!
Now, that's a surprise...
Ohh!!!
Amazing!!!
So it's finished ?!!
FAIRY T

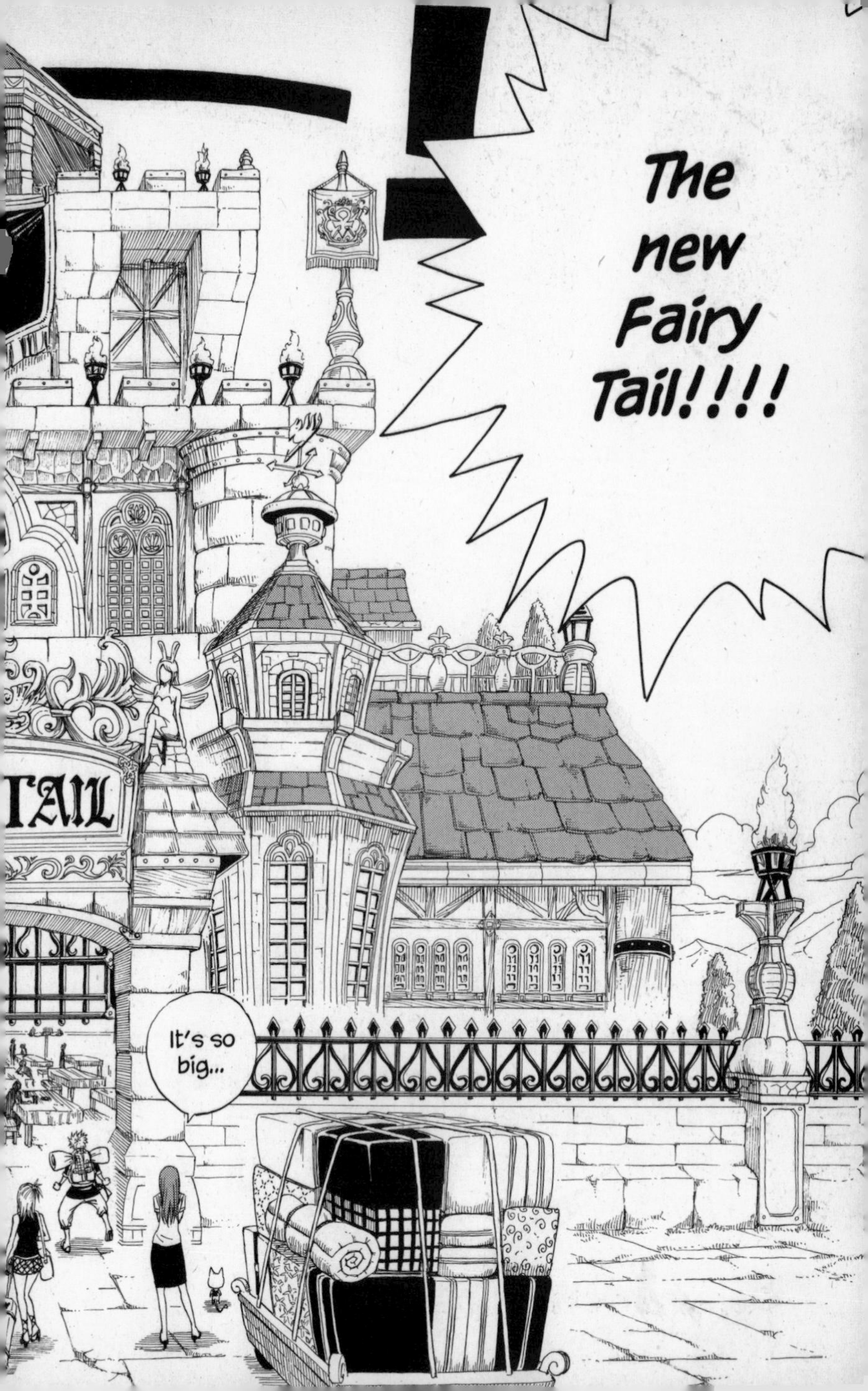
The new Fairy Tail!!!!
TAIL
It's so big...

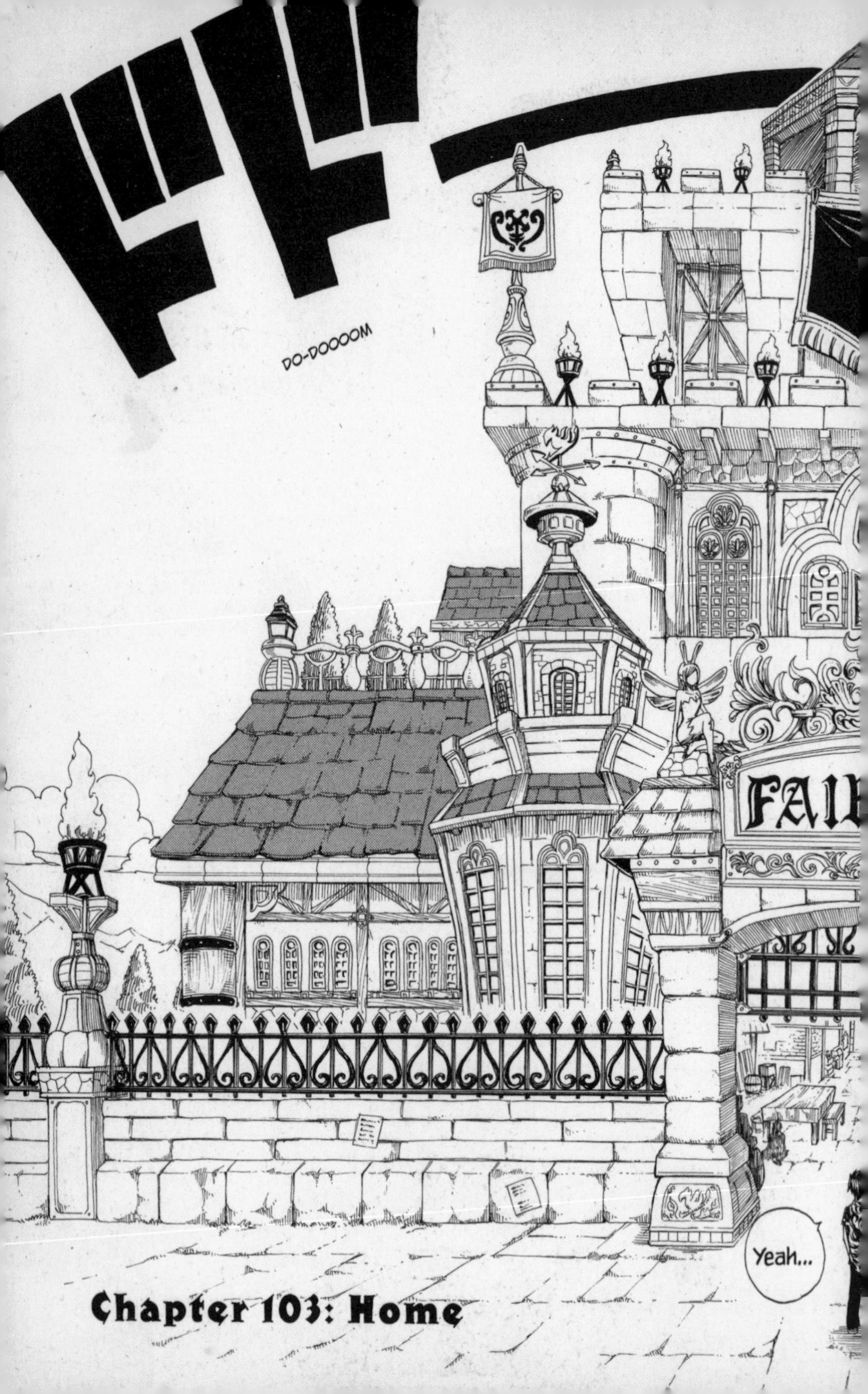
DO-DOOOOM
FAI
Yeah...
Chapter 103: Home

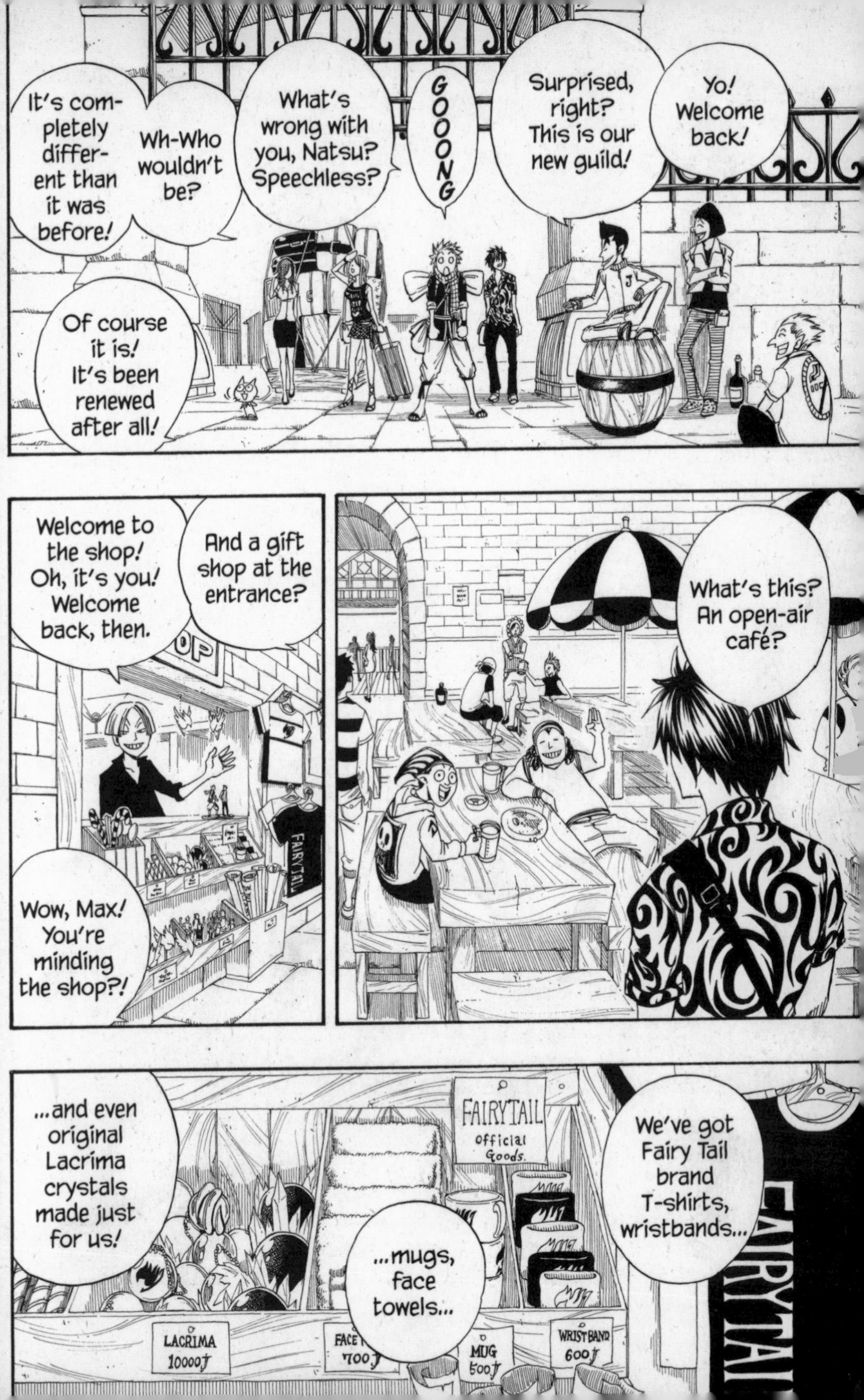
Yo! Welcome back!
Surprised, right? This is our new guild!
GOOONG
What's wrong with you, Natsu? Speechless?
Wh-Who wouldn't be?
It's completely different than it was before!
Of course it is! It's been renewed after all!
What's this? An open-air café?
And a gift shop at the entrance?
Welcome to the shop! Oh, it's you! Welcome back, then.
FAIRY TAIL
Wow, Max! You're minding the shop?!
We've got Fairy Tail brand T-shirts, wristbands...
FAIRY TAIL Official Goods.
...mugs, face towels...
...and even original Lacrima crystals made just for us!
WRISTBAND 600J
MUG 500J
LACRIMA 10000J
FAIRY TAIL

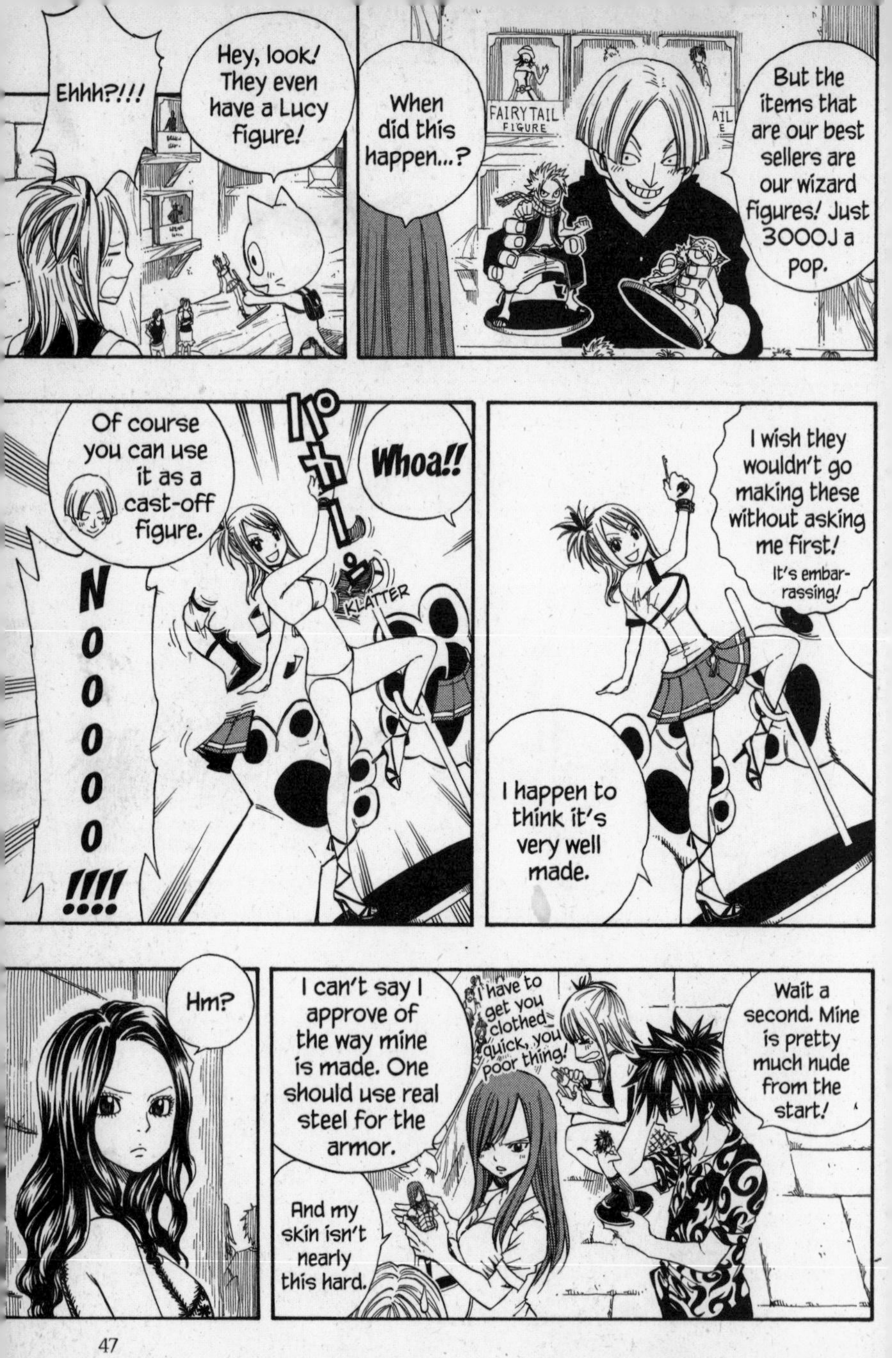
FAIRY TAIL
FIGURE
But the items that are our best sellers are our wizard figures! Just 3000J a pop.
When did this happen...?
Hey, look! They even have a Lucy figure!
Ehhh?!!!
I wish they wouldn't go making these without asking me first!
It's embarrassing!
I happen to think it's very well made.
Whoa!!
パカーッ
KLATTER
Of course you can use it as a cast-off figure.
Noooooo!!!!
Wait a second. Mine is pretty much nude from the start!
I have to get you clothed quick, you poor thing!
I can't say I approve of the way mine is made. One should use real steel for the armor.
And my skin isn't nearly this hard.
Hm?

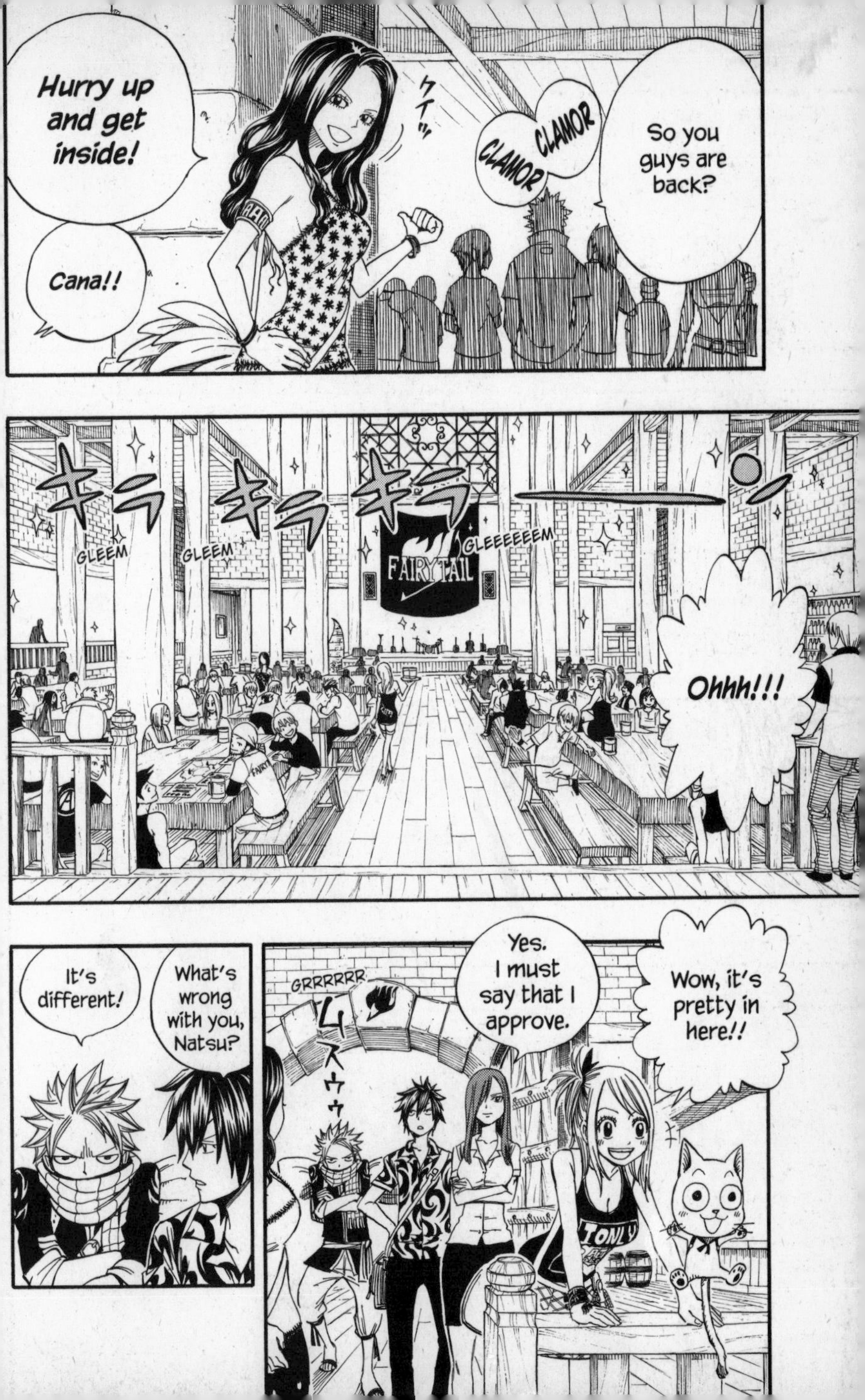
So you guys are back?
CLAMOR
CLAMOR
Hurry up and get inside!
Cana!!
Ohhh!!!
GLEEEEEEM
GLEEM
GLEEM
Wow, it's pretty in here!!
Yes. I must say that I approve.
GRRRRRR
What's wrong with you, Natsu?
It's different!

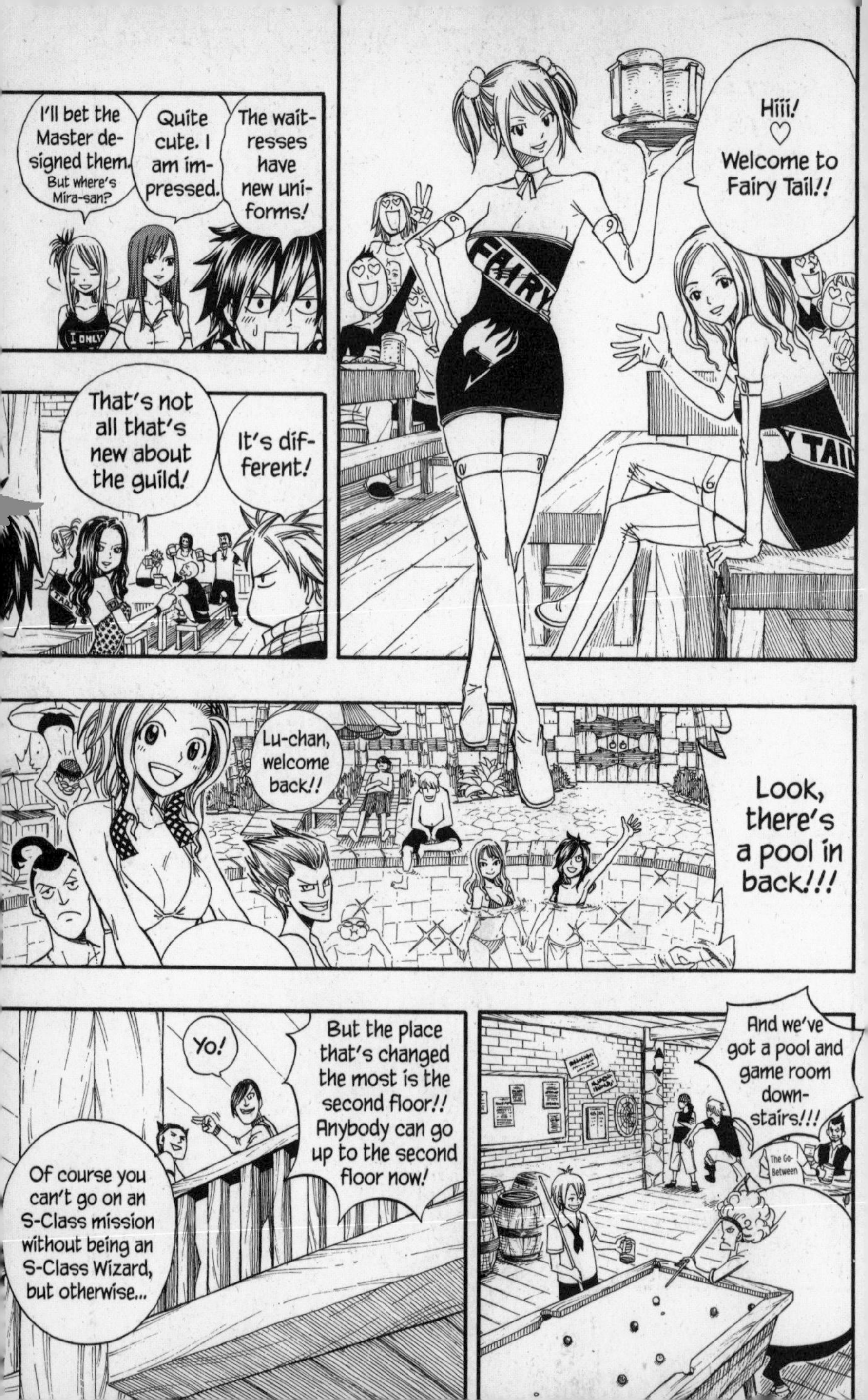
Hiii! ♡ Welcome to Fairy Tail!!
The wait-resses have new uni-forms!
Quite cute. I am im-pressed.
I'll bet the Master de-signed them.
But where's Mira-san?
It's dif-ferent!
That's not all that's new about the guild!
Look, there's a pool in back!!!
Lu-chan, welcome back!!
And we've got a pool and game room down-stairs!!!
The Go-Between
But the place that's changed the most is the second floor!! Anybody can go up to the second floor now!
Yo!
Of course you can't go on an S-Class mission without being an S-Class Wizard, but otherwise...

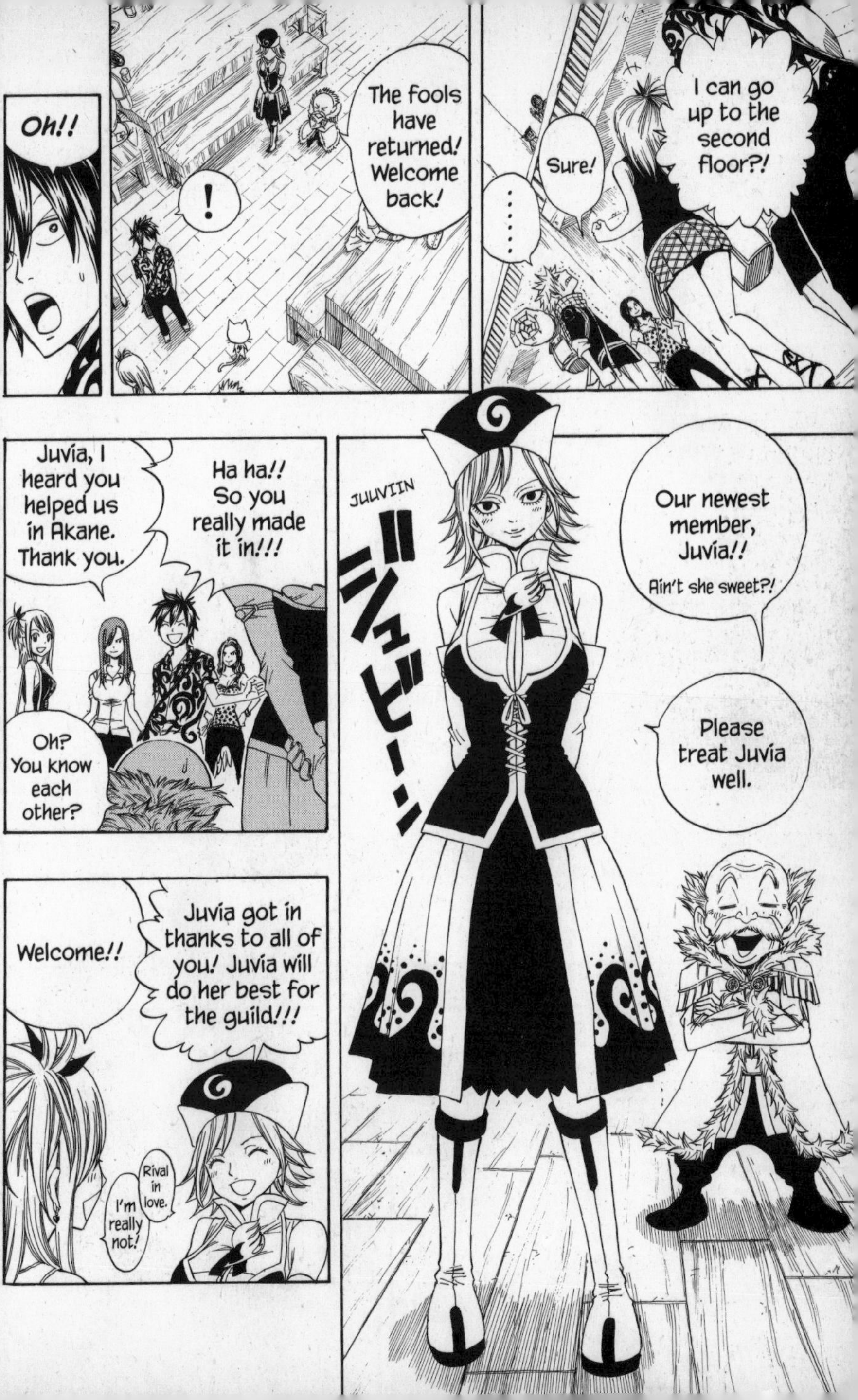
I can go up to the second floor?!
Sure!
......
The fools have returned! Welcome back!
!
Oh!!
Our newest member, Juvia!! Ain't she sweet?!
JUUVIIN
ジュビーン
Please treat Juvia well.
Ha ha!! So you really made it in!!!
Juvia, I heard you helped us in Akane. Thank you.
Oh? You know each other?
Juvia got in thanks to all of you! Juvia will do her best for the guild!!!
Welcome!!
Rival in love.
I'm really not!

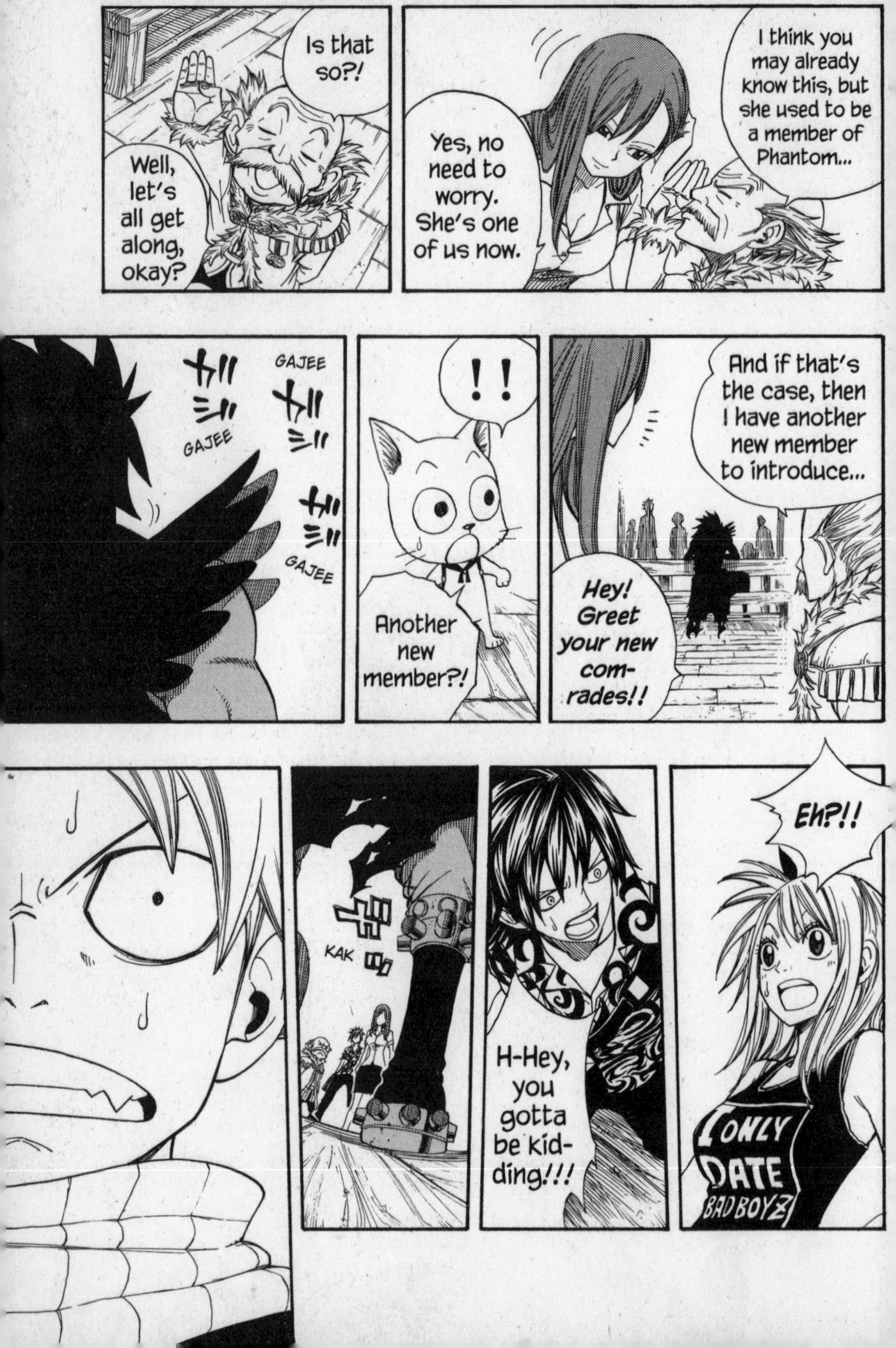
I think you may already know this, but she used to be a member of Phantom...
Yes, no need to worry. She's one of us now.
Is that so?!
Well, let's all get along, okay?
And if that's the case, then I have another new member to introduce...
Hey! Greet your new com-rades!!
!!
Another new member?!
GAJEE
GAJEE
GAJEE
Eh?!!
ONLY DATE BAD BOYZ
H-Hey, you gotta be kid-ding!!!
KAK

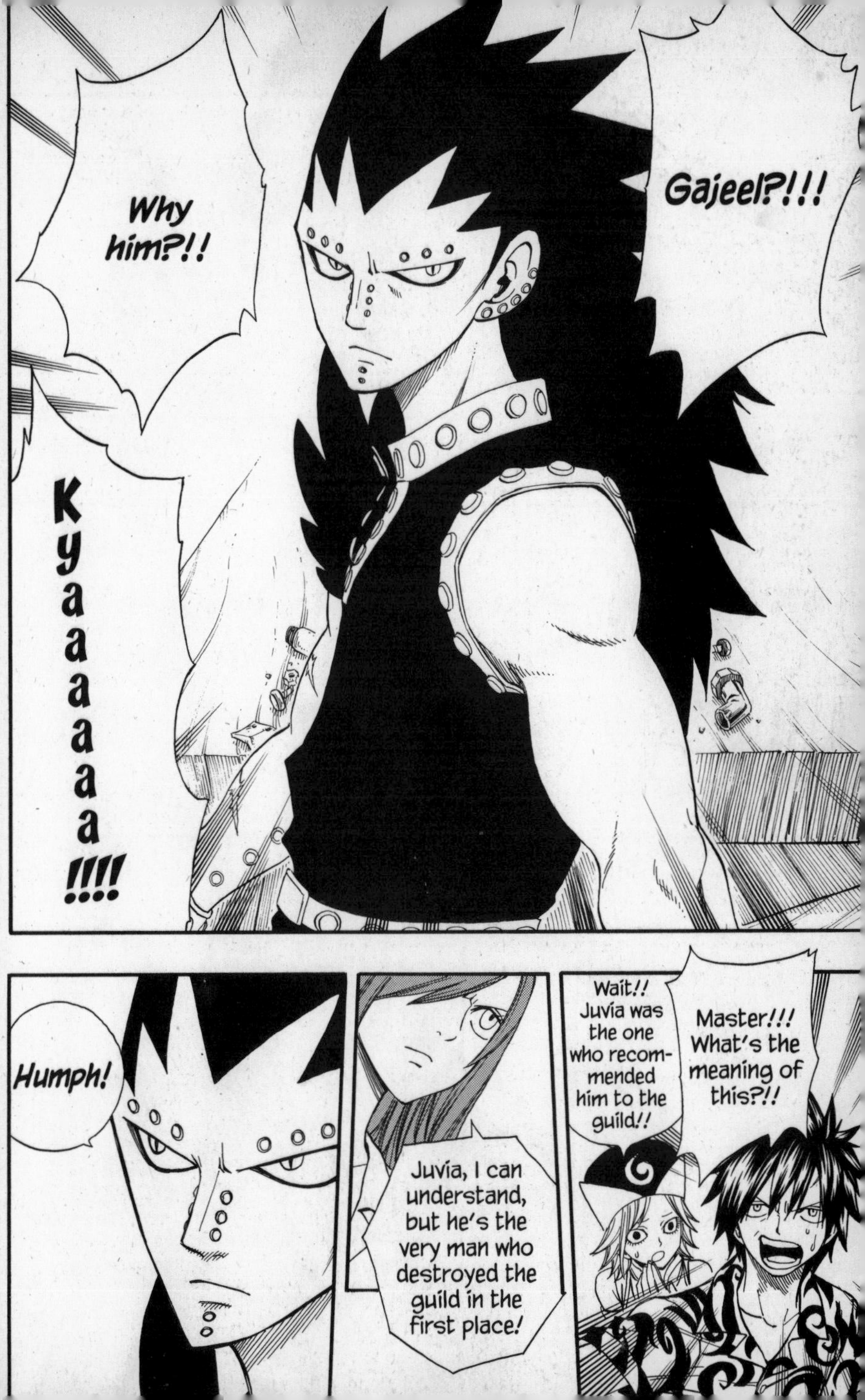
Gajeel?!!!
Why him?!!
Kyaaaaaaa!!!!
Master!!! What's the meaning of this?!!
Wait!! Juvia was the one who recom-mended him to the guild!!
Juvia, I can understand, but he's the very man who destroyed the guild in the first place!
Humph!

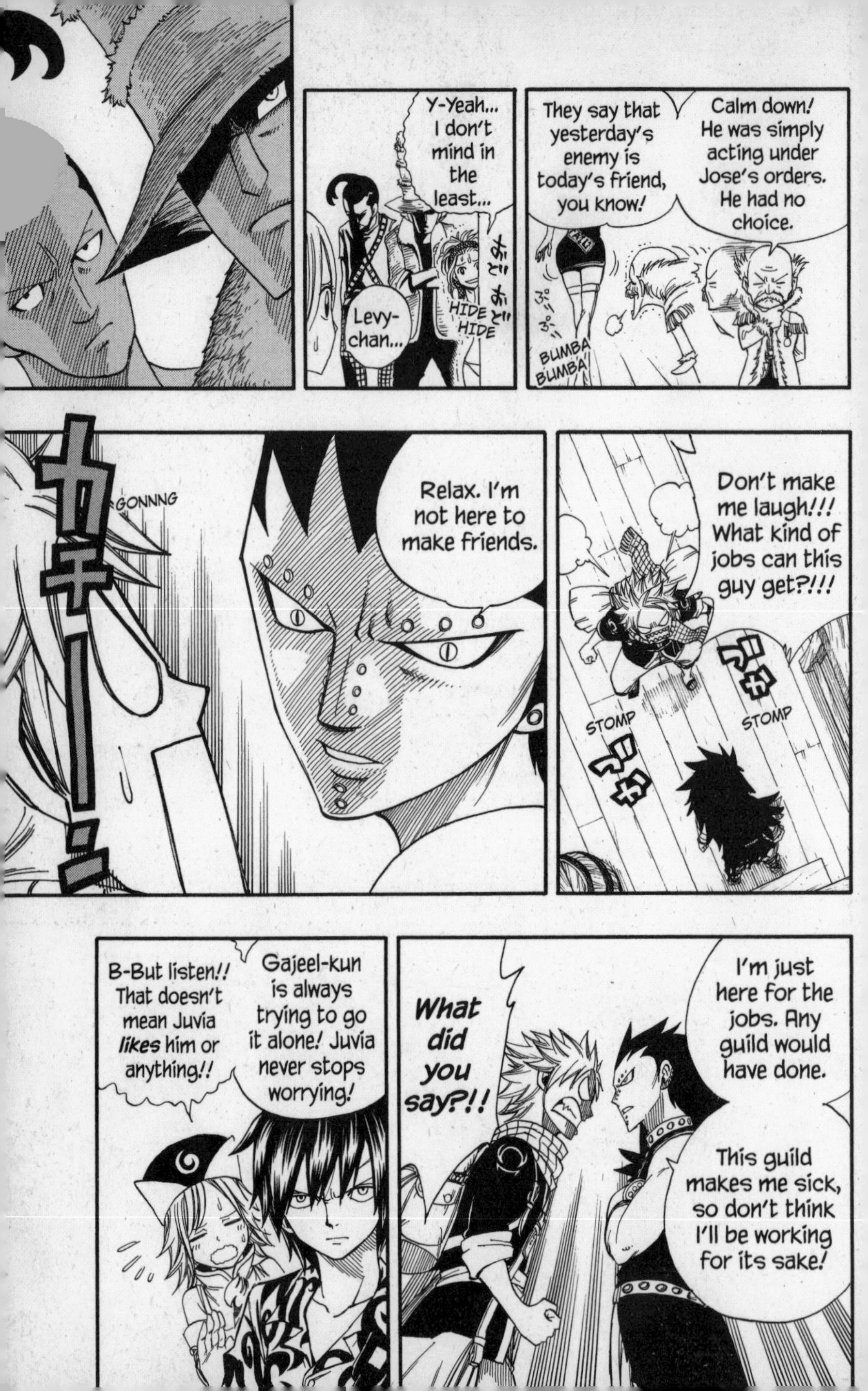
Calm down! He was simply acting under Jose's orders. He had no choice.
They say that yesterday's enemy is today's friend, you know!
BUMBA BUMBA
Y-Yeah... I don't mind in the least...
HIDE HIDE
Levy-chan...
Don't make me laugh!!! What kind of jobs can this guy get?!!!
STOMP
STOMP
Relax. I'm not here to make friends.
GONNNG
I'm just here for the jobs. Any guild would have done.
This guild makes me sick, so don't think I'll be working for its sake!
What did you say?!!
Gajeel-kun is always trying to go it alone! Juvia never stops worrying!
B-But listen!! That doesn't mean Juvia *likes* him or anything!!

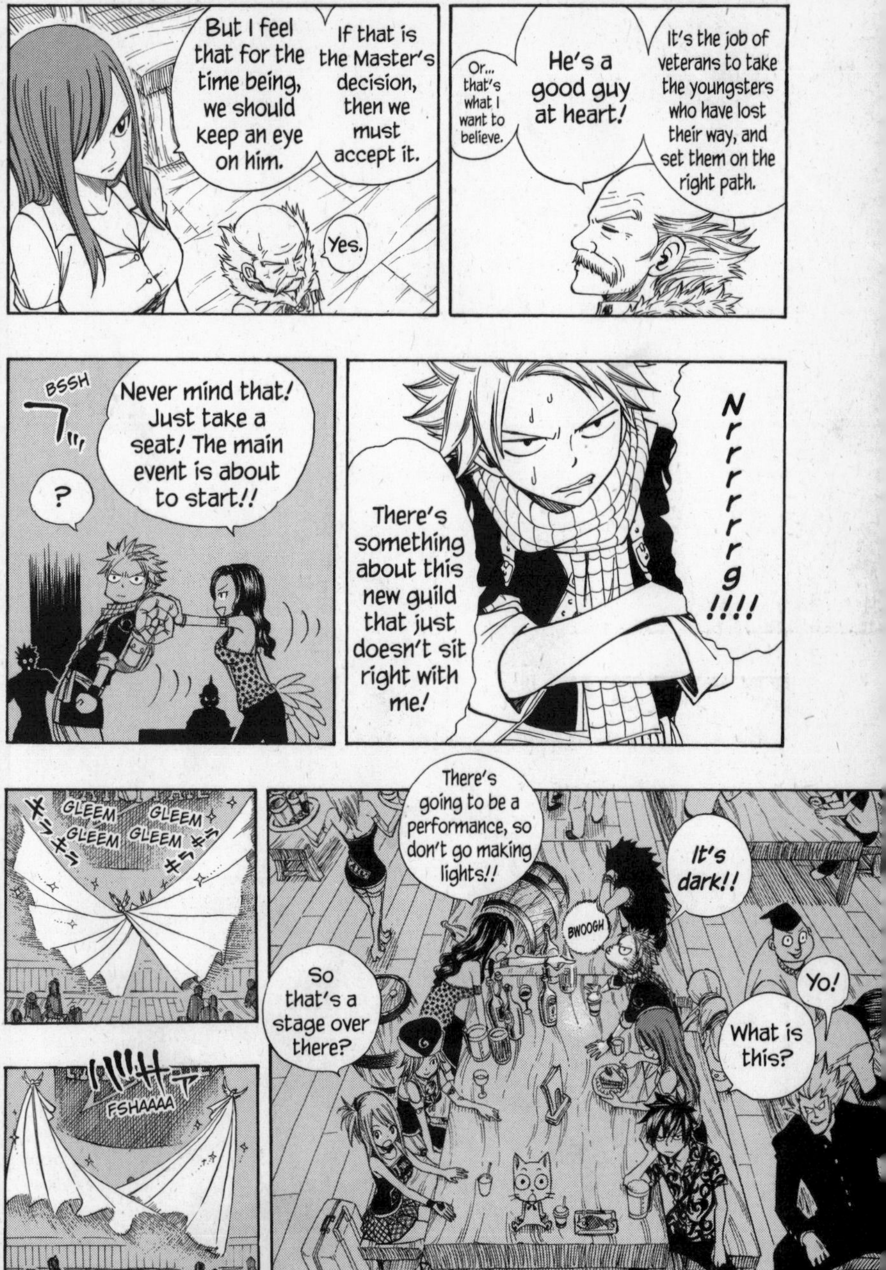
It's the job of veterans to take the youngsters who have lost their way, and set them on the right path.
He's a good guy at heart!
Or... that's what I want to believe.
If that is the Master's decision, then we must accept it.
But I feel that for the time being, we should keep an eye on him.
Yes.
Nrrrrrrg!!!!
There's something about this new guild that just doesn't sit right with me!
BSSH
Never mind that! Just take a seat! The main event is about to start!!
?
There's going to be a performance, so don't go making lights!!
It's dark!!
BWOOGH
Yo!
What is this?
So that's a stage over there?
GLEEM GLEEM GLEEM GLEEM
FSHAAAA

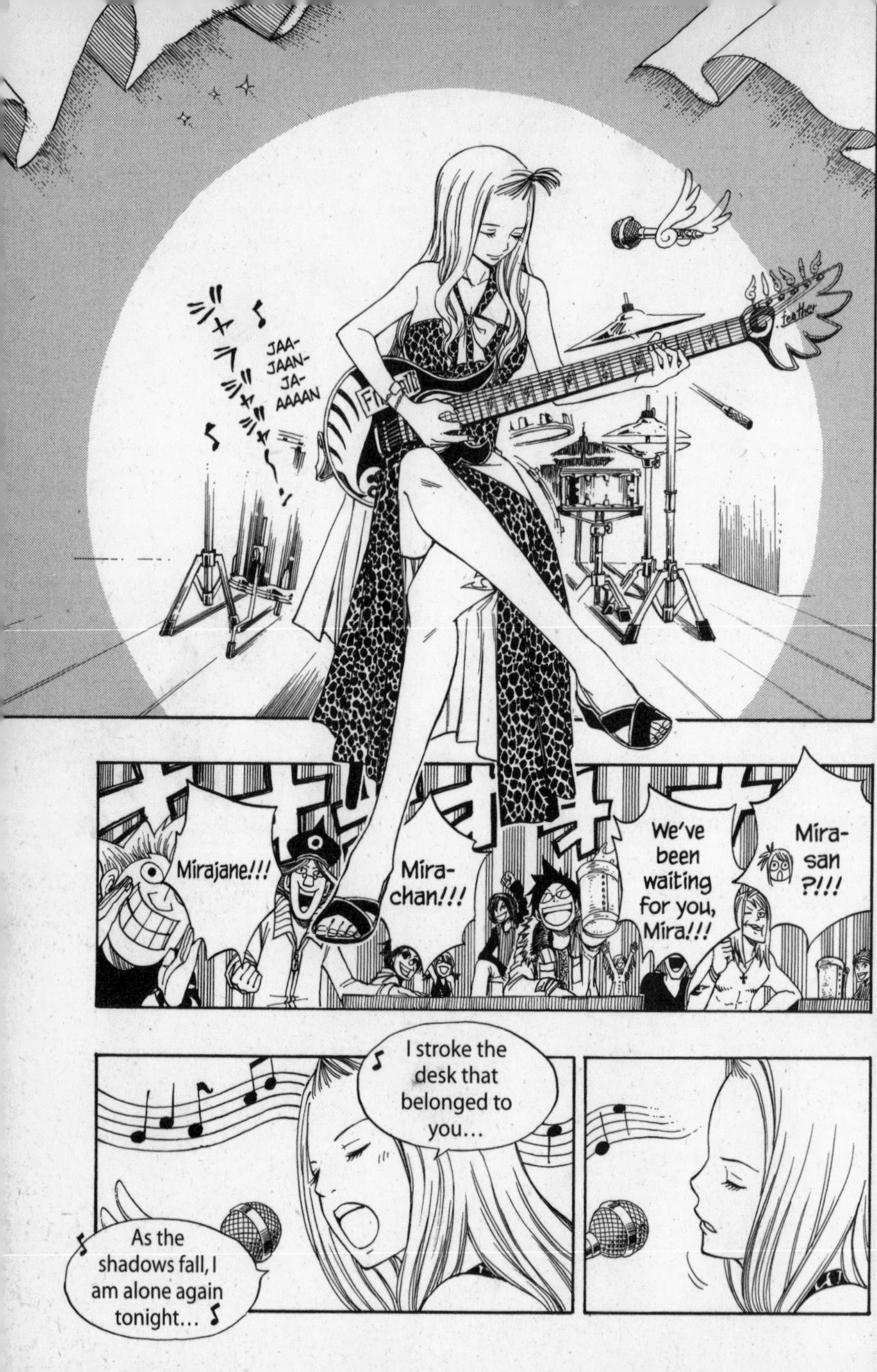
JAA-JAAN-JA-AAAAN
Mira-san?!!!
We've been waiting for you, Mira!!!
Mira-chan!!!
Mirajane!!!
I stroke the desk that belonged to you…
As the shadows fall, I am alone again tonight…

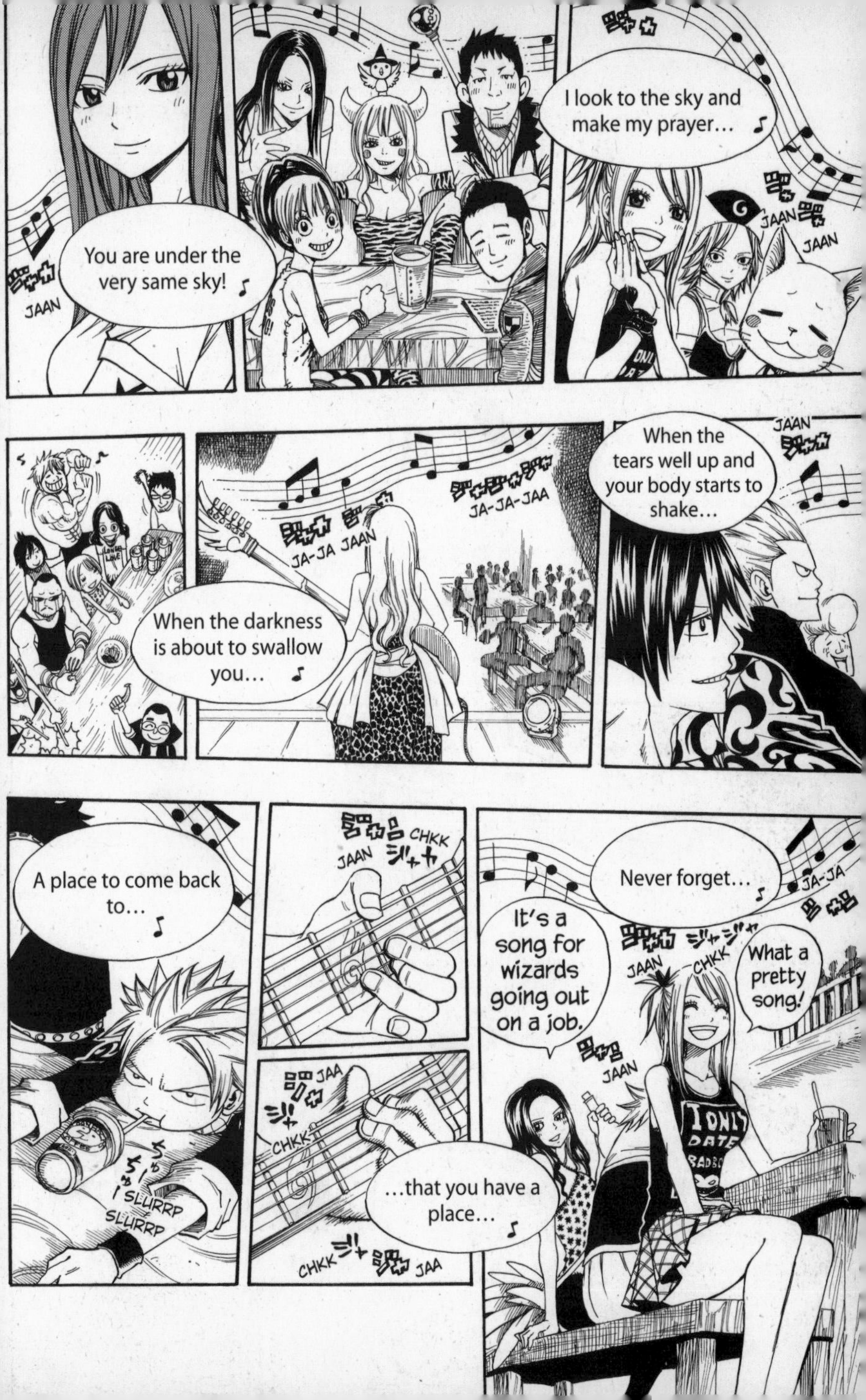
I look to the sky and make my prayer…
JAAN
JAAN
You are under the very same sky!
JAAN
JAAN
When the tears well up and your body starts to shake…
JA-JA-JAA
JA-JA JAAN
When the darkness is about to swallow you…
JA-JA
Never forget…
What a pretty song!
JAAN
CHKK
It's a song for wizards going out on a job.
JAAN
CHKK
JAAN
JAA
CHKK
…that you have a place…
CHKK
JAA
A place to come back to…
SLURRP
SLURRP

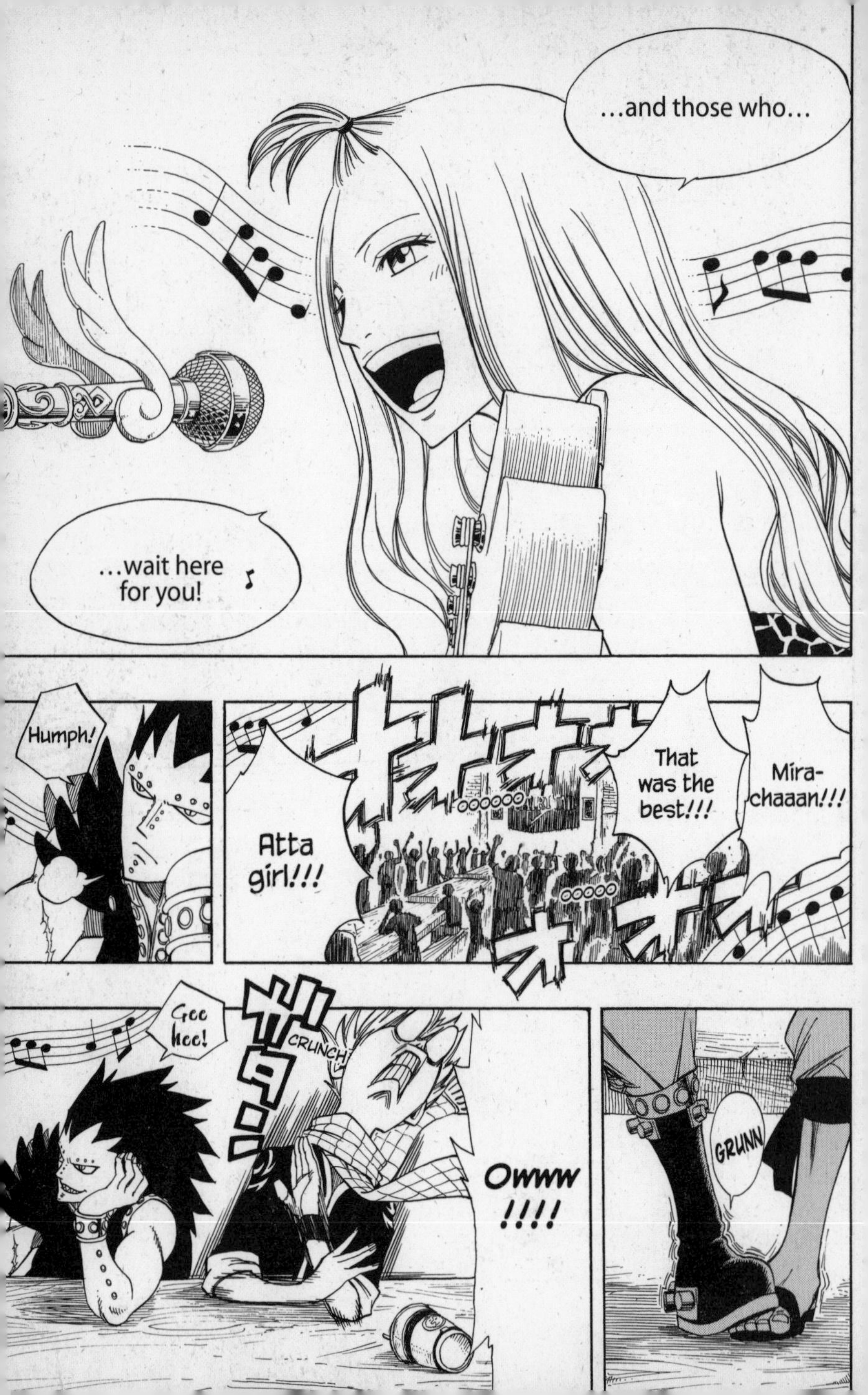
…and those who…
…wait here for you!
Mira-chaaan!!!
That was the best!!!
Atta girl!!!
Humph!
GRUNN
CRUNCH
Gee hee!
Owww!!!!

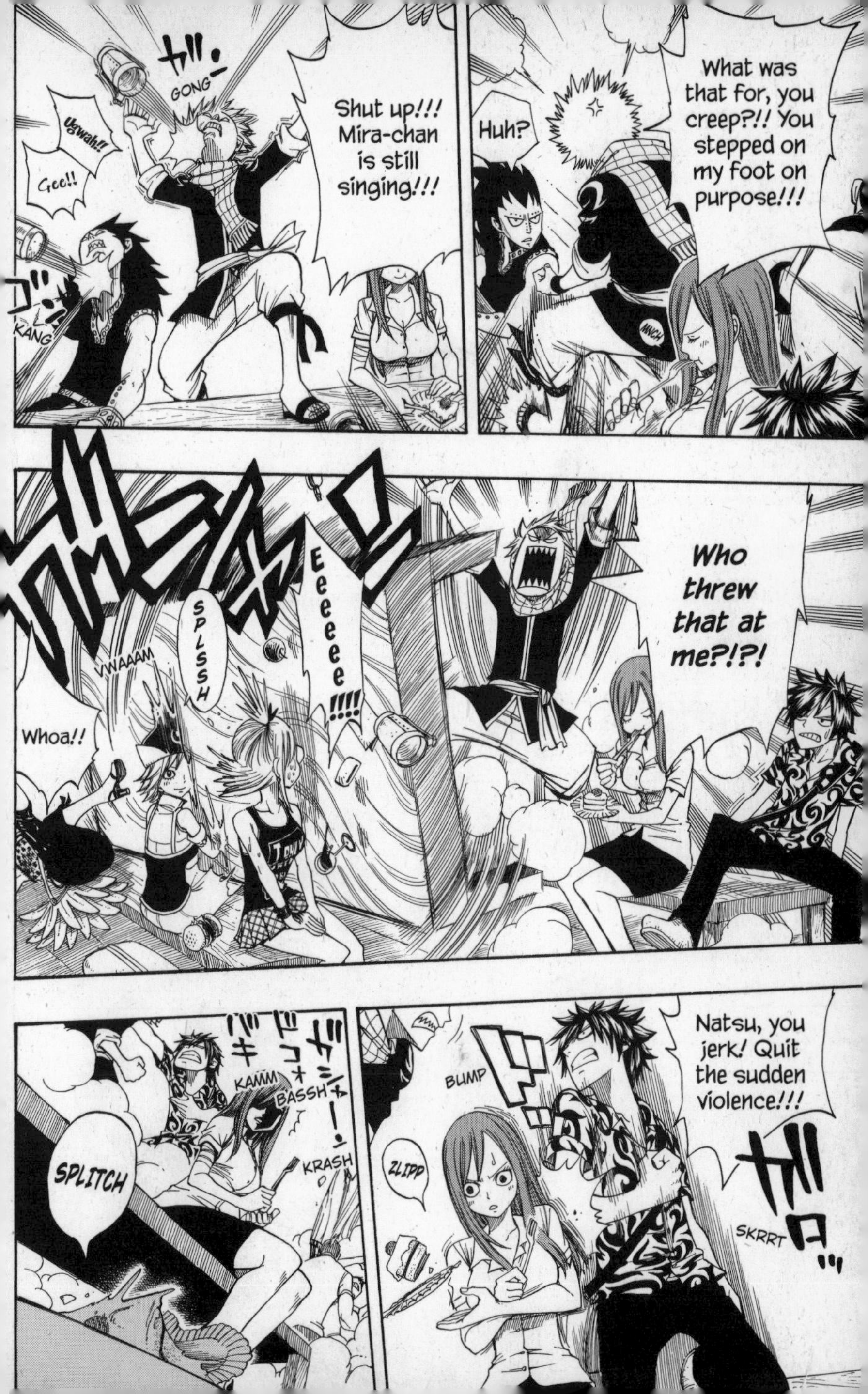
What was that for, you creep?!! You stepped on my foot on purpose!!!
Huh?
MNCH
Shut up!!! Mira-chan is still singing!!!
GONG
Ugwah!!
Gee!!
KANG
Who threw that at me?!?!
Eeeeee!!!!
SPLSSH
VWAAAM
Whoa!!
Natsu, you jerk! Quit the sudden violence!!!
SKRRT
BUMP
ZLIPP
KAMM
BASSH
KRASH
SPLITCH

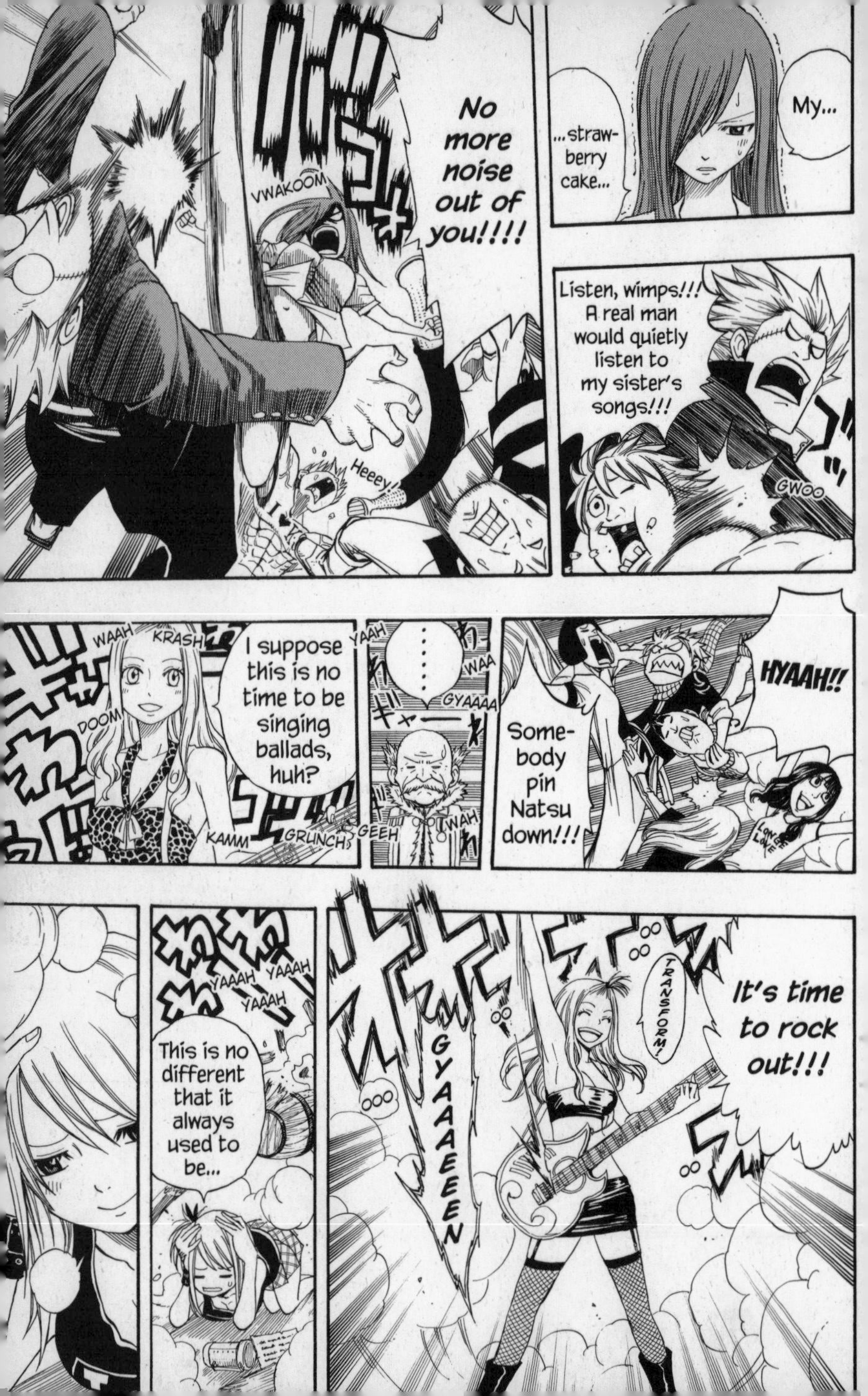
My...
...straw-
berry
cake...
Listen, wimps!!!
A real man
would quietly
listen to
my sister's
songs!!!
GWOO
No
more
noise
out of
you!!!!
VWAKOOM
Heeey
HYAAH!!
Some-
body
pin
Natsu
down!!!
LONG LOVE
......
YAAH
WAA
GYAAAA
WAH
GEEH
I suppose
this is no
time to be
singing
ballads,
huh?
WAAH
KRASH
DOOM
KAMM
GRUNCH
It's time
to rock
out!!!
TRANSFORM!
GYAAAAEEEN
YAAAH
YAAAH
YAAAH
This is no
different
that it
always
used to
be...

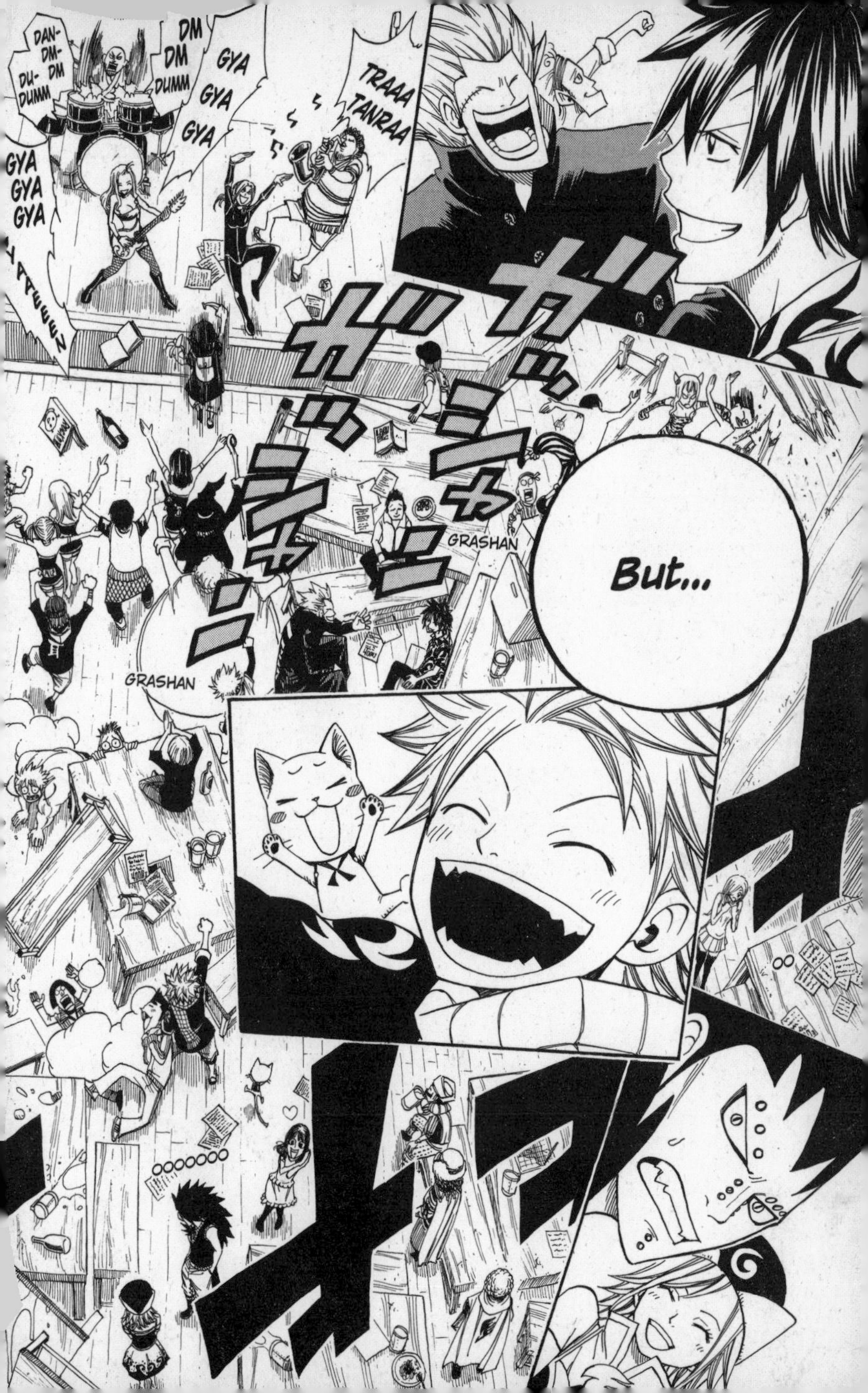
TRAAA TANRAA
GYA GYA GYA
DM DM DUMM
DAN-DM-DM DU-DUMM
GYA GYA GYA
YAAEEEN
GRASHAN
But...
GRASHAN

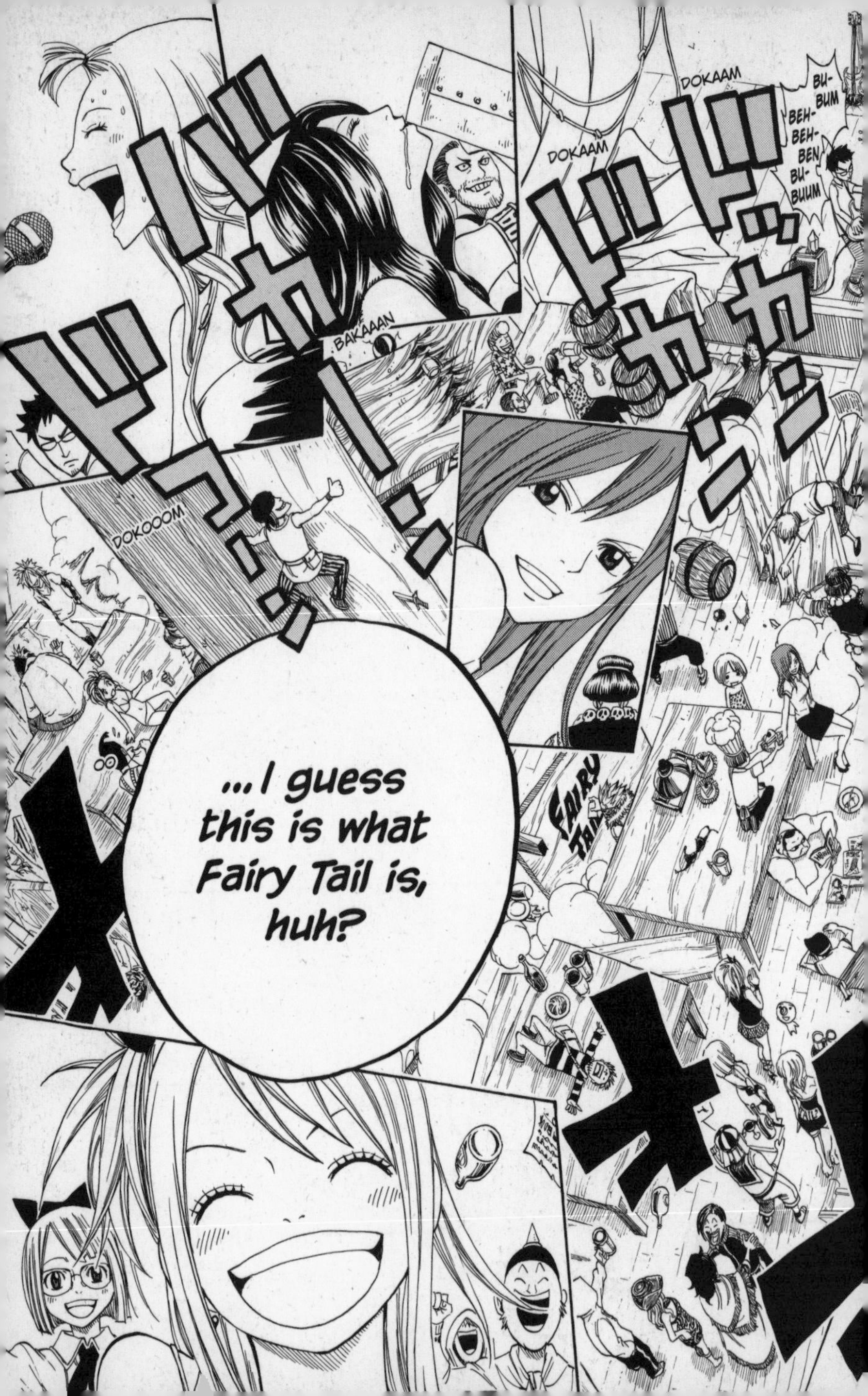
DOKAAM
BU-BUM
BEH-BEH-BEN
BU-BUUM
DOKAAM
BAKAAAN
DOKOOOM
...I guess this is what Fairy Tail is, huh?

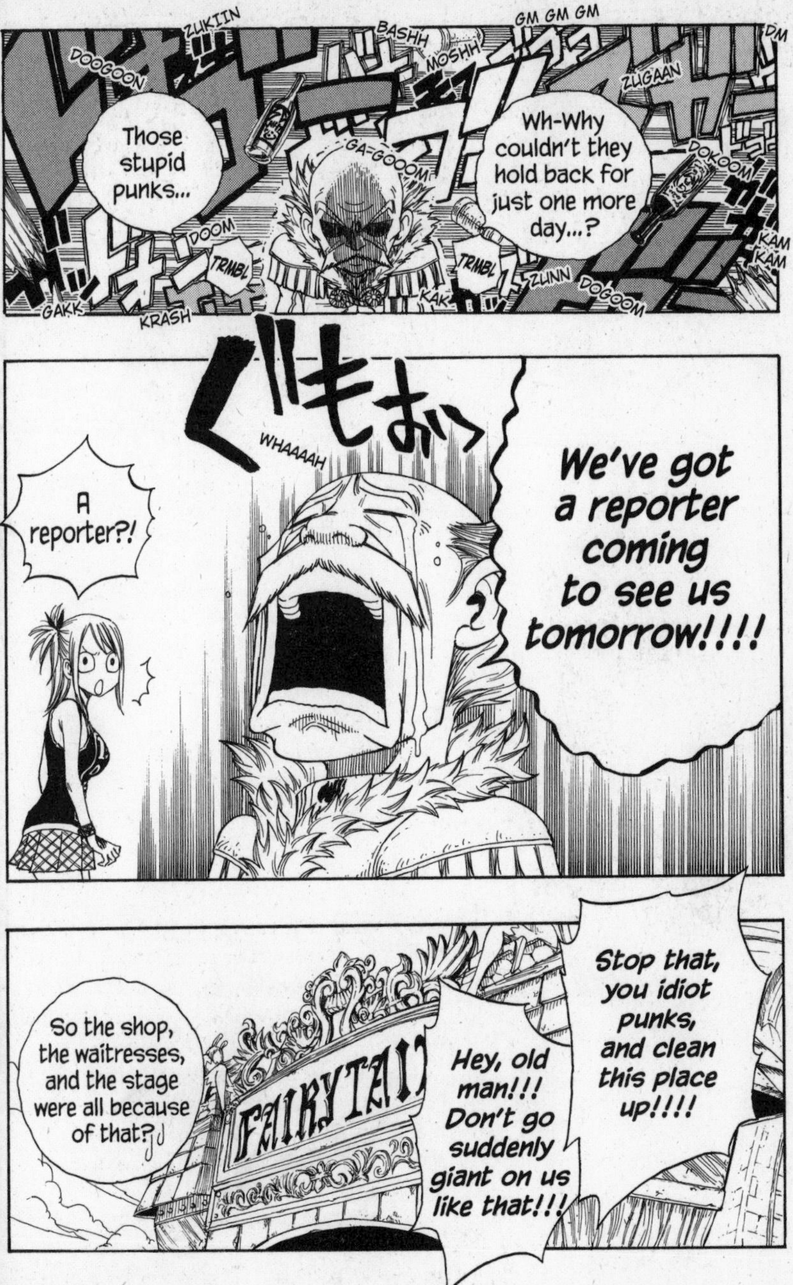
DM
GM GM GM
ZUGAAN
BASHH
MOSHH
ZUKIIN
DOOGOON
Wh-Why couldn't they hold back for just one more day...?
DOKOOM
GA-GOOOM
Those stupid punks...
KAM KAM
DOGOOM
ZUNN
TRMBL
KAK
TRMBL
DOOM
KRASH
GAKK
WHAAAAH
We've got a reporter coming to see us tomorrow!!!!
A reporter?!
Stop that, you idiot punks, and clean this place up!!!!
Hey, old man!!! Don't go suddenly giant on us like that!!!
FAIRY TAIL
So the shop, the waitresses, and the stage were all because of that?

FAIRY TAIL

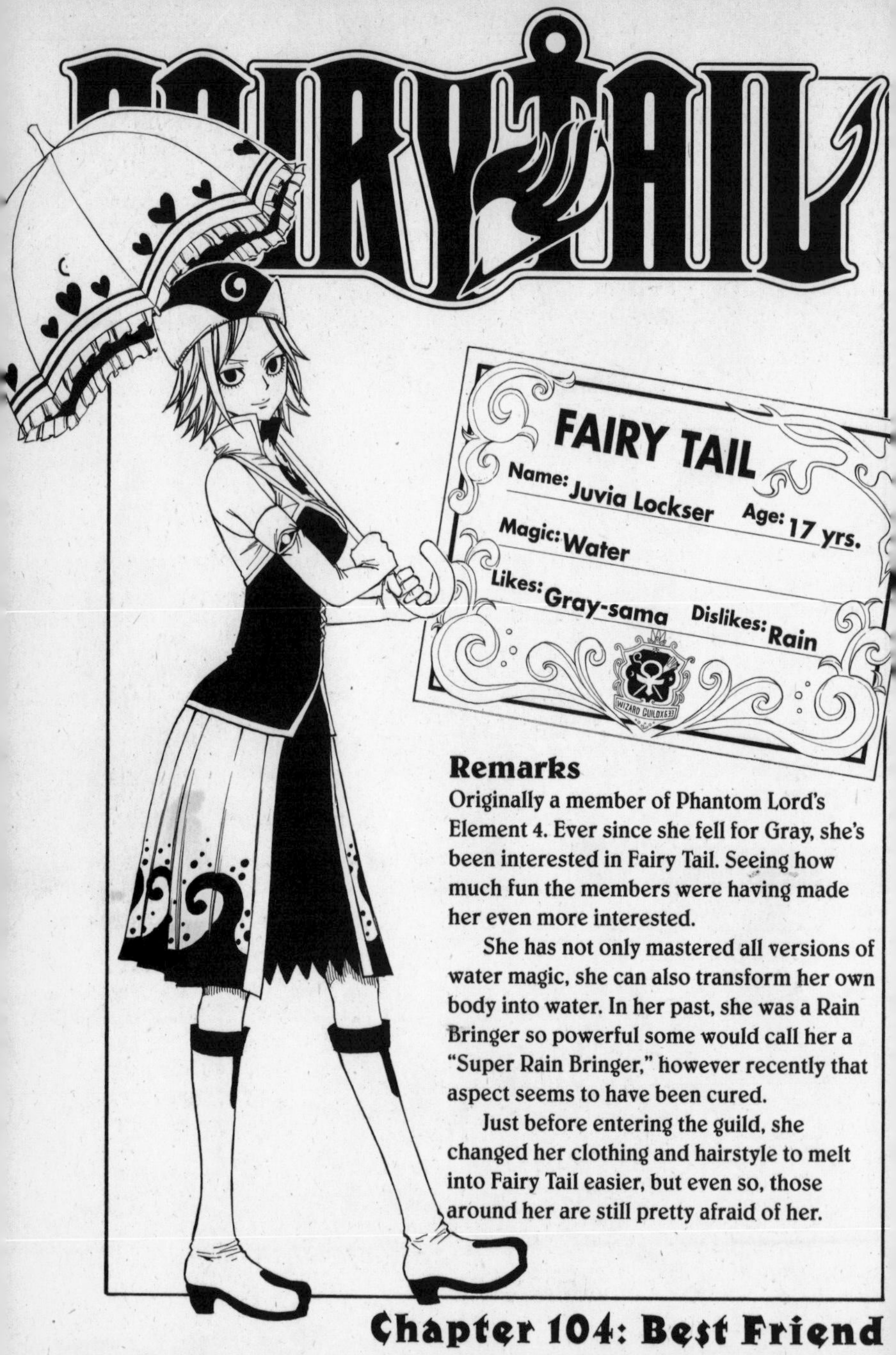

FAIRY TAIL

Name: Juvia Lockser Age: 17 yrs.

Magic: Water

Likes: Gray-sama Dislikes: Rain

WIZARD GUILDX633

Remarks

Originally a member of Phantom Lord's Element 4. Ever since she fell for Gray, she's been interested in Fairy Tail. Seeing how much fun the members were having made her even more interested.

She has not only mastered all versions of water magic, she can also transform her own body into water. In her past, she was a Rain Bringer so powerful some would call her a "Super Rain Bringer," however recently that aspect seems to have been cured.

Just before entering the guild, she changed her clothing and hairstyle to melt into Fairy Tail easier, but even so, those around her are still pretty afraid of her.

Chapter 104: Best Friend

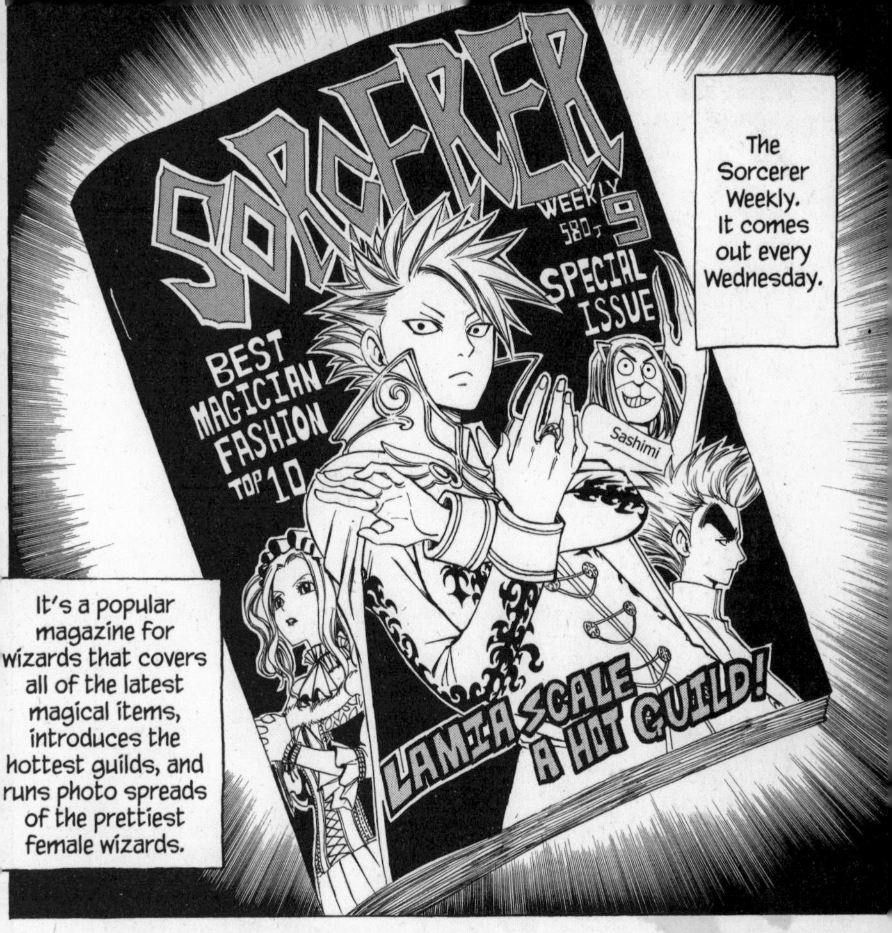
The Sorcerer Weekly. It comes out every Wednesday.
SORCERER
WEEKLY 9
580J
SPECIAL ISSUE
BEST MAGICIAN FASHION TOP 10
Sashimi
LAMIA SCALE A HOT GUILD!
It's a popular magazine for wizards that covers all of the latest magical items, introduces the hottest guilds, and runs photo spreads of the prettiest female wizards.

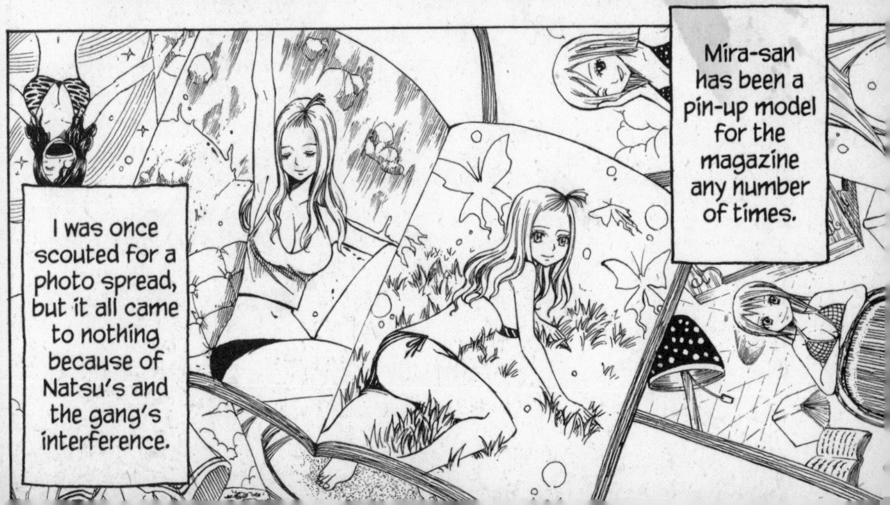
Mira-san has been a pin-up model for the magazine any number of times.
I was once scouted for a photo spread, but it all came to nothing because of Natsu's and the gang's interference.

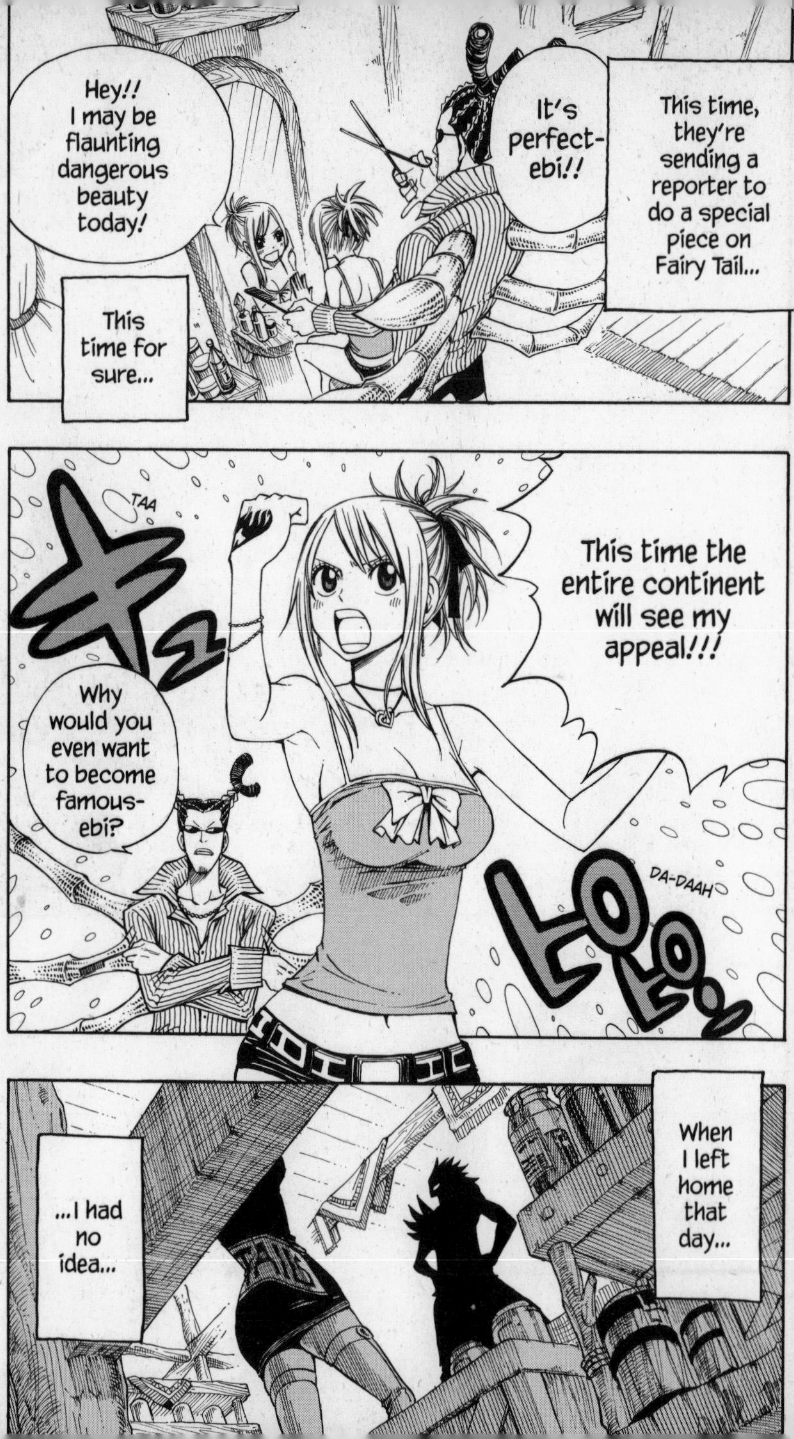
This time, they're sending a reporter to do a special piece on Fairy Tail...
It's perfect-ebi!!
Hey!! I may be flaunting dangerous beauty today!
This time for sure...
This time the entire continent will see my appeal!!!
DA-DAAH
TAA
Why would you even want to become famous-ebi?
When I left home that day...
...I had no idea...

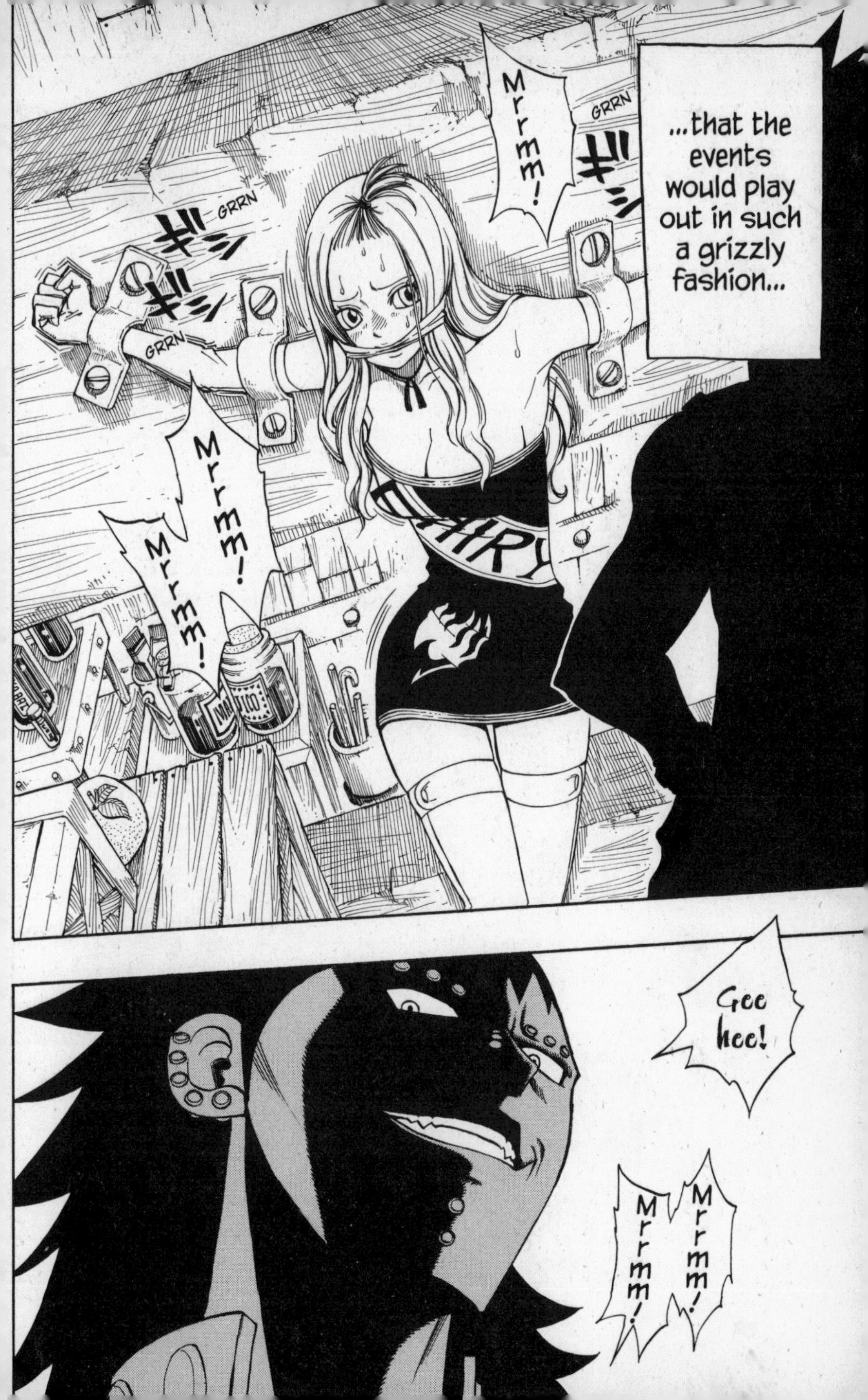
...that the events would play out in such a grizzly fashion...
GRRN
ギシ
Mrrmm!
GRRN
ギシ
ギシ
GRRN
Mrrmm!
Mrrmm!
Gee hee!
Mrrmm!
Mrrmm!

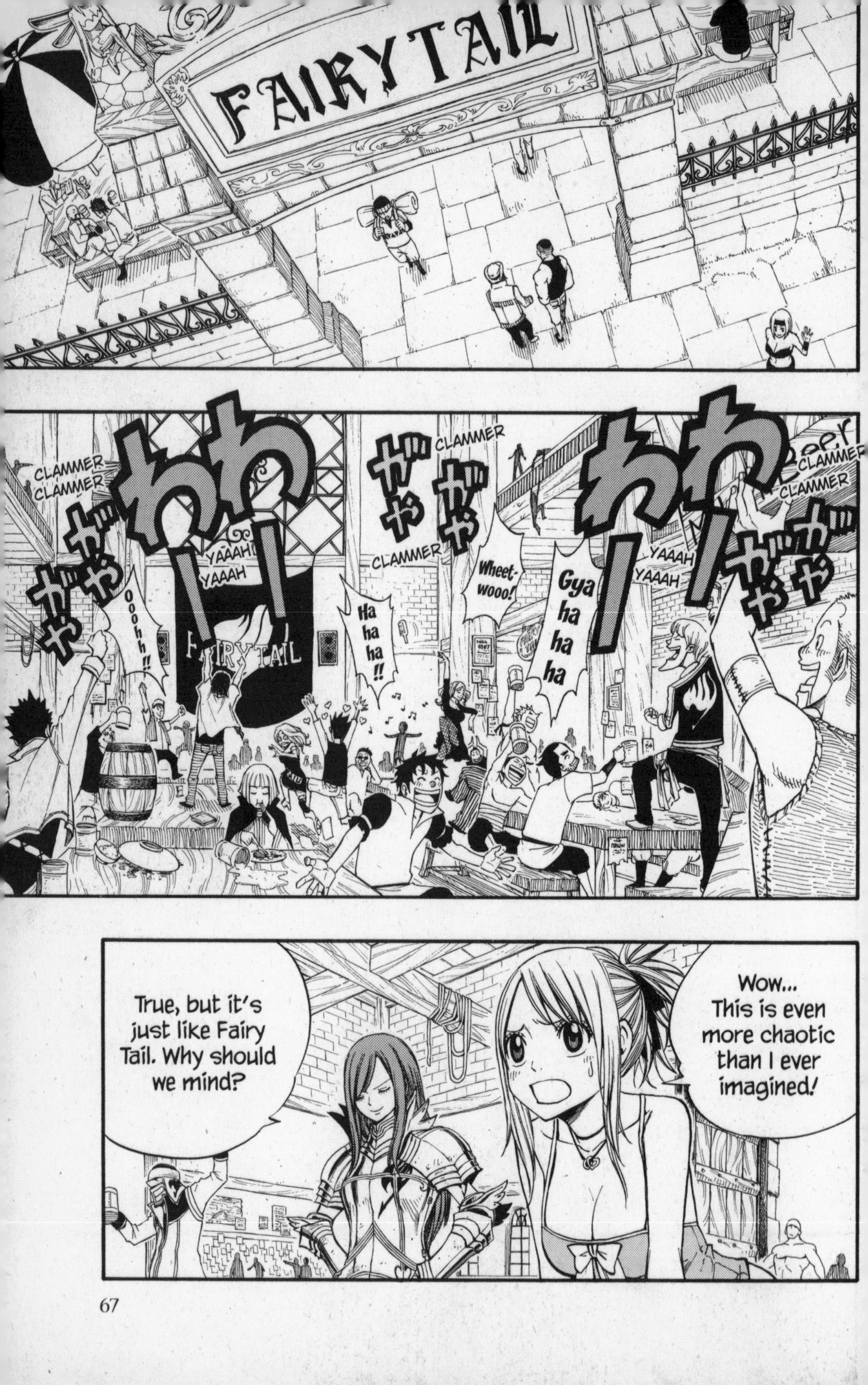
FAIRY TAIL
CLAMMER CLAMMER
ガヤガヤ
YAAAH YAAAH
Gya ha ha ha ha
Wheet-wooo!
CLAMMER
ガヤガヤ
CLAMMER
Ha ha ha!!
YAAAH YAAAH
Ooohh!!
FAIRY TAIL
CLAMMER CLAMMER
ガヤガヤ
Wow... This is even more chaotic than I ever imagined!
True, but it's just like Fairy Tail. Why should we mind?

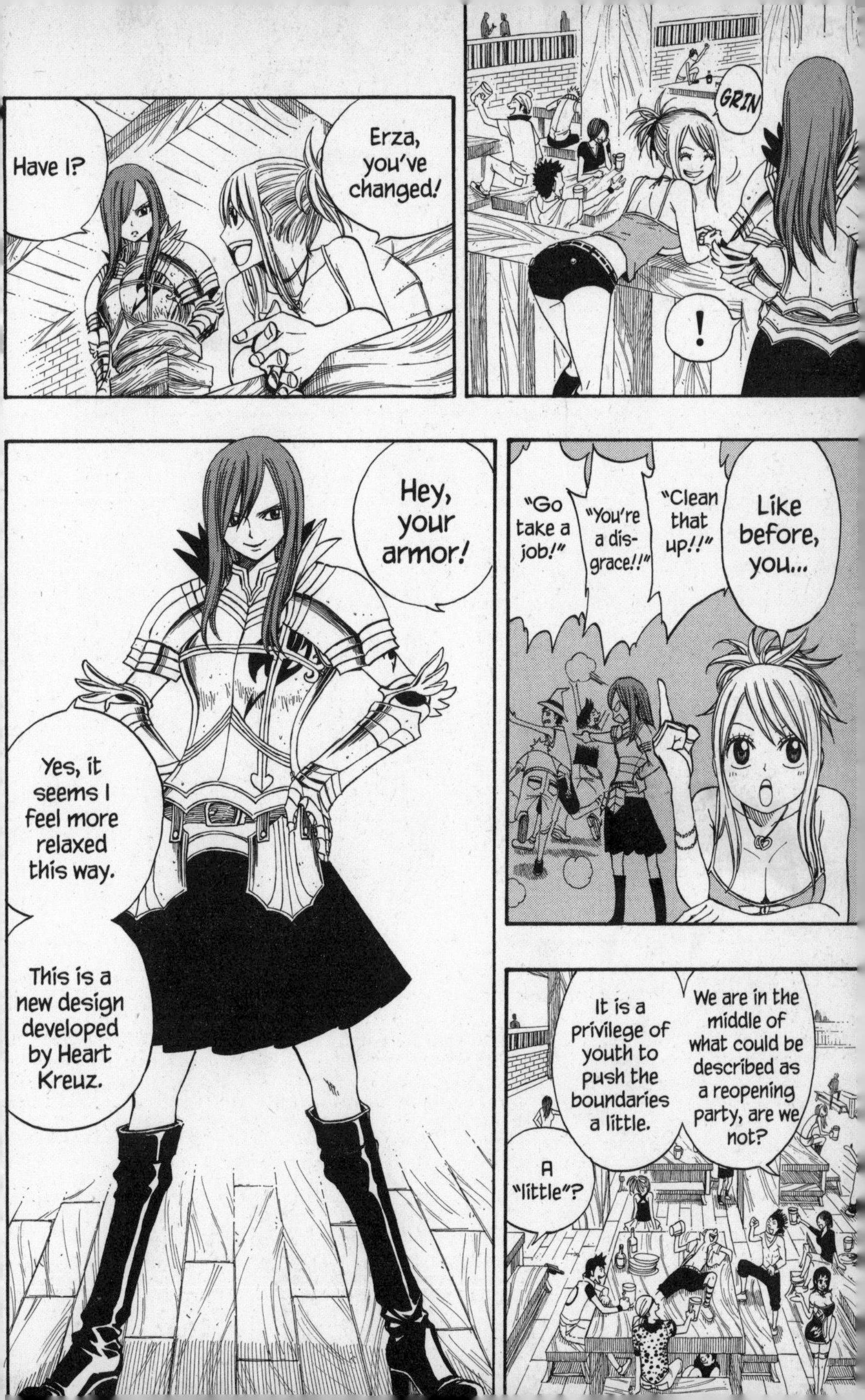
GRIN
!
Erza, you've changed!
Have I?
Like before, you...
"Clean that up!!"
"You're a dis-grace!!"
"Go take a job!"
We are in the middle of what could be described as a reopening party, are we not?
It is a privilege of youth to push the boundaries a little.
A "little"?
Hey, your armor!
Yes, it seems I feel more relaxed this way.
This is a new design developed by Heart Kreuz.

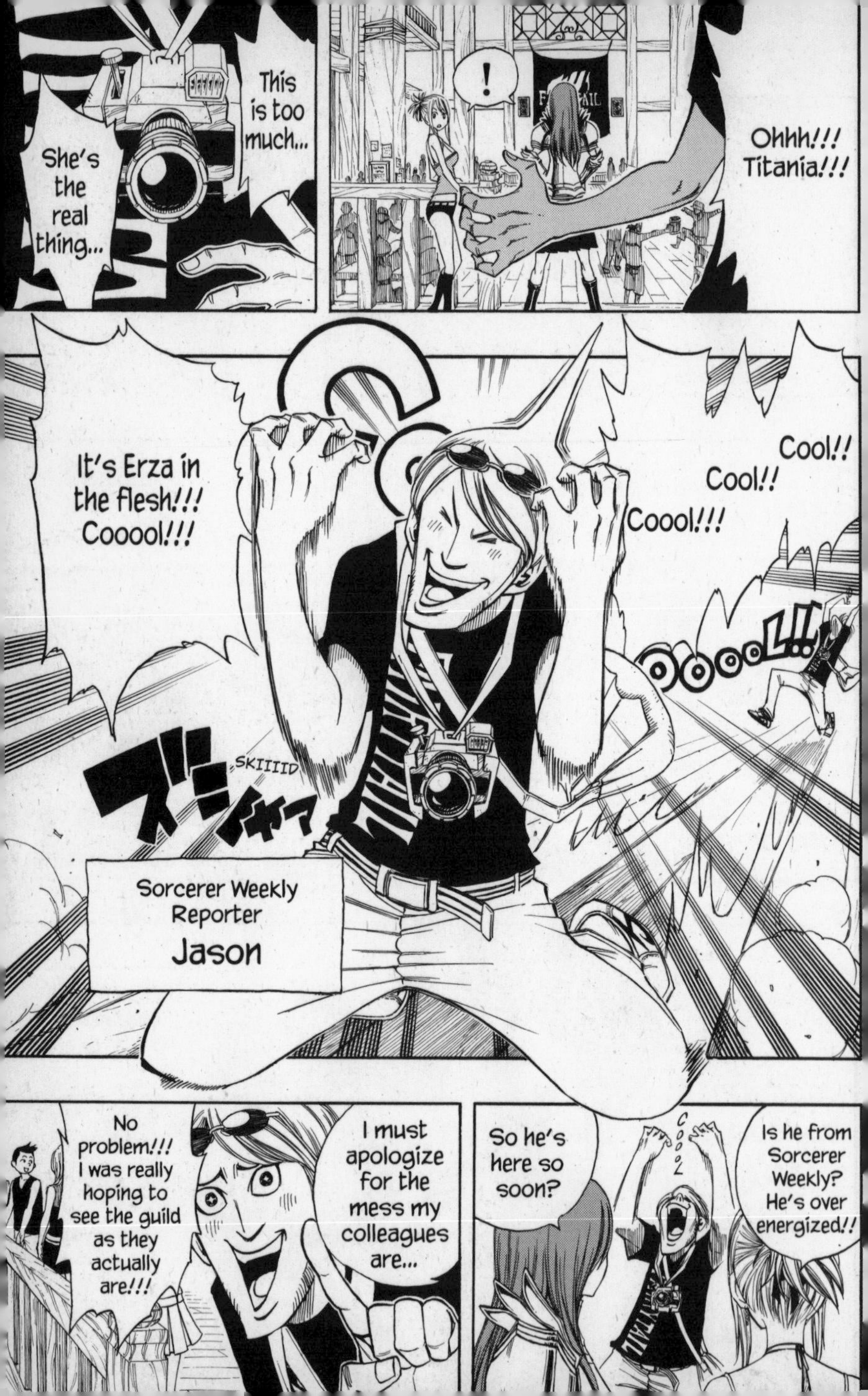

Ohhh!!! Titania!!!
!
This is too much...
She's the real thing...
Cool!!
Cool!!
Coool!!!
OOOOOL!!
It's Erza in the flesh!!! Cooool!!!
SKIIIID
Sorcerer Weekly Reporter
Jason
Is he from Sorcerer Weekly? He's over energized!!
COOOL
So he's here so soon?
I must apologize for the mess my colleagues are...
No problem!!! I was really hoping to see the guild as they actually are!!!

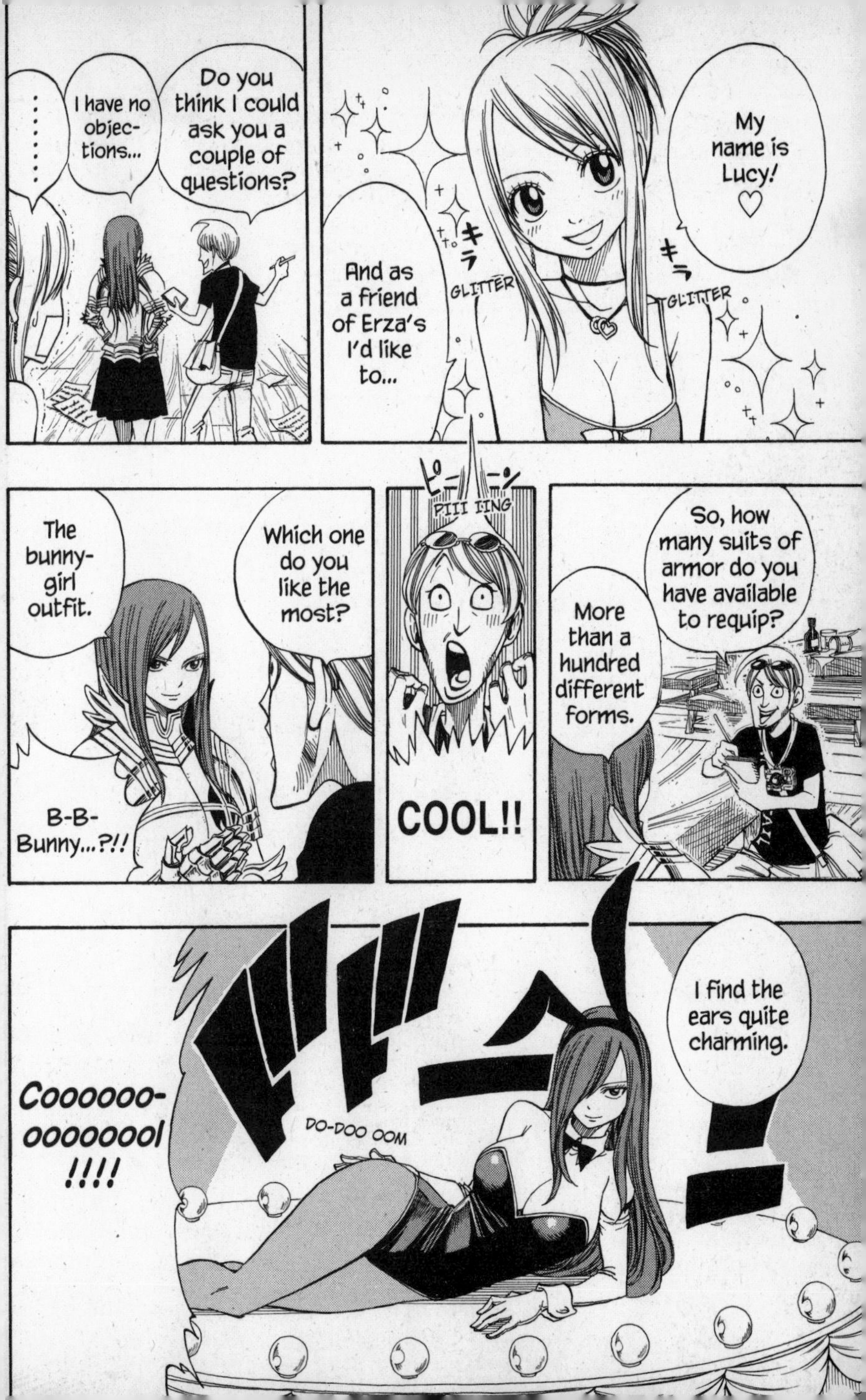
My name is Lucy! ♡
キラ
GLITTER
キラ
GLITTER
And as a friend of Erza's I'd like to...
Do you think I could ask you a couple of questions?
I have no objections...
......
So, how many suits of armor do you have available to requip?
More than a hundred different forms.
ピーン
PIII IING
COOL!!
Which one do you like the most?
The bunny-girl outfit.
B-B-Bunny...?!!
I find the ears quite charming.
DO-DOO OOM
Cooooooo-oooooool!!!!

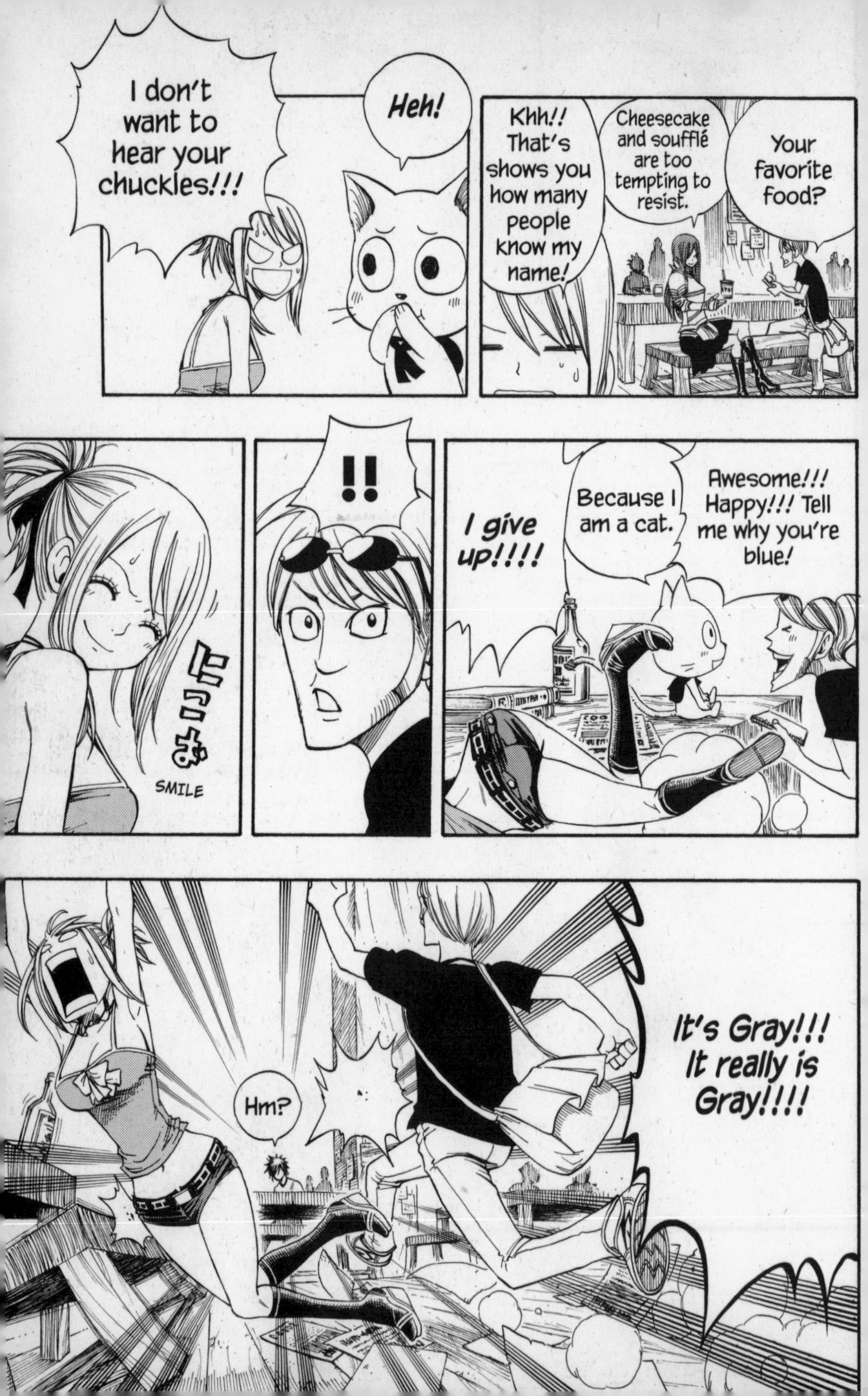
Your favorite food?
Cheesecake and soufflé are too tempting to resist.
Khh!! That's shows you how many people know my name!
Heh!
I don't want to hear your chuckles!!!
Awesome!!! Happy!!! Tell me why you're blue!
Because I am a cat.
I give up!!!!
!!
SMILE
It's Gray!!! It really is Gray!!!!
Hm?

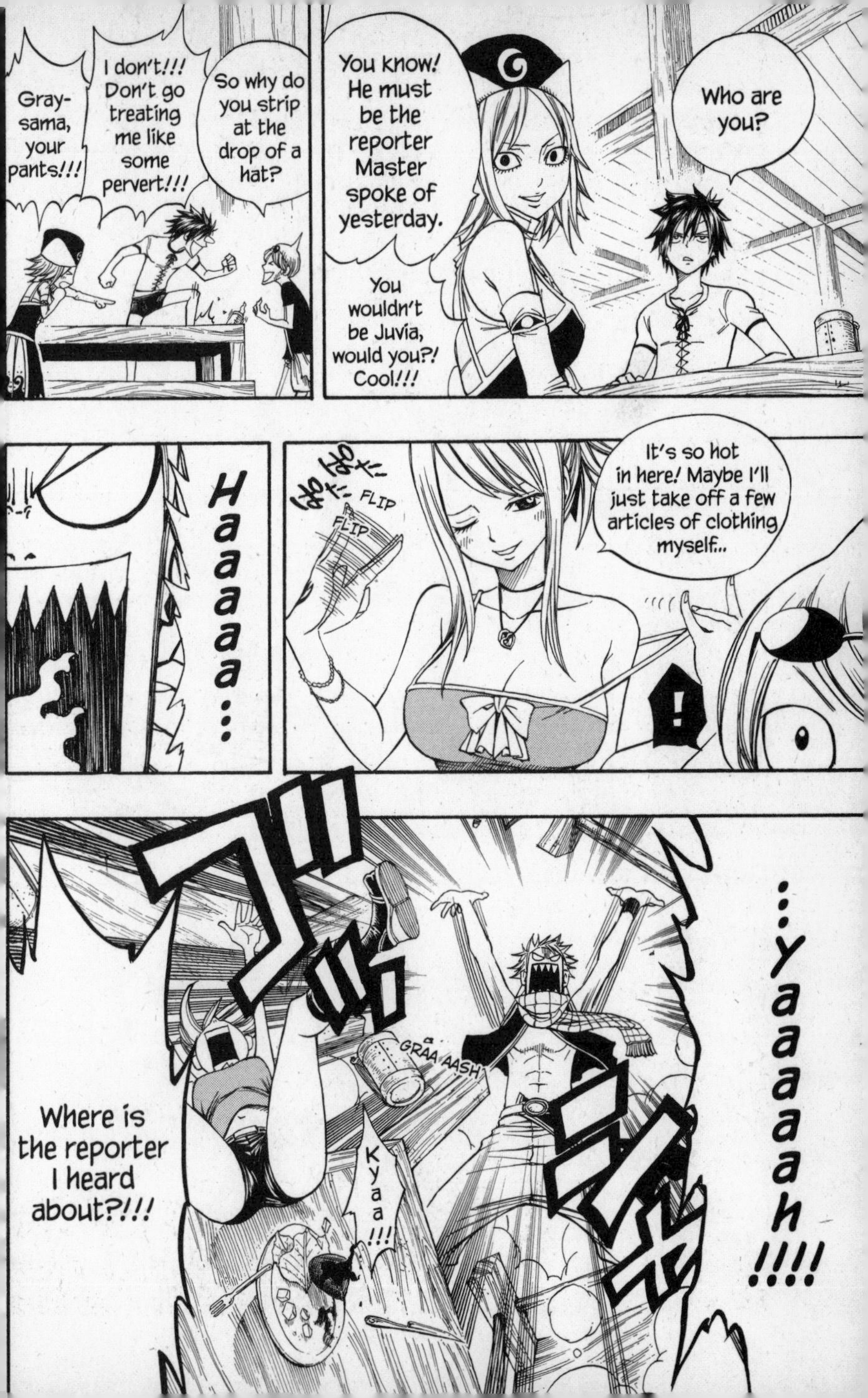

Who are you?
You know! He must be the reporter Master spoke of yesterday.
You wouldn't be Juvia, would you?! Cool!!!
So why do you strip at the drop of a hat?
I don't!!! Don't go treating me like some pervert!!!
Gray-sama, your pants!!!
It's so hot in here! Maybe I'll just take off a few articles of clothing myself...
FLIP
FLIP
!
Haaaaaa...
...Yaaaaaaah!!!!
GRAAAASH
Kyaaa!!!
Where is the reporter I heard about?!!!

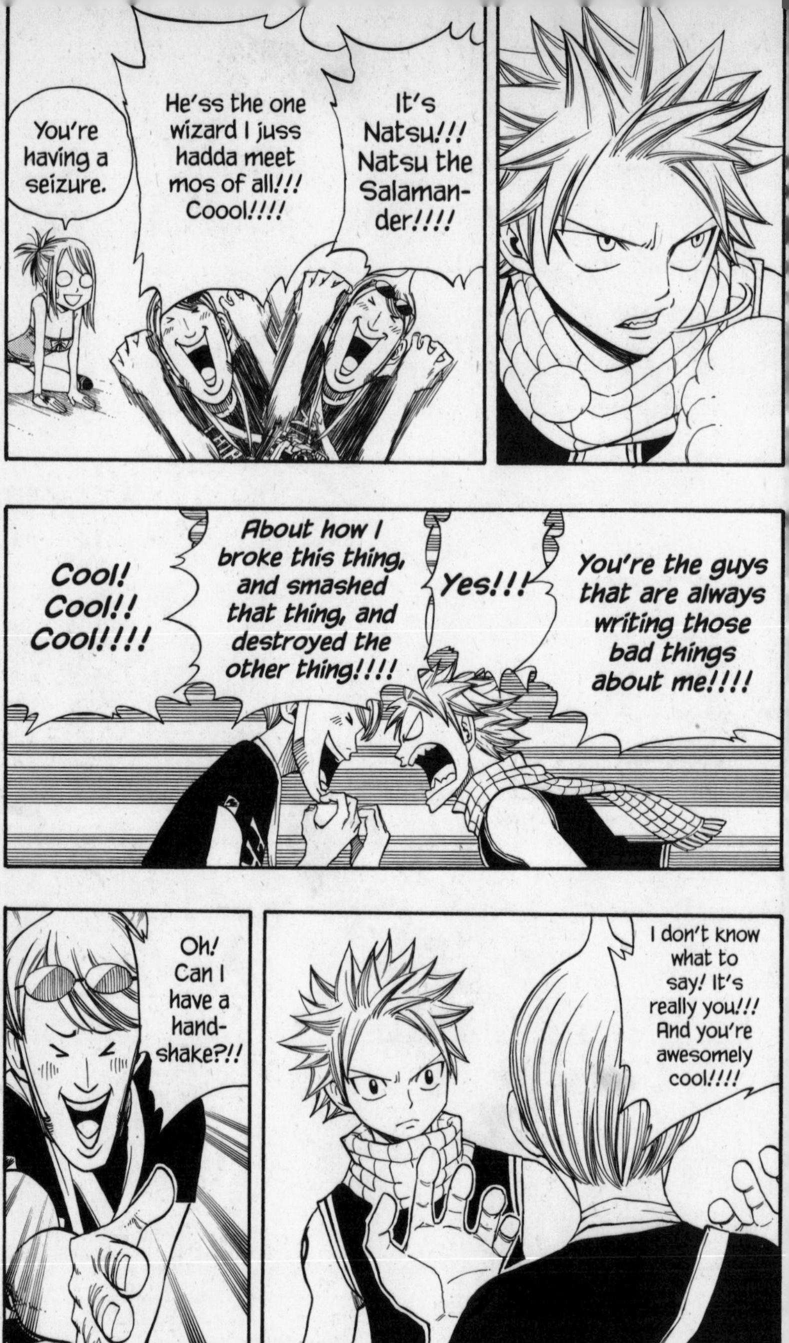
It's Natsu!!! Natsu the Salamander!!!!
He'ss the one wizard I juss hadda meet mos of all!!! Coool!!!!
You're having a seizure.
You're the guys that are always writing those bad things about me!!!!
Yes!!!
About how I broke this thing, and smashed that thing, and destroyed the other thing!!!!
Cool! Cool!! Cool!!!!
I don't know what to say! It's really you!!! And you're awesomely cool!!!!
Oh! Can I have a handshake?!!

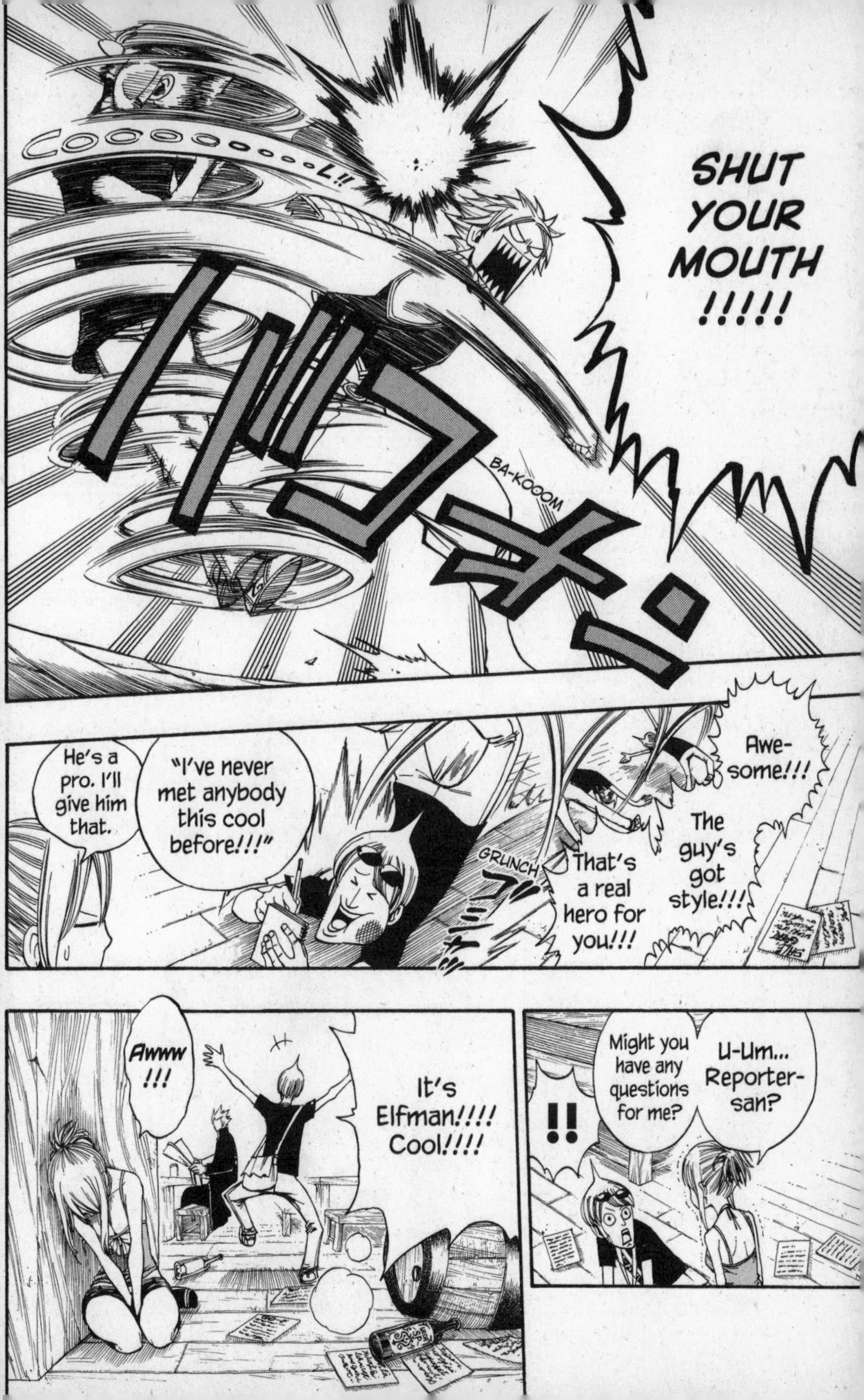
SHUT YOUR MOUTH!!!!!
Coooooooo...L!!
BA-KOOOM
Awe-some!!!
The guy's got style!!!
That's a real hero for you!!!
GRUNCH
"I've never met anybody this cool before!!!"
He's a pro. I'll give him that.
U-Um... Reporter-san?
Might you have any questions for me?
!!
It's Elfman!!!! Cool!!!!
Awww!!!

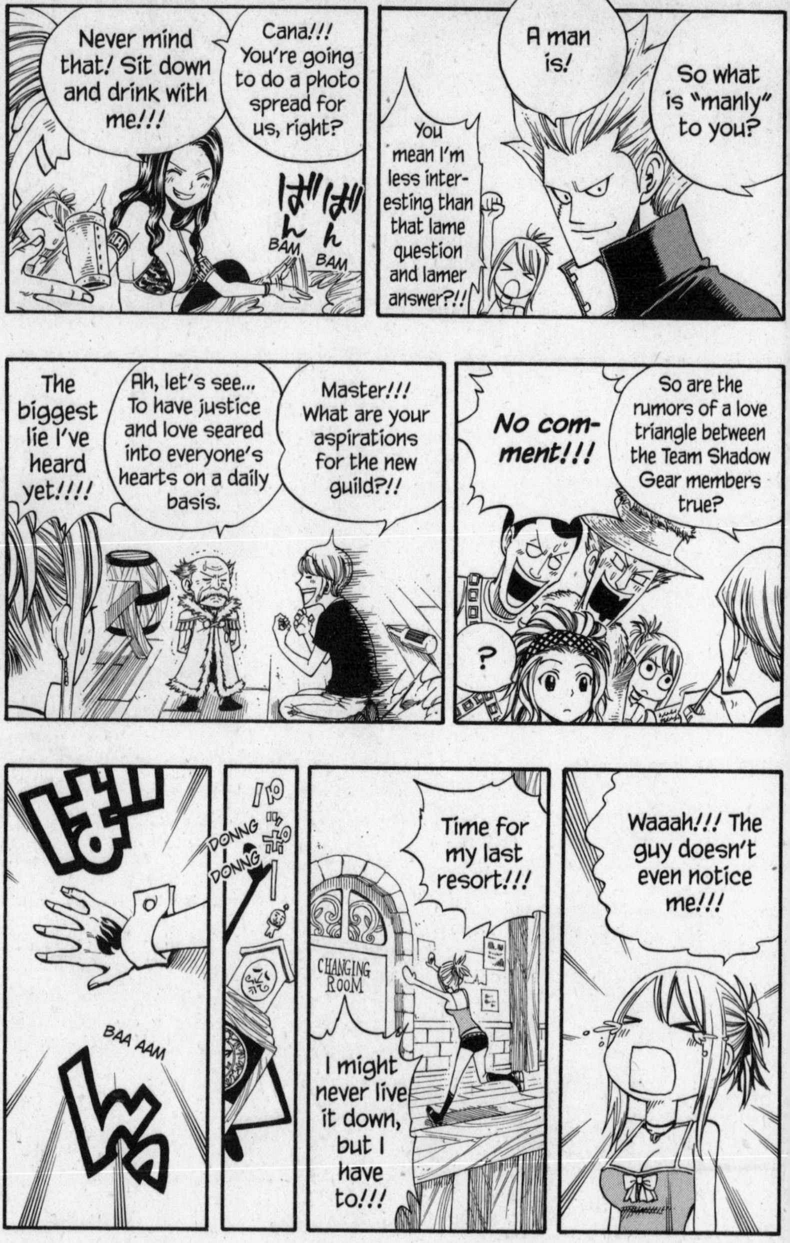
So what is "manly" to you?
A man is!
You mean I'm less interesting than that lame question and lamer answer?!!
Cana!!! You're going to do a photo spread for us, right?
Never mind that! Sit down and drink with me!!!
ばん ばん
BAM BAM
So are the rumors of a love triangle between the Team Shadow Gear members true?
No comment!!!
?
Master!!! What are your aspirations for the new guild?!!
Ah, let's see... To have justice and love seared into everyone's hearts on a daily basis.
The biggest lie I've heard yet!!!!
Waaah!!! The guy doesn't even notice me!!!
Time for my last resort!!!
CHANGING ROOM
I might never live it down, but I have to!!!
DONNG DONNG
BAA AAM

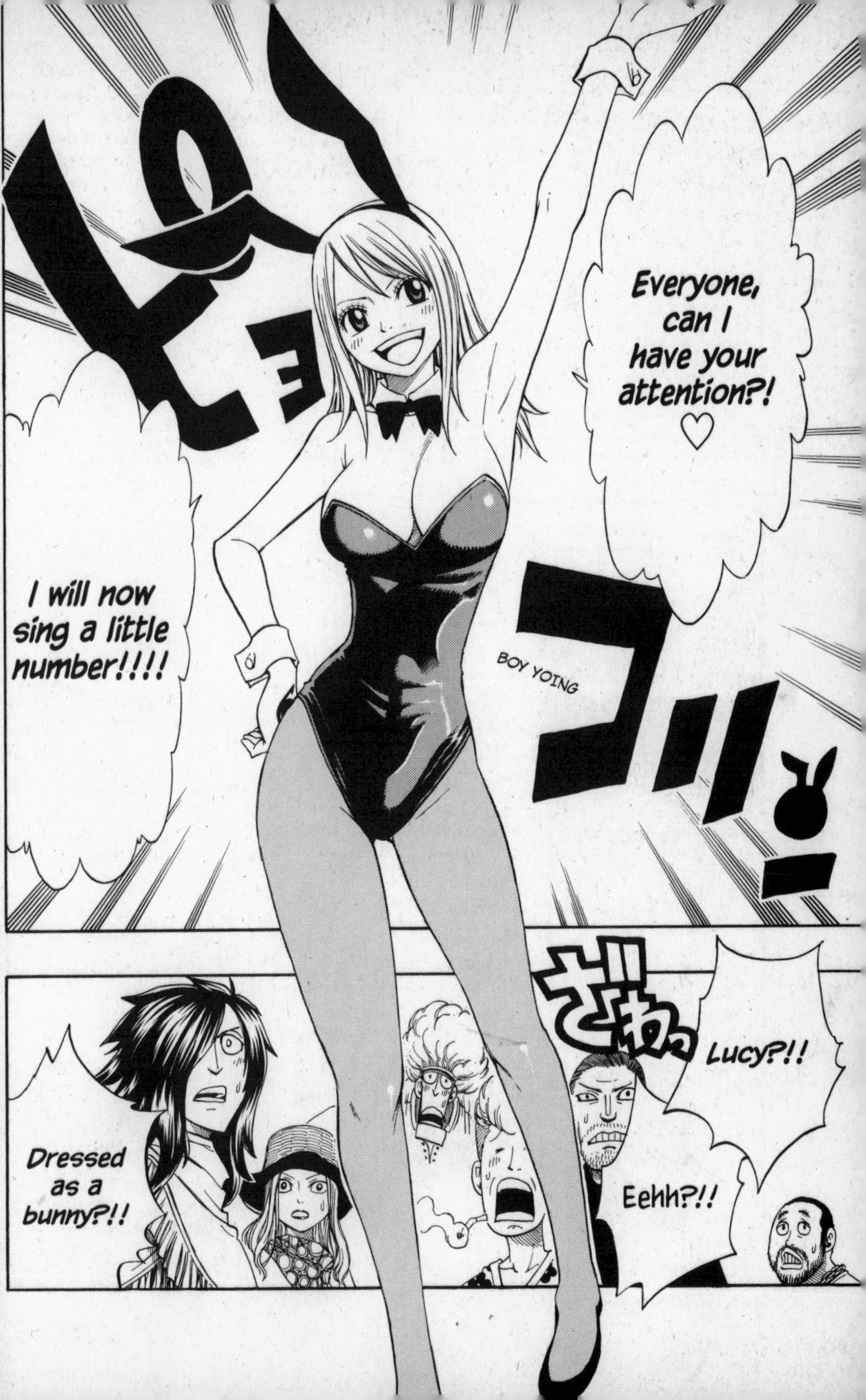
Everyone, can I have your attention?! ♡
I will now sing a little number!!!!
BOY YOING
ざわっ
Lucy?!!
Eehh?!!
Dressed as a bunny?!!

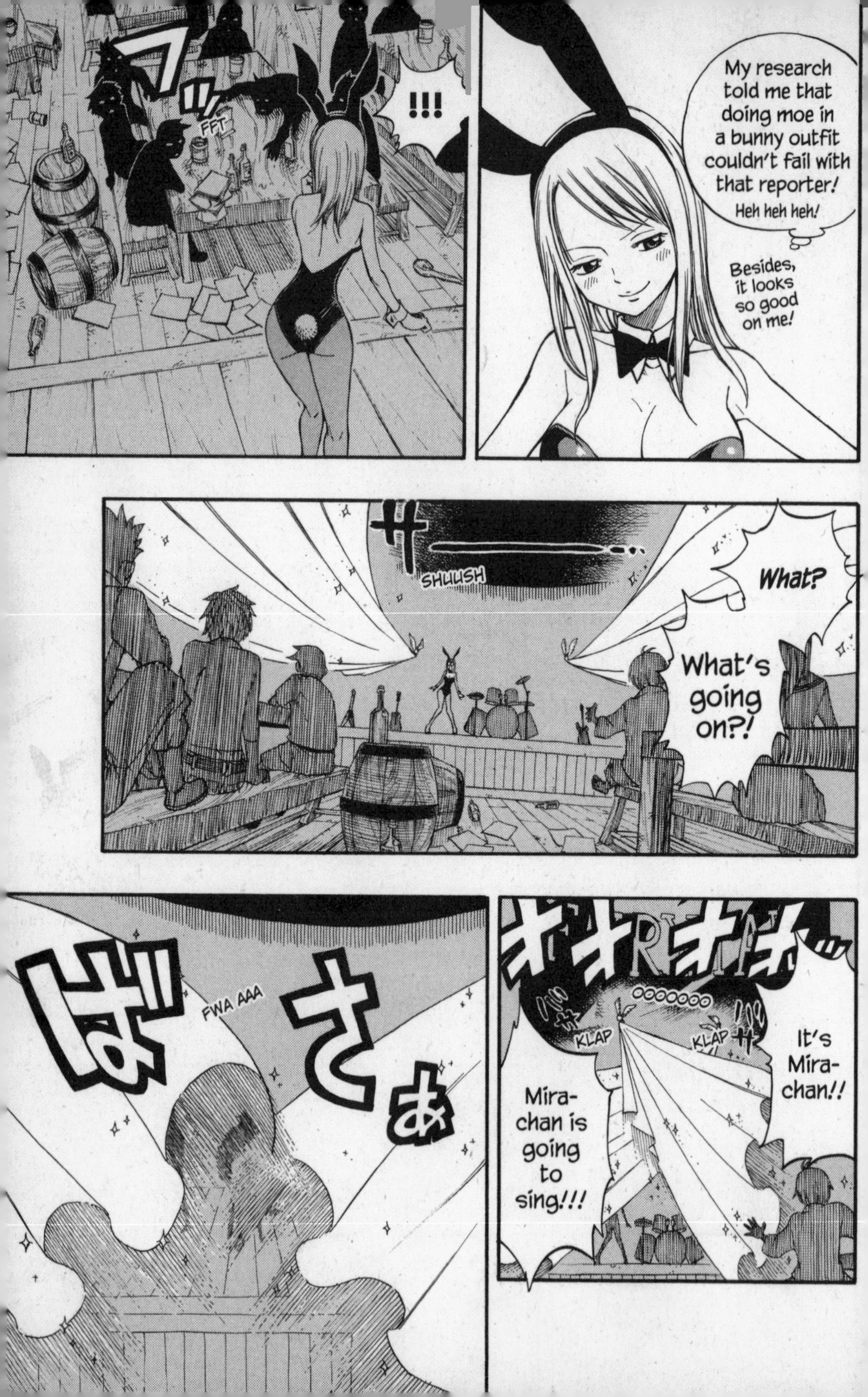

My research told me that doing moe in a bunny outfit couldn't fail with that reporter!
Heh heh heh!
Besides, it looks so good on me!
!!!
FFT
What?
What's going on?!
SHUUSH
It's Mira-chan!!
KLAP
oooooooo
KLAP
Mira-chan is going to sing!!!
FWA AAA
ばさぁ

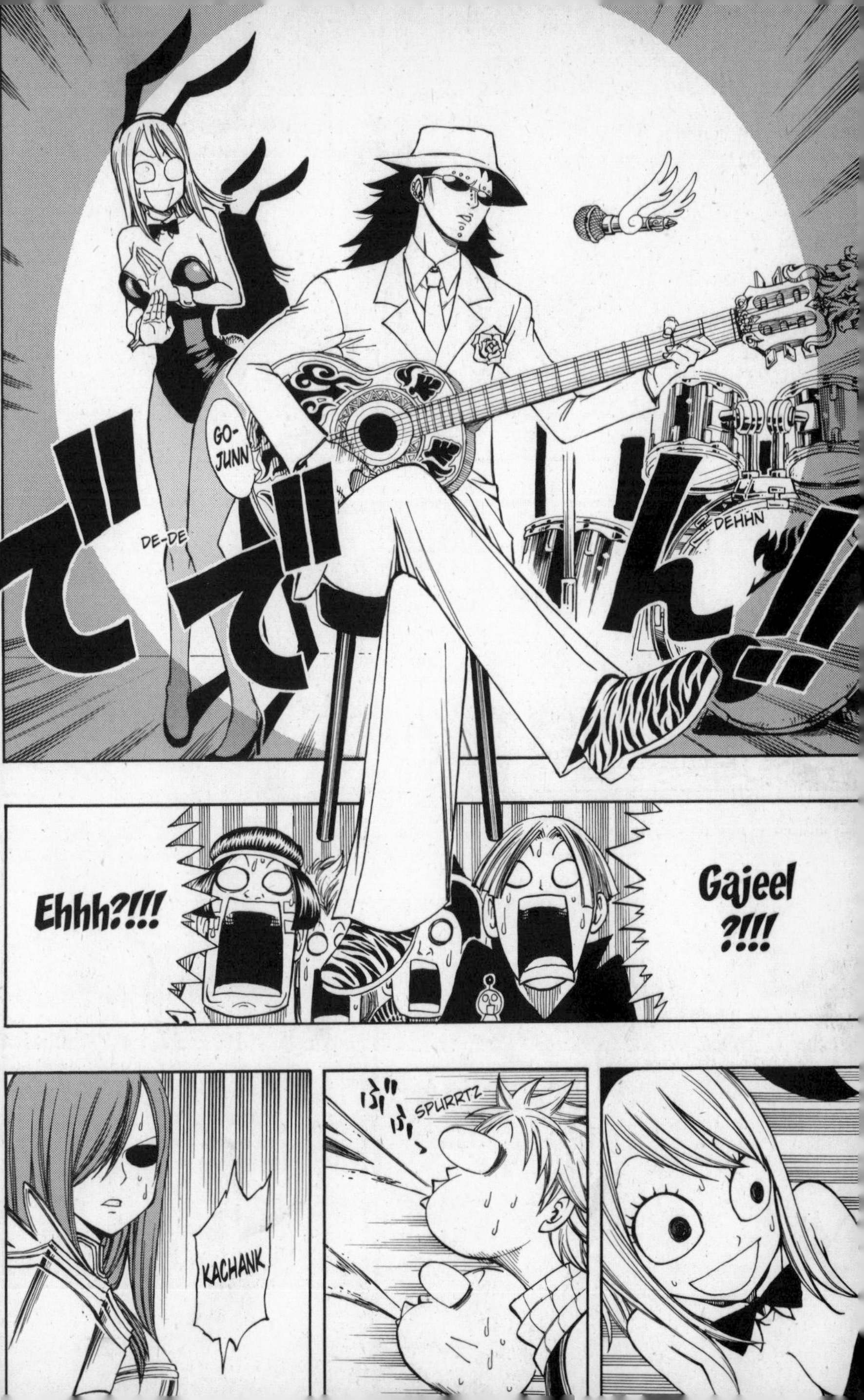
GO-JUNN
ででん!!
DEHHN
DE-DE
Gajeel ?!!!
Ehhh?!!!
SPURRTZ
KACHANK

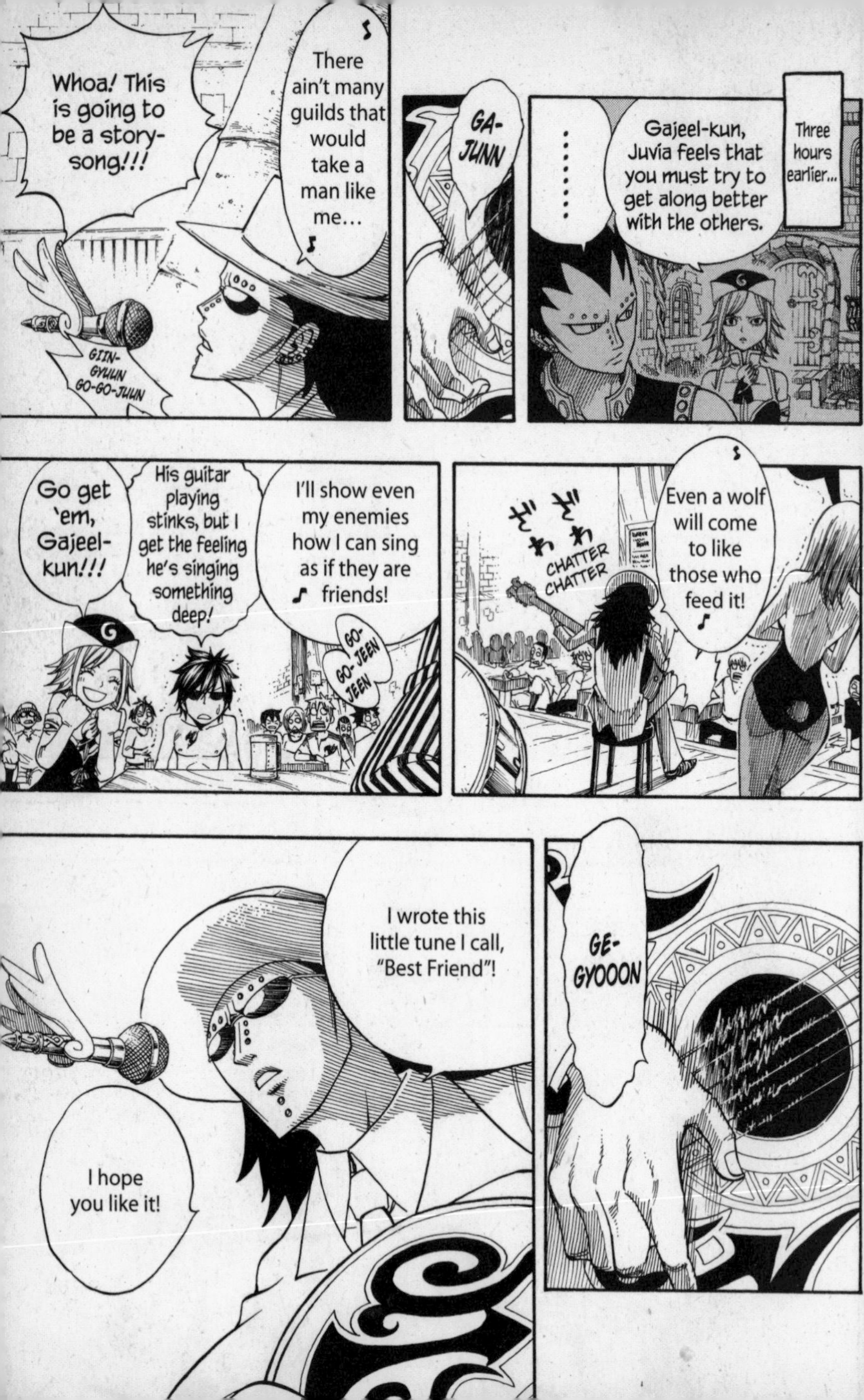
Three hours earlier...
Gajeel-kun, Juvia feels that you must try to get along better with the others.
......
GA-JUNN
There ain't many guilds that would take a man like me...
Whoa! This is going to be a story-song!!!
GIIN-GYUUN GO-GO-JUUN
Even a wolf will come to like those who feed it!
ざわざわ
CHATTER CHATTER
I'll show even my enemies how I can sing as if they are friends!
GO-GO-JEEN JEEN
His guitar playing stinks, but I get the feeling he's singing something deep!
Go get 'em, Gajeel-kun!!!
GE-GYOOON
I wrote this little tune I call, "Best Friend"!
I hope you like it!

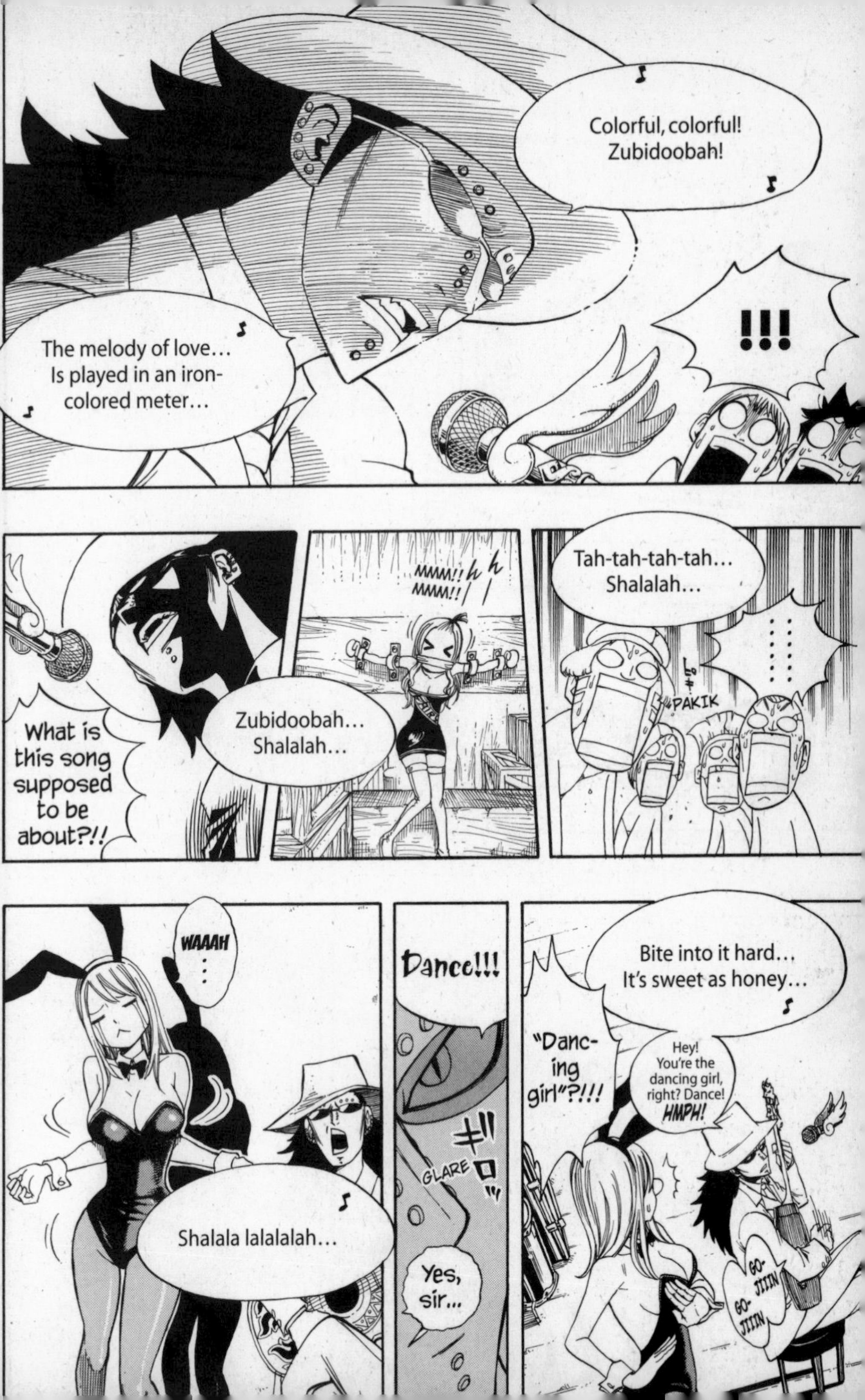
Colorful, colorful! Zubidoobah!
!!!
The melody of love… Is played in an iron-colored meter…
Tah-tah-tah-tah… Shalalah…
……
PAKIK
MMM!! MMM!!
Zubidoobah… Shalalah…
What is this song supposed to be about?!!
Bite into it hard… It's sweet as honey…
Hey! You're the dancing girl, right? Dance! HMPH!
"Danc-ing girl"?!!!
GO-JIIIN GO-JIIIN
Dance!!!
GLARE
Yes, sir...
WAAAH …
Shalala lalalalah…

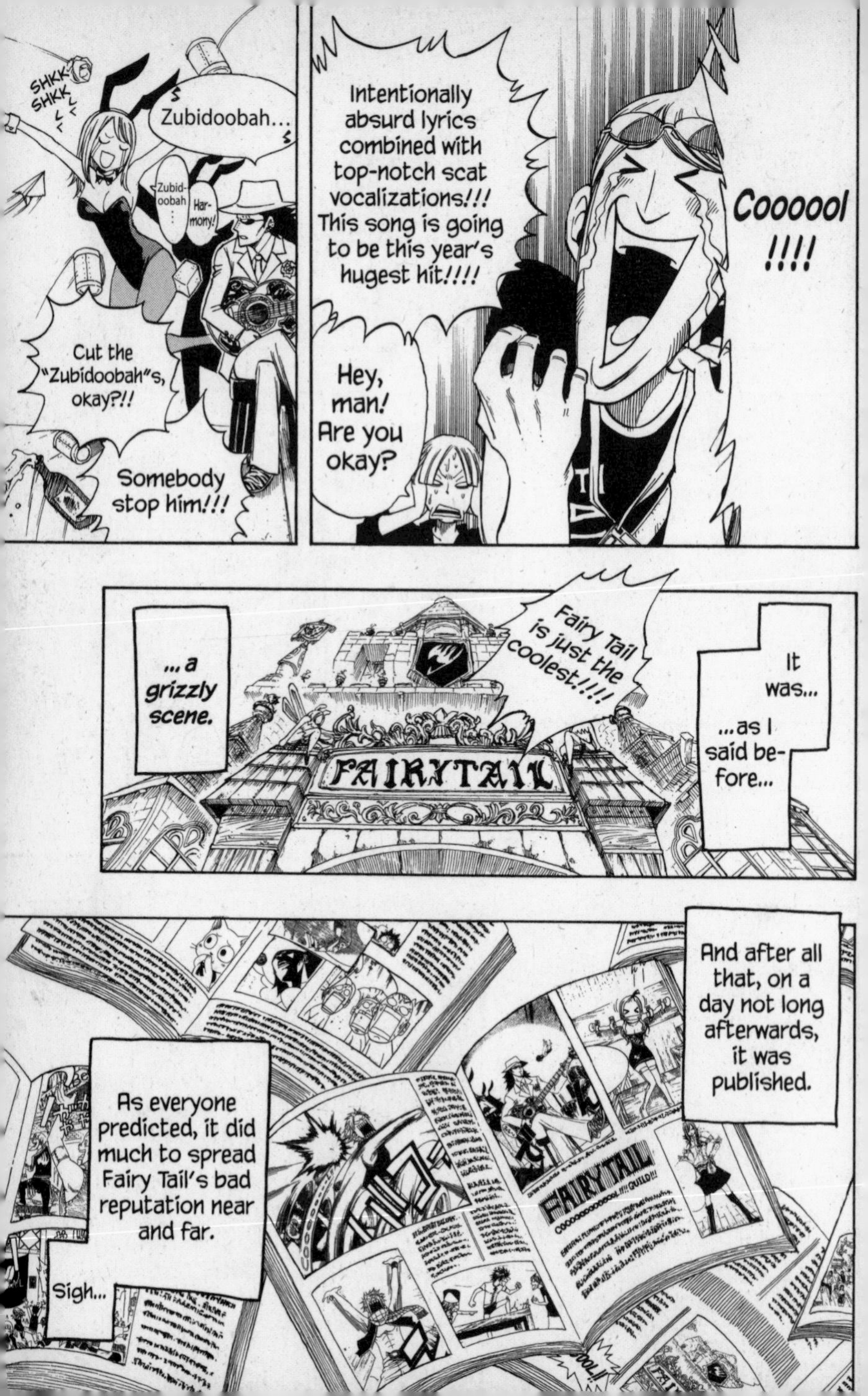
Cooooool !!!!
Intentionally absurd lyrics combined with top-notch scat vocalizations!!! This song is going to be this year's hugest hit!!!!
Hey, man! Are you okay?
Zubidoobah...
Harmony!
Zubid-oobah...
SHKK SHKK
Cut the "Zubidoobah"s, okay?!!
Somebody stop him!!!
It was...
...as I said before...
Fairy Tail is just the coolest!!!!
FAIRYTAIL
...a grizzly scene.
And after all that, on a day not long afterwards, it was published.
FAIRYTAIL
As everyone predicted, it did much to spread Fairy Tail's bad reputation near and far.
Sigh...

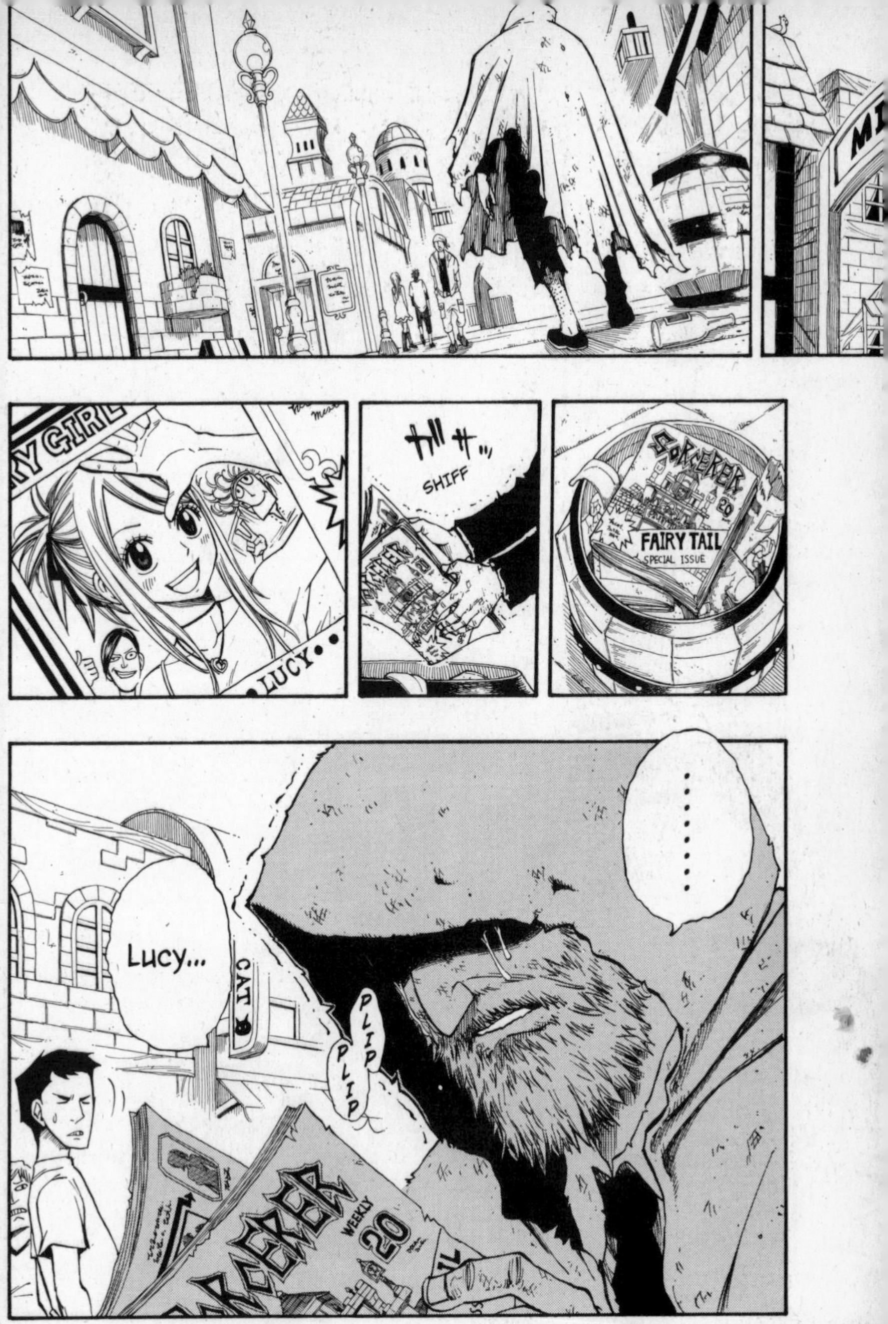
SORCERER
20
FAIRY TAIL
SPECIAL ISSUE
SHIFF
RY GIRL
LUCY..
......
Lucy...
CAT
PLIP PLIP
SORCERER
WEEKLY
20

FAIRY TAIL

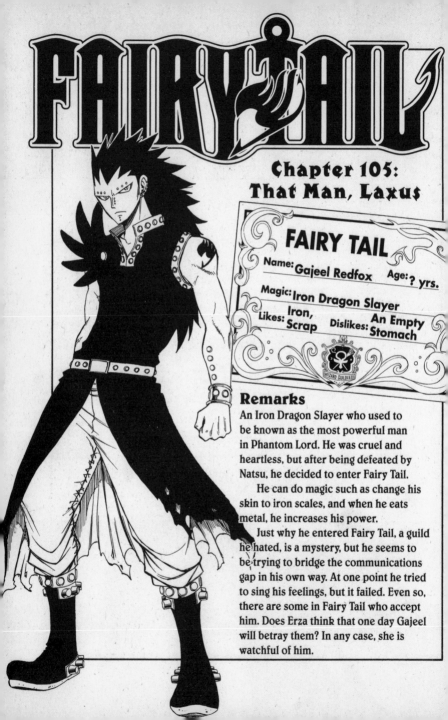

Chapter 105: That Man, Laxus

FAIRY TAIL

Name: Gajeel Redfox   Age: ? yrs.

Magic: Iron Dragon Slayer

Likes: Iron, Scrap   Dislikes: An Empty Stomach

WIZARD GUILD(KSS)

Remarks

An Iron Dragon Slayer who used to be known as the most powerful man in Phantom Lord. He was cruel and heartless, but after being defeated by Natsu, he decided to enter Fairy Tail.

He can do magic such as change his skin to iron scales, and when he eats metal, he increases his power.

Just why he entered Fairy Tail, a guild he hated, is a mystery, but he seems to be trying to bridge the communications gap in his own way. At one point he tried to sing his feelings, but it failed. Even so, there are some in Fairy Tail who accept him. Does Erza think that one day Gajeel will betray them? In any case, she is watchful of him.

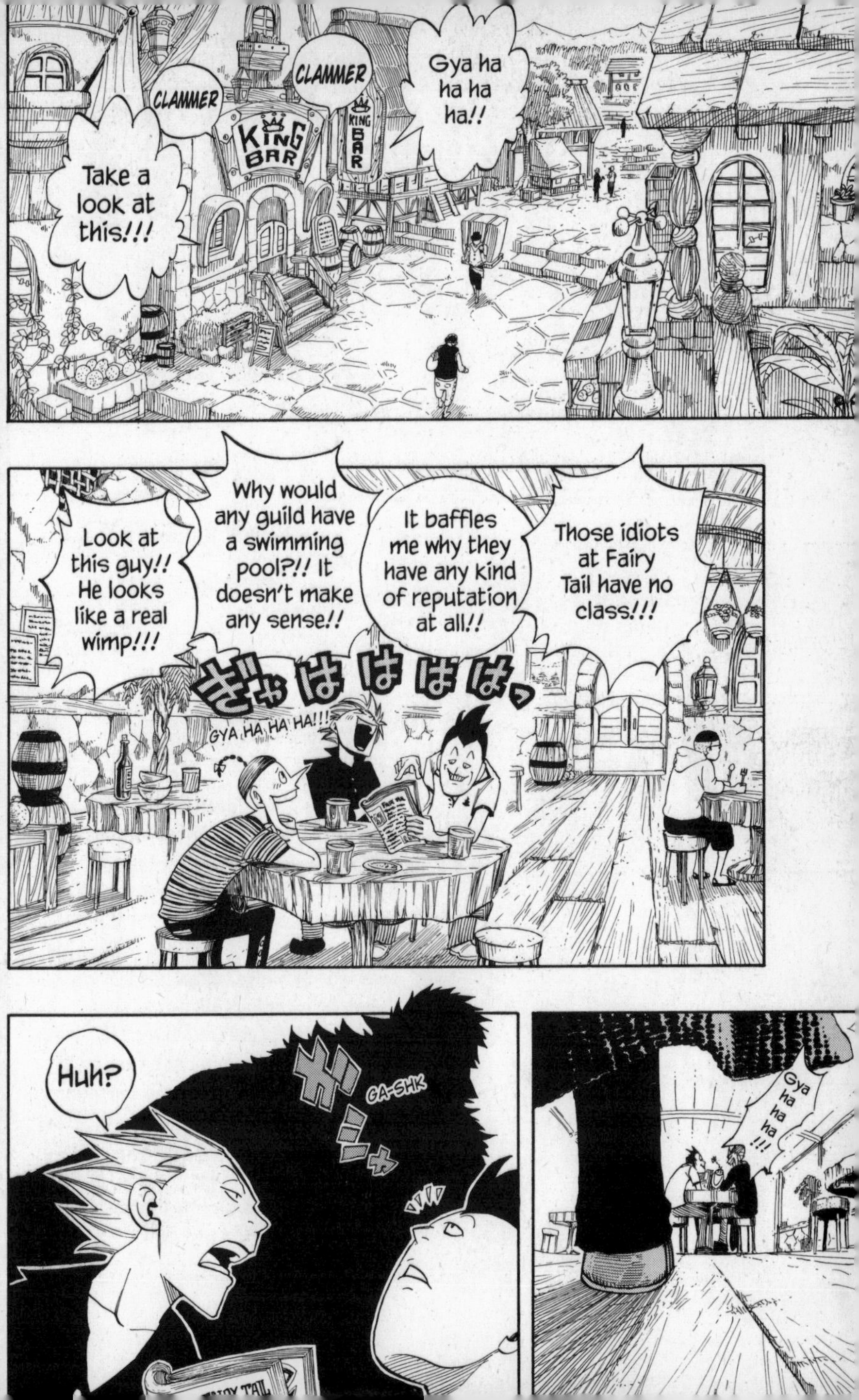
Gya ha ha ha ha!!
CLAMMER
KING BAR
KING BAR
CLAMMER
Take a look at this!!!
Those idiots at Fairy Tail have no class!!!
It baffles me why they have any kind of reputation at all!!
Why would any guild have a swimming pool?!! It doesn't make any sense!!
Look at this guy!! He looks like a real wimp!!!
ぎゃははははっ
GYA HA HA HA!!!
Gya ha ha ha!!!
Huh?
ガシッ
GA-SHK

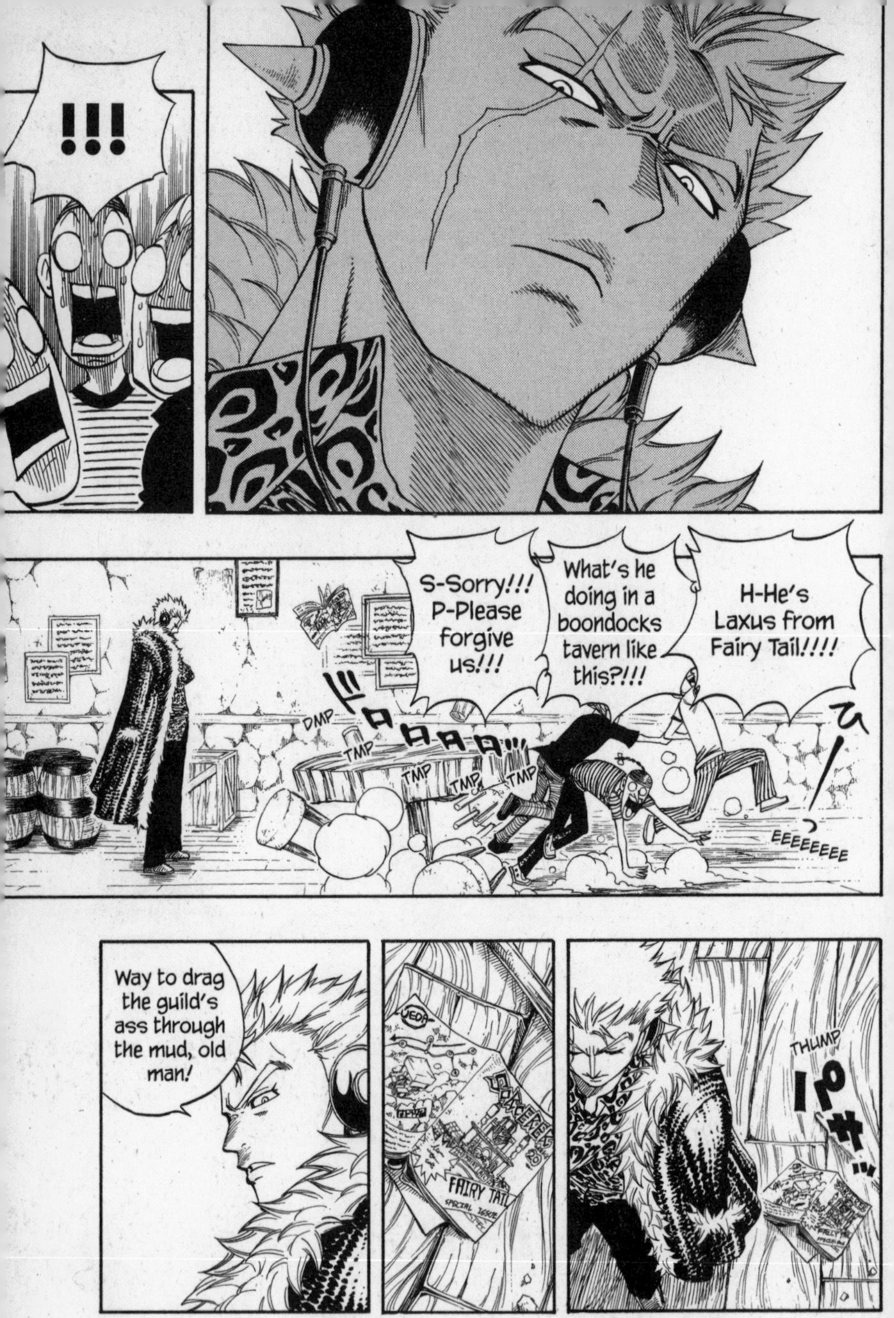
!!!
H-He's Laxus from Fairy Tail!!!!
What's he doing in a boondocks tavern like this?!!!
S-Sorry!!! P-Please forgive us!!!
EEEEEEEE
DMP
TMP
TMP
TMP
TMP
THUMP
FAIRY TAIL
SPECIAL ISSUE
Way to drag the guild's ass through the mud, old man!

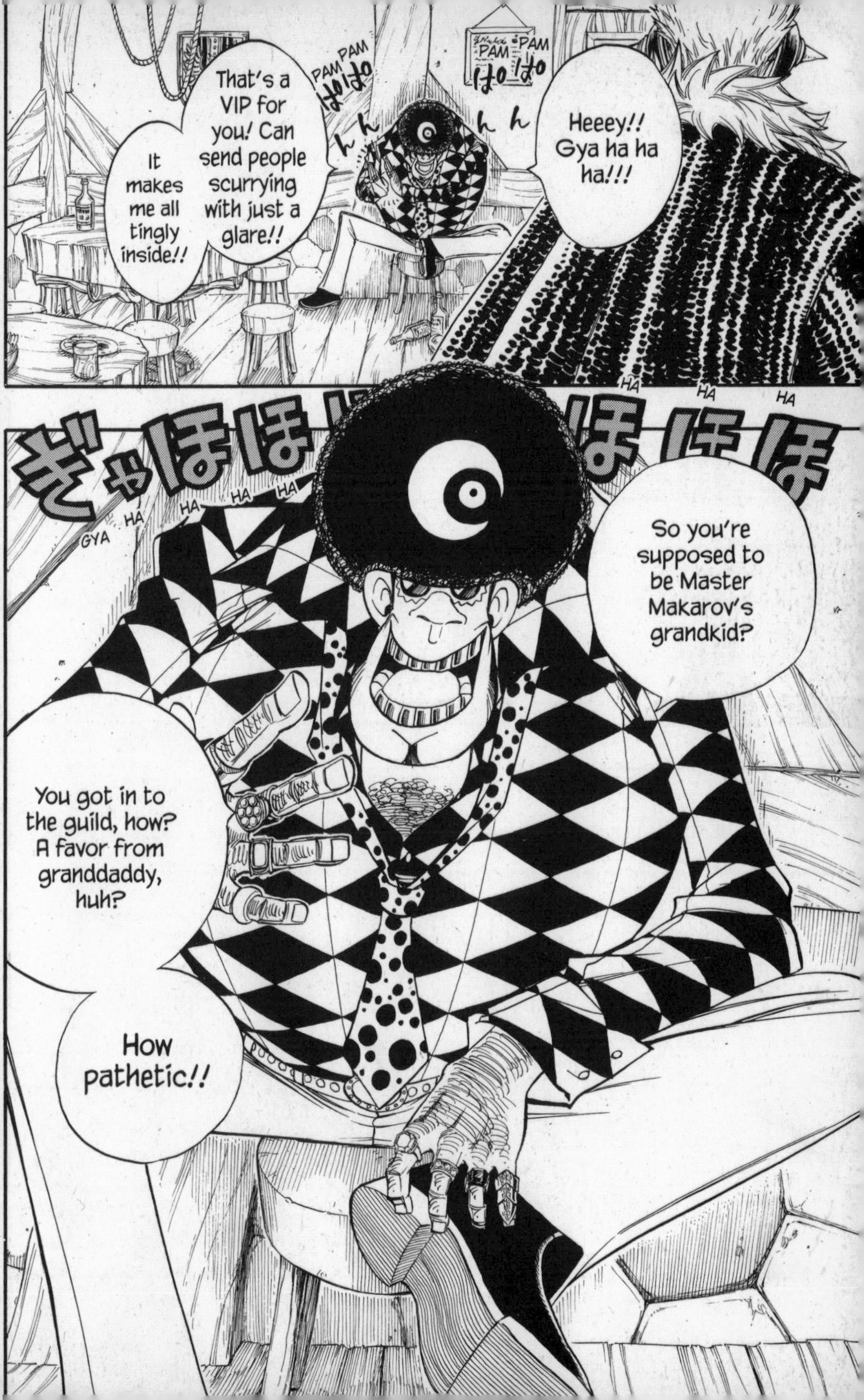
Heeey!! Gya ha ha ha!!!
PAM PAM
PAM PAM
That's a VIP for you! Can send people scurrying with just a glare!!
It makes me all tingly inside!!
HA HA HA HA HA HA HA GYA
So you're supposed to be Master Makarov's grandkid?
You got in to the guild, how? A favor from granddaddy, huh?
How pathetic!!

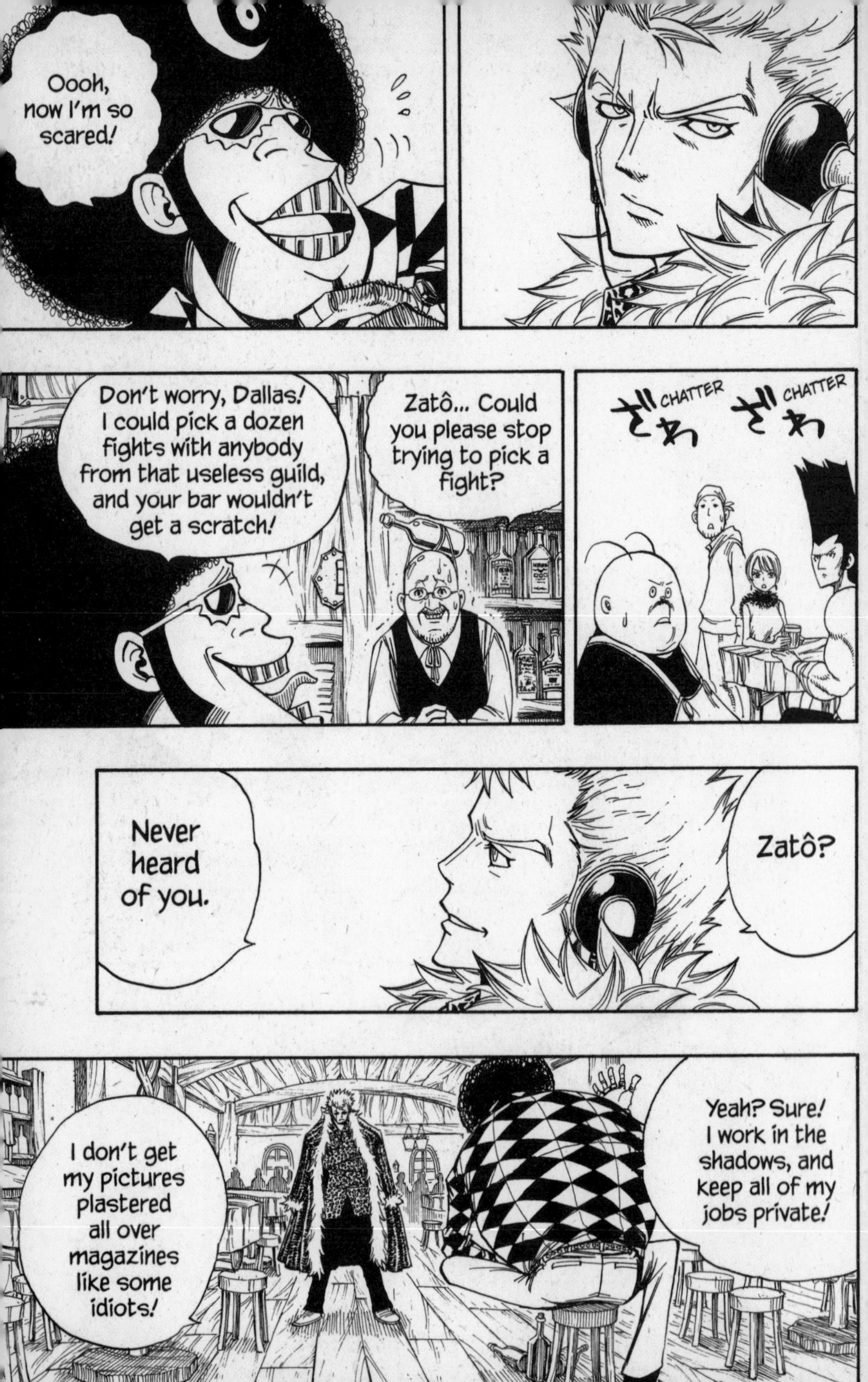

Oooh, now I'm so scared!
ざわ ざわ
CHATTER CHATTER
Zatô... Could you please stop trying to pick a fight?
Don't worry, Dallas! I could pick a dozen fights with anybody from that useless guild, and your bar wouldn't get a scratch!
Zatô?
Never heard of you.
Yeah? Sure! I work in the shadows, and keep all of my jobs private!
I don't get my pictures plastered all over magazines like some idiots!

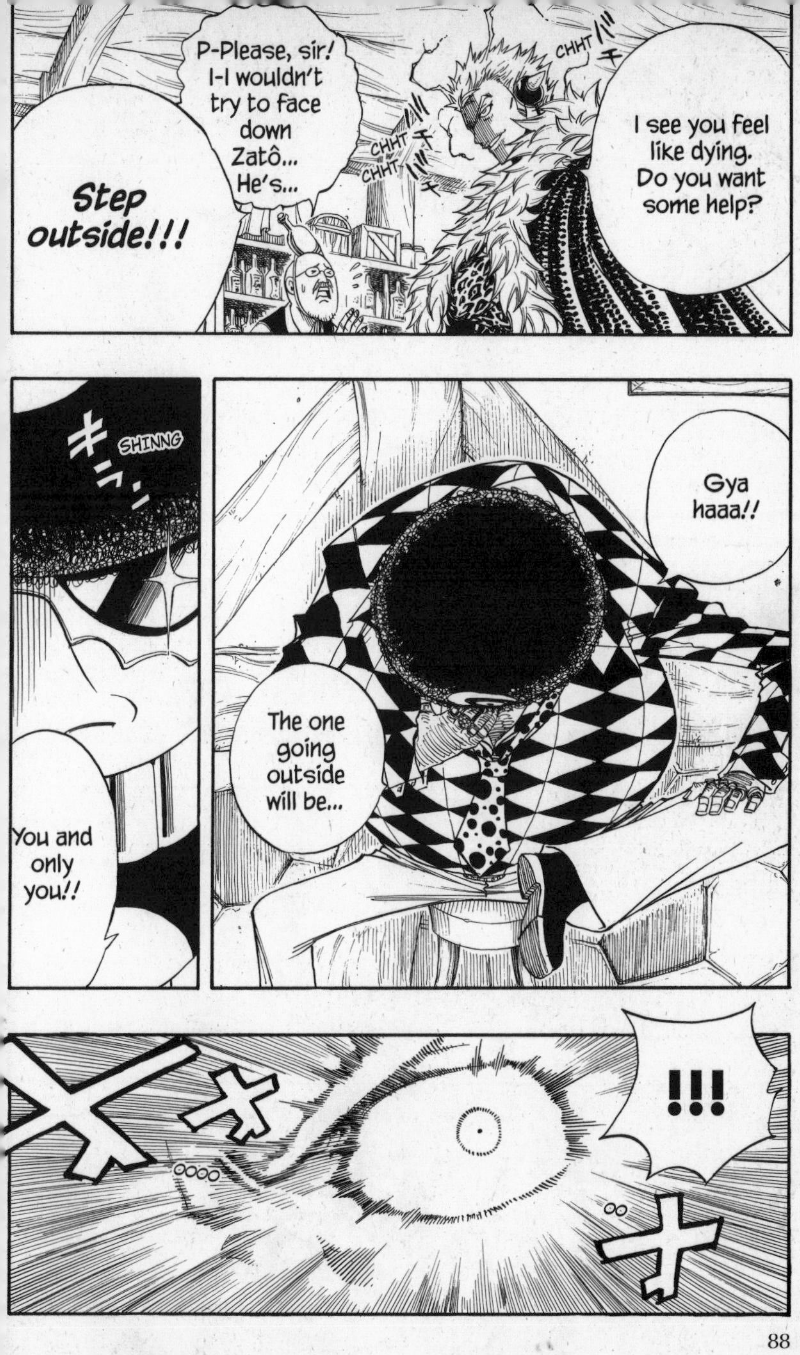
CHHT
I see you feel like dying. Do you want some help?
P-Please, sir! I-I wouldn't try to face down Zatô... He's...
CHHT
CHHT
Step outside!!!
Gya haaa!!
The one going outside will be...
SHINNG
You and only you!!
!!!

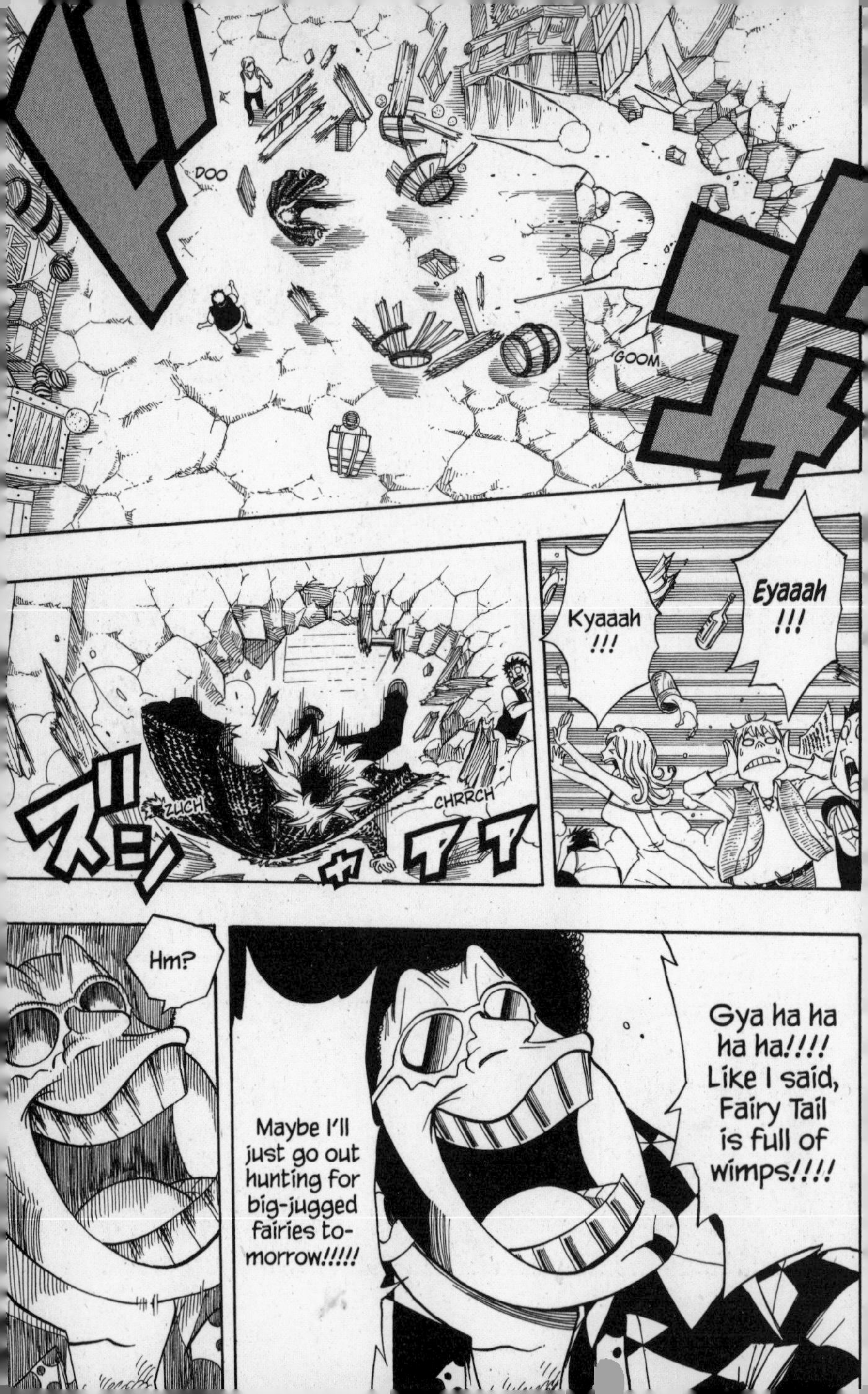
GOOM
DOO
Eyaaah!!!
Kyaaah!!!
CHRRCH
ZUCH
Gya ha ha ha ha!!!! Like I said, Fairy Tail is full of wimps!!!!
Maybe I'll just go out hunting for big-jugged fairies to-morrow!!!!!
Hm?

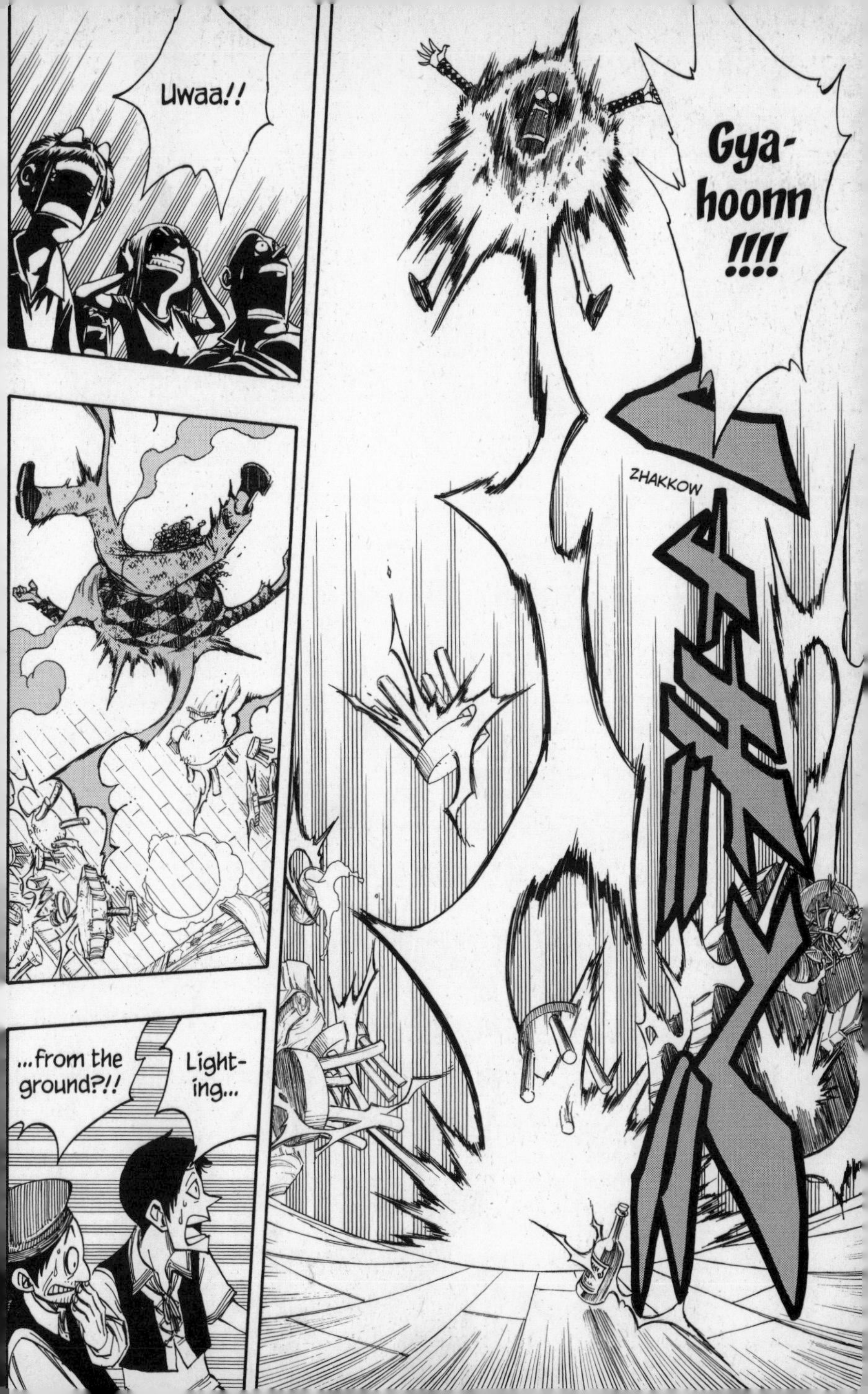
Gya-hoonn!!!!
ZHAKKOW
Uwaa!!
Light-ing...
...from the ground?!!

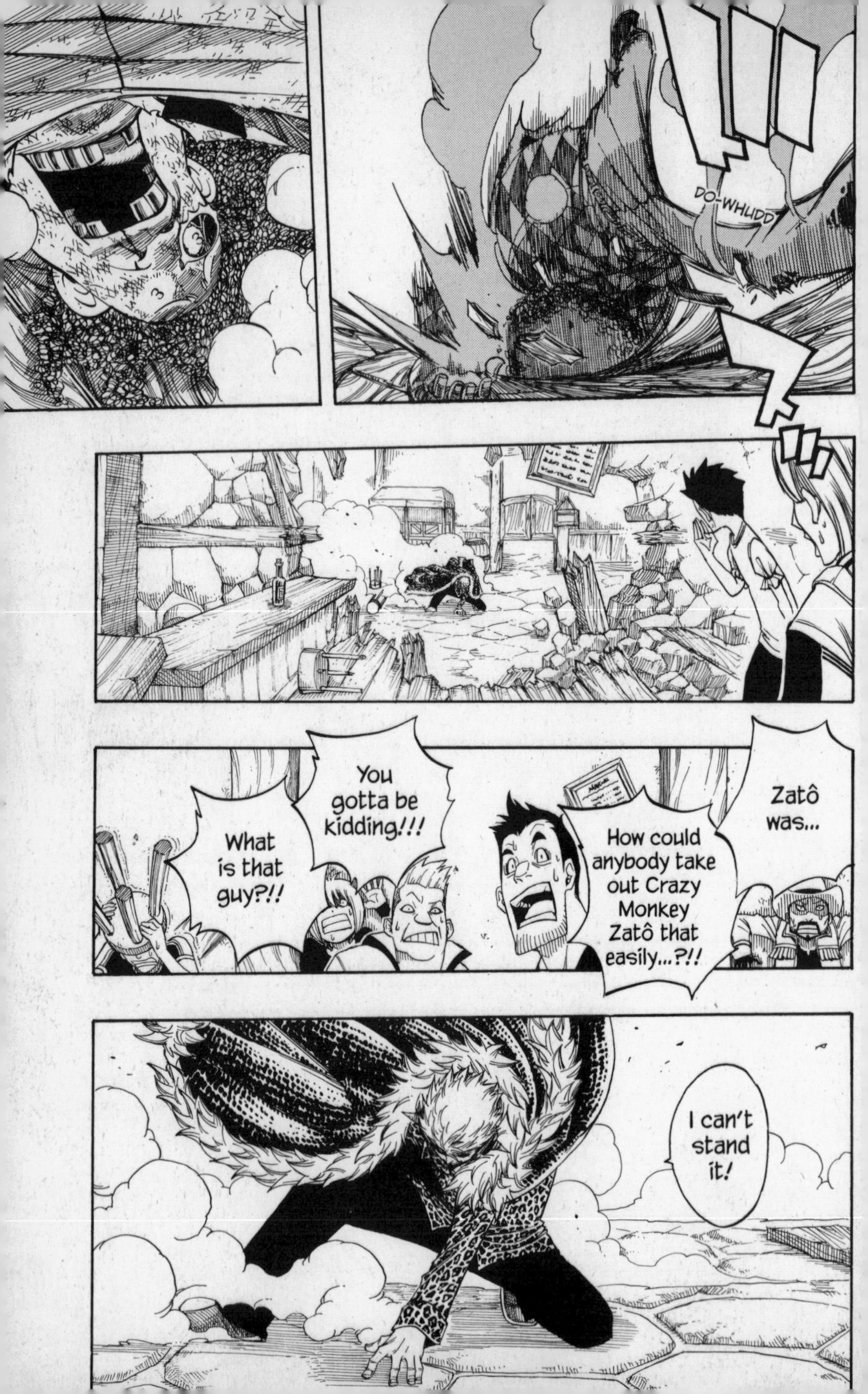

DO-WHUDD
Zatô was...
How could anybody take out Crazy Monkey Zatô that easily...?!!
You gotta be kidding!!!
What is that guy?!!
I can't stand it!

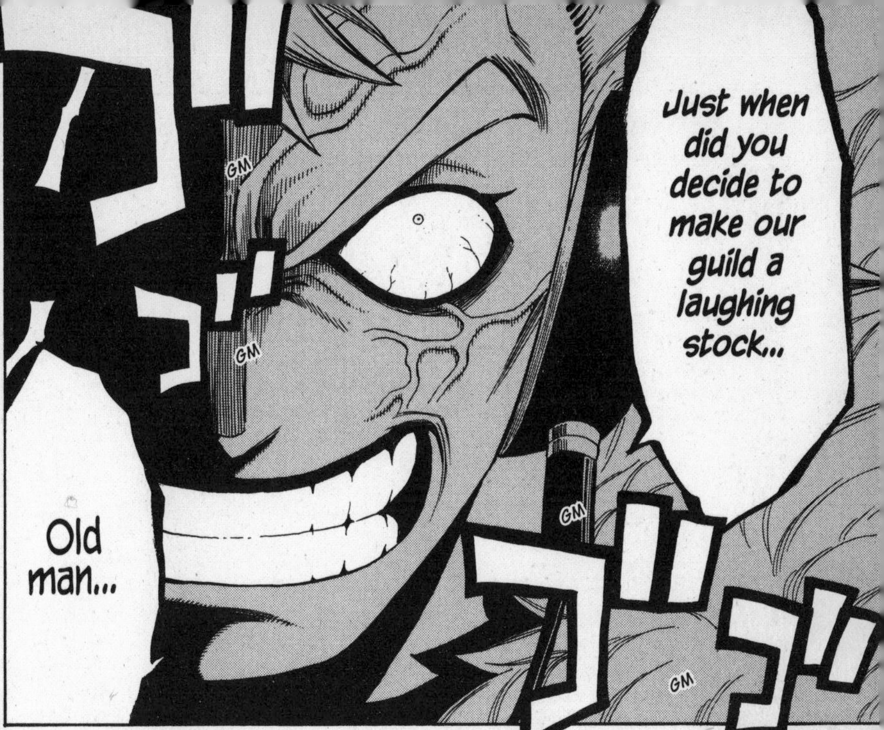
Just when did you decide to make our guild a laughing stock...
GM
GM
GM
GM
Old man...

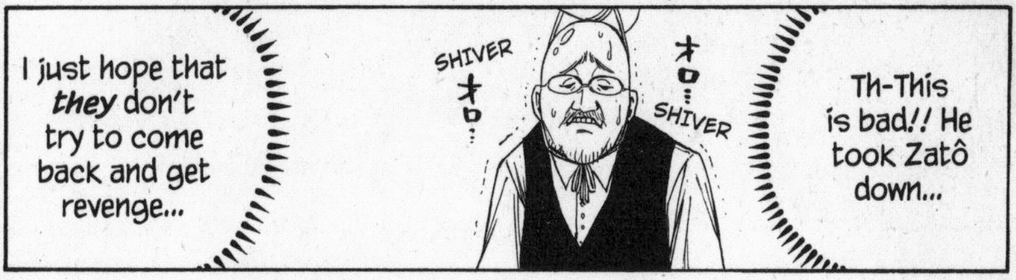
Th-This is bad!! He took Zatô down...
オロ...
SHIVER
SHIVER
オロ...
I just hope that *they* don't try to come back and get revenge...

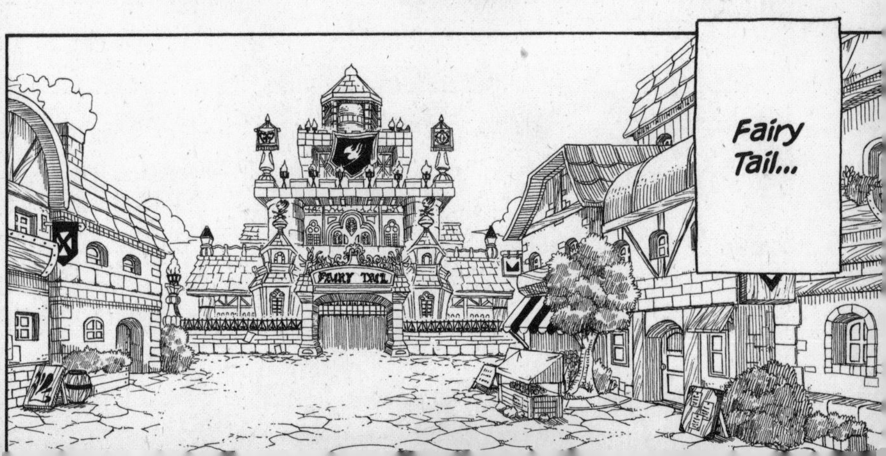
Fairy Tail...
FAIRY TAIL

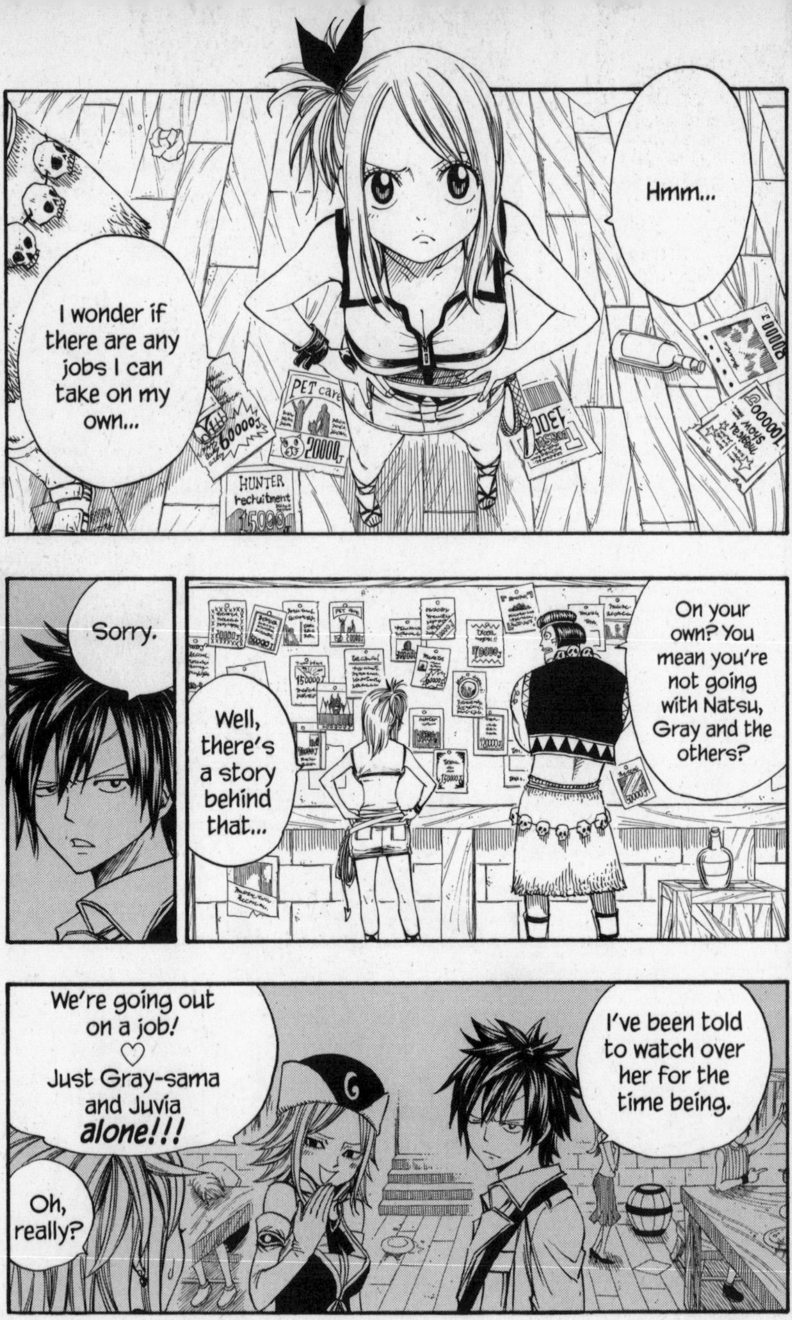
Hmm...
I wonder if there are any jobs I can take on my own...
PET care
HUNTER recruitment
On your own? You mean you're not going with Natsu, Gray and the others?
Well, there's a story behind that...
Sorry.
I've been told to watch over her for the time being.
We're going out on a job! ♡ Just Gray-sama and Juvia ***alone!!!***
Oh, really?

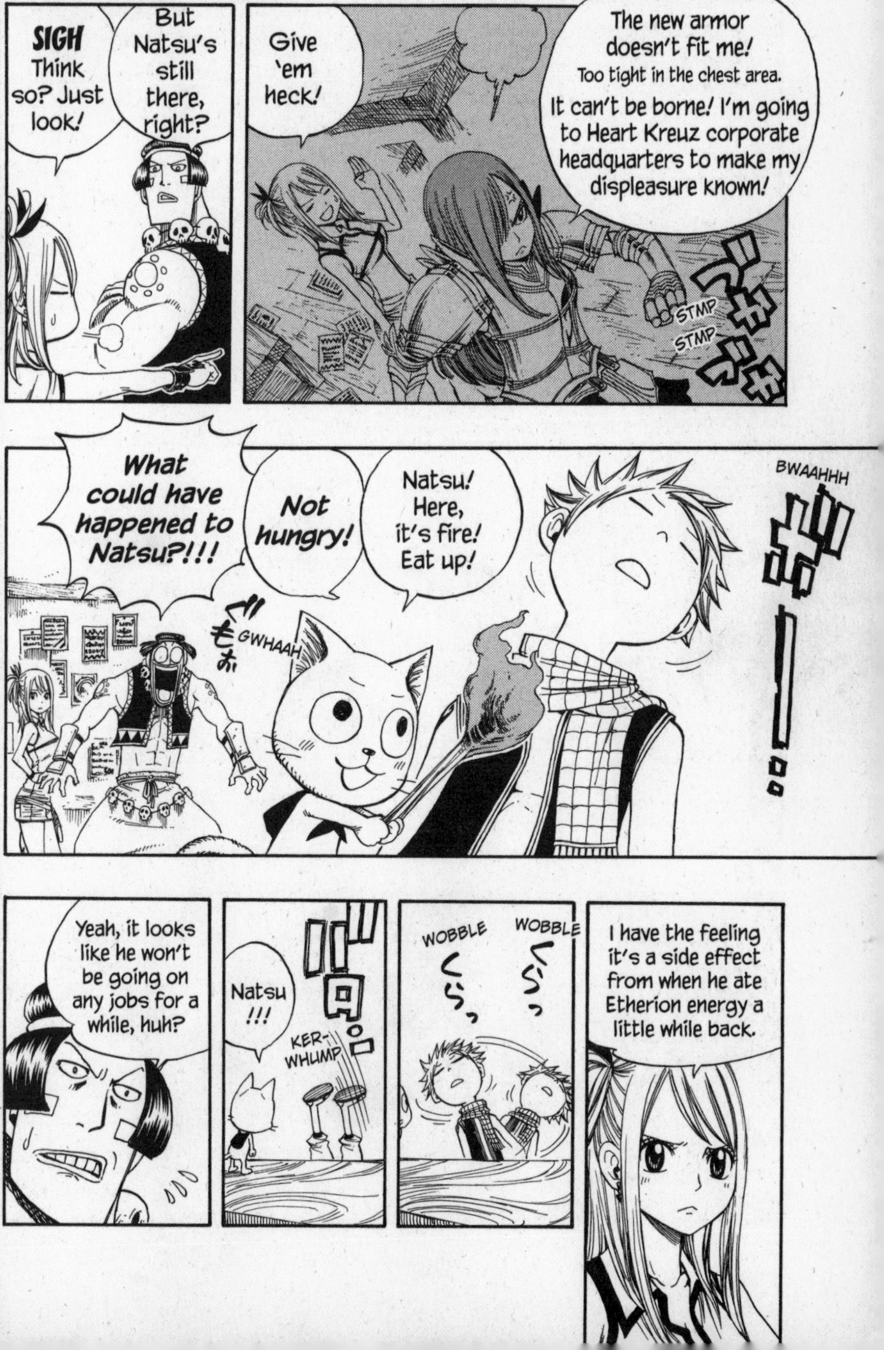
The new armor doesn't fit me!
Too tight in the chest area.
It can't be borne! I'm going to Heart Kreuz corporate headquarters to make my displeasure known!
STMP
STMP
Give 'em heck!
But Natsu's still there, right?
SIGH
Think so? Just look!
BWAAHHH
Natsu! Here, it's fire! Eat up!
Not hungry!
What could have happened to Natsu?!!!
GWHAAH
I have the feeling it's a side effect from when he ate Etherion energy a little while back.
WOBBLE
WOBBLE
Natsu!!!
KER-WHUMP
Yeah, it looks like he won't be going on any jobs for a while, huh?

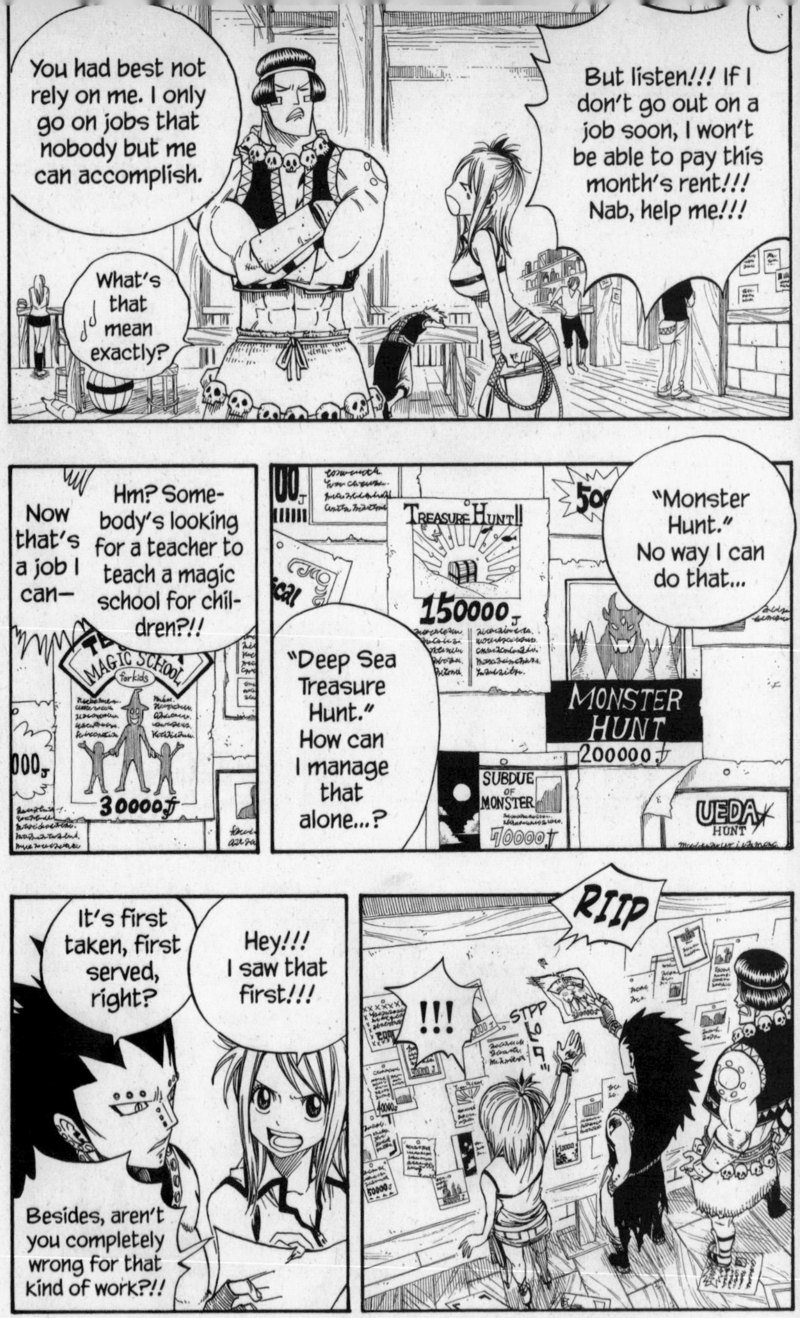
But listen!!! If I don't go out on a job soon, I won't be able to pay this month's rent!!! Nab, help me!!!
You had best not rely on me. I only go on jobs that nobody but me can accomplish.
What's that mean exactly?
"Monster Hunt." No way I can do that...
MONSTER HUNT
200000 J
UEDA HUNT
SUBDUE OF MONSTER
70000 J
TREASURE HUNT!!
150000 J
"Deep Sea Treasure Hunt." How can I manage that alone...?
Hm? Somebody's looking for a teacher to teach a magic school for children?!!
Now that's a job I can—
MAGIC SCHOOL
for kids
30000 J
RIIP
!!!
STPP
Hey!!! I saw that first!!!
It's first taken, first served, right?
Besides, aren't you completely wrong for that kind of work?!!

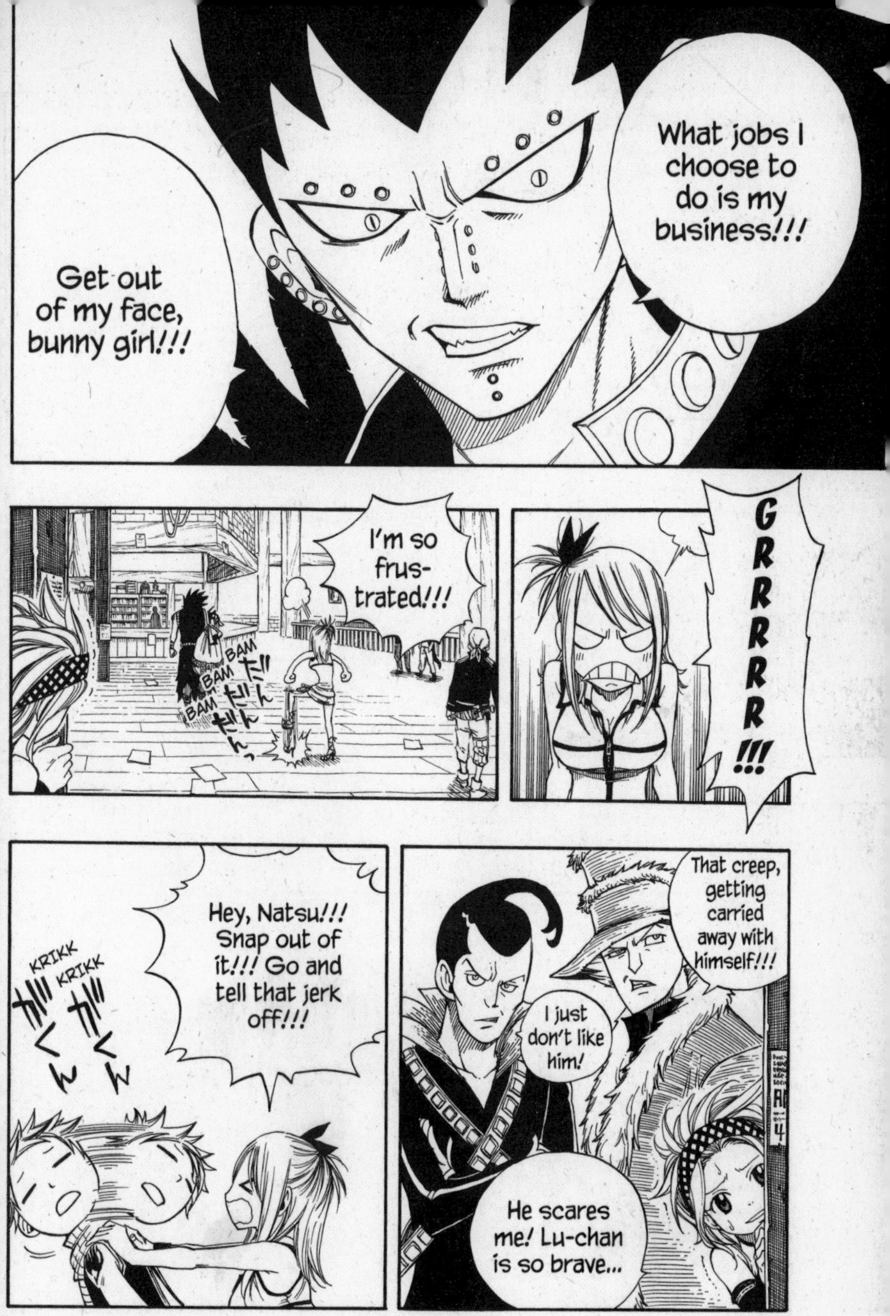
What jobs I choose to do is my business!!!
Get out of my face, bunny girl!!!
GRRRRRR!!!
I'm so frus-trated!!!
BAM BAM BAM
That creep, getting carried away with himself!!!
I just don't like him!
He scares me! Lu-chan is so brave...
Hey, Natsu!!! Snap out of it!!! Go and tell that jerk off!!!
KRIKK KRIKK

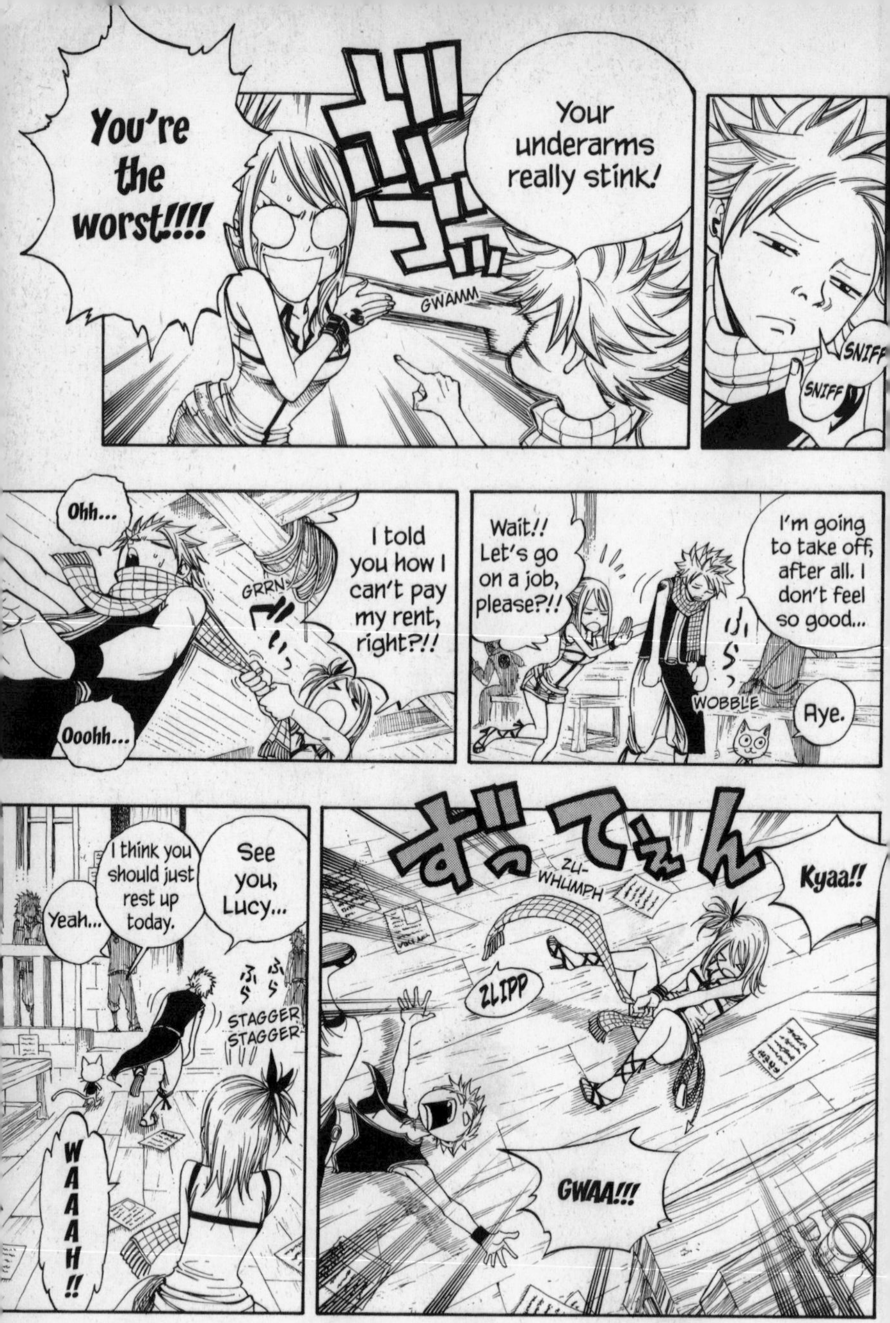
SNIFF
SNIFF
Your underarms really stink!
GWAMM
You're the worst!!!!
I'm going to take off, after all. I don't feel so good...
Aye.
ふらっ
WOBBLE
Wait!! Let's go on a job, please?!!
I told you how I can't pay my rent, right?!!
GRRN
Ohh...
Ooohh...
ずってぇん
ZU-WHUMPH
Kyaa!!
ZLIPP
GWAA!!!
See you, Lucy...
I think you should just rest up today.
Yeah...
ふら ふら
STAGGER STAGGER
WAAAAH!!

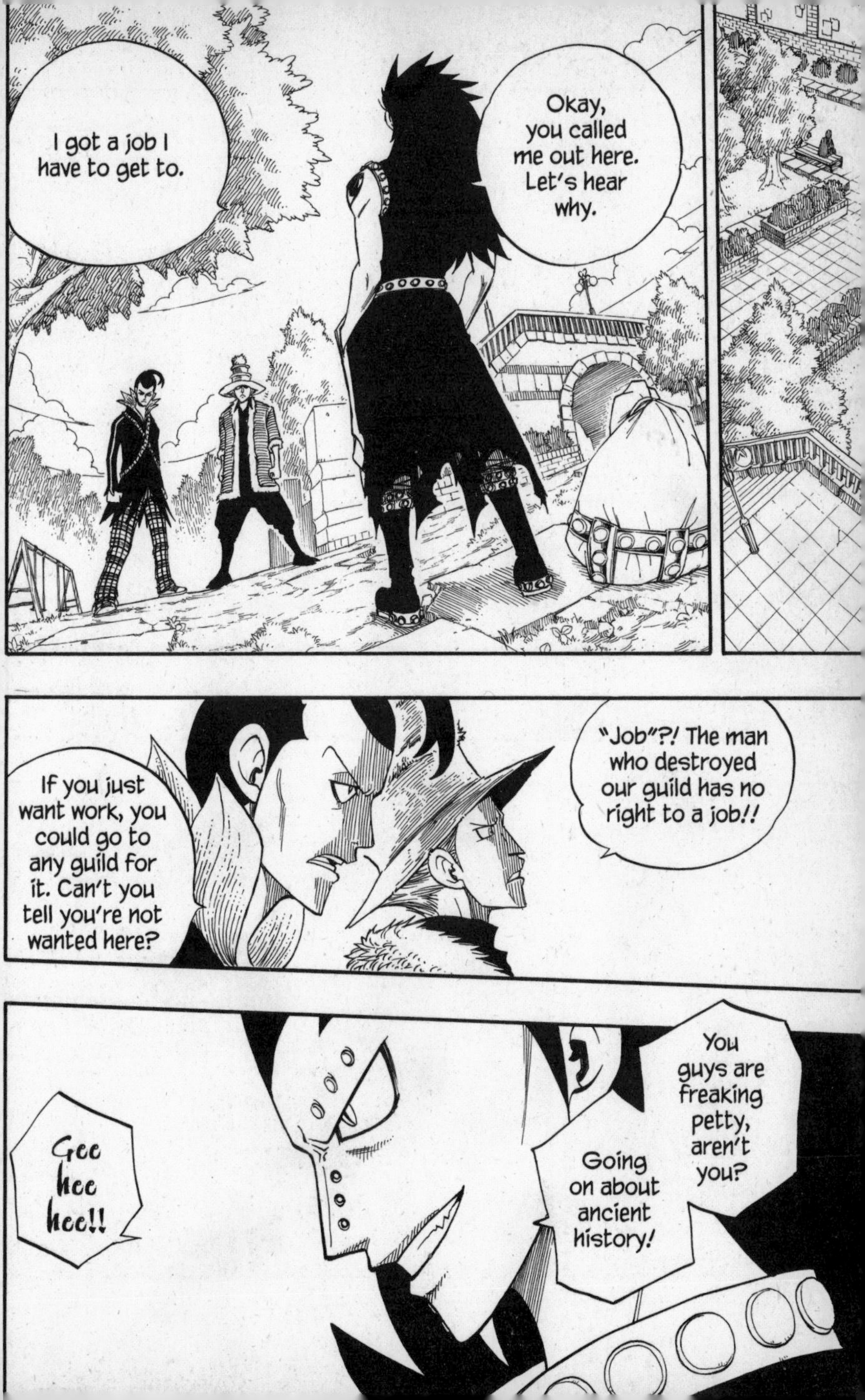
Okay, you called me out here. Let's hear why.
I got a job I have to get to.
"Job"?! The man who destroyed our guild has no right to a job!!
If you just want work, you could go to any guild for it. Can't you tell you're not wanted here?
You guys are freaking petty, aren't you?
Going on about ancient history!
Gee hee hee!!

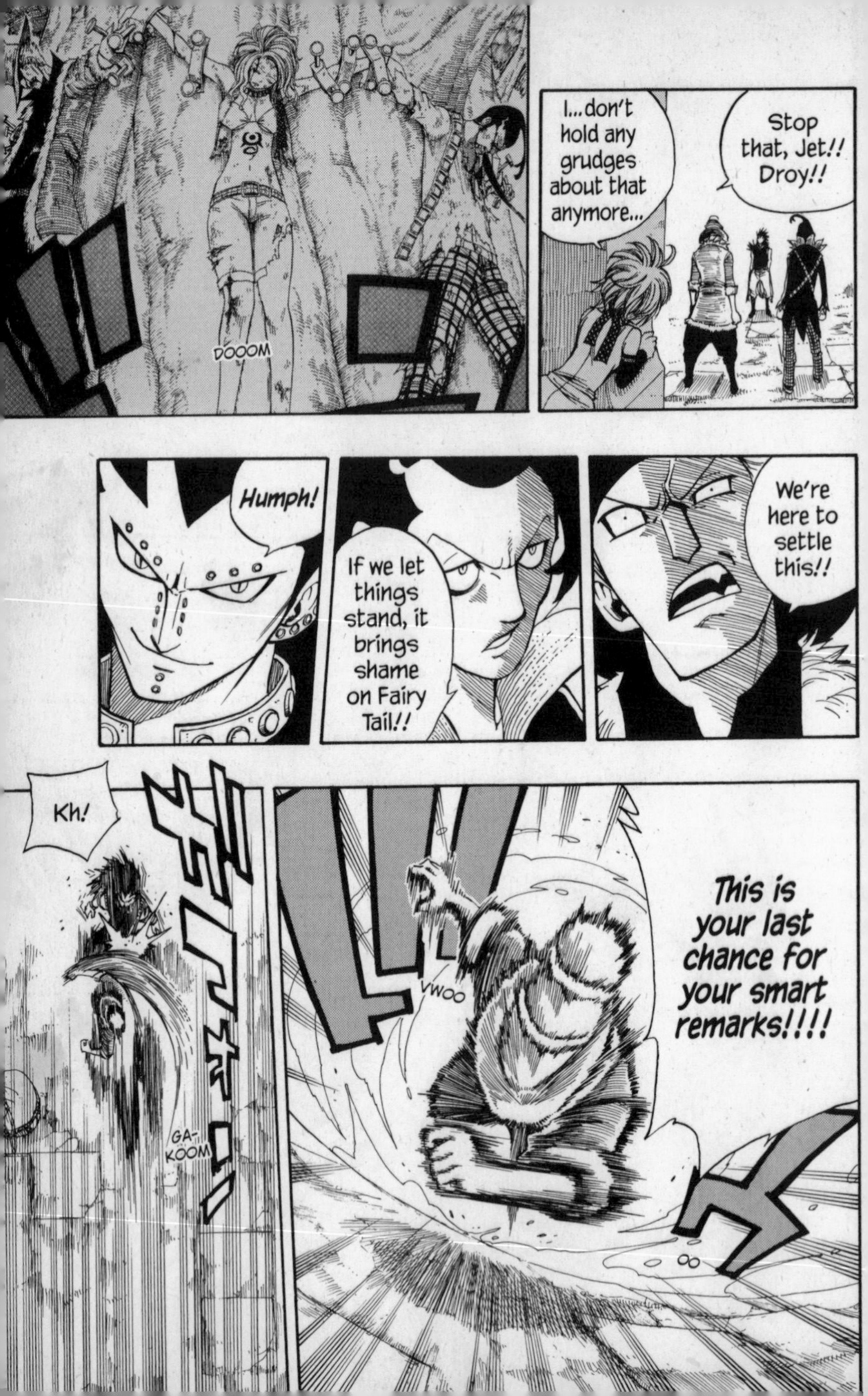
Stop that, Jet!! Droy!!
I...don't hold any grudges about that anymore...
DOOOM
We're here to settle this!!
If we let things stand, it brings shame on Fairy Tail!!
Humph!
This is your last chance for your smart remarks!!!!
VWOO
Kh!
GA-KOOM

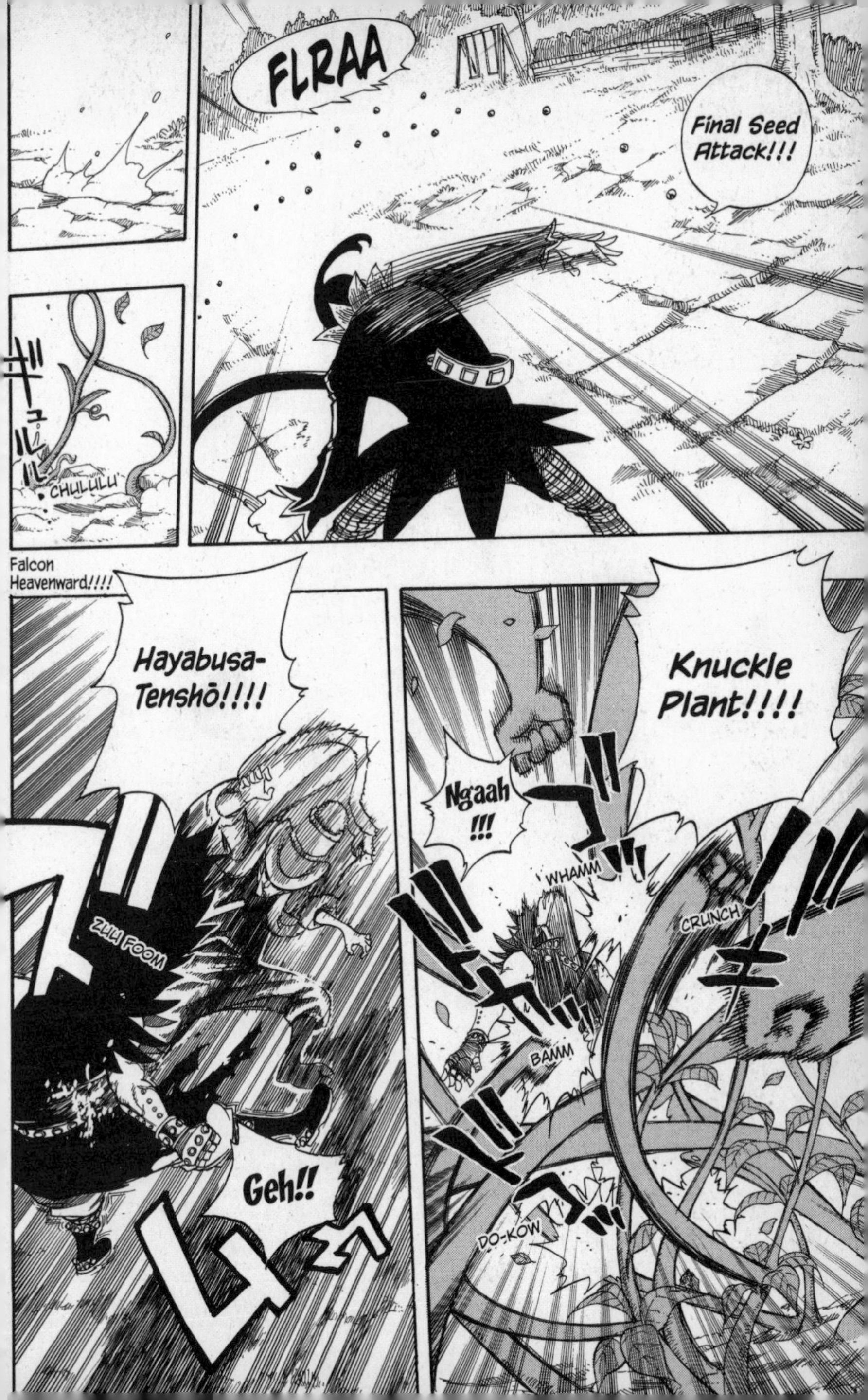
FLRAA
Final Seed Attack!!!
ギュルル
CHULULU
Knuckle Plant!!!!
Ngaah!!!
WHAMM
CRUNCH
BAMM
DO-KOW
Hayabusa-Tenshō!!!!
Falcon Heavenward!!!!
ZULI FOOM
Geh!!

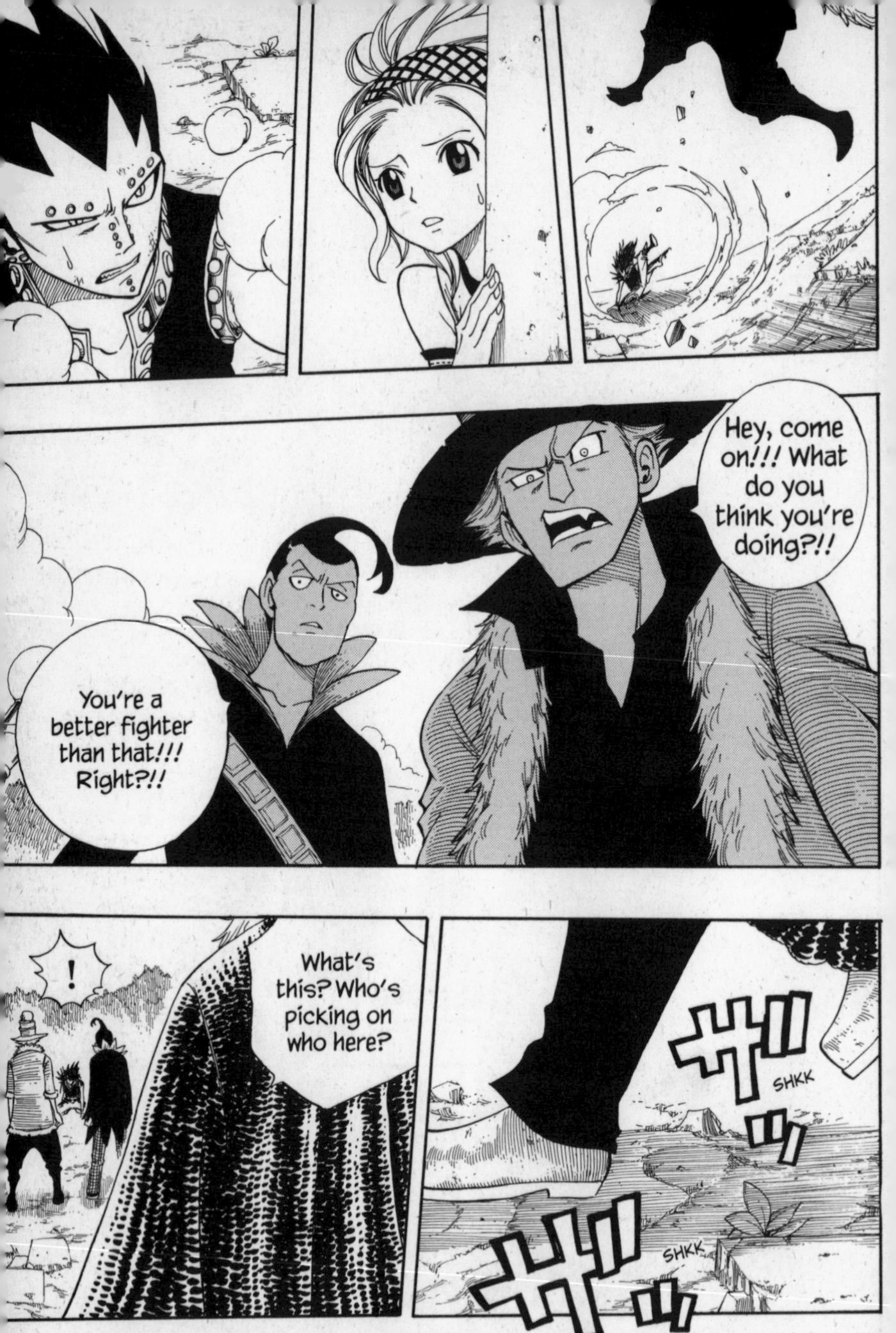

Hey, come on!!! What do you think you're doing?!!
You're a better fighter than that!!! Right?!!
SHKK
SHKK
What's this? Who's picking on who here?
!

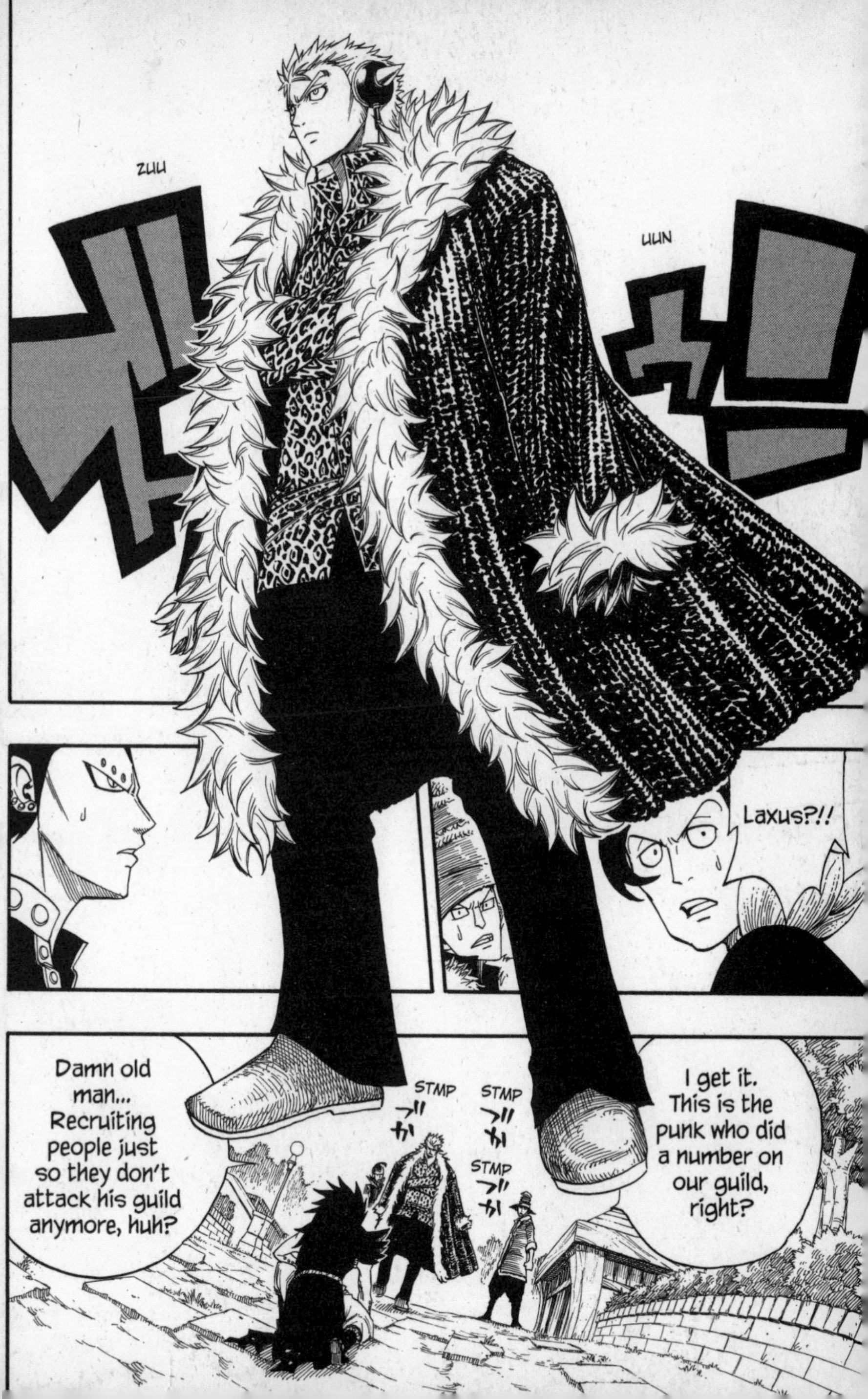
ZUU
UUN
Laxus?!!
I get it. This is the punk who did a number on our guild, right?
STMP
STMP
STMP
Damn old man... Recruiting people just so they don't attack his guild anymore, huh?

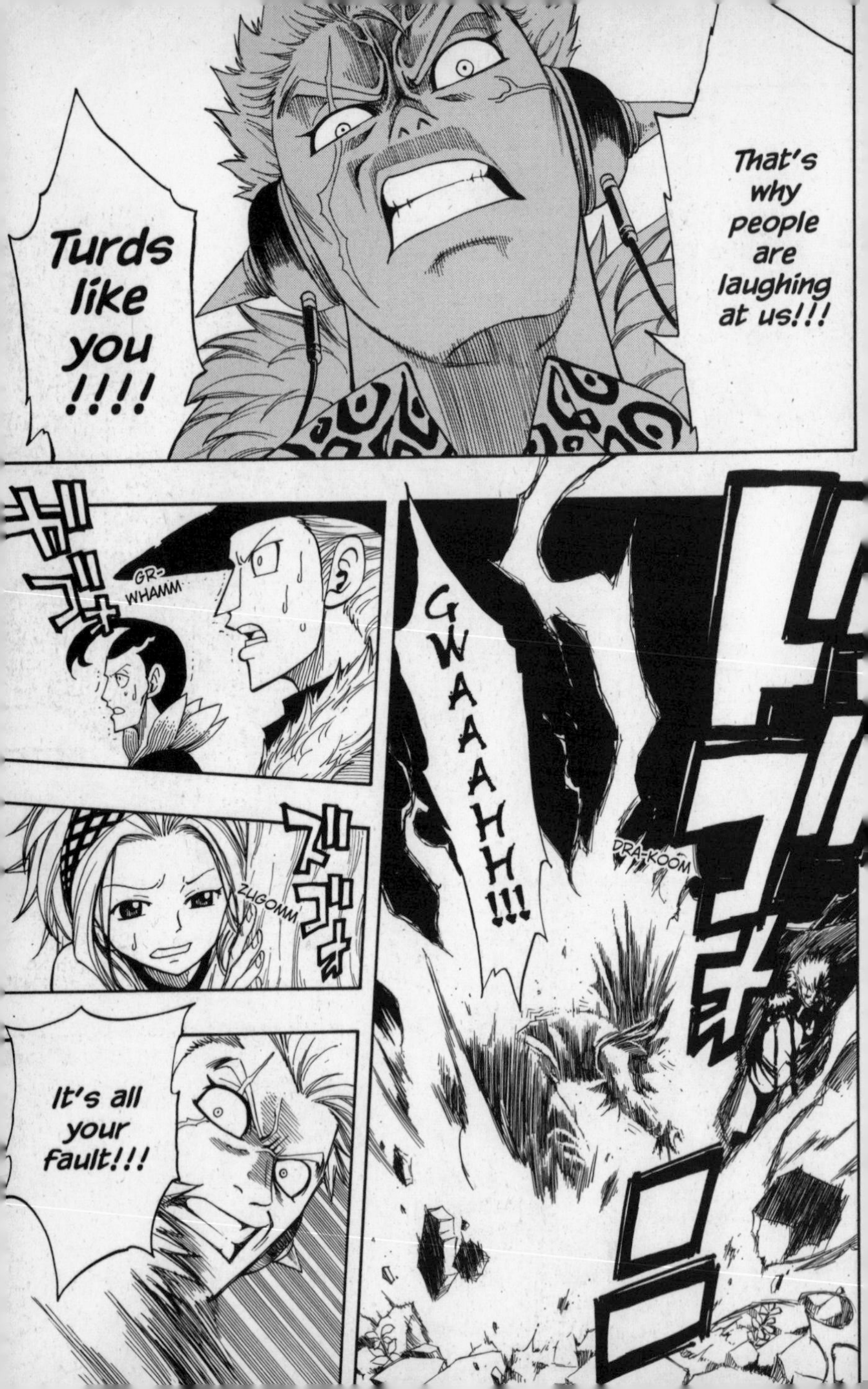
That's why people are laughing at us!!!
Turds like you !!!!
GWAAAHH!!!
DRA-KOOM
GR-WHAMM
ZUGOMM
It's all your fault!!!

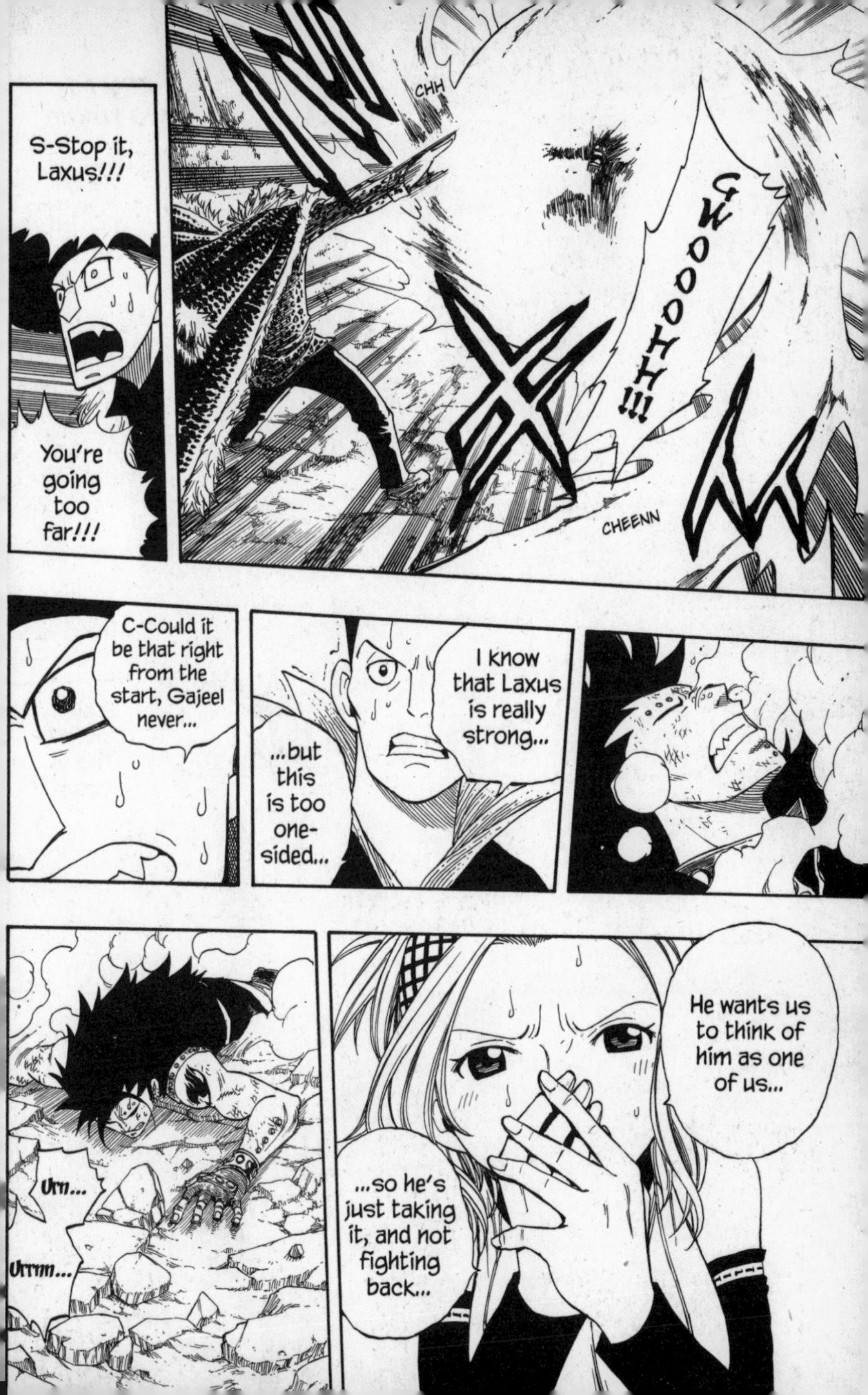
GWOOOOHH!!!
CHH
CHEENN
S-Stop it, Laxus!!!
You're going too far!!!
I know that Laxus is really strong...
...but this is too one-sided...
C-Could it be that right from the start, Gajeel never...
He wants us to think of him as one of us...
...so he's just taking it, and not fighting back...
Urn...
Urrrn...

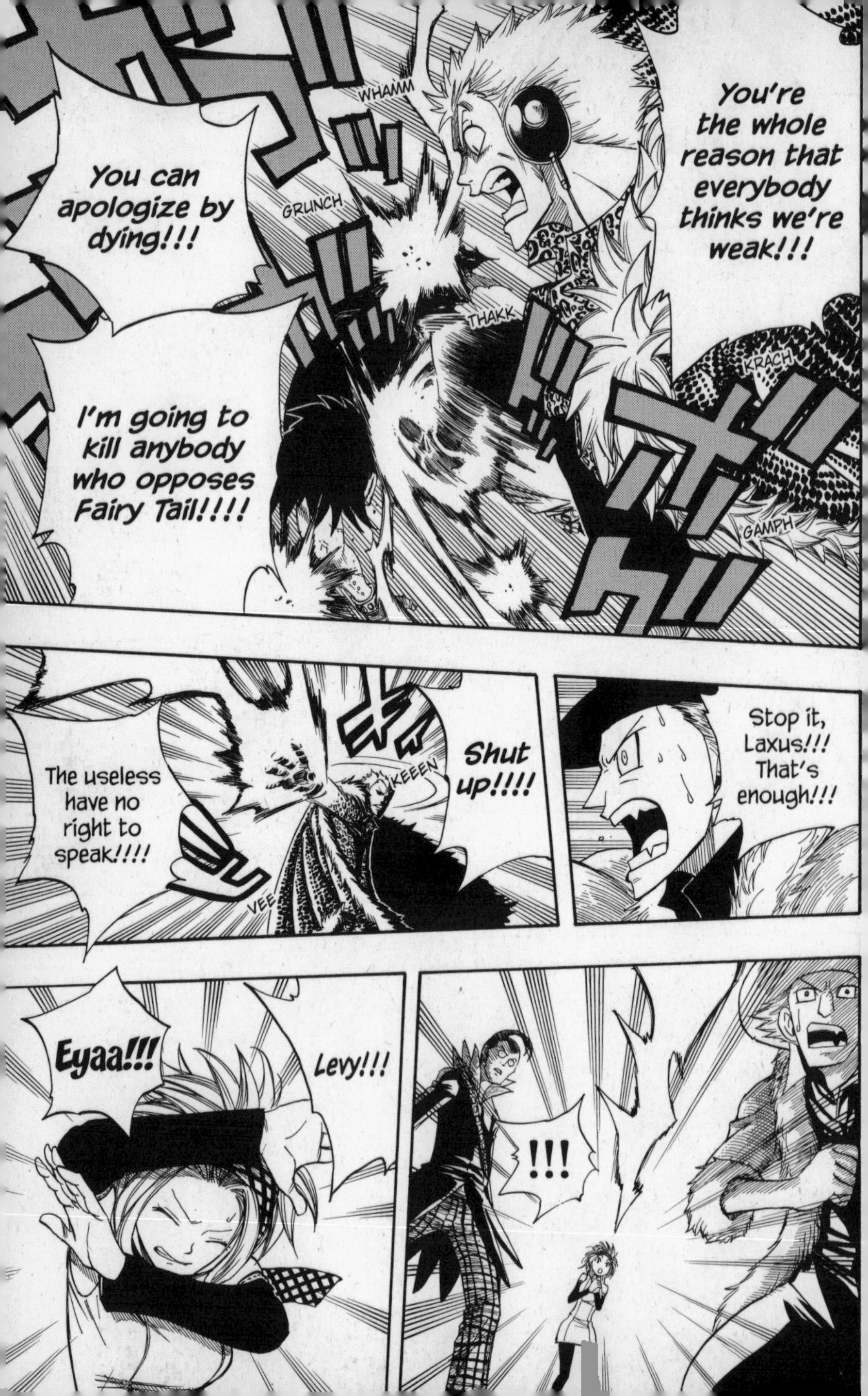
You're the whole reason that everybody thinks we're weak!!!
WHAMM
GRUNCH
THAKK
KRACH
GAMPH
You can apologize by dying!!!
I'm going to kill anybody who opposes Fairy Tail!!!!
Stop it, Laxus!!! That's enough!!!
Shut up!!!!
KEEEN
The useless have no right to speak!!!!
VEE
!!!
Levy!!!
Eyaa!!!

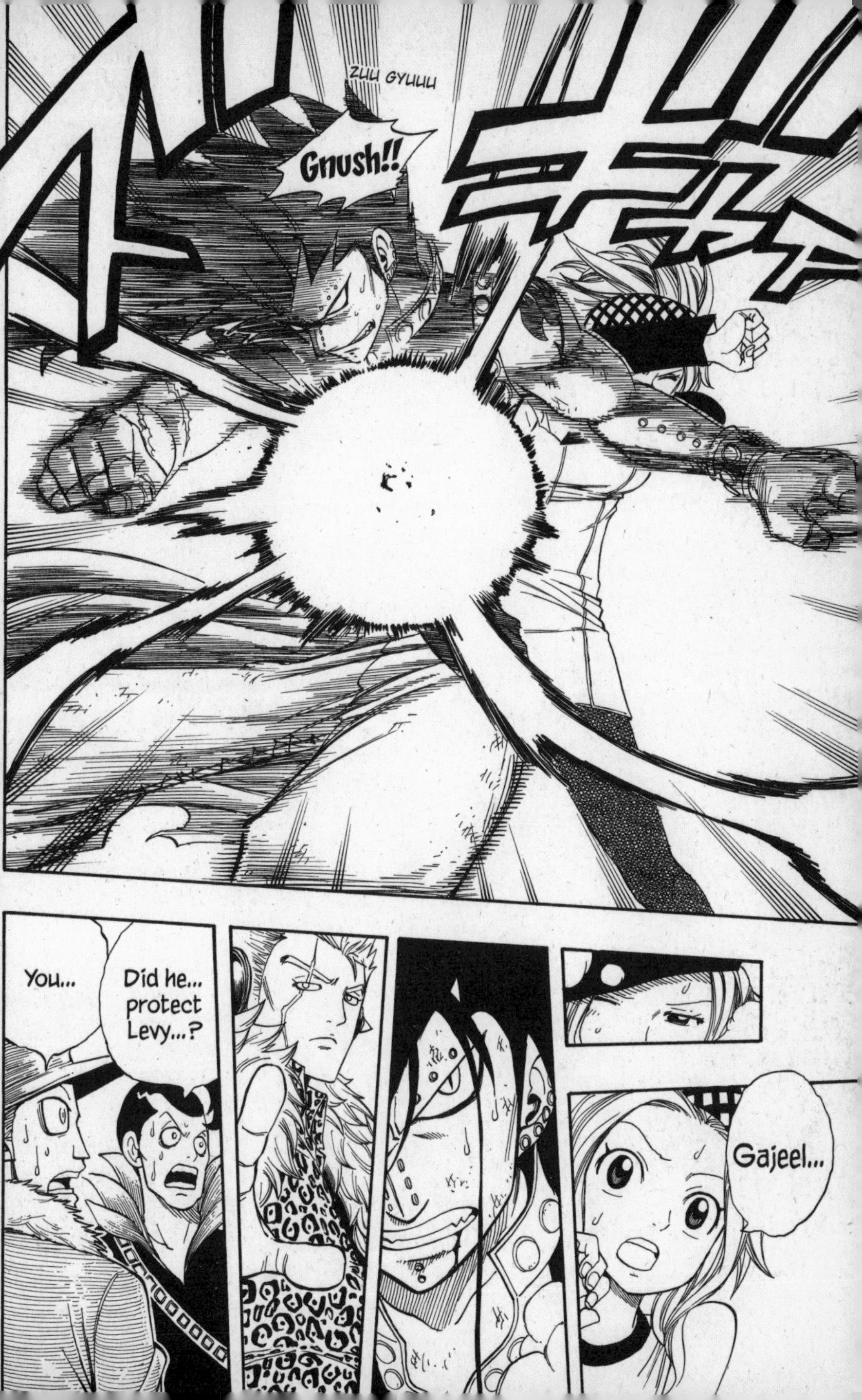
ZUU GYUUU
Gnush!!
Gajeel...
Did he... protect Levy...?
You...

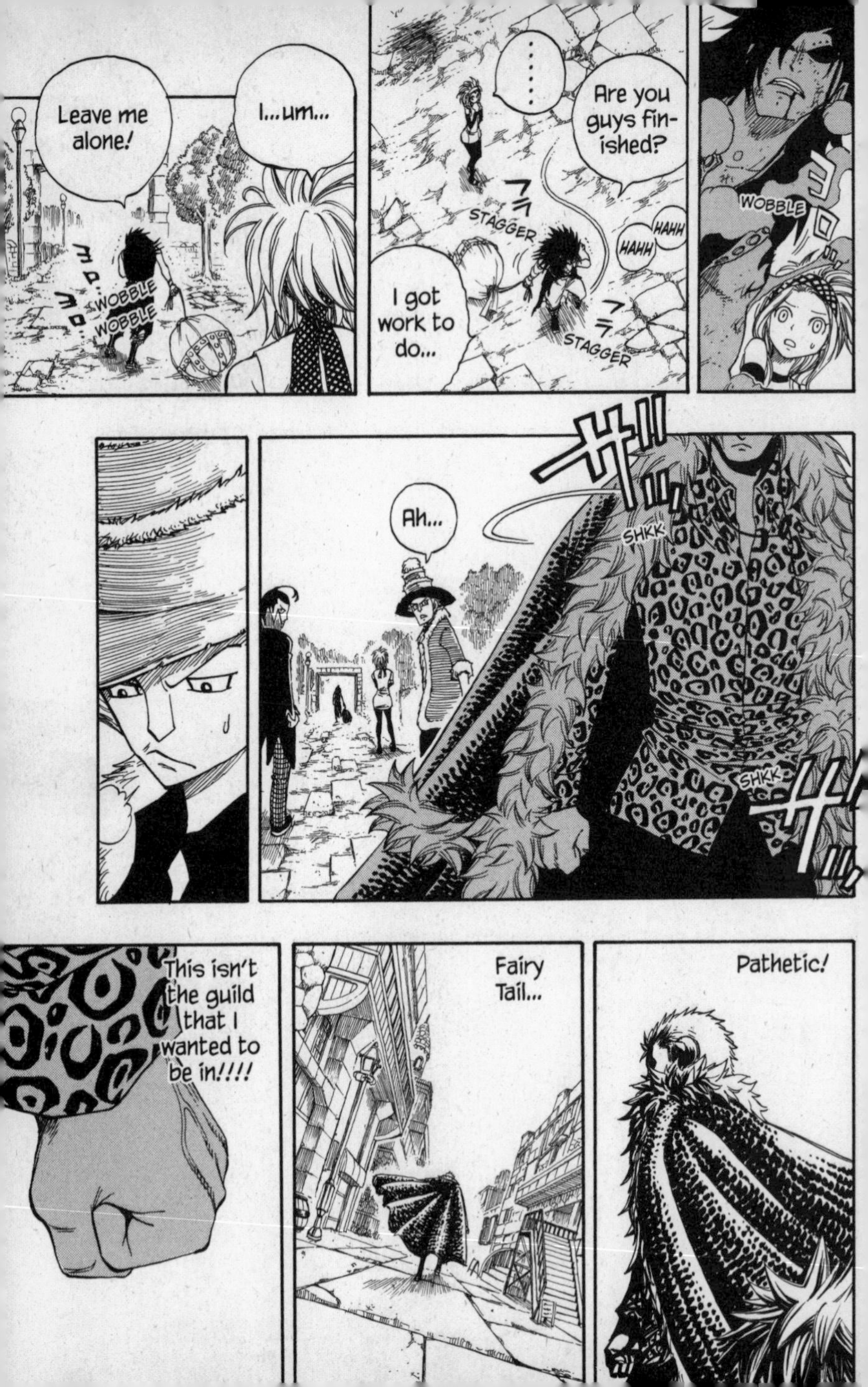
WOBBLE
......
Are you guys fin-ished?
STAGGER
HAHH
HAHH
I got work to do...
STAGGER
I...um...
Leave me alone!
WOBBLE
WOBBLE
Ah...
SHKK
SHKK
Pathetic!
Fairy Tail...
This isn't the guild that I wanted to be in!!!!

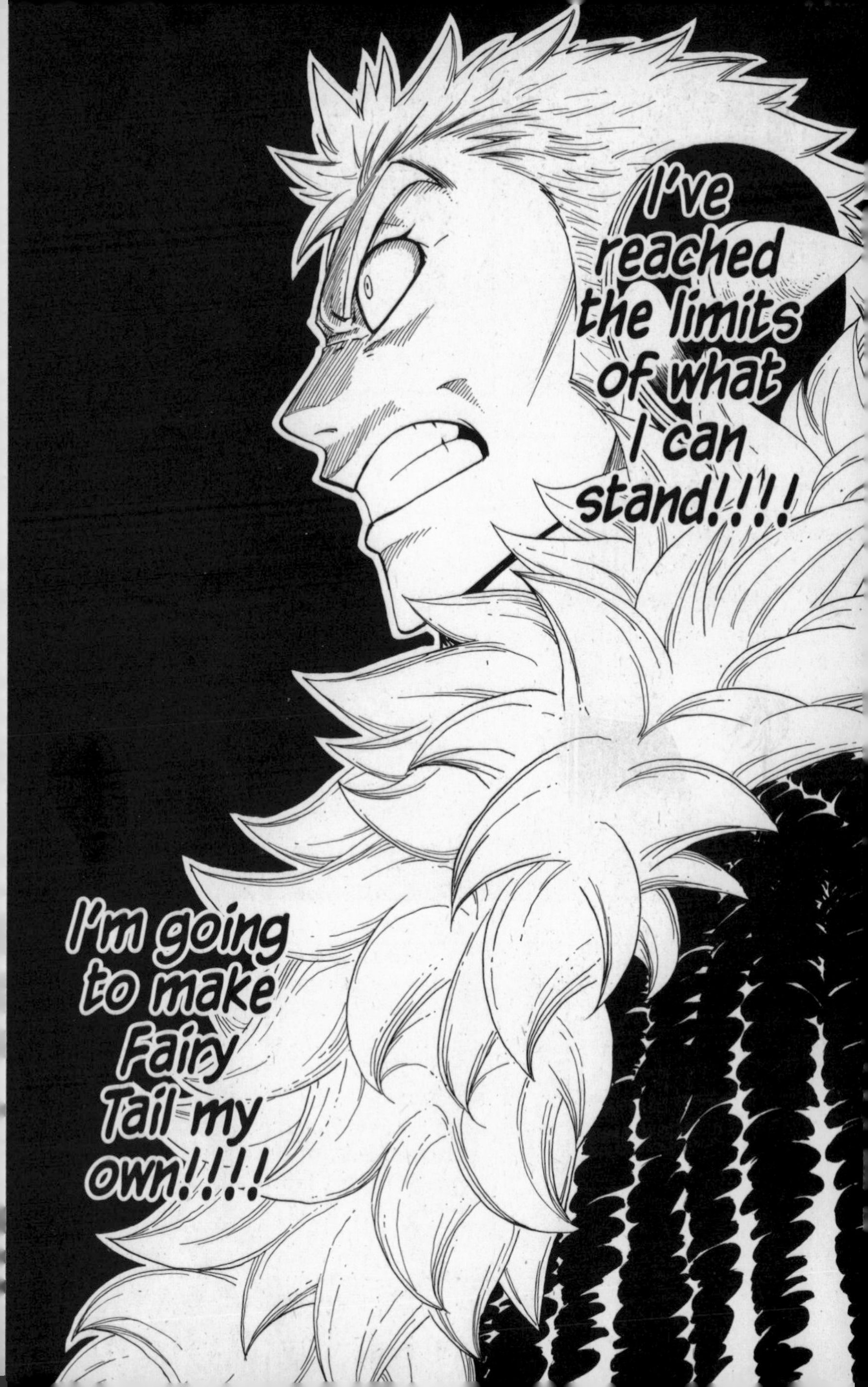
I've reached the limits of what I can stand!!!!
I'm going to make Fairy Tail my own!!!!

FAIRY TAIL

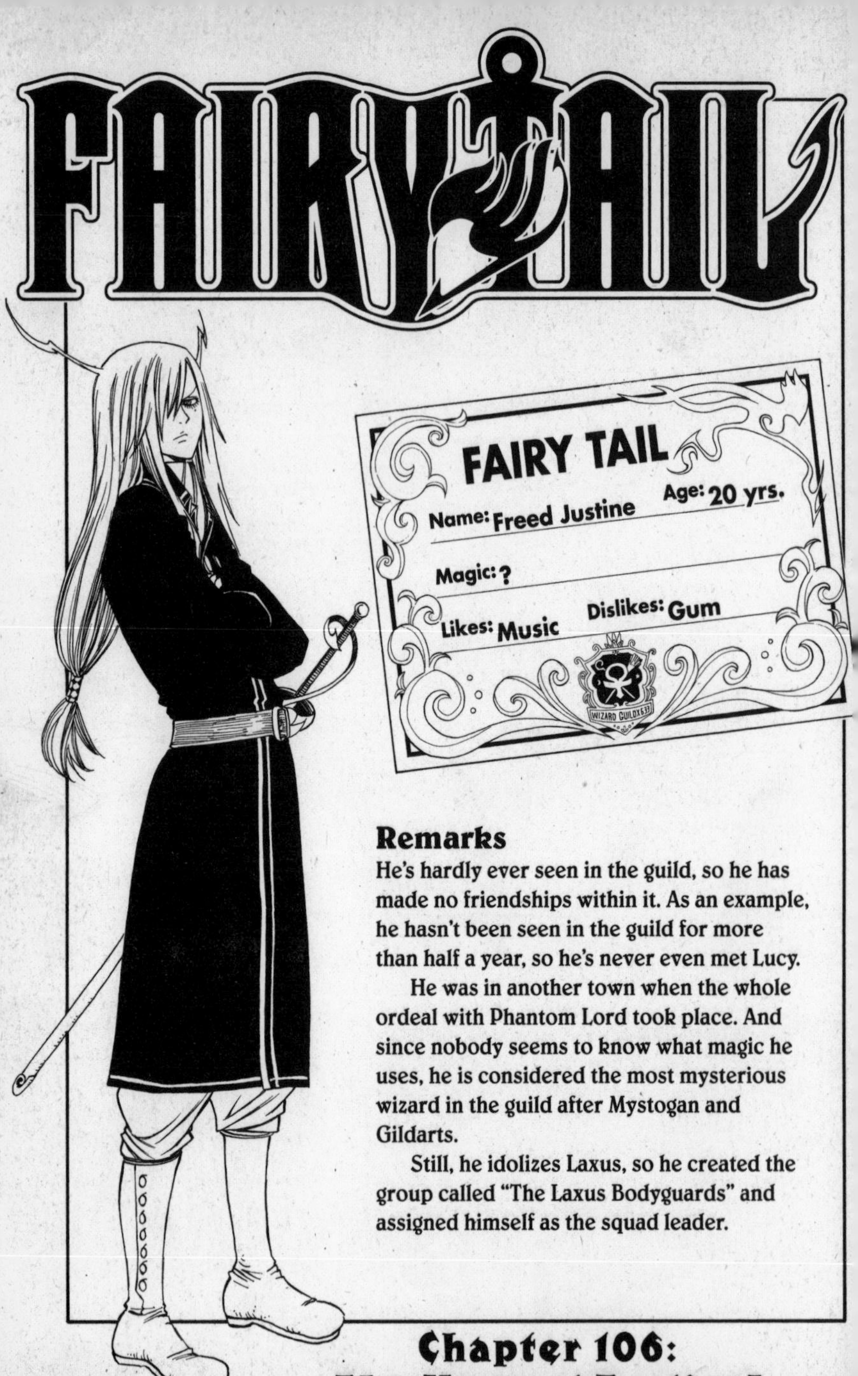

FAIRY TAIL

Name: Freed Justine   Age: 20 yrs.

Magic: ?

Likes: Music   Dislikes: Gum

WIZARD GUILDX639

Remarks

He's hardly ever seen in the guild, so he has made no friendships within it. As an example, he hasn't been seen in the guild for more than half a year, so he's never even met Lucy.

He was in another town when the whole ordeal with Phantom Lord took place. And since nobody seems to know what magic he uses, he is considered the most mysterious wizard in the guild after Mystogan and Gildarts.

Still, he idolizes Laxus, so he created the group called "The Laxus Bodyguards" and assigned himself as the squad leader.

Chapter 106: The Harvest Festival

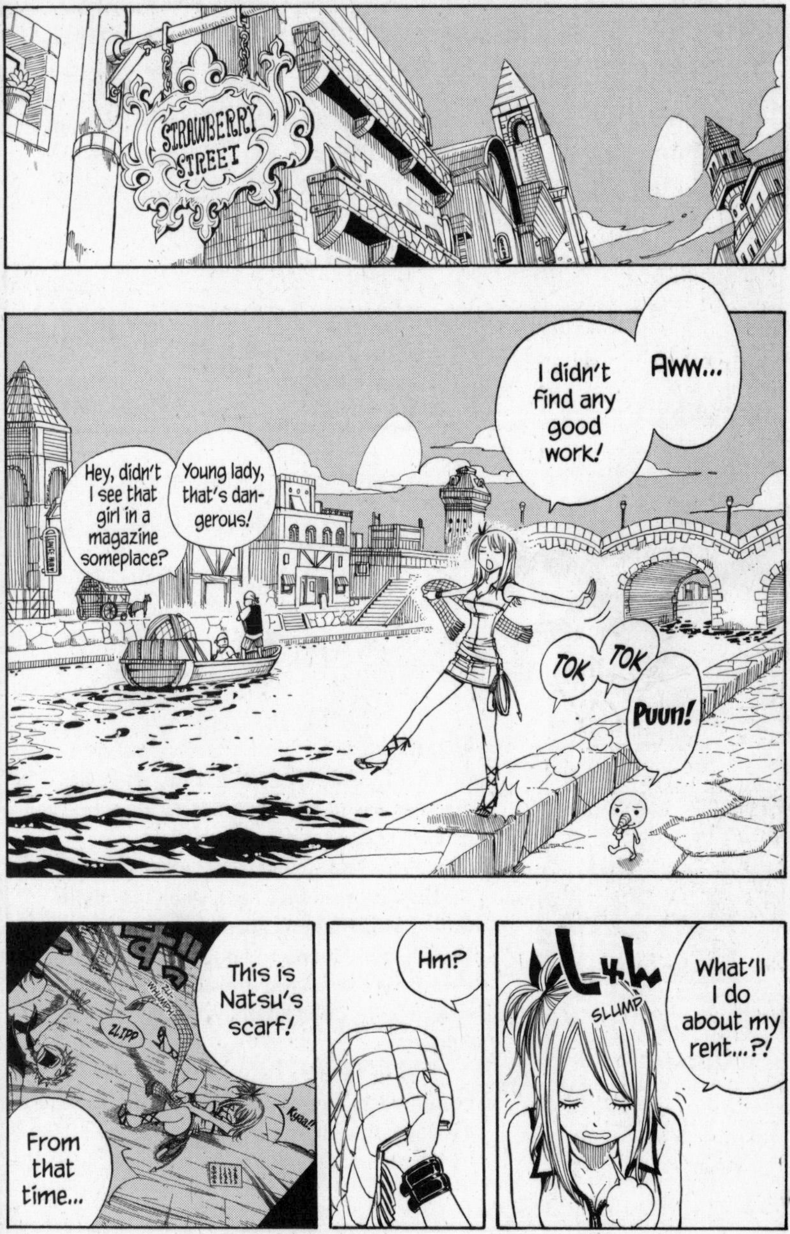
STRAWBERRY STREET
Aww...
I didn't find any good work!
TOK TOK
Puun!
Young lady, that's dangerous!
Hey, didn't I see that girl in a magazine someplace?
What'll I do about my rent...?!
SLUMP
Hm?
This is Natsu's scarf!
ZLIPP
Kyaa!
From that time...

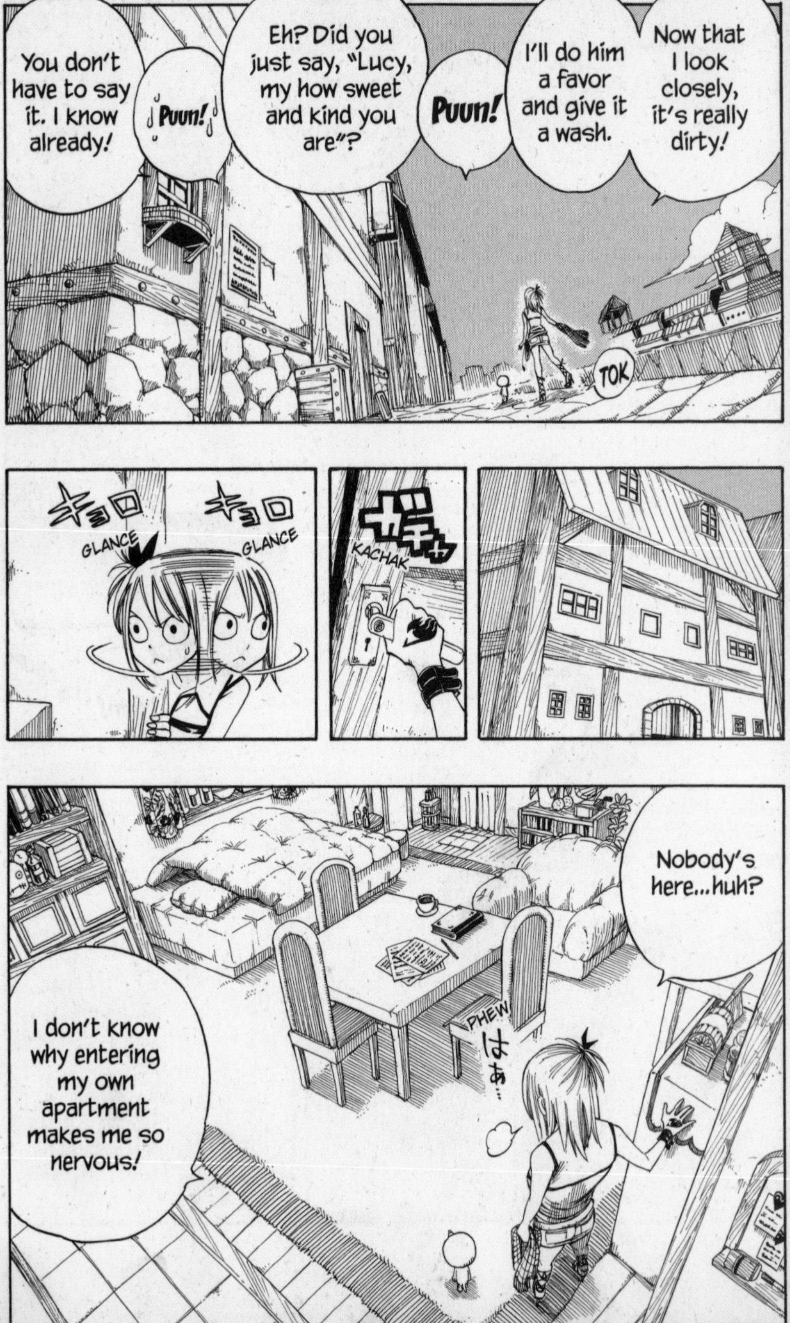
Now that I look closely, it's really dirty!
I'll do him a favor and give it a wash.
Puun!
Eh? Did you just say, "Lucy, my how sweet and kind you are"?
Puun!
You don't have to say it. I know already!
TOK
ガチャ
KACHAK
キョロ
GLANCE
キョロ
GLANCE
Nobody's here...huh?
PHEW
はぁ…
I don't know why entering my own apartment makes me so nervous!

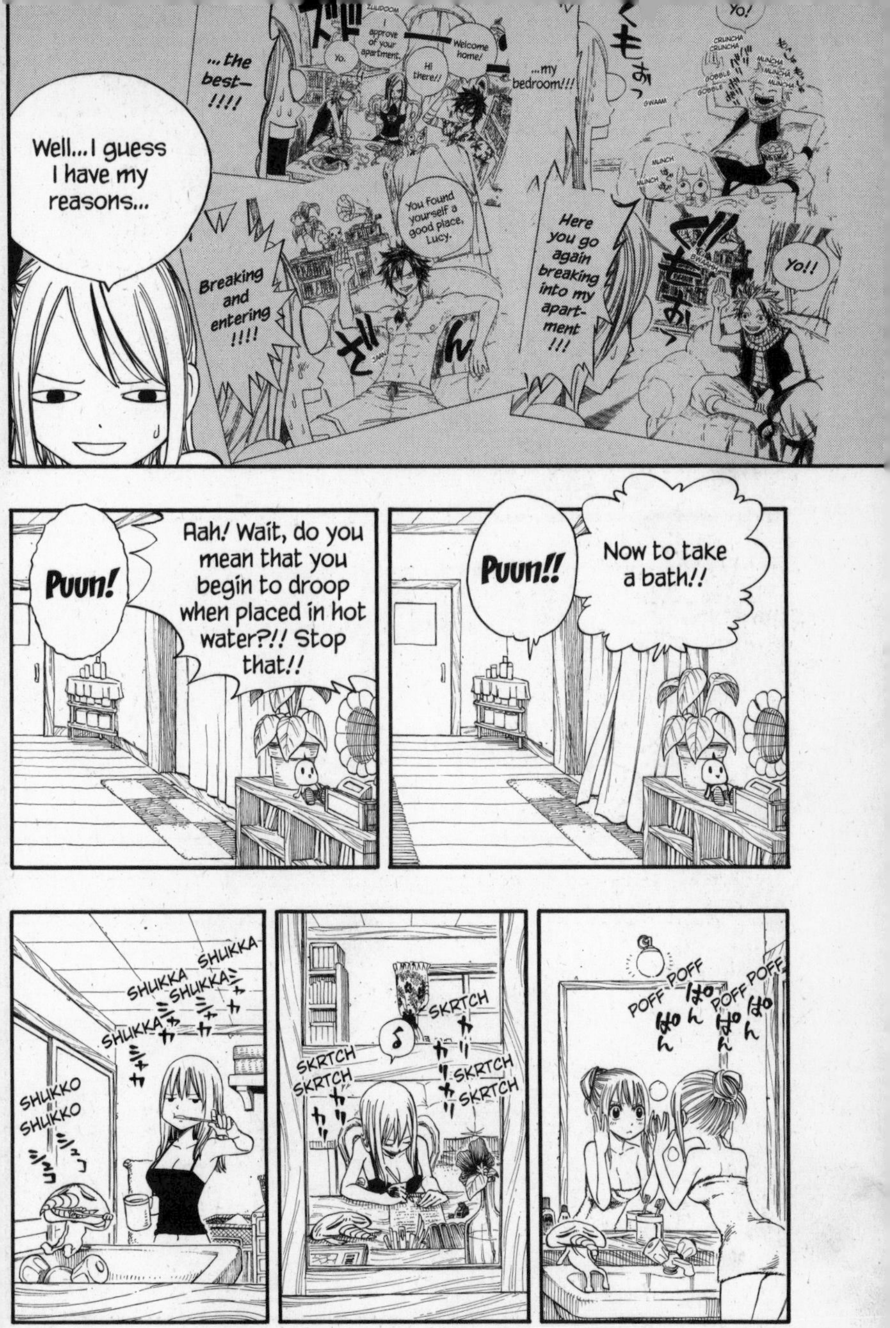
Yo!
CRUNCHA CRUNCHA
MUNCHA MUNCHA
GOBBLE GOBBLE
GWAAM
MUNCH MUNCH
Yo!!
Here you go again breaking into my apartment!!!
...my bedroom!!!
You found yourself a good place, Lucy.
Breaking and entering!!!!
Welcome home!
Hi there!!
I approve of your apartment.
Yo.
ZUUDOOM
...the best—!!!!
Well...I guess I have my reasons...
Now to take a bath!!
Puun!!
Aah! Wait, do you mean that you begin to droop when placed in hot water?!! Stop that!!
Puun!
POFF POFF
POFF POFF
SKRTCH
SKRTCH SKRTCH
SKRTCH SKRTCH
SHUKKA SHUKKA
SHUKKA SHUKKA
SHUKKO SHUKKO

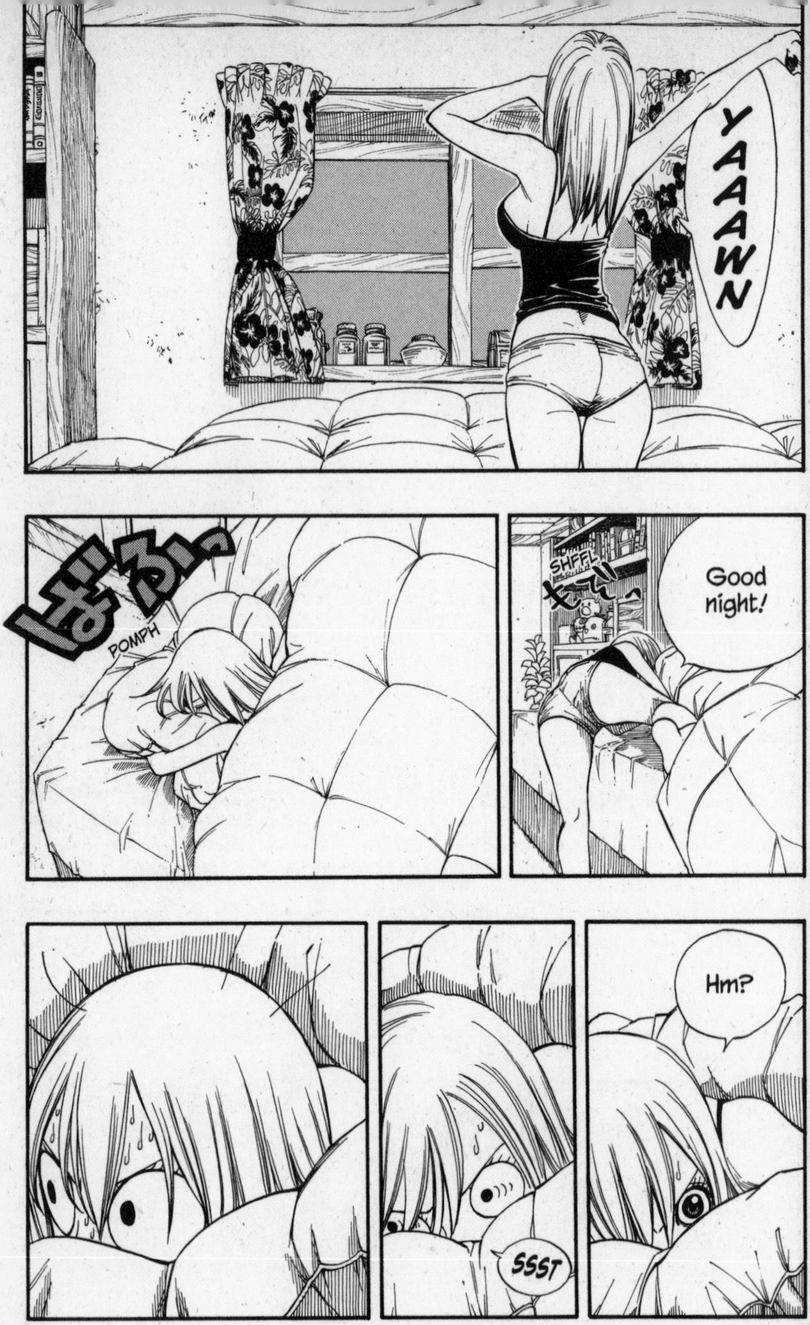
YAAAWN
SHFFL
Good night!
POMPH
Hm?
SSST

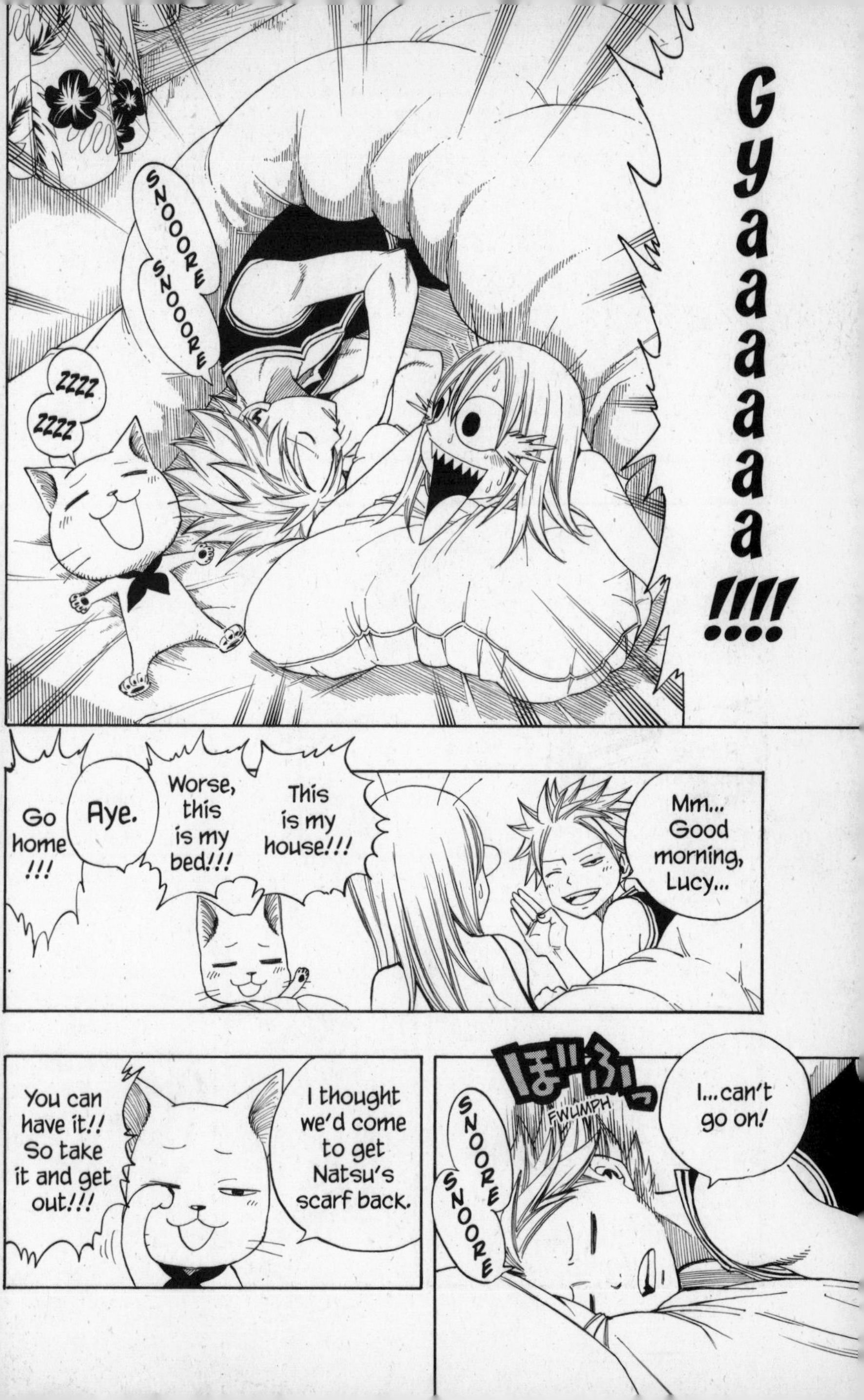
Gyaaaaaa!!!!
SNOOORE SNOOORE
ZZZZ ZZZZ
Mm... Good morning, Lucy...
This is my house!!!
Worse, this is my bed!!!
Aye.
Go home!!!
I...can't go on!
ぼふっ
FWUMPH
SNOORE SNOORE
I thought we'd come to get Natsu's scarf back.
You can have it!! So take it and get out!!!

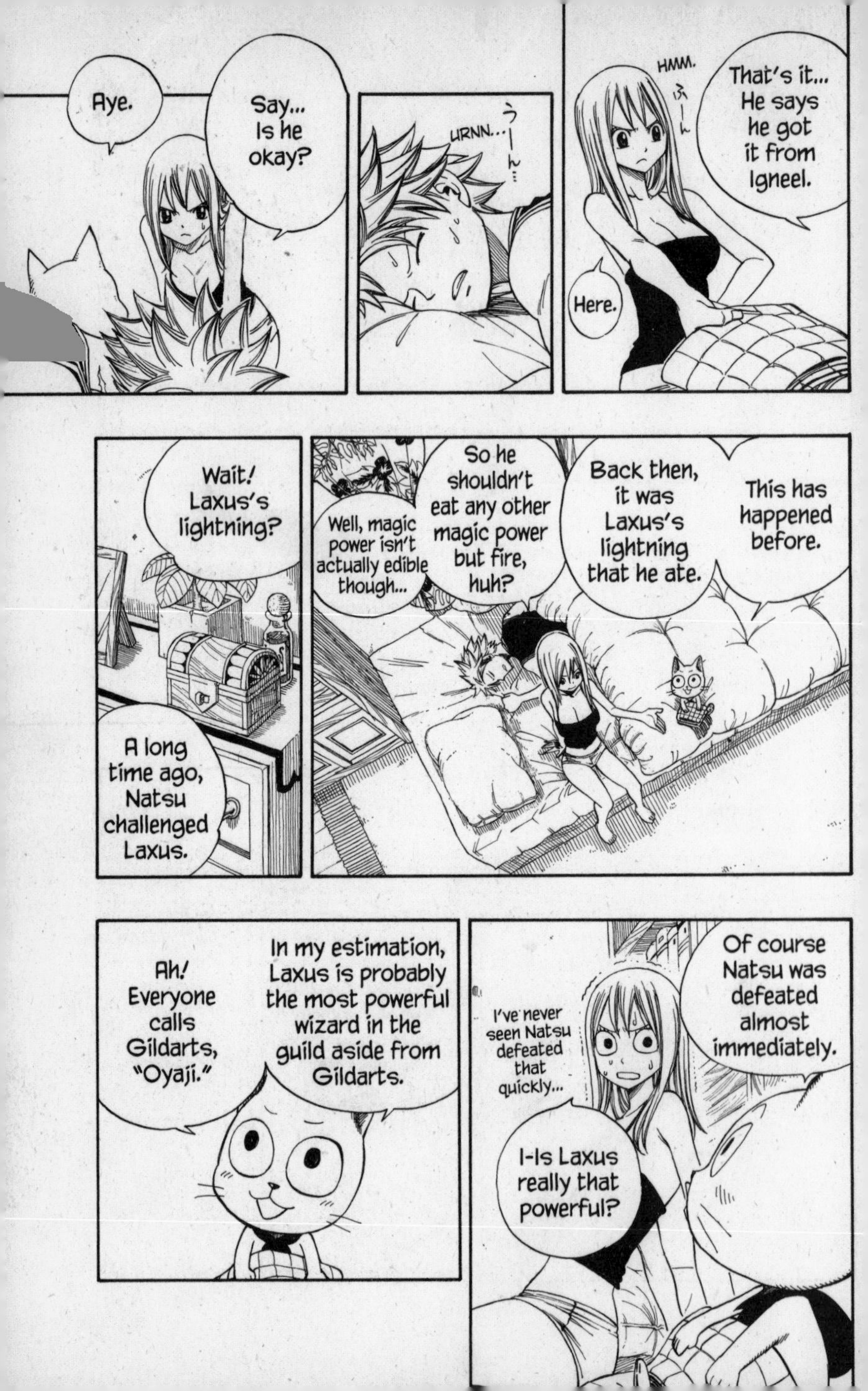

That's it... He says he got it from Igneel.
HMM.
ふーん
Here.
URNN...
うーん...
Say... Is he okay?
Aye.
This has happened before.
Back then, it was Laxus's lightning that he ate.
So he shouldn't eat any other magic power but fire, huh?
Well, magic power isn't actually edible though...
Wait! Laxus's lightning?
A long time ago, Natsu challenged Laxus.
Of course Natsu was defeated almost immediately.
I've never seen Natsu defeated that quickly...
I-Is Laxus really that powerful?
In my estimation, Laxus is probably the most powerful wizard in the guild aside from Gildarts.
Ah! Everyone calls Gildarts, "Oyaji."

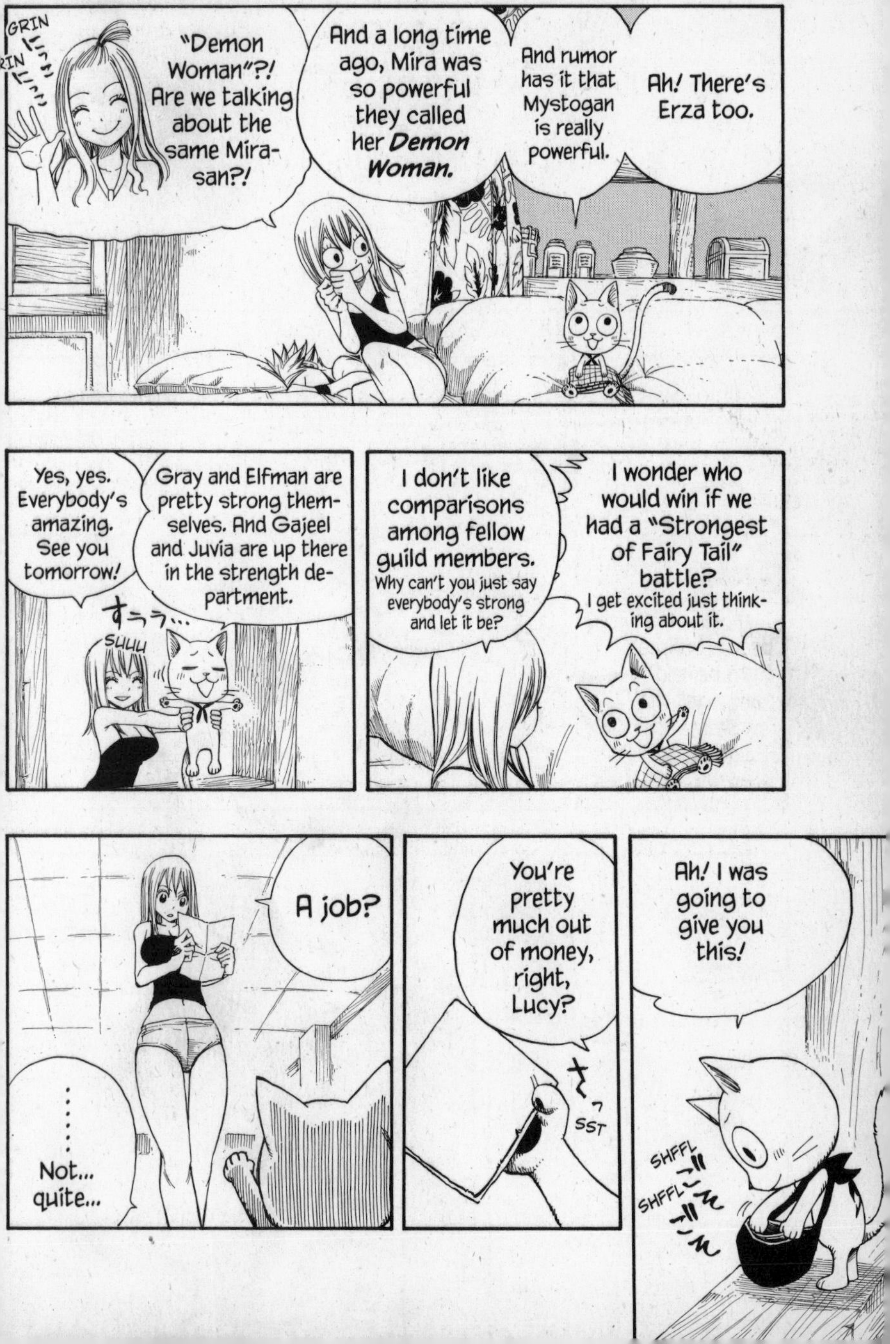
Ah! There's Erza too.
And rumor has it that Mystogan is really powerful.
And a long time ago, Mira was so powerful they called her *Demon Woman.*
GRIN
RIN
"Demon Woman"?! Are we talking about the same Mira-san?!
I wonder who would win if we had a "Strongest of Fairy Tail" battle? I get excited just thinking about it.
I don't like comparisons among fellow guild members. Why can't you just say everybody's strong and let it be?
Gray and Elfman are pretty strong themselves. And Gajeel and Juvia are up there in the strength department.
Yes, yes. Everybody's amazing. See you tomorrow!
SUUU
Ah! I was going to give you this!
SHFFL
SHFFL
You're pretty much out of money, right, Lucy?
SST
A job?
...... Not... quite...

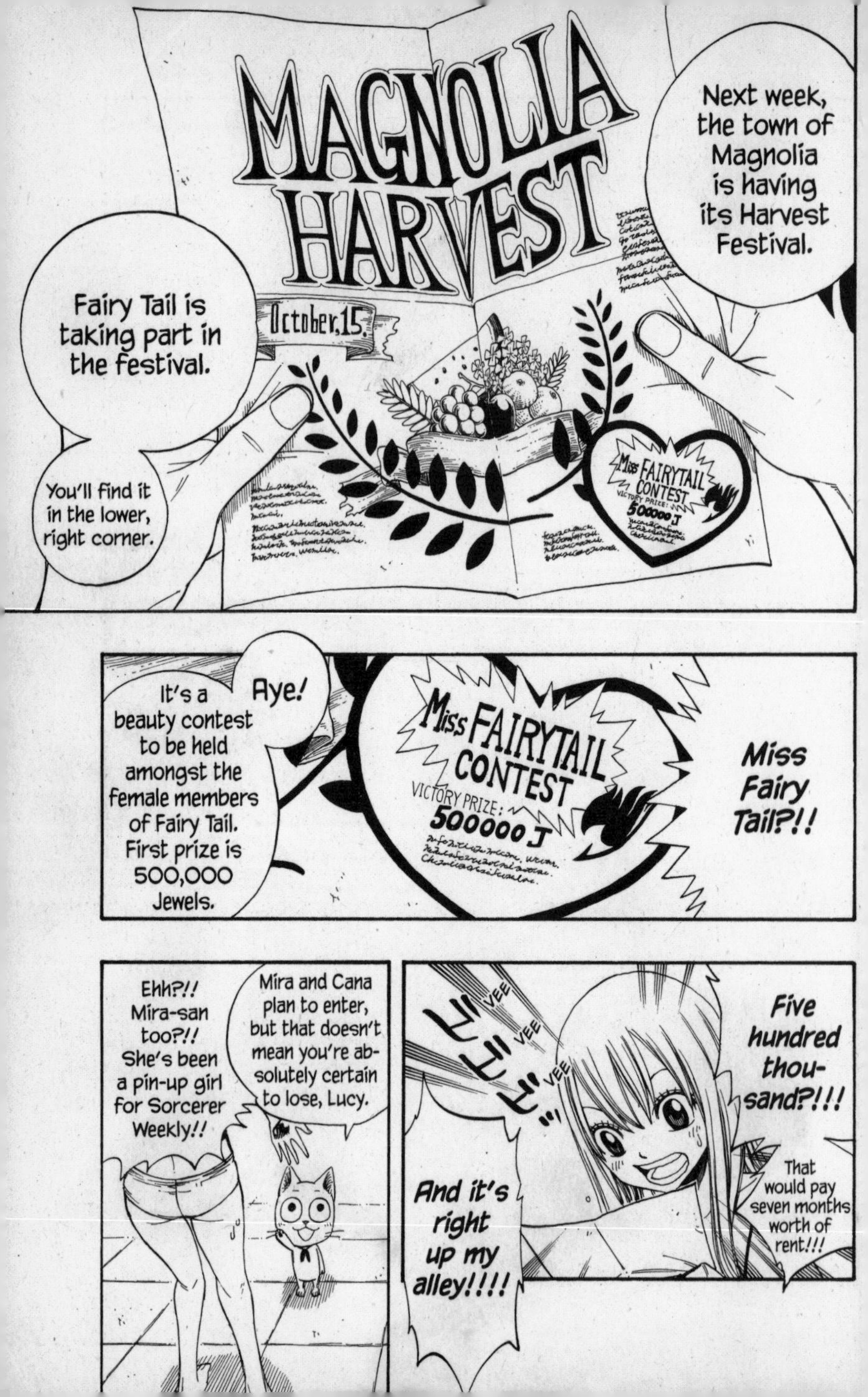
Next week, the town of Magnolia is having its Harvest Festival.
MAGNOLIA HARVEST
October.15.
Fairy Tail is taking part in the festival.
You'll find it in the lower, right corner.
Miss FAIRYTAIL CONTEST
VICTORY PRIZE: 500000 J
Miss Fairy Tail?!!
Miss FAIRYTAIL CONTEST
VICTORY PRIZE: 500000 J
Aye!
It's a beauty contest to be held amongst the female members of Fairy Tail. First prize is 500,000 Jewels.
Five hundred thou-sand?!!!
That would pay seven months worth of rent!!!
VEE VEE VEE
And it's right up my alley!!!!
Mira and Cana plan to enter, but that doesn't mean you're ab-solutely certain to lose, Lucy.
Ehh?!! Mira-san too?!! She's been a pin-up girl for Sorcerer Weekly!!

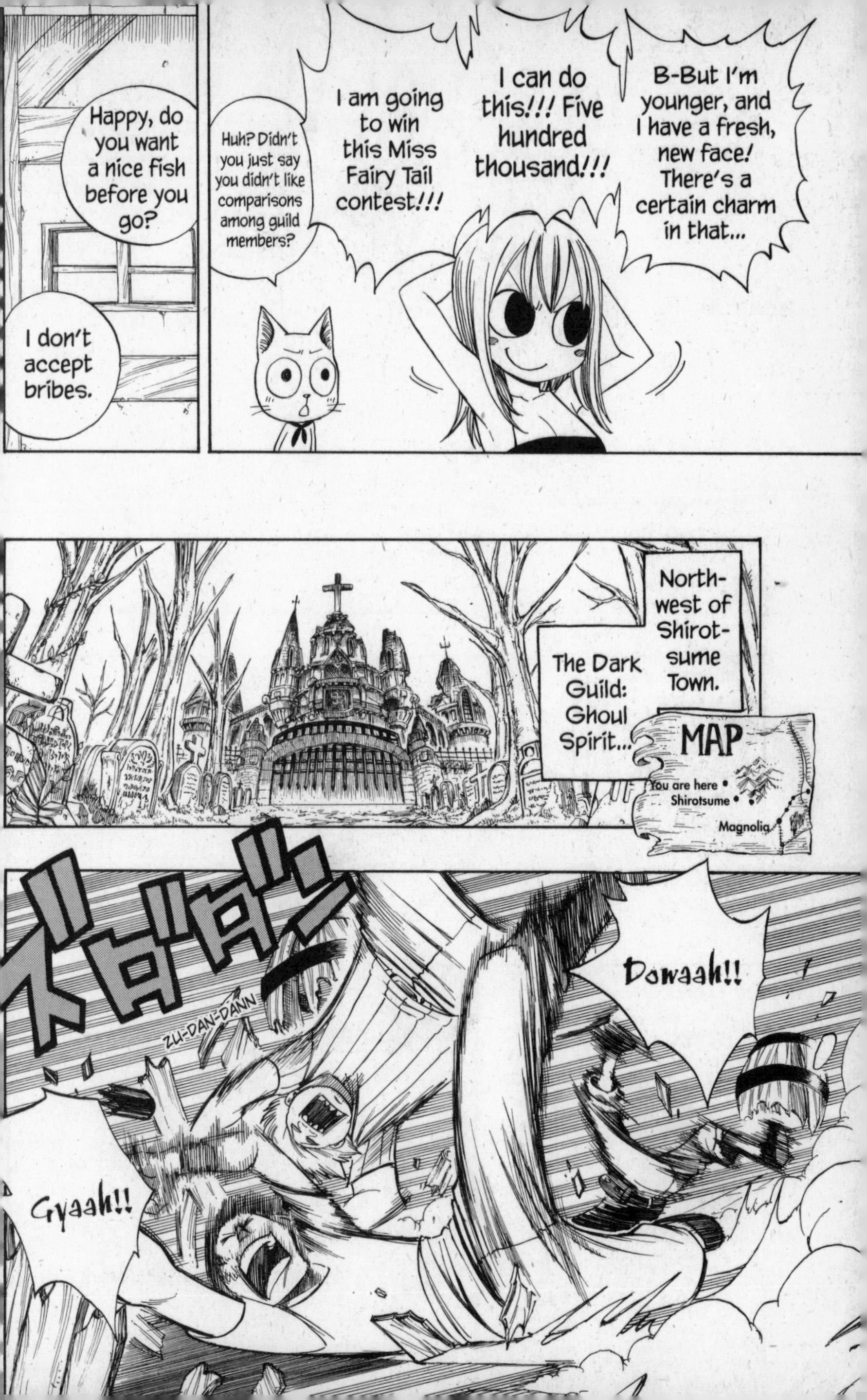
B-But I'm younger, and I have a fresh, new face! There's a certain charm in that...
I can do this!!! Five hundred thousand!!!
I am going to win this Miss Fairy Tail contest!!!
Huh? Didn't you just say you didn't like comparisons among guild members?
Happy, do you want a nice fish before you go?
I don't accept bribes.
North-west of Shirotsume Town.
The Dark Guild: Ghoul Spirit...
MAP
You are here
Shirotsume
Magnolia
Dowaah!!
ZU-DAN-DANN
Gyaah!!

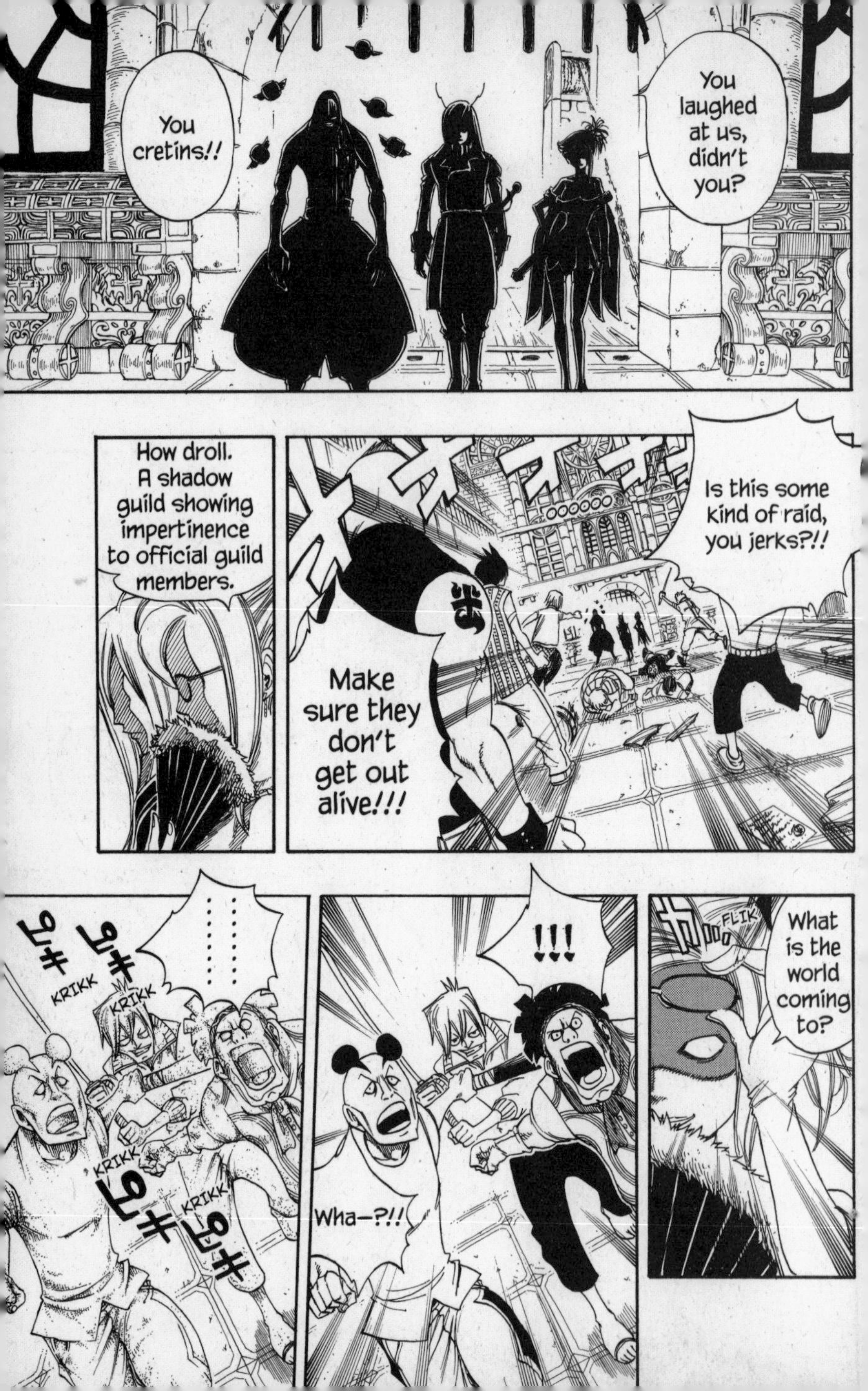
You laughed at us, didn't you?
You cretins!!
Is this some kind of raid, you jerks?!!
Make sure they don't get out alive!!!
How droll. A shadow guild showing impertinence to official guild members.
FLIK
What is the world coming to?
!!!
Wha–?!!
......
KRIKK
KRIKK
KRIKK
KRIKK

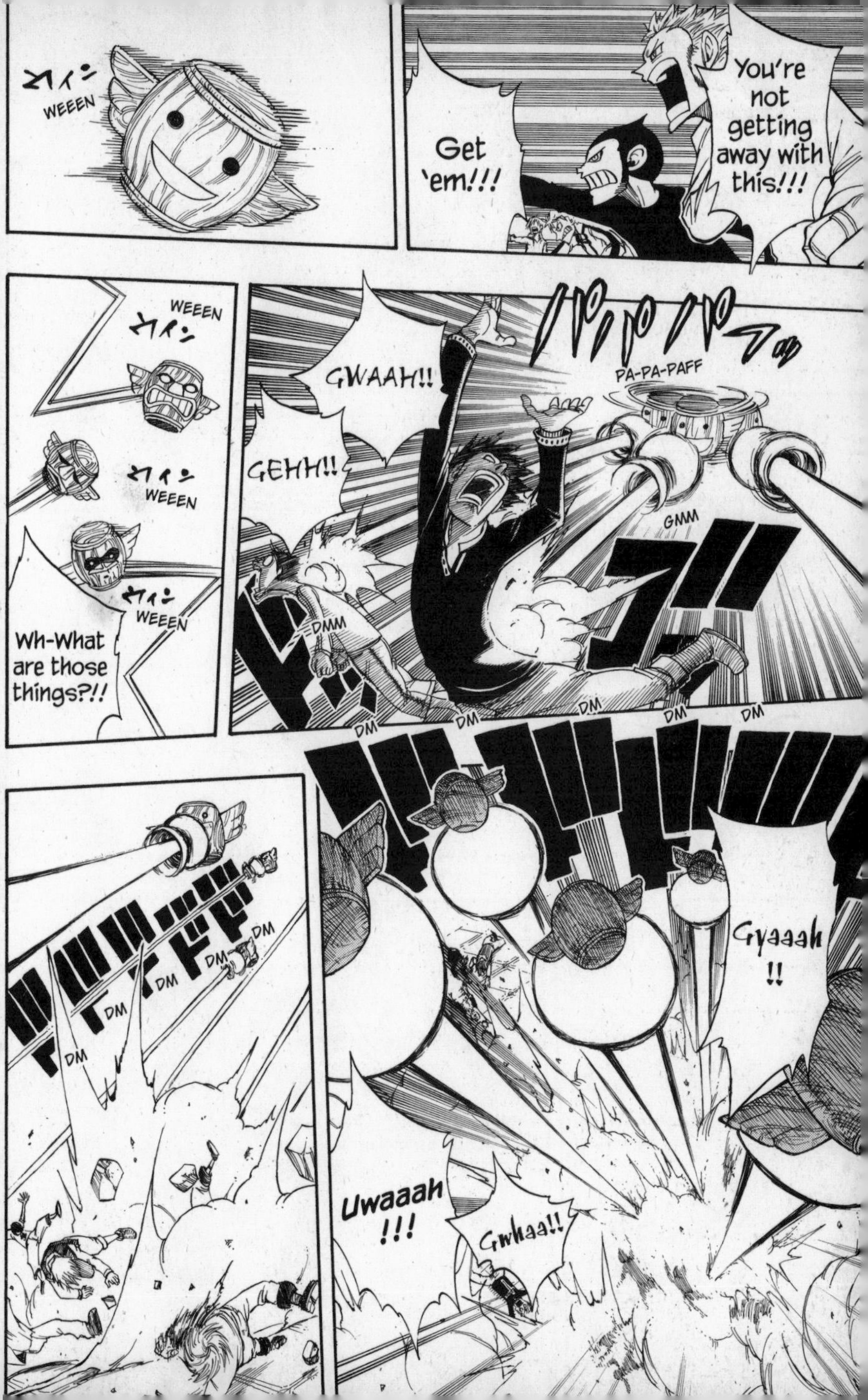

You're not getting away with this!!!
Get 'em!!!
WEEEN
PA-PA-PAFF
GWAAH!!
GEHH!!
GMM
DMM
DM
DM
DM
DM
DM
WEEEN
WEEEN
WEEEN
Wh-What are those things?!!
Gyaaah!!
Gwhaa!!
Uwaaah!!!
DM
DM
DM
DM
DM

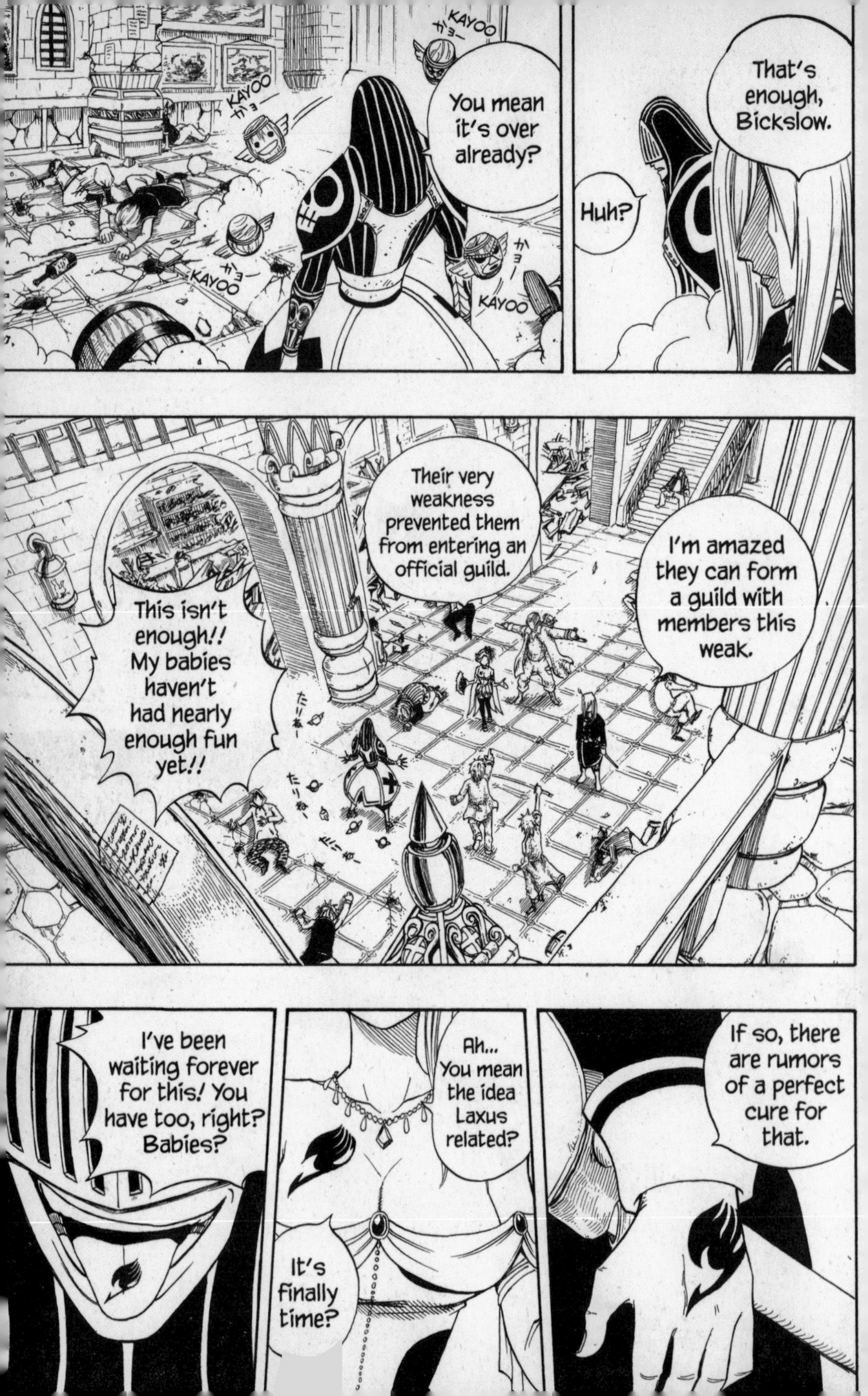
That's enough, Bickslow.
Huh?
KAYOO
カヨー
You mean it's over already?
KAYOO
カヨー
KAYOO
カヨー
KAYOO
カヨー
I'm amazed they can form a guild with members this weak.
Their very weakness prevented them from entering an official guild.
This isn't enough!! My babies haven't had nearly enough fun yet!!
たりねー
たりねー
If so, there are rumors of a perfect cure for that.
Ah... You mean the idea Laxus related?
It's finally time?
I've been waiting forever for this! You have too, right? Babies?

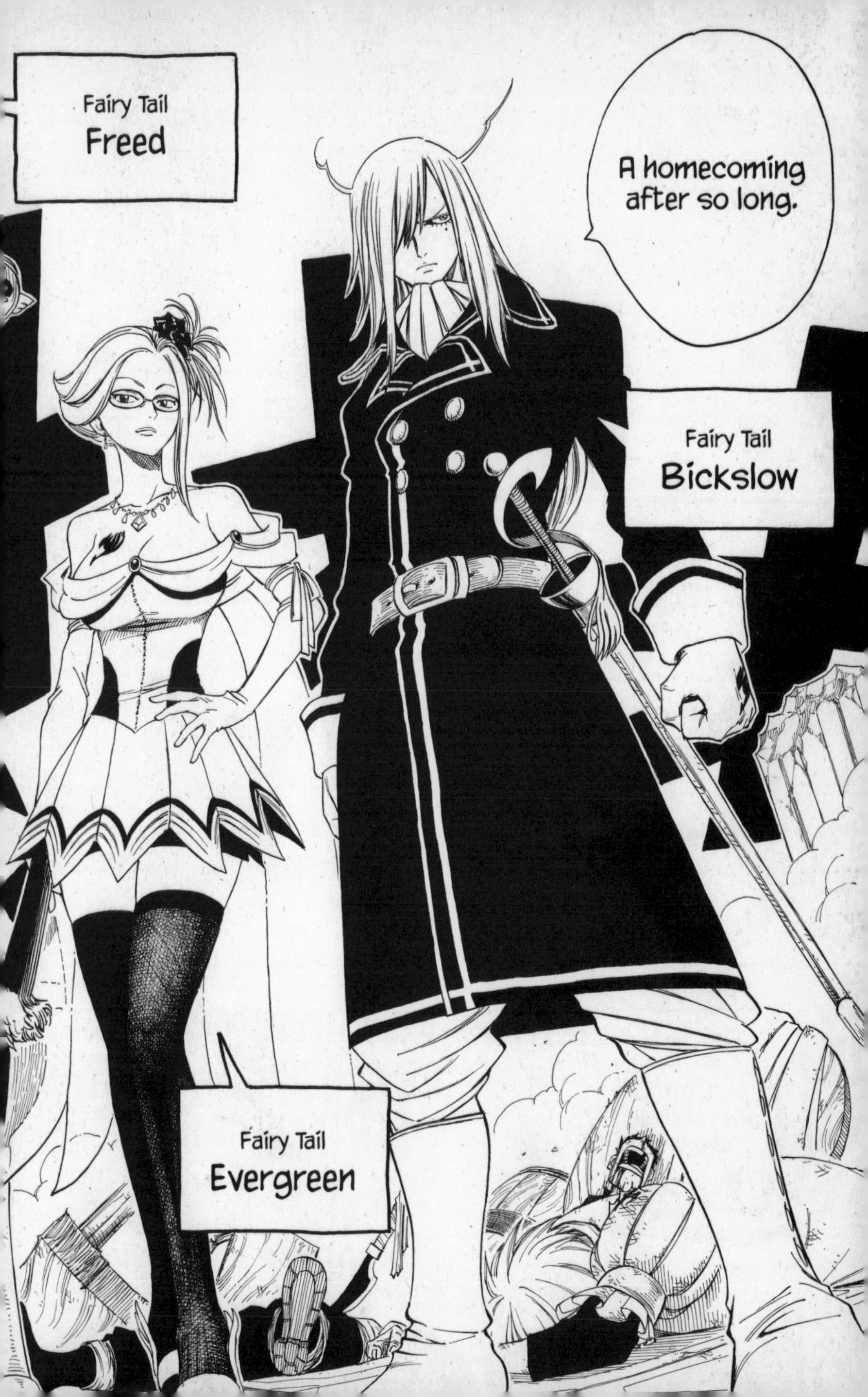
A homecoming after so long.
Fairy Tail Freed
Fairy Tail Bickslow
Fairy Tail Evergreen

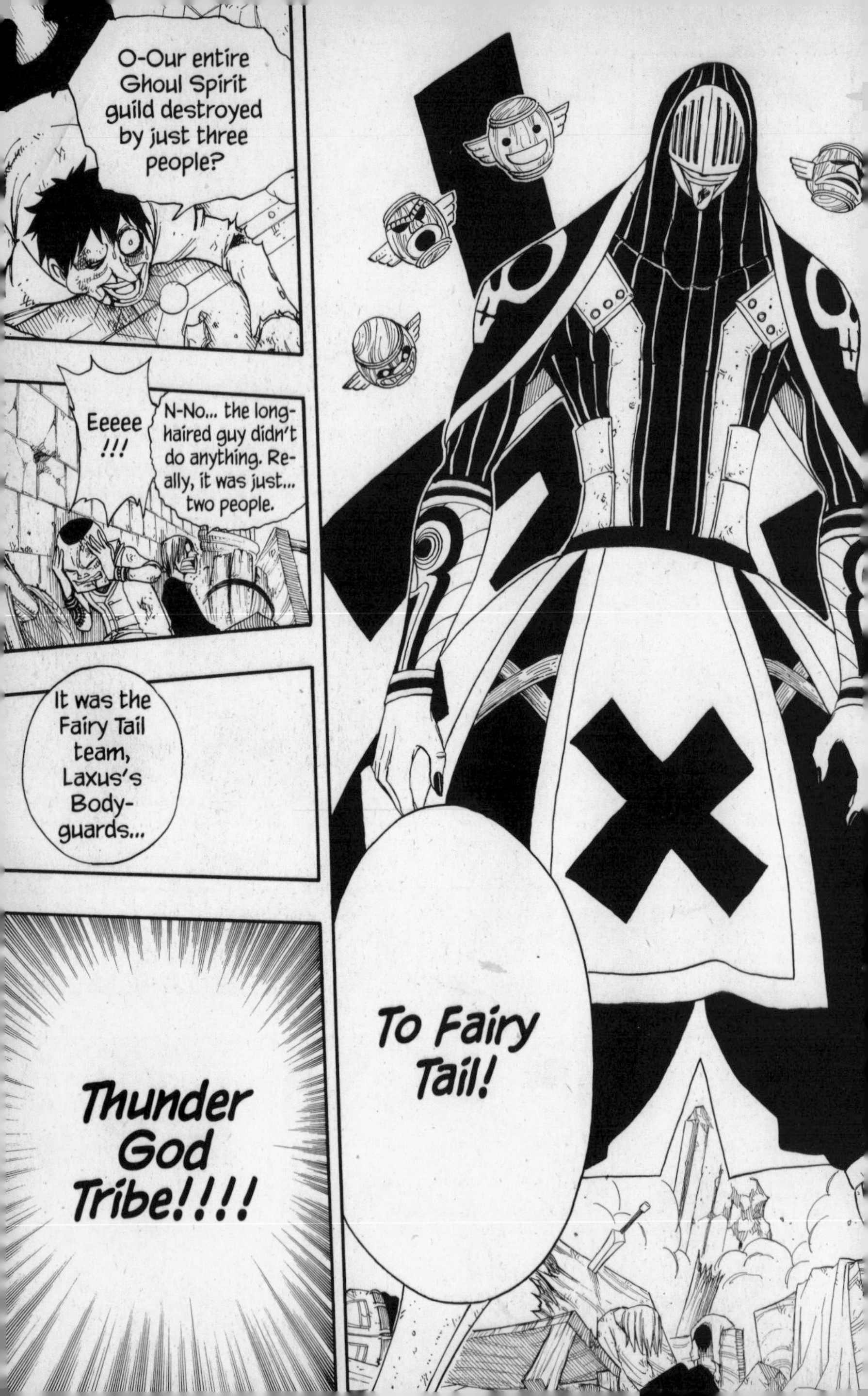
To Fairy Tail!
O-Our entire Ghoul Spirit guild destroyed by just three people?
N-No... the long-haired guy didn't do anything. Really, it was just... two people.
Eeeee !!!
It was the Fairy Tail team, Laxus's Bodyguards...
Thunder God Tribe!!!!

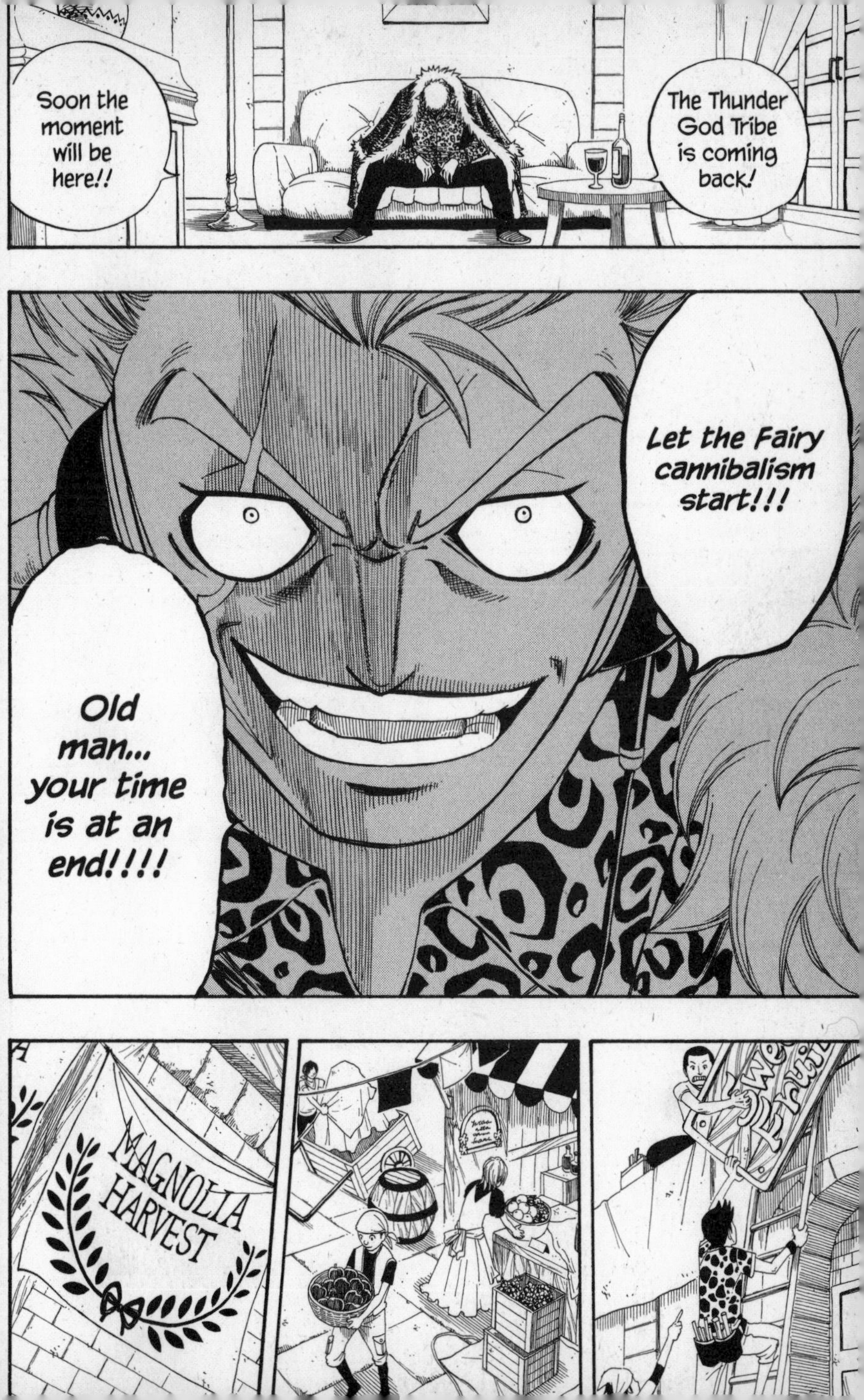
The Thunder God Tribe is coming back!
Soon the moment will be here!!
Let the Fairy cannibalism start!!!
Old man... your time is at an end!!!!
MAGNOLIA HARVEST

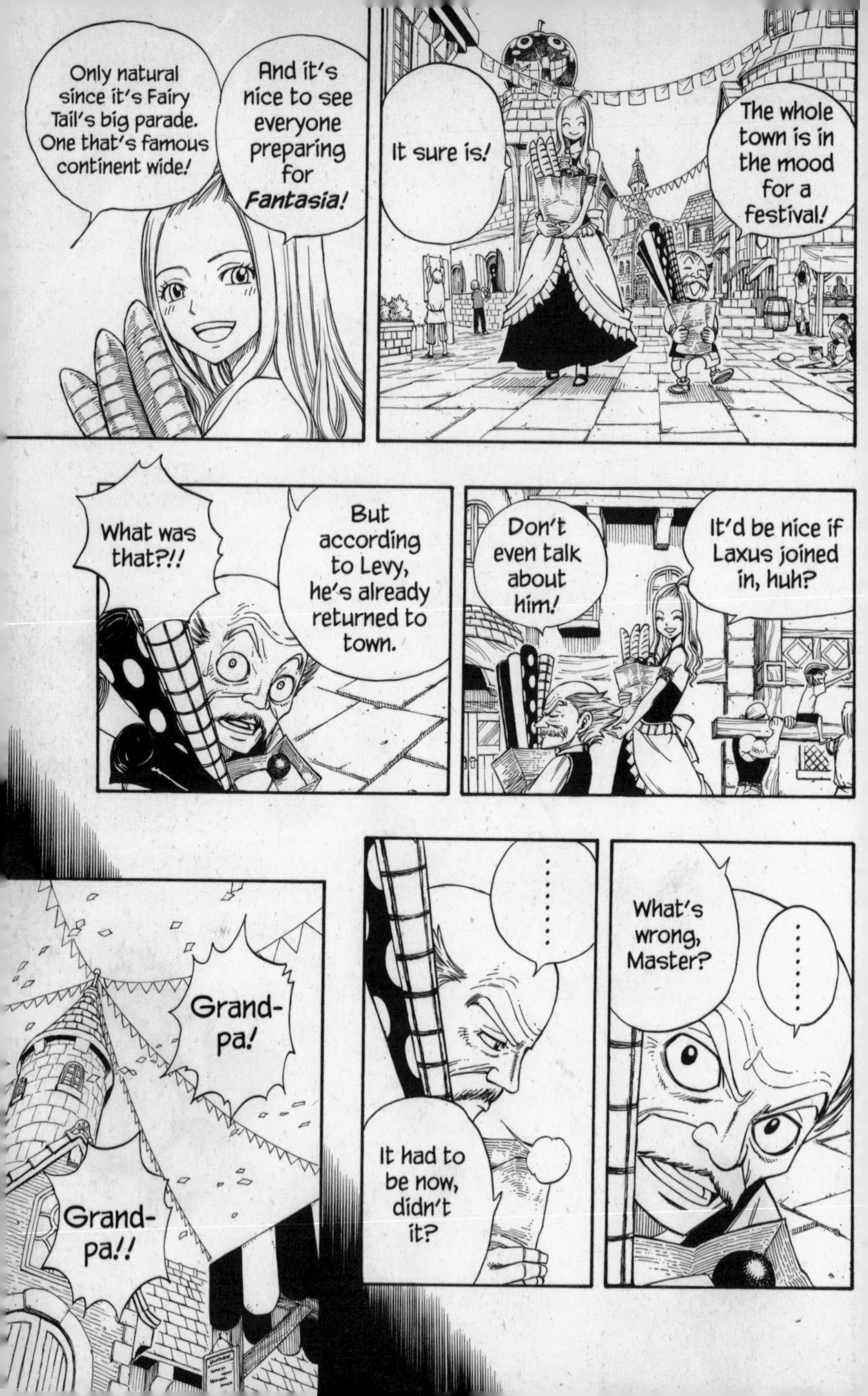
The whole town is in the mood for a festival!
It sure is!
And it's nice to see everyone preparing for *Fantasia!*
Only natural since it's Fairy Tail's big parade. One that's famous continent wide!
It'd be nice if Laxus joined in, huh?
Don't even talk about him!
But according to Levy, he's already returned to town.
What was that?!!
......
What's wrong, Master?
......
It had to be now, didn't it?
Grand-pa!
Grand-pa!!

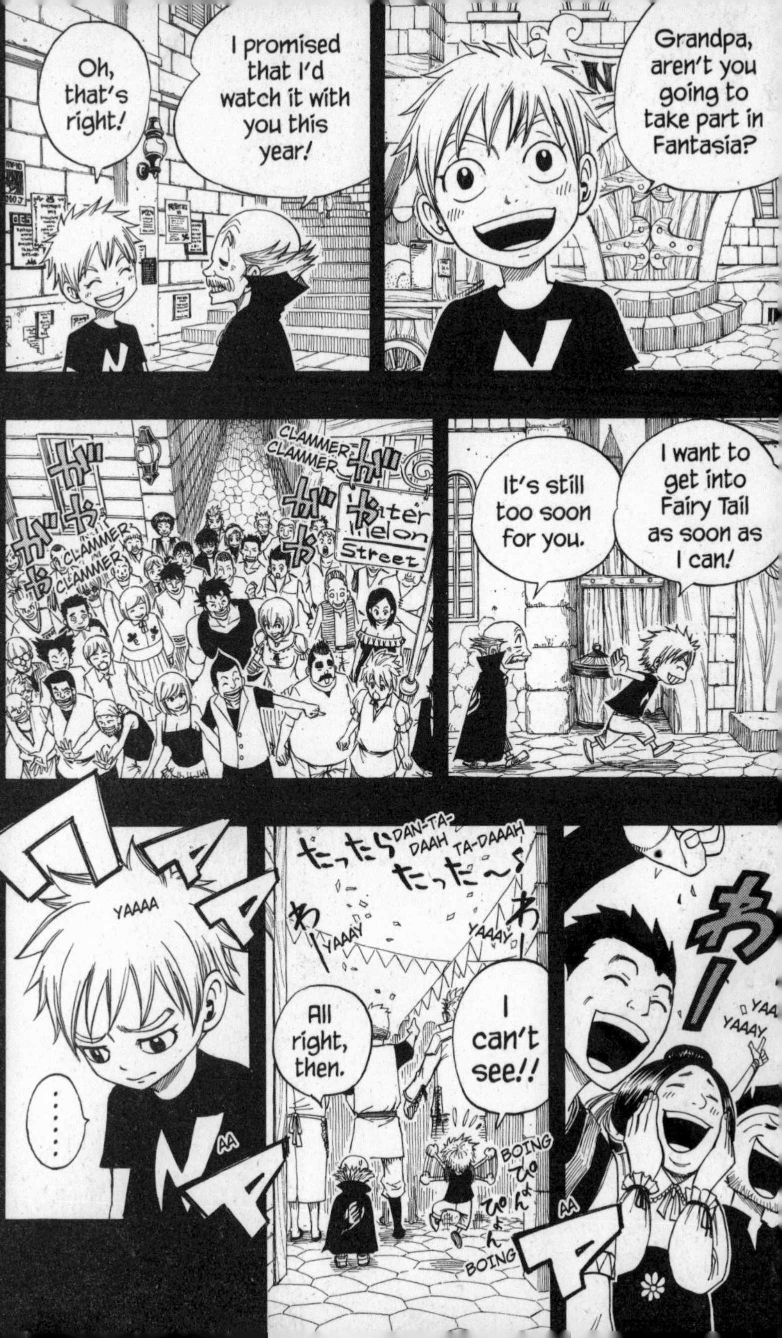
Grandpa, aren't you going to take part in Fantasia?
I promised that I'd watch it with you this year!
Oh, that's right!
I want to get into Fairy Tail as soon as I can!
It's still too soon for you.
ガヤ CLAMMER CLAMMER
ガヤ
ガヤ CLAMMER CLAMMER
Street
あー!
YAA YAAAY
AA
たったら DAN-TA-DAAH
たった~ TA-DAAAH
わー YAAAY
わー YAAAY
I can't see!!
All right, then.
ぴょん BOING
ぴょん BOING
YAAAA
......
AA

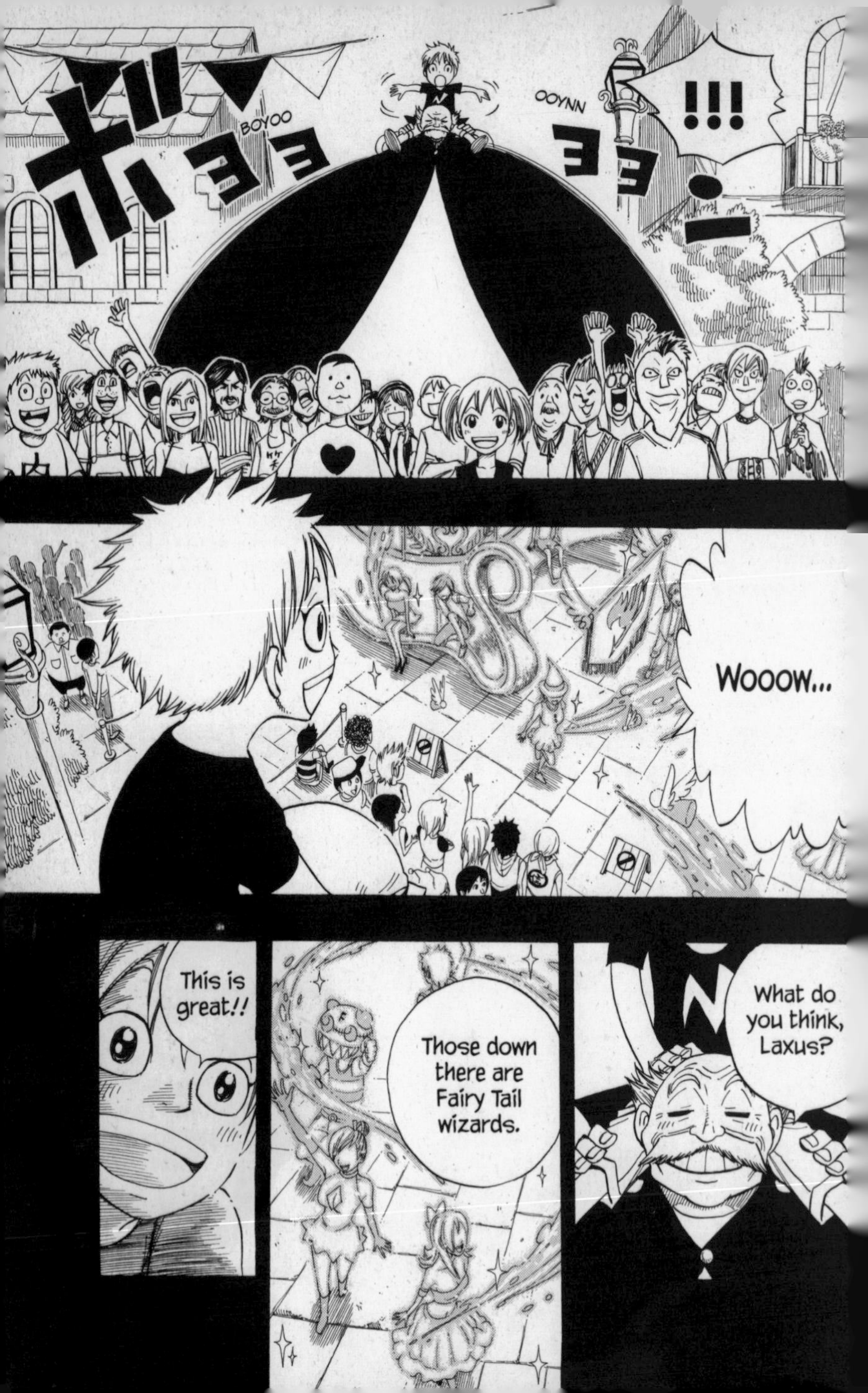
!!!
OOYNN
BOYOO
WOOOW...
What do you think, Laxus?
Those down there are Fairy Tail wizards.
This is great!!

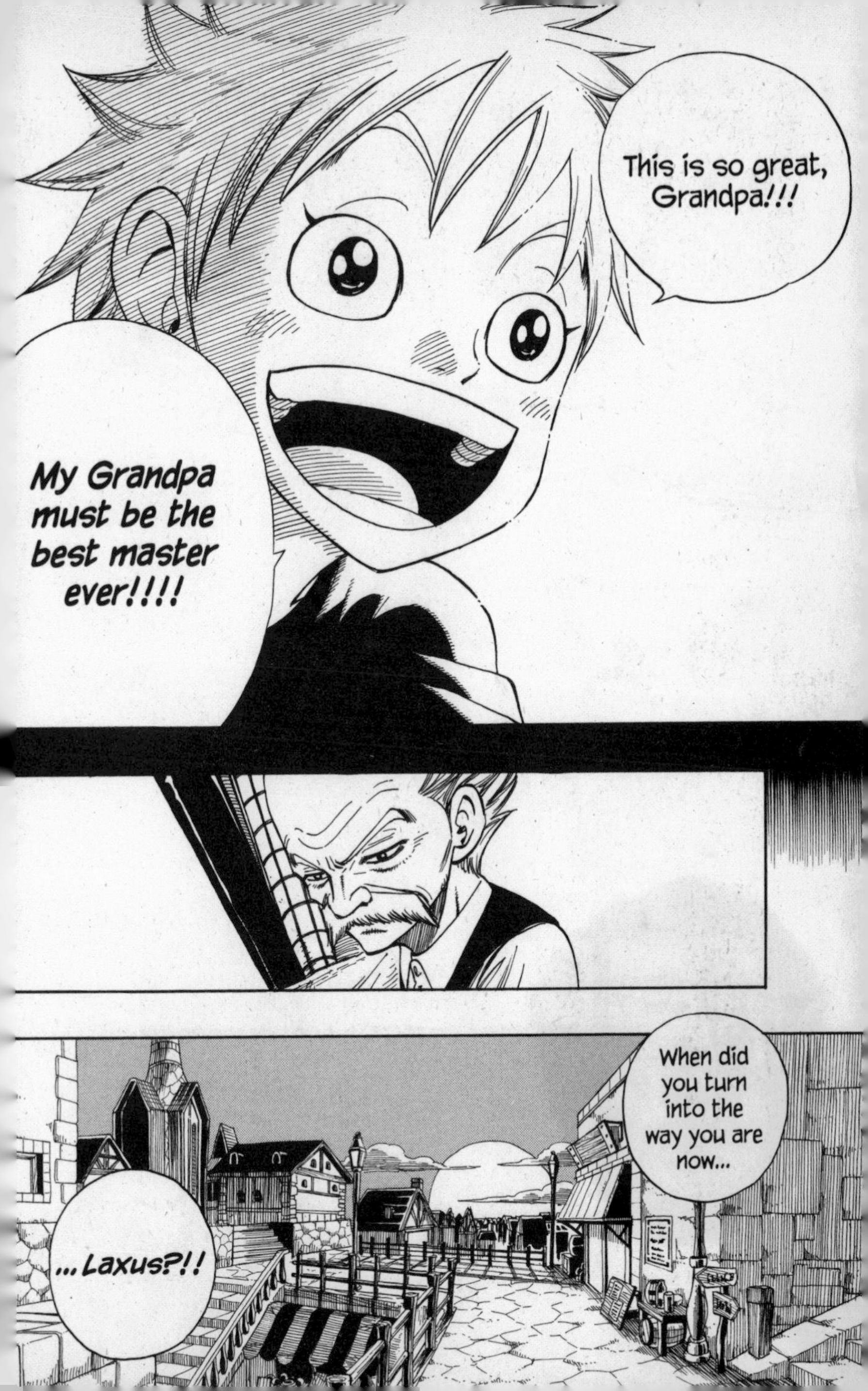
This is so great, Grandpa!!!
My Grandpa must be the best master ever!!!!
When did you turn into the way you are now...
...Laxus?!!

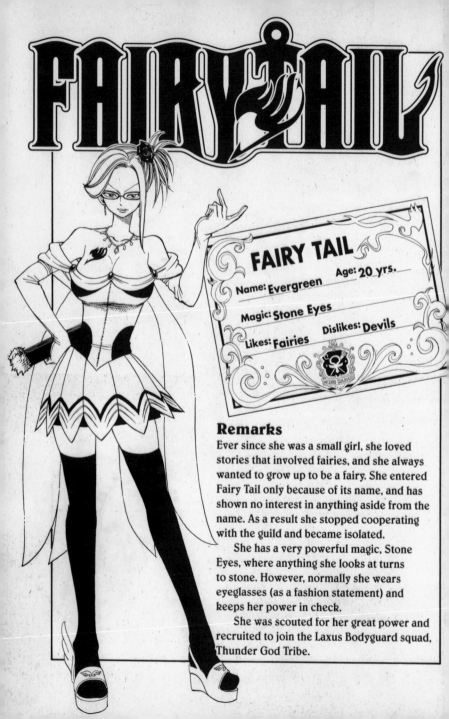

FAIRY TAIL

FAIRY TAIL

Name: Evergreen   Age: 20 yrs.

Magic: Stone Eyes

Likes: Fairies   Dislikes: Devils

WIZARD GUILDERS

Remarks

Ever since she was a small girl, she loved
stories that involved fairies, and she always
wanted to grow up to be a fairy. She entered
Fairy Tail only because of its name, and has
shown no interest in anything aside from the
name. As a result she stopped cooperating
with the guild and became isolated.

   She has a very powerful magic, Stone
Eyes, where anything she looks at turns
to stone. However, normally she wears
eyeglasses (as a fashion statement) and
keeps her power in check.

   She was scouted for her great power and
recruited to join the Laxus Bodyguard squad,
Thunder God Tribe.

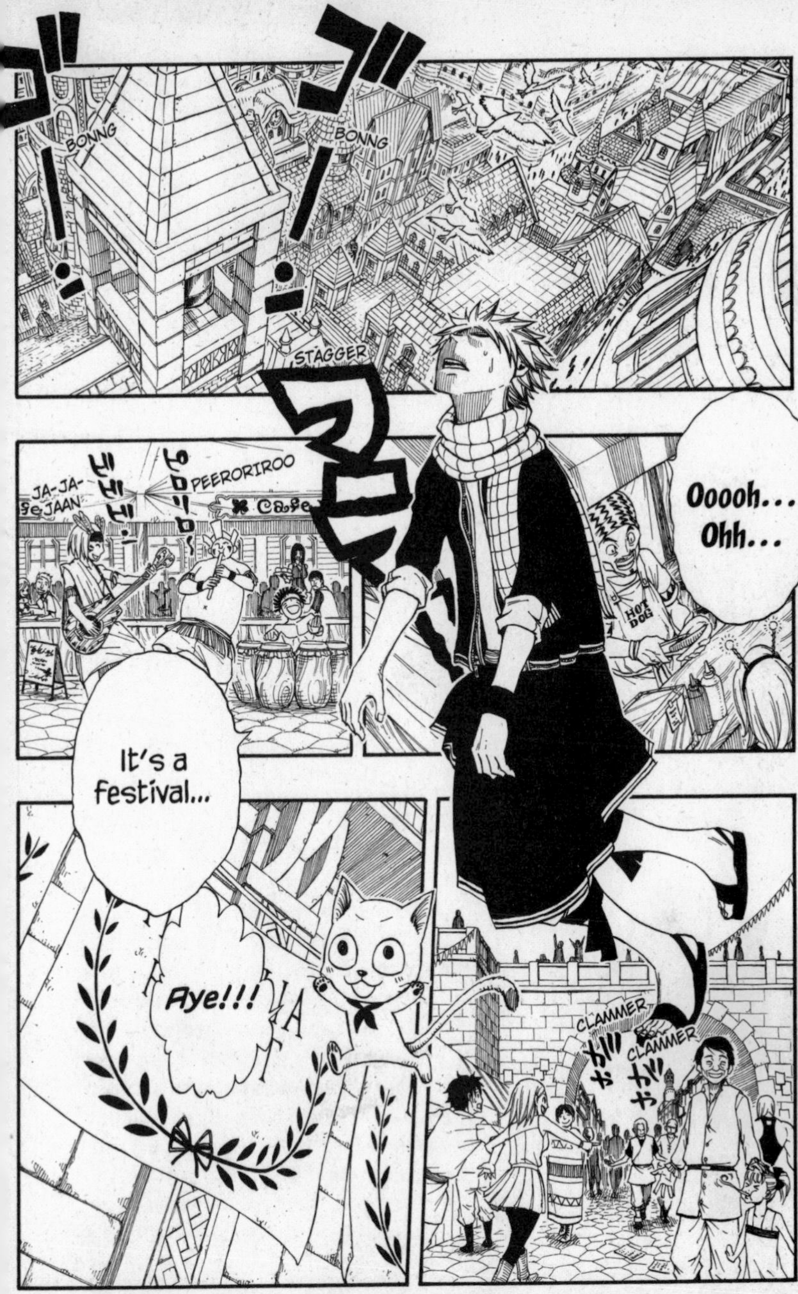
BONNG
BONNG
STAGGER
Ooooh... Ohh...
HOT DOG
PEERORIROO
JA-JA-JAAN
Cafe
It's a festival...
CLAMMER
CLAMMER
Aye!!!

Chapter 107: The Battle of Fairy Tail

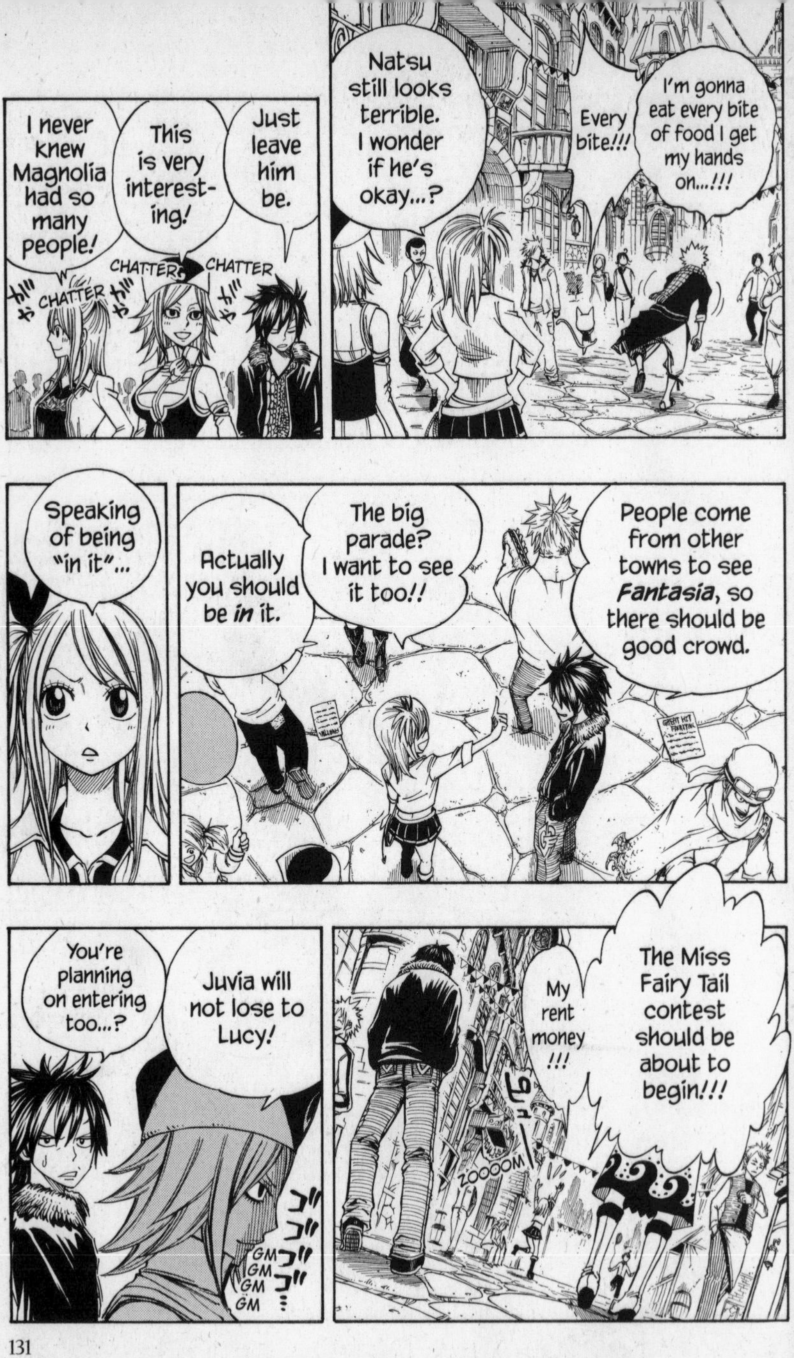
I'm gonna eat every bite of food I get my hands on...!!!
Every bite!!!
Natsu still looks terrible. I wonder if he's okay...?
Just leave him be.
This is very interest-ing!
I never knew Magnolia had so many people!
CHATTER
CHATTER
CHATTER
People come from other towns to see *Fantasia*, so there should be good crowd.
The big parade? I want to see it too!!
Actually you should be *in* it.
Speaking of being "in it"...
The Miss Fairy Tail contest should be about to begin!!!
My rent money!!!
ZOOOOM
Juvia will not lose to Lucy!
You're planning on entering too...?
GM GM GM GM

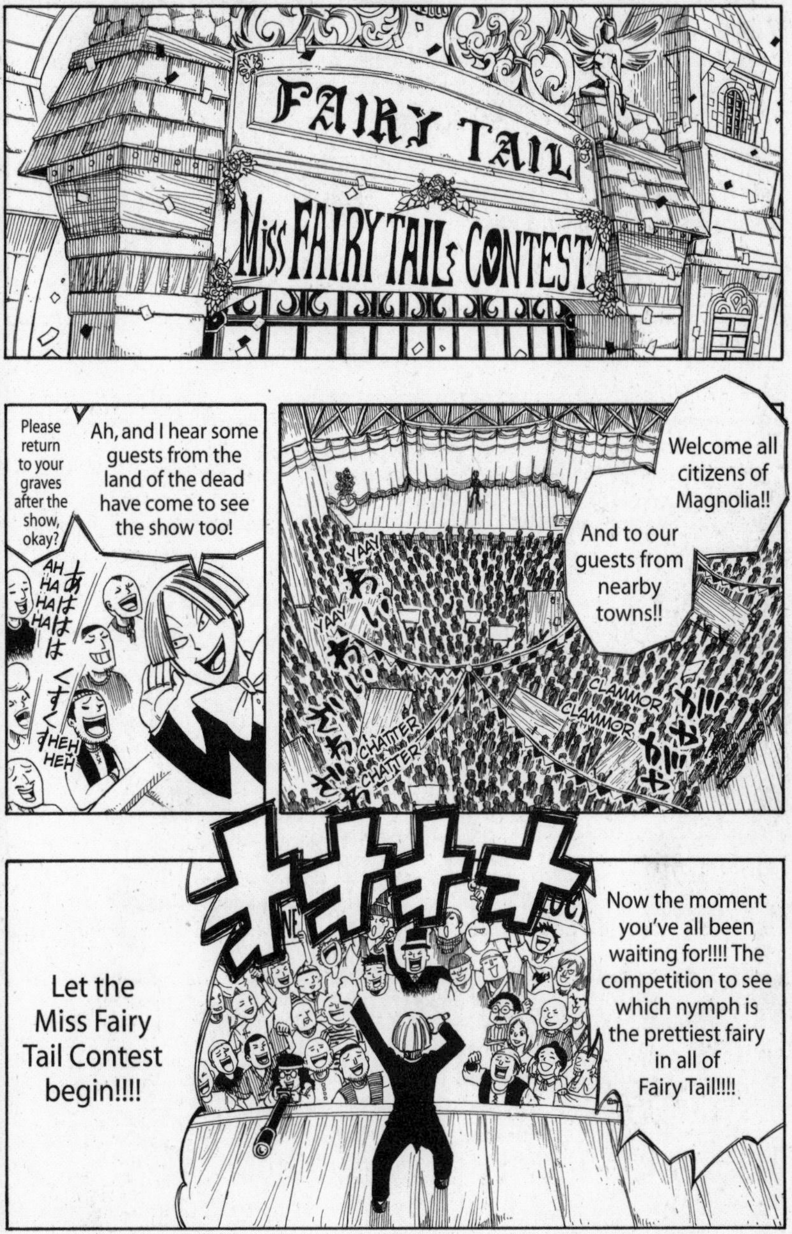
FAIRY TAIL
Miss FAIRY TAIL CONTEST
Welcome all citizens of Magnolia!!
And to our guests from nearby towns!!
わーい YAAY
わーい YAAY
ガヤガヤ CLAMMOR CLAMMOR
ざわざわ CHATTER CHATTER
Ah, and I hear some guests from the land of the dead have come to see the show too!
Please return to your graves after the show, okay?
あははは AH HA HA HA
くすくす HEH HEH
オオオオ
Now the moment you've all been waiting for!!!! The competition to see which nymph is the prettiest fairy in all of Fairy Tail!!!!
Let the Miss Fairy Tail Contest begin!!!!

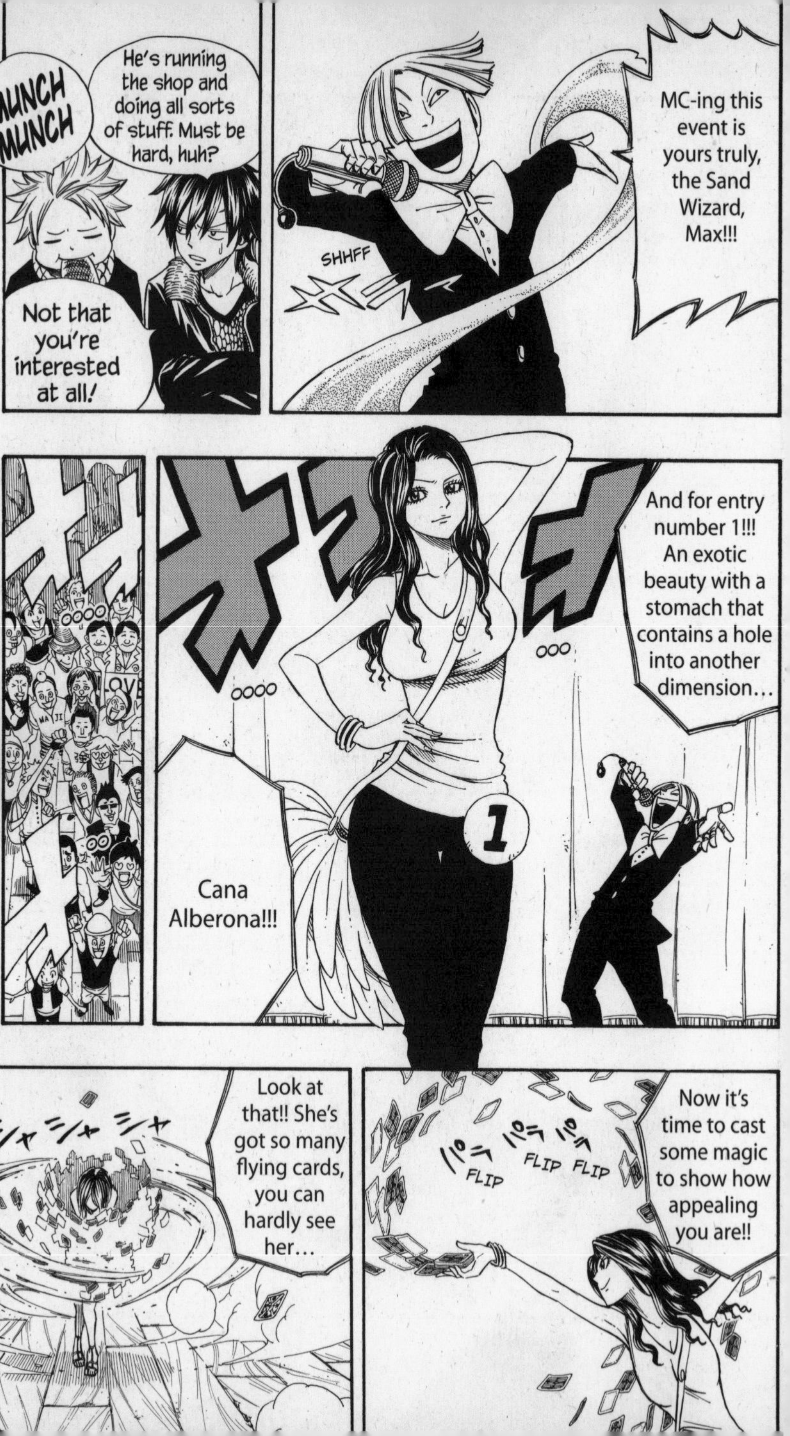
MC-ing this event is yours truly, the Sand Wizard, Max!!!
SHHFF
He's running the shop and doing all sorts of stuff. Must be hard, huh?
MUNCH MUNCH
Not that you're interested at all!
And for entry number 1!!! An exotic beauty with a stomach that contains a hole into another dimension…
OOO
OOOO
1
Cana Alberona!!!
OOOO
LOVE
Now it's time to cast some magic to show how appealing you are!!
FLIP FLIP
FLIP
Look at that!! She's got so many flying cards, you can hardly see her…

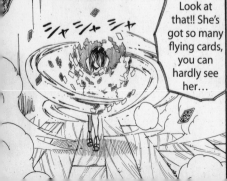

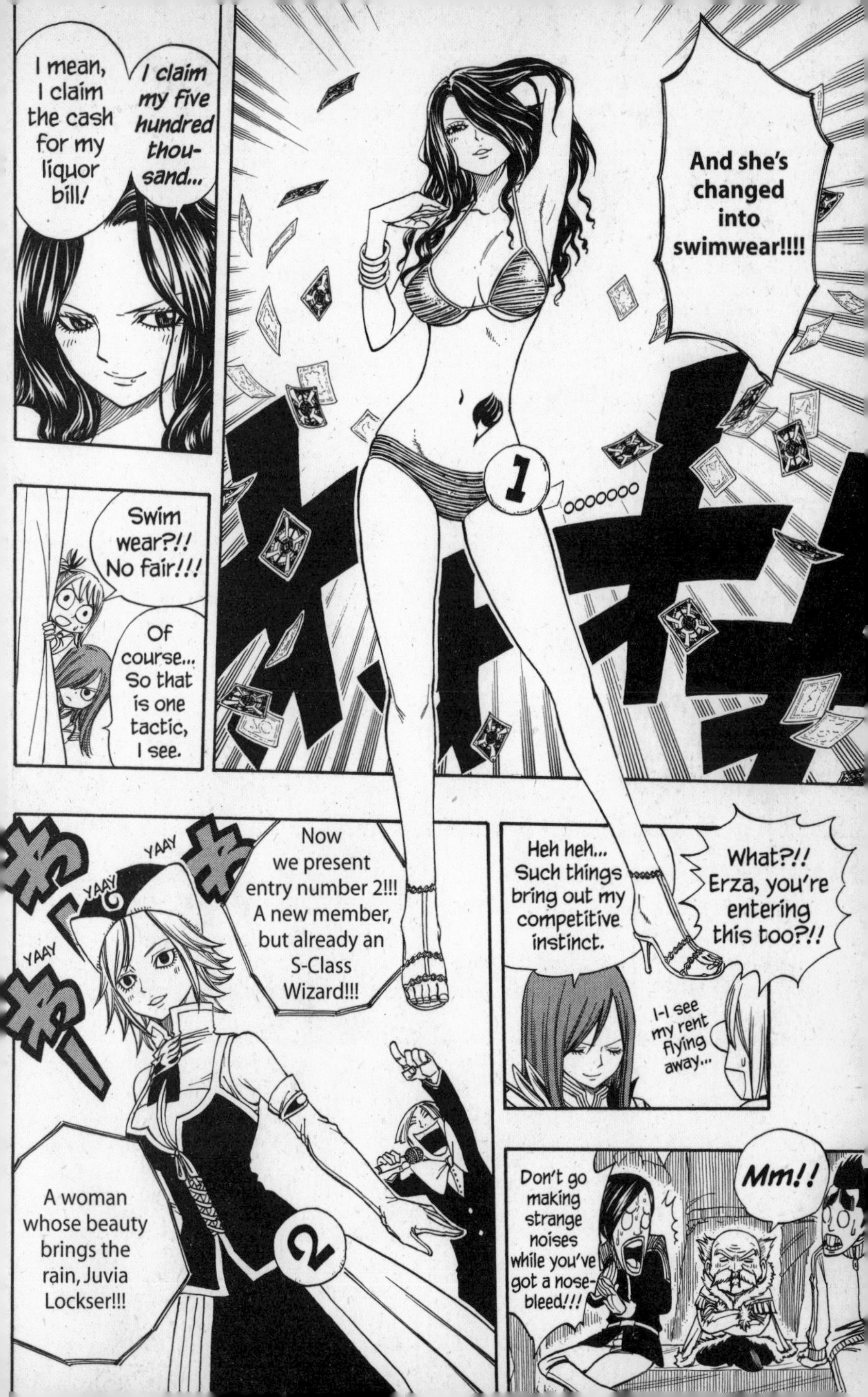
And she's changed into swimwear!!!!
oooooo
I claim my five hundred thousand...
I mean, I claim the cash for my liquor bill!
Swim wear?!! No fair!!!
Of course... So that is one tactic, I see.
What?!! Erza, you're entering this too?!!
Heh heh... Such things bring out my competitive instinct.
I-I see my rent flying away...
Mm!!
Don't go making strange noises while you've got a nose-bleed!!!
Now we present entry number 2!!! A new member, but already an S-Class Wizard!!!
YAAY
YAAY
YAAY
A woman whose beauty brings the rain, Juvia Lockser!!!

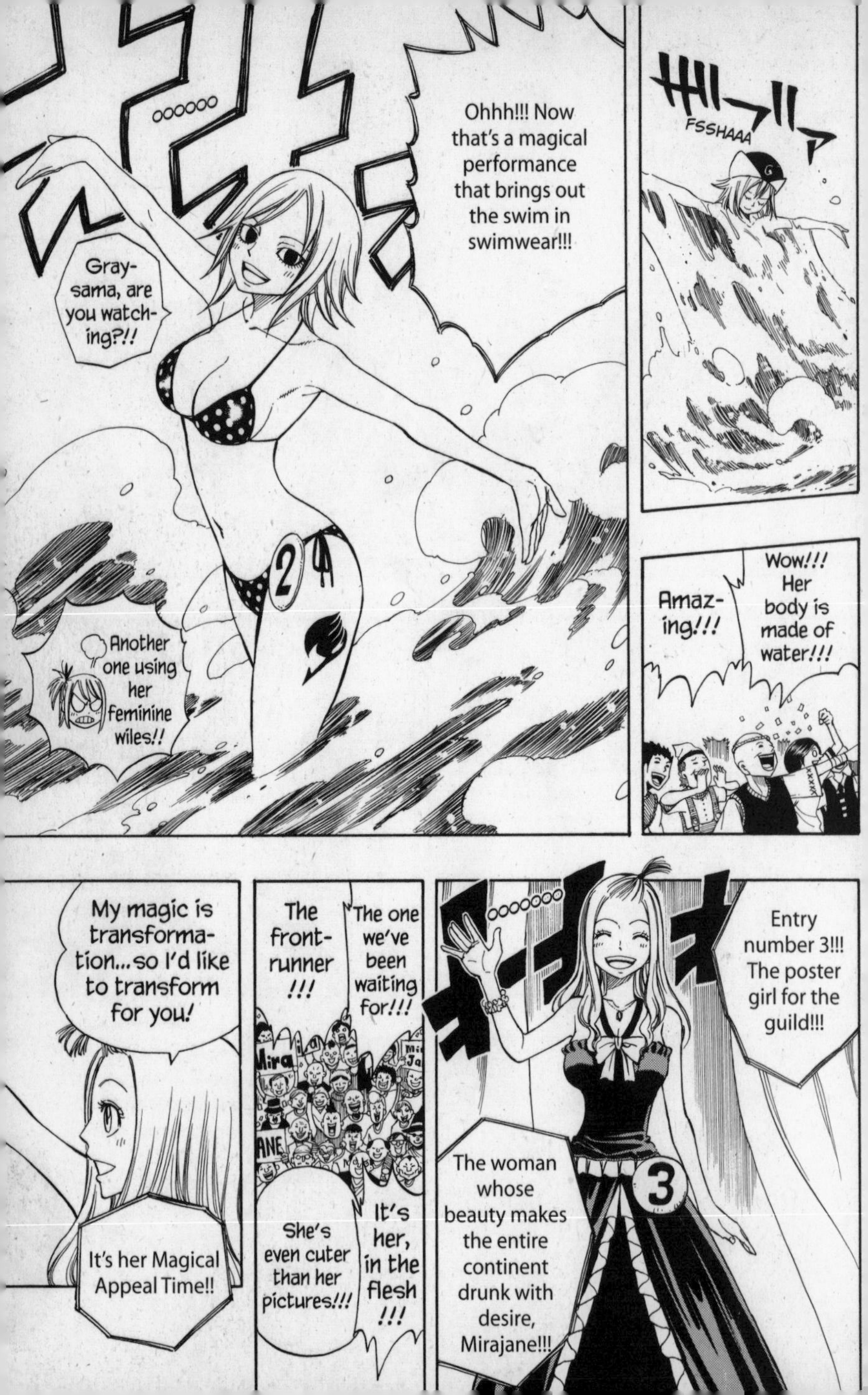
FSSHAAA
Wow!!! Her body is made of water!!!
Amazing!!!
Ohhh!!! Now that's a magical performance that brings out the swim in swimwear!!!
oooooo
Gray-sama, are you watching?!!
Another one using her feminine wiles!!
oooooooo
Entry number 3!!! The poster girl for the guild!!!
The woman whose beauty makes the entire continent drunk with desire, Mirajane!!!
The one we've been waiting for!!!
The front-runner!!!
It's her, in the flesh!!!
She's even cuter than her pictures!!!
My magic is transformation...so I'd like to transform for you!
It's her Magical Appeal Time!!

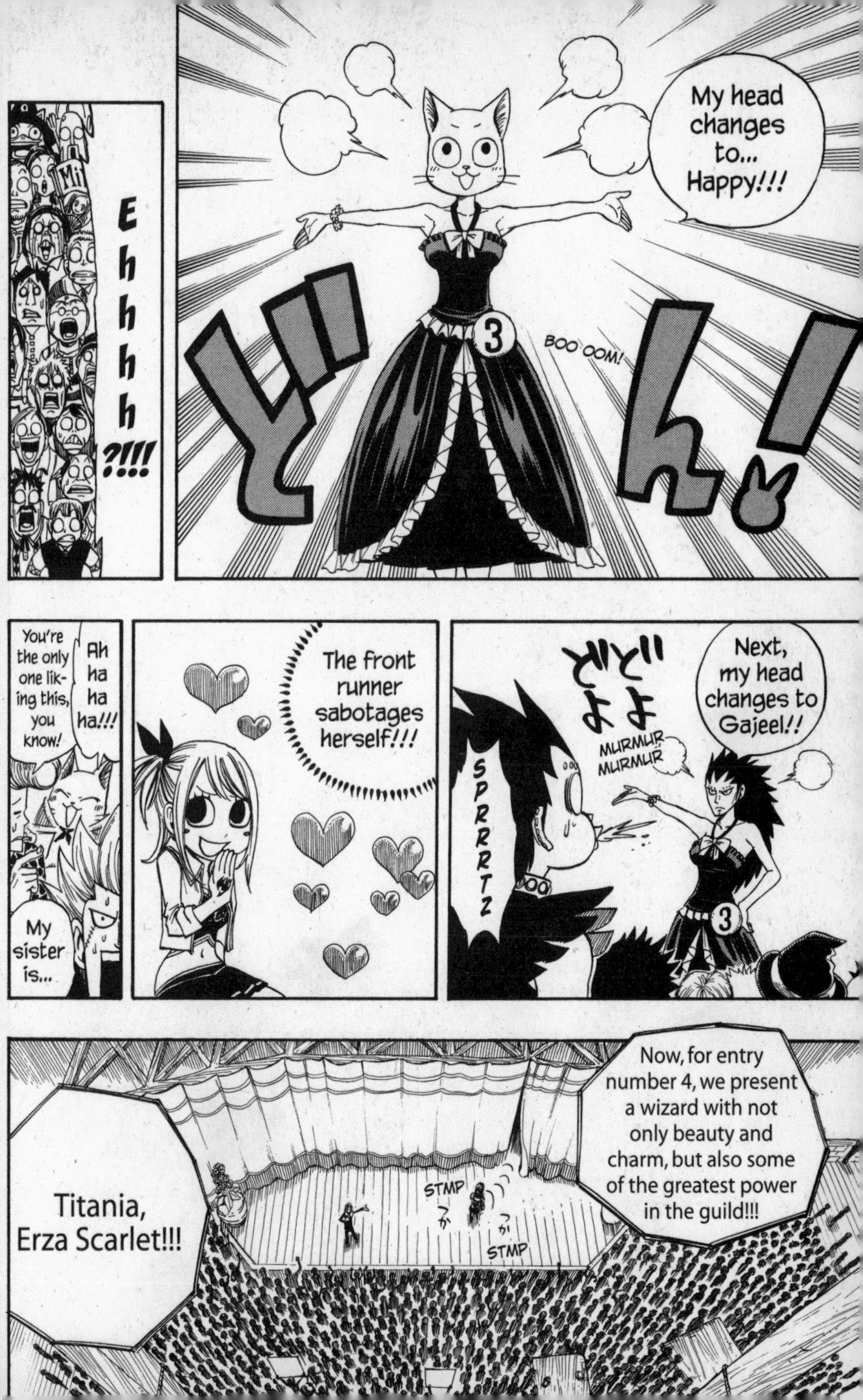

My head changes to... Happy!!!
どん!
BOO OOM!
Ehhhh?!!!
Next, my head changes to Gajeel!!
どよどよ
MURMUR MURMUR
SPRRRTZ
The front runner sabotages herself!!!
Ah ha ha ha!!!
You're the only one liking this, you know!
My sister is...
Now, for entry number 4, we present a wizard with not only beauty and charm, but also some of the greatest power in the guild!!!
STMP
つか
つか
STMP
Titania, Erza Scarlet!!!

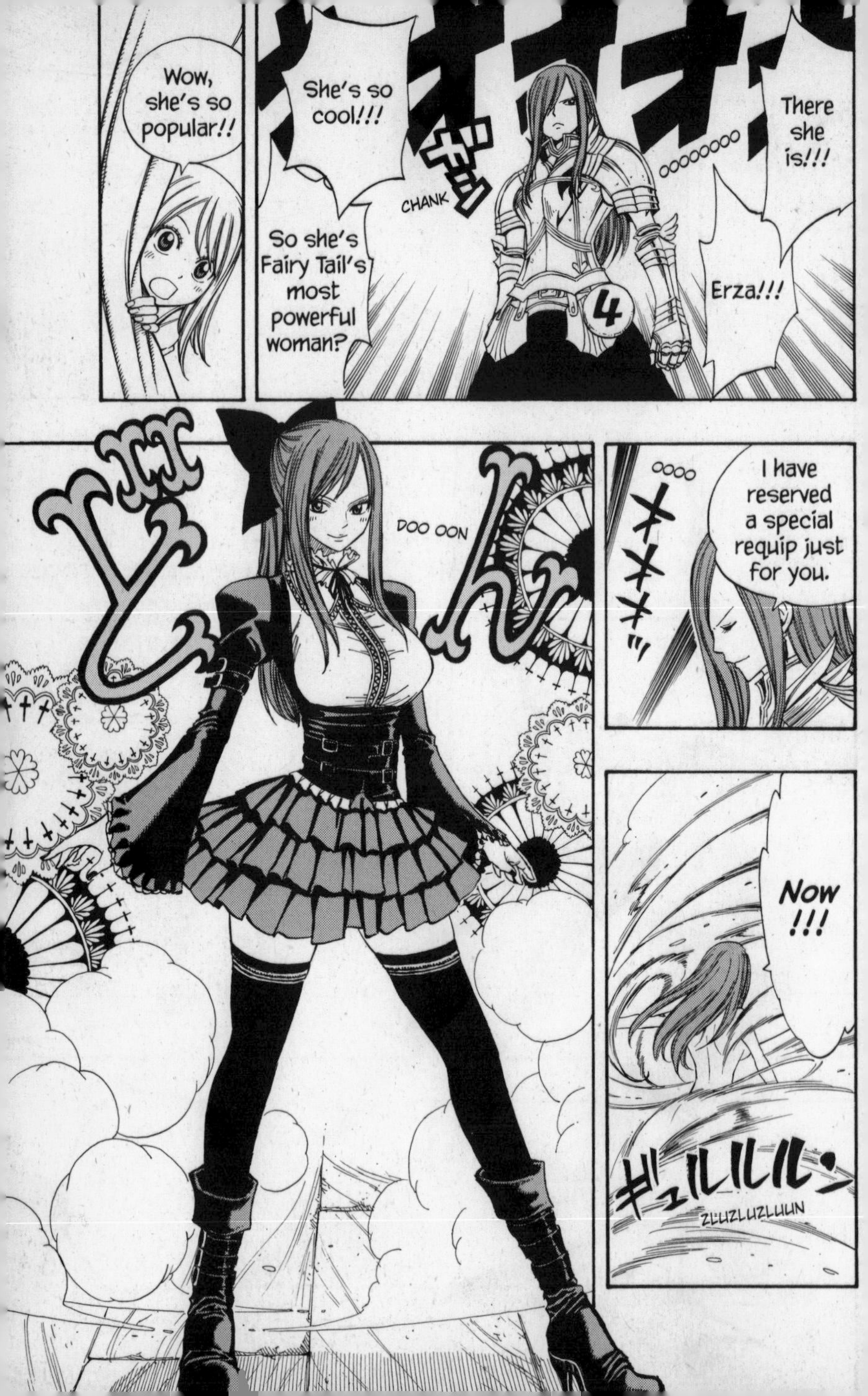
There she is!!!
Erza!!!
OOOOOOOO
She's so cool!!!
CHANK
So she's Fairy Tail's most powerful woman?
Wow, she's so popular!!
OOOO
I have reserved a special requip just for you.
Now!!!
ZLUZLUZLUUN
DOO OON

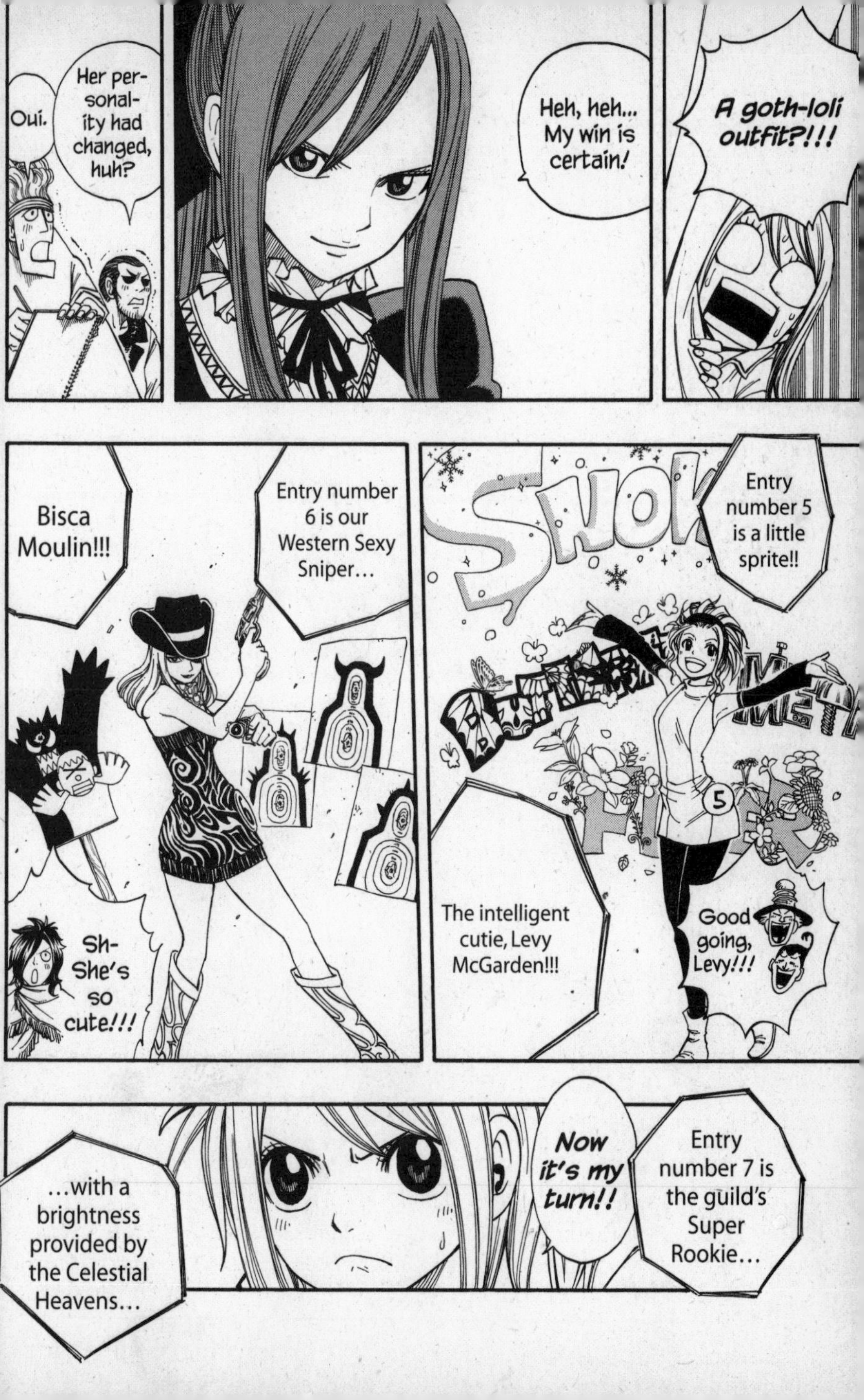
A goth-loli outfit?!!!
Heh, heh... My win is certain!
Her personality had changed, huh?
Oui.
Entry number 5 is a little sprite!!
The intelligent cutie, Levy McGarden!!!
Good going, Levy!!!
Entry number 6 is our Western Sexy Sniper…
Bisca Moulin!!!
Sh-She's so cute!!!
Entry number 7 is the guild's Super Rookie…
Now it's my turn!!
…with a brightness provided by the Celestial Heavens…

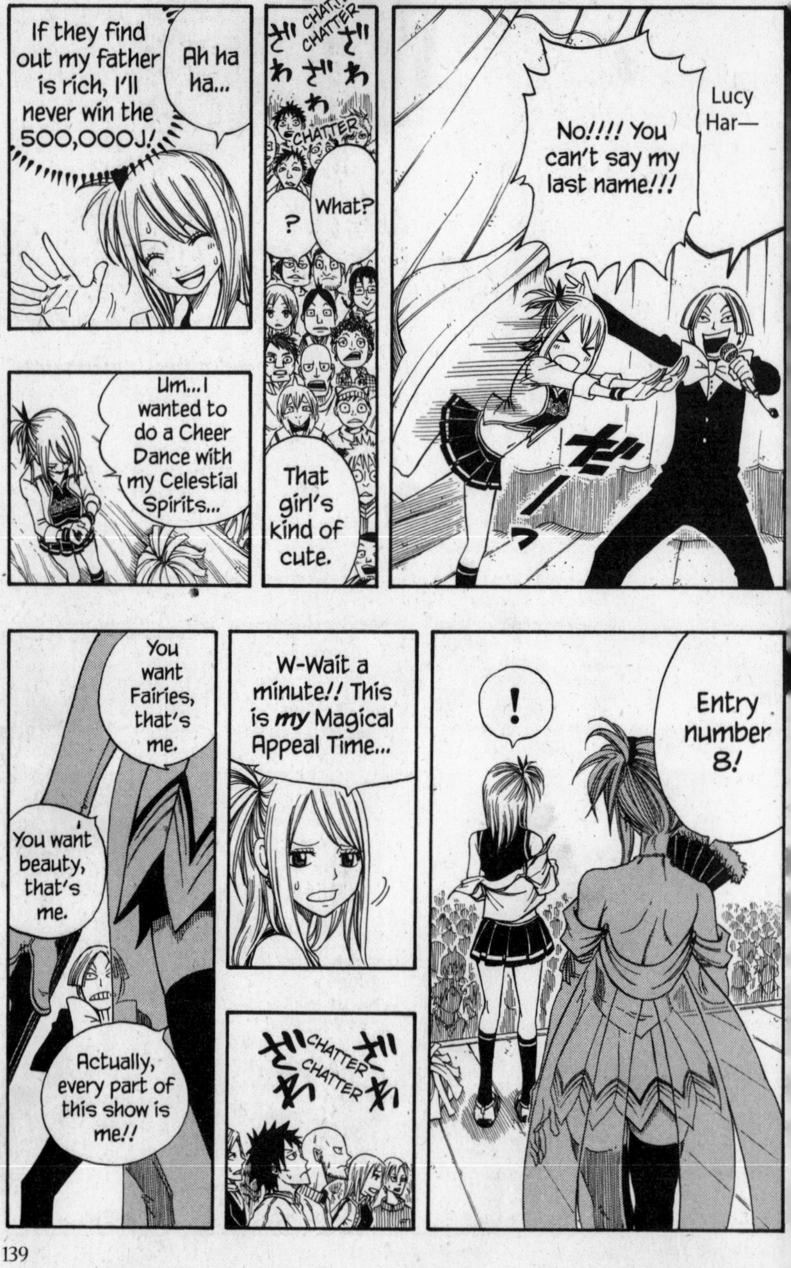
Lucy Har—
No!!!! You can't say my last name!!!
ざわざわ
CHATTER CHATTER
ざわ
CHATTER
What?
?
That girl's kind of cute.
Ah ha ha...
If they find out my father is rich, I'll never win the 500,000J!
Um...I wanted to do a Cheer Dance with my Celestial Spirits...
Entry number 8!
!
W-Wait a minute!! This is *my* Magical Appeal Time...
ざわざわ
CHATTER CHATTER
You want Fairies, that's me.
You want beauty, that's me.
Actually, every part of this show is me!!

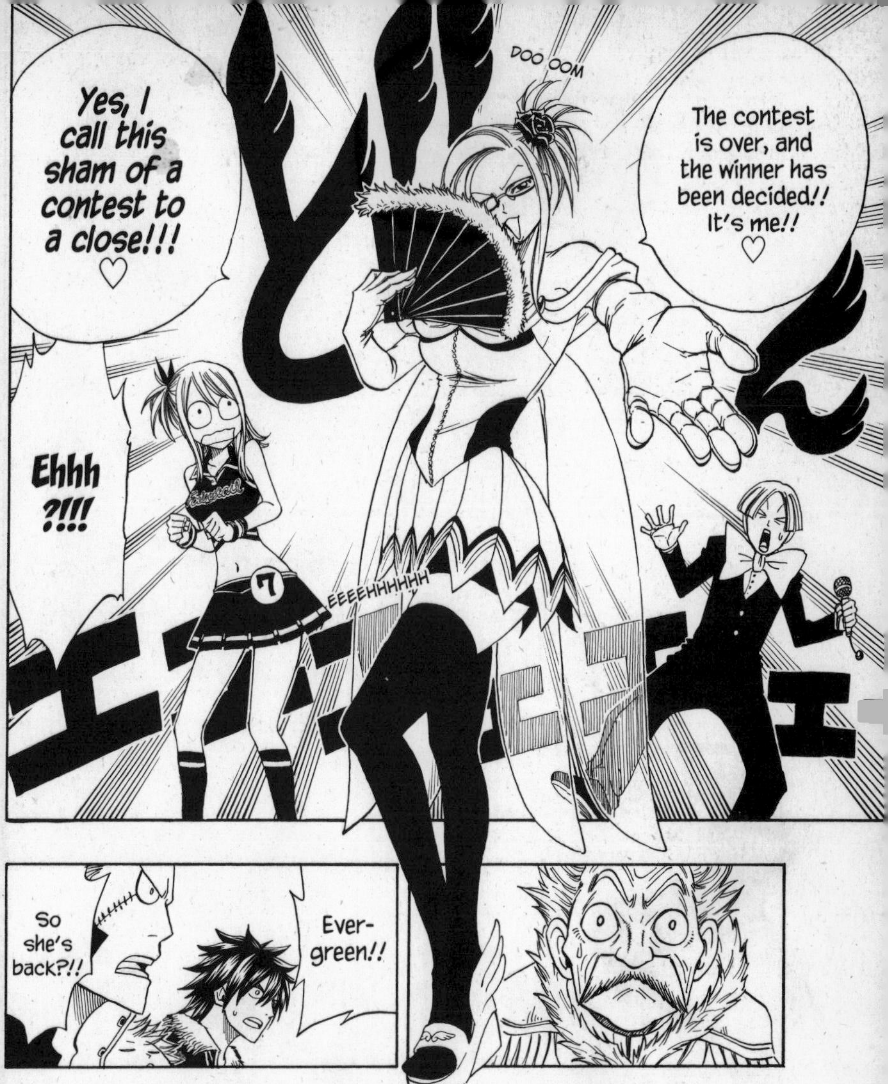
DOO OOM
The contest is over, and the winner has been decided!! It's me!! ♡
Yes, I call this sham of a contest to a close!!! ♡
Ehhh ?!!!
EEEEHHHHHH
Ever-green!!
So she's back?!!
But what about my 500,000 Jewels?!
You're the judges!!! Everybody vote now!!!
The Miss Fairy Tail Contest will be decided by votes from you readers!!

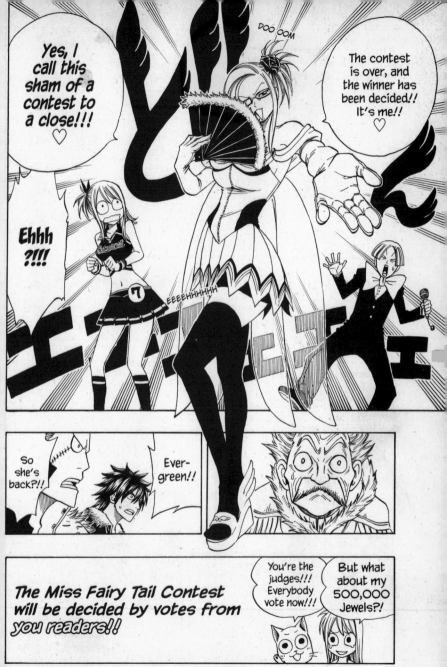

The contest was held during the magazine serialization of Fairy Tail, and voting has been completed. Votes are now being tallied.

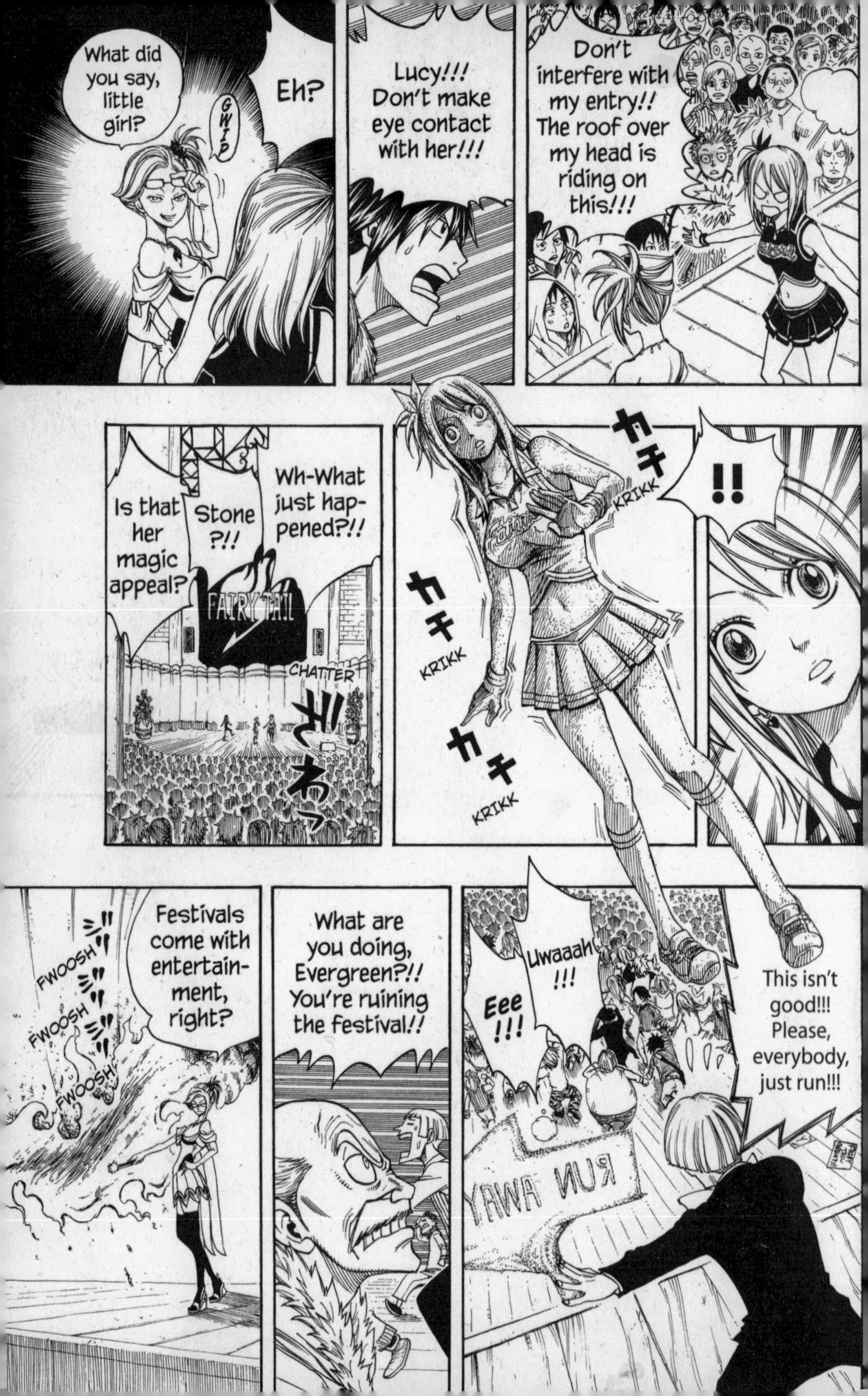
Don't interfere with my entry!! The roof over my head is riding on this!!!
Lucy!!! Don't make eye contact with her!!!
Eh?
GWIP
What did you say, little girl?
!!
カチ KRIKK
カチ KRIKK
カチ KRIKK
Wh-What just happened?!!
Stone ?!!
Is that her magic appeal?
FAIRY TAIL
CHATTER
This isn't good!!! Please, everybody, just run!!!
Uwaaah !!!
Eee !!!
What are you doing, Evergreen?!! You're ruining the festival!!
Festivals come with entertain-ment, right?
FWOOSH
FWOOSH
FWOOSH

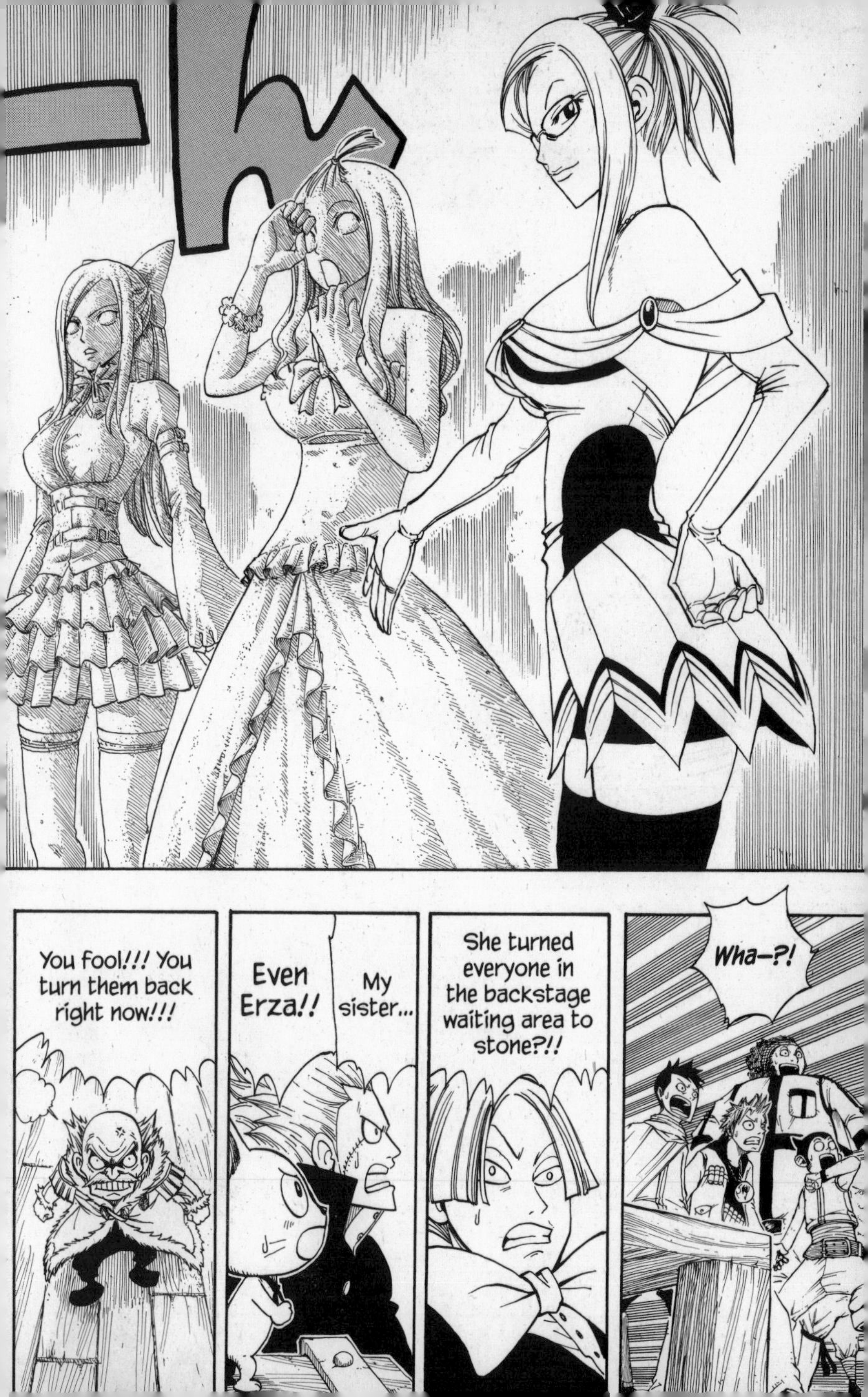
Wha–?!
She turned everyone in the backstage waiting area to stone?!!
My sister...
Even Erza!!
You fool!!! You turn them back right now!!!

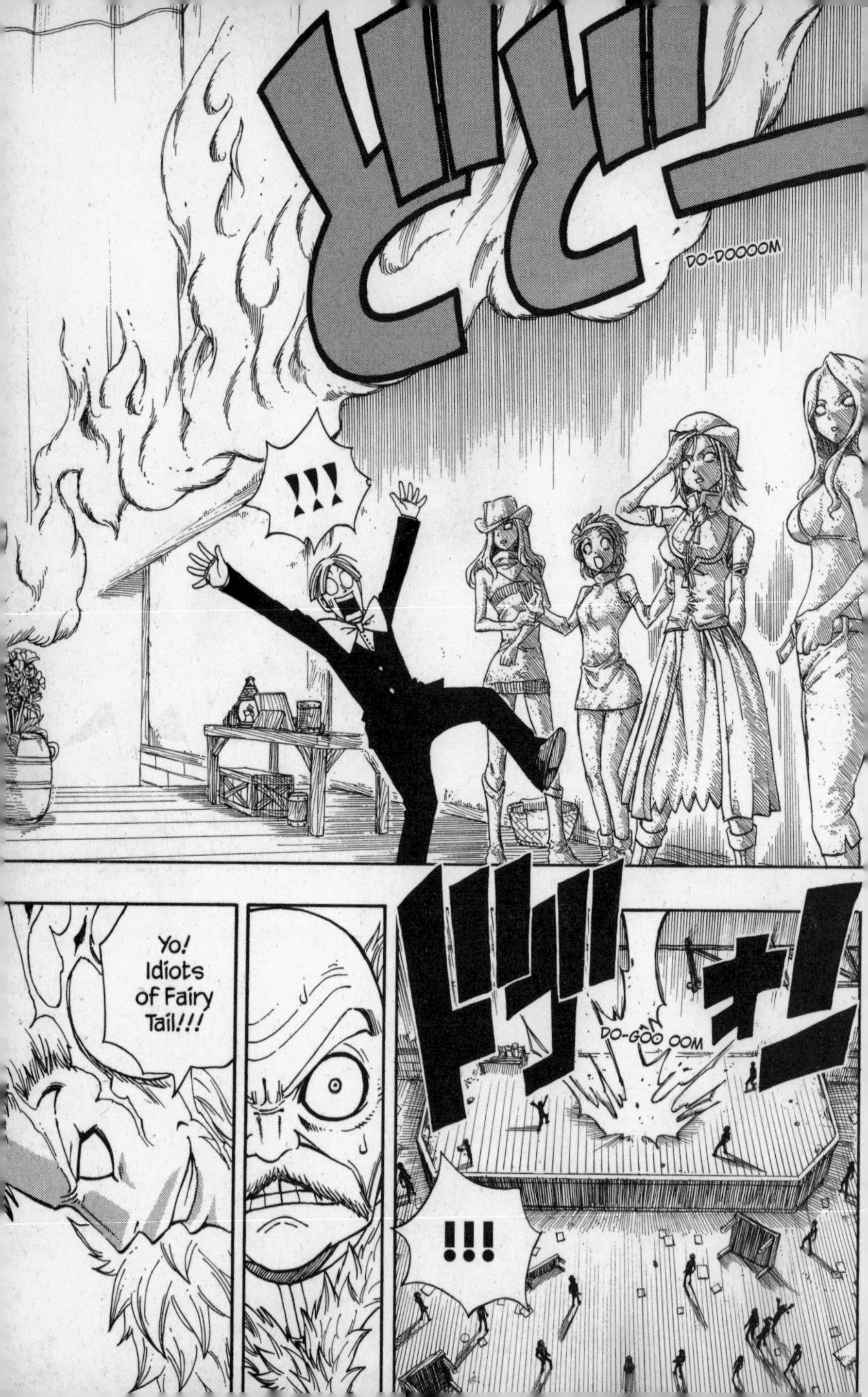
DO-DOOOOM
!!!
DO-GOO OOM
!!!
Yo! Idiots of Fairy Tail!!!

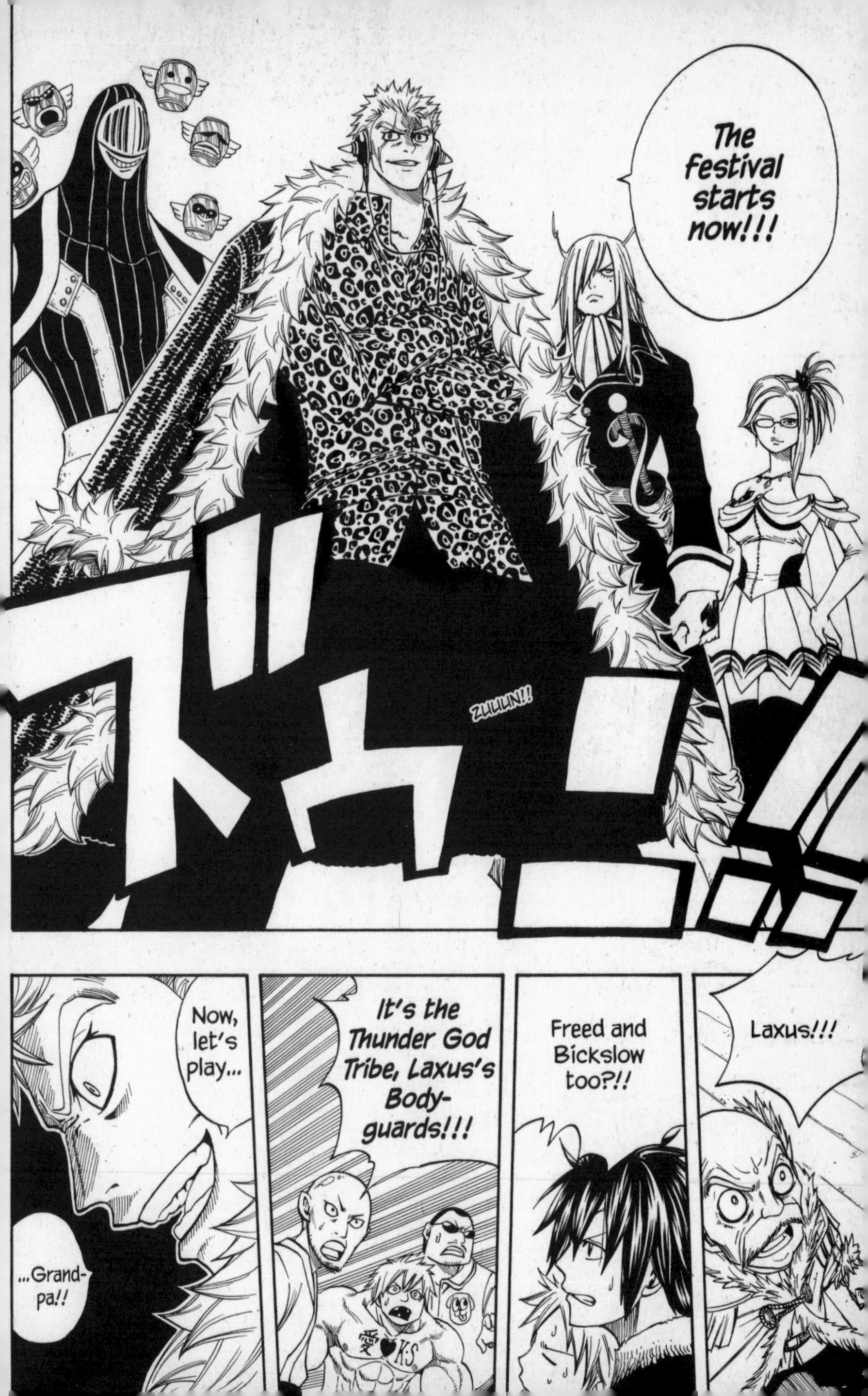
The festival starts now!!!
ZULLUN!!
Laxus!!!
Freed and Bickslow too?!!
It's the Thunder God Tribe, Laxus's Body-guards!!!
Now, let's play...
...Grand-pa!!

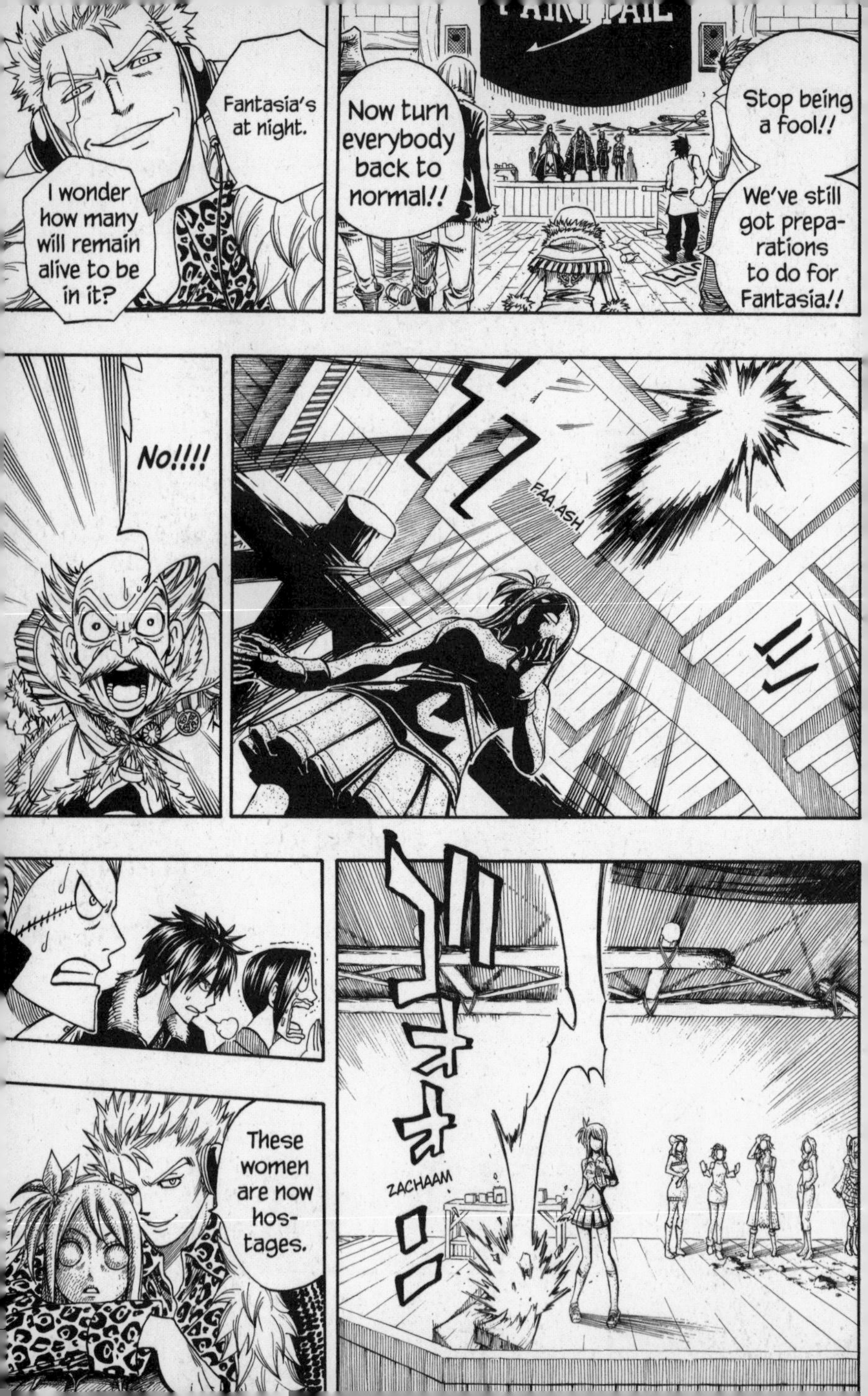
Stop being a fool!!
We've still got preparations to do for Fantasia!!
Now turn everybody back to normal!!
Fantasia's at night.
I wonder how many will remain alive to be in it?
FAA ASH
No!!!!
ZACHAAM
These women are now hostages.

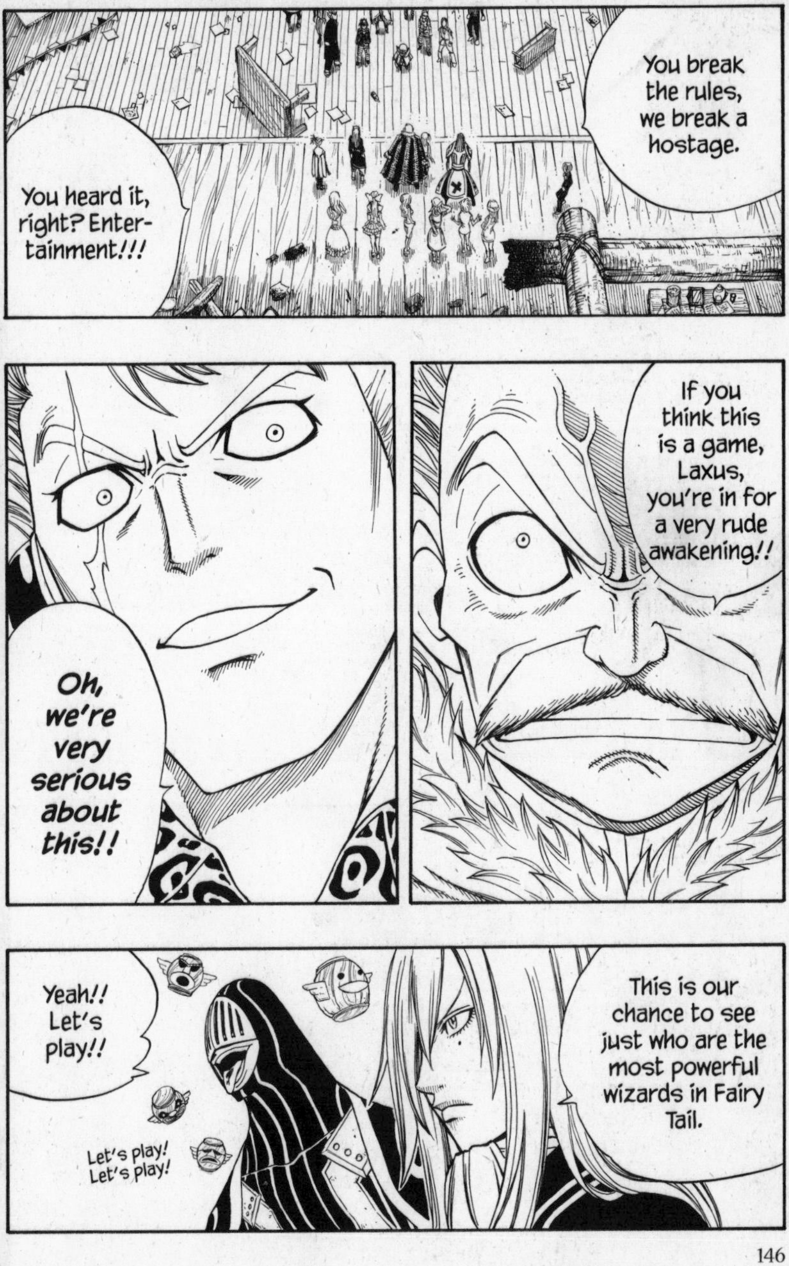
You break the rules, we break a hostage.
You heard it, right? Enter-tainment!!!
If you think this is a game, Laxus, you're in for a very rude awakening!!
Oh, we're very serious about this!!
This is our chance to see just who are the most powerful wizards in Fairy Tail.
Yeah!! Let's play!!
Let's play! Let's play!

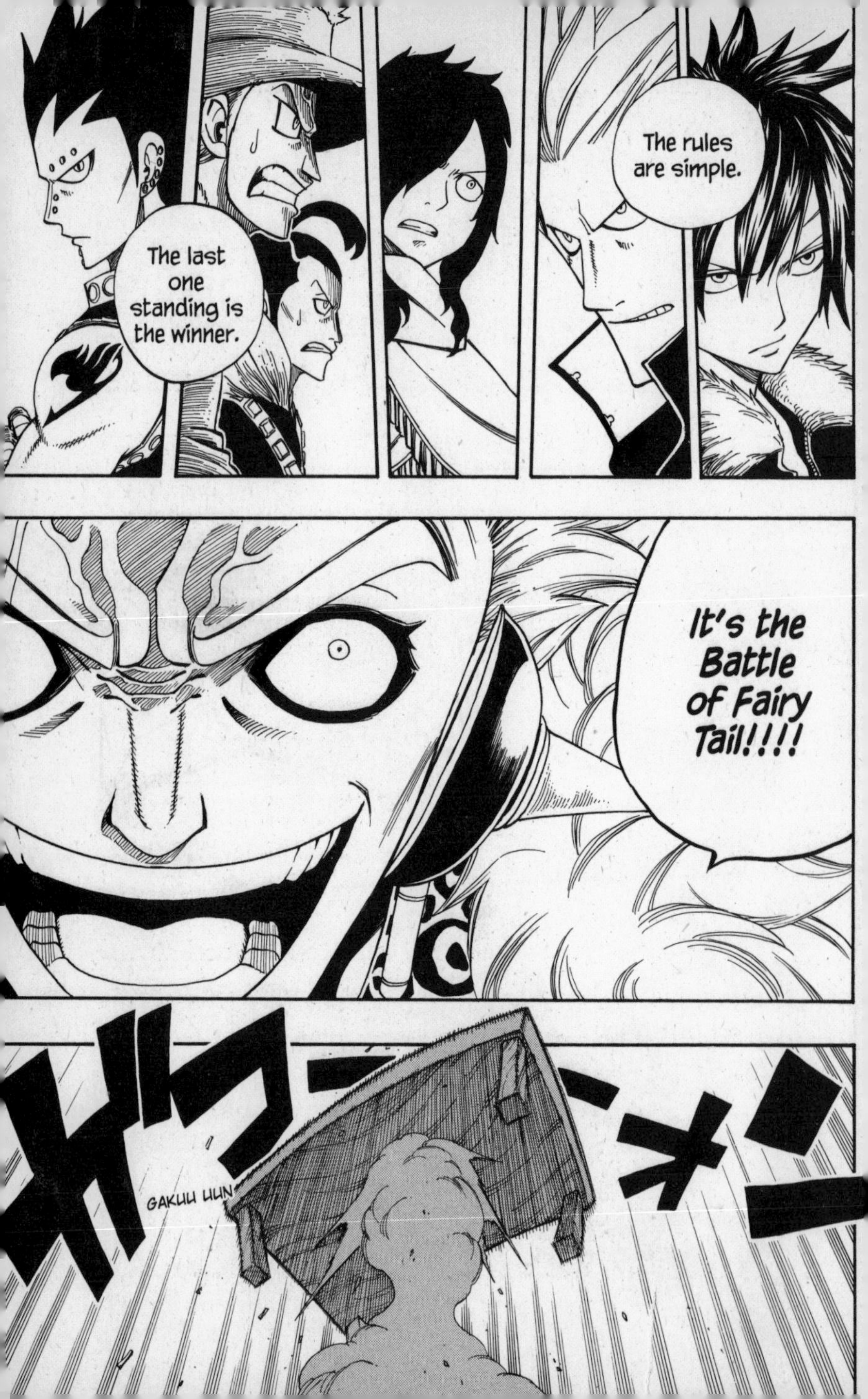
The rules are simple.
The last one standing is the winner.
It's the Battle of Fairy Tail!!!!
GAKUU UUN

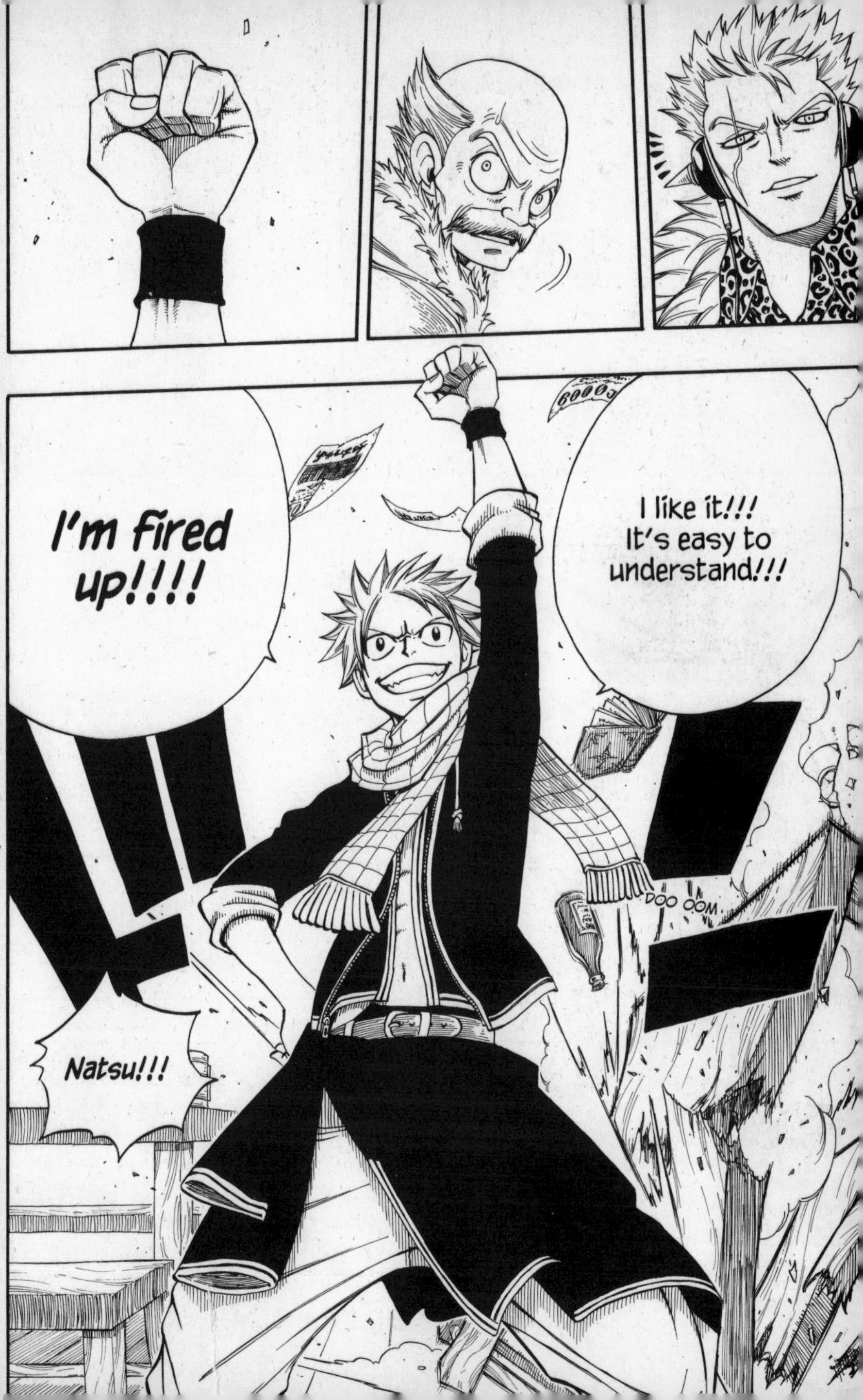
I like it!!! It's easy to understand!!!
DOO OOM
I'm fired up!!!!
Natsu!!!

FAIRY TAIL

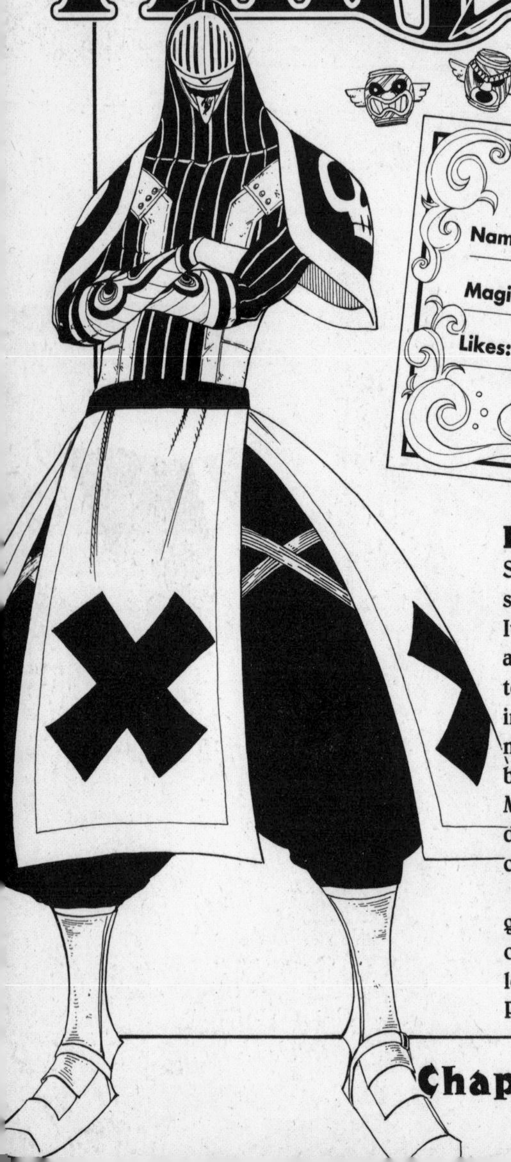

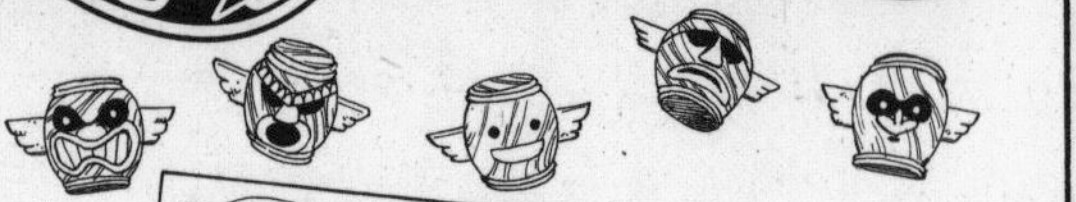

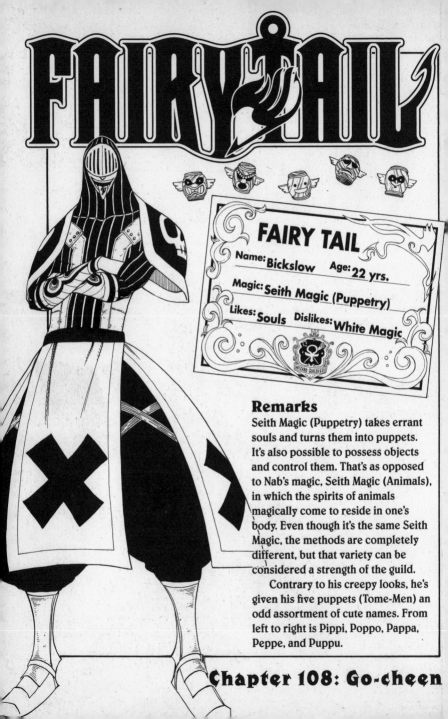

FAIRY TAIL

Name: Bickslow Age: 22 yrs.

Magic: Seith Magic (Puppetry)

Likes: Souls Dislikes: White Magic

WIZARD GUILD X633

Remarks

Seith Magic (Puppetry) takes errant souls and turns them into puppets. It's also possible to possess objects and control them. That's as opposed to Nab's magic, Seith Magic (Animals), in which the spirits of animals magically come to reside in one's body. Even though it's the same Seith Magic, the methods are completely different, but that variety can be considered a strength of the guild.

Contrary to his creepy looks, he's given his five puppets (Tome-Men) an odd assortment of cute names. From left to right is Pippi, Poppo, Pappa, Peppe, and Puppu.

Chapter 108: Go-cheen

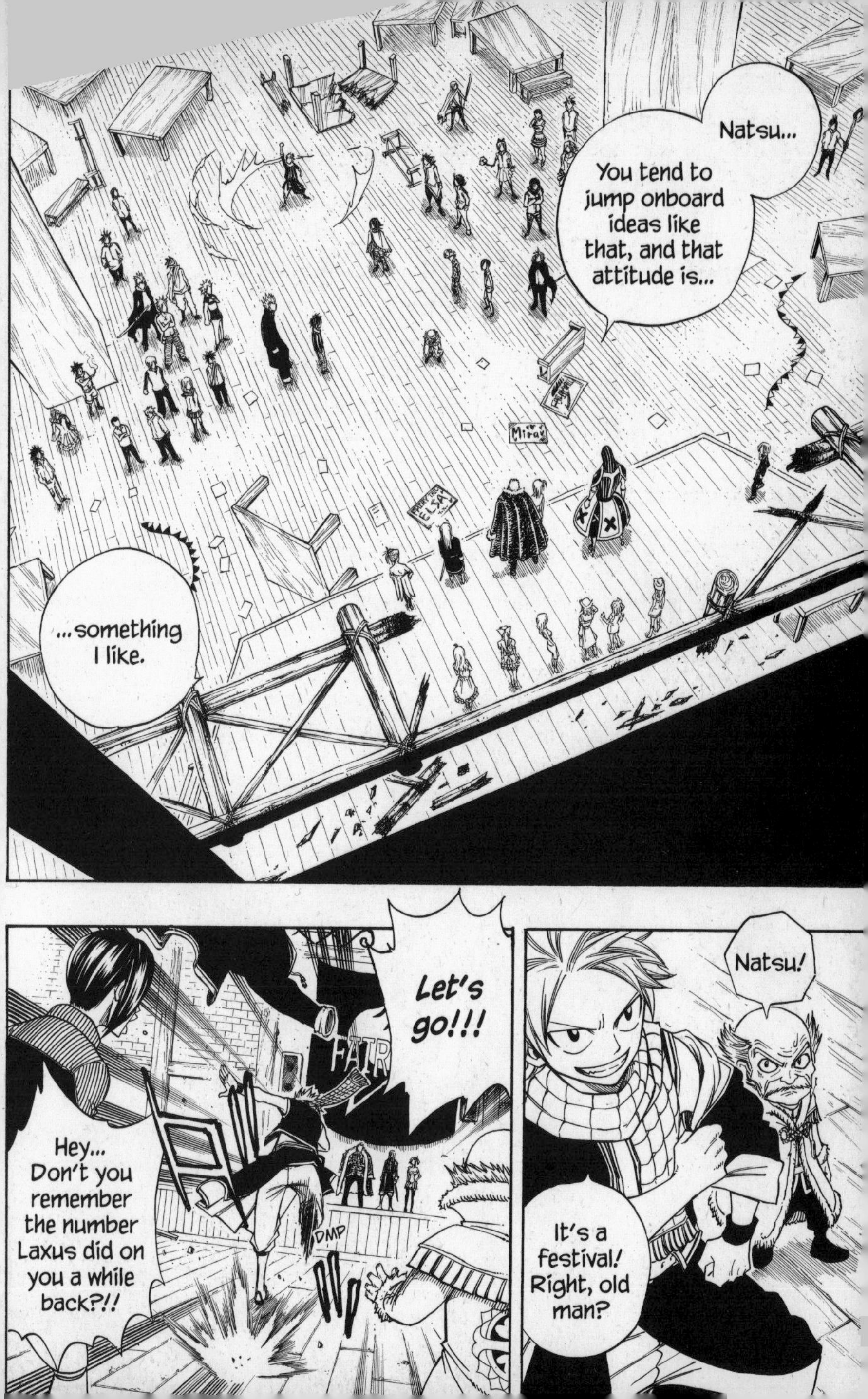
Natsu...
You tend to jump onboard ideas like that, and that attitude is...
...something I like.
Natsu!
It's a festival! Right, old man?
Let's go!!!
Hey... Don't you remember the number Laxus did on you a while back?!!
DMP

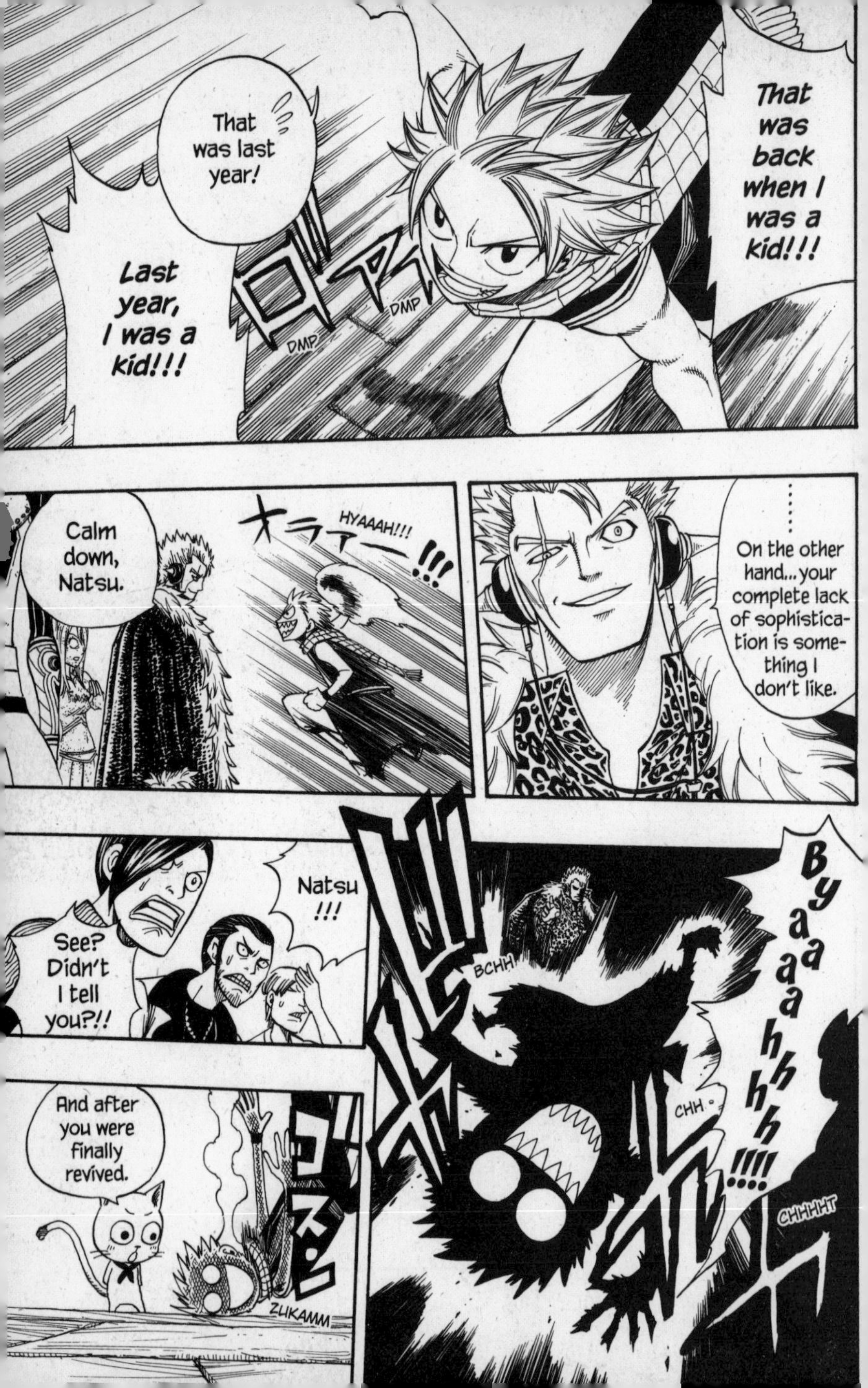
That was back when I was a kid!!!
That was last year!
DMP
DMP
Last year, I was a kid!!!
......
On the other hand...your complete lack of sophistication is something I don't like.
HYAAAH!!!
Calm down, Natsu.
Byaaaahhhh!!!!
BCHH
CHH
CHHHHT
Natsu!!!
See? Didn't I tell you?!!
And after you were finally revived.
ZUKAMM

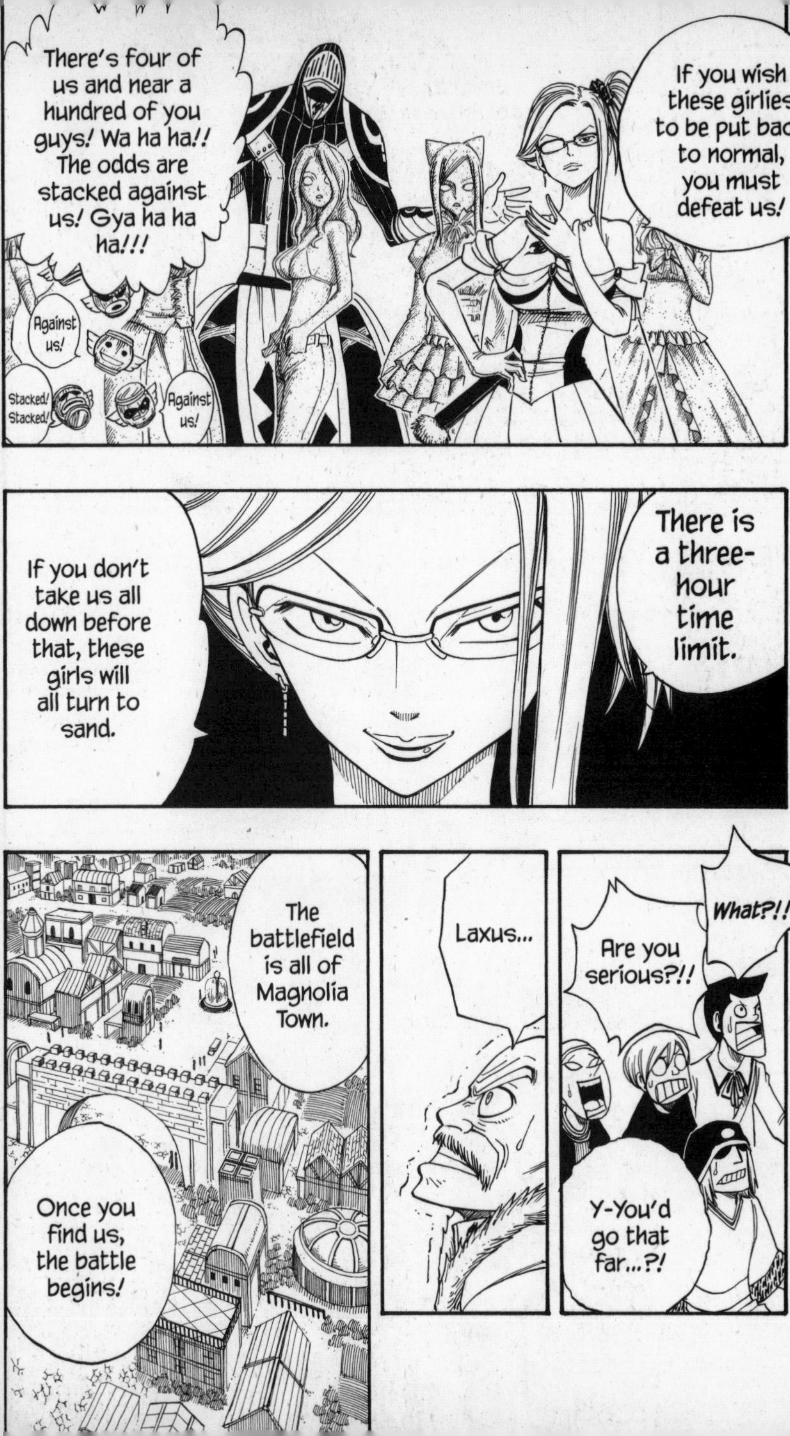
If you wish these girlies to be put back to normal, you must defeat us!
There's four of us and near a hundred of you guys! Wa ha ha!! The odds are stacked against us! Gya ha ha ha!!!
Against us!
Against us!
Stacked! Stacked!
There is a three-hour time limit.
If you don't take us all down before that, these girls will all turn to sand.
What?!!
Are you serious?!!
Y-You'd go that far...?!
Laxus...
The battlefield is all of Magnolia Town.
Once you find us, the battle begins!

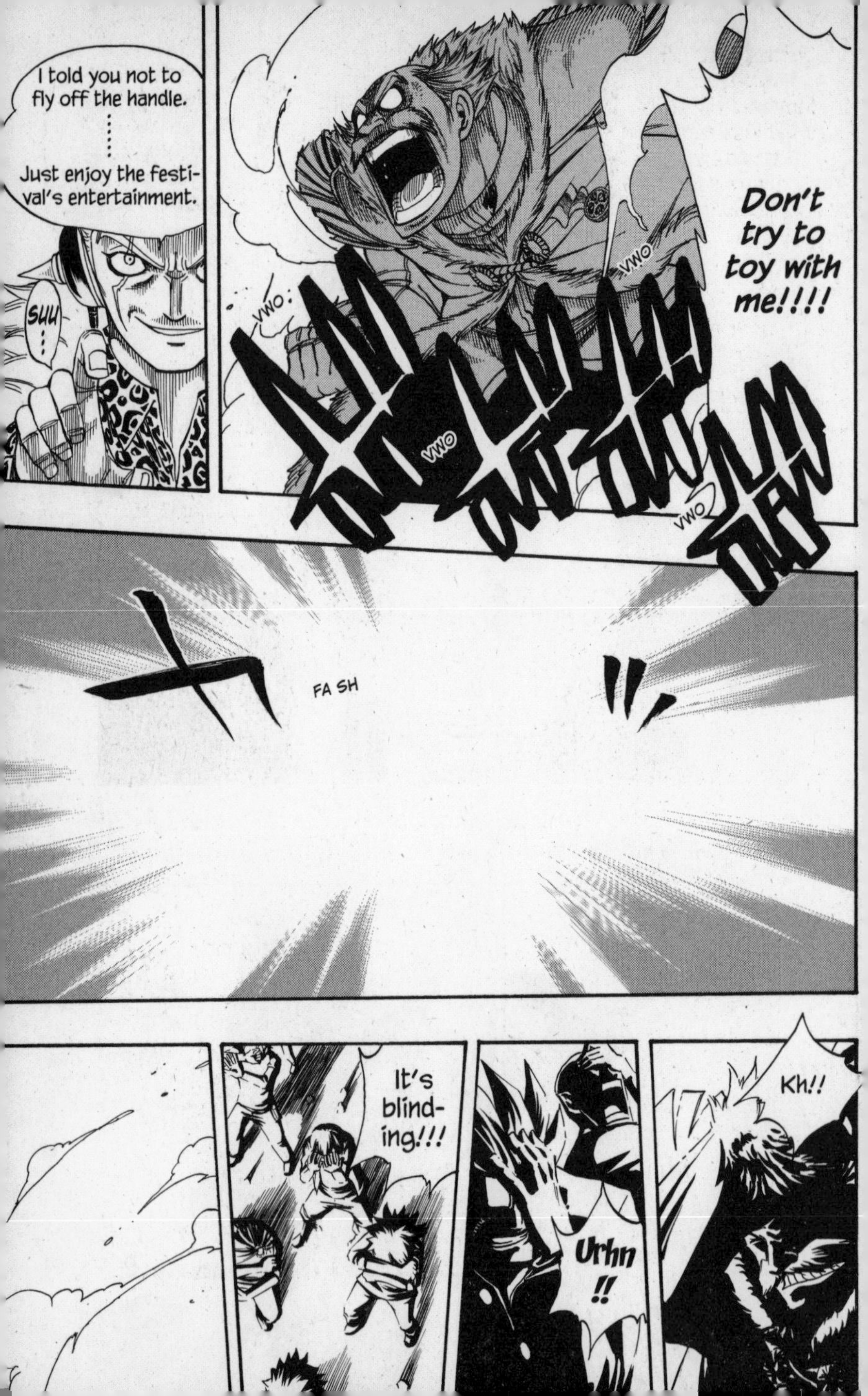
Don't try to toy with me!!!!
VWO
VWO
VWO
VWO
I told you not to fly off the handle.
Just enjoy the festival's entertainment.
SUU
FA SH
Kh!!
Urhn !!
It's blinding!!!

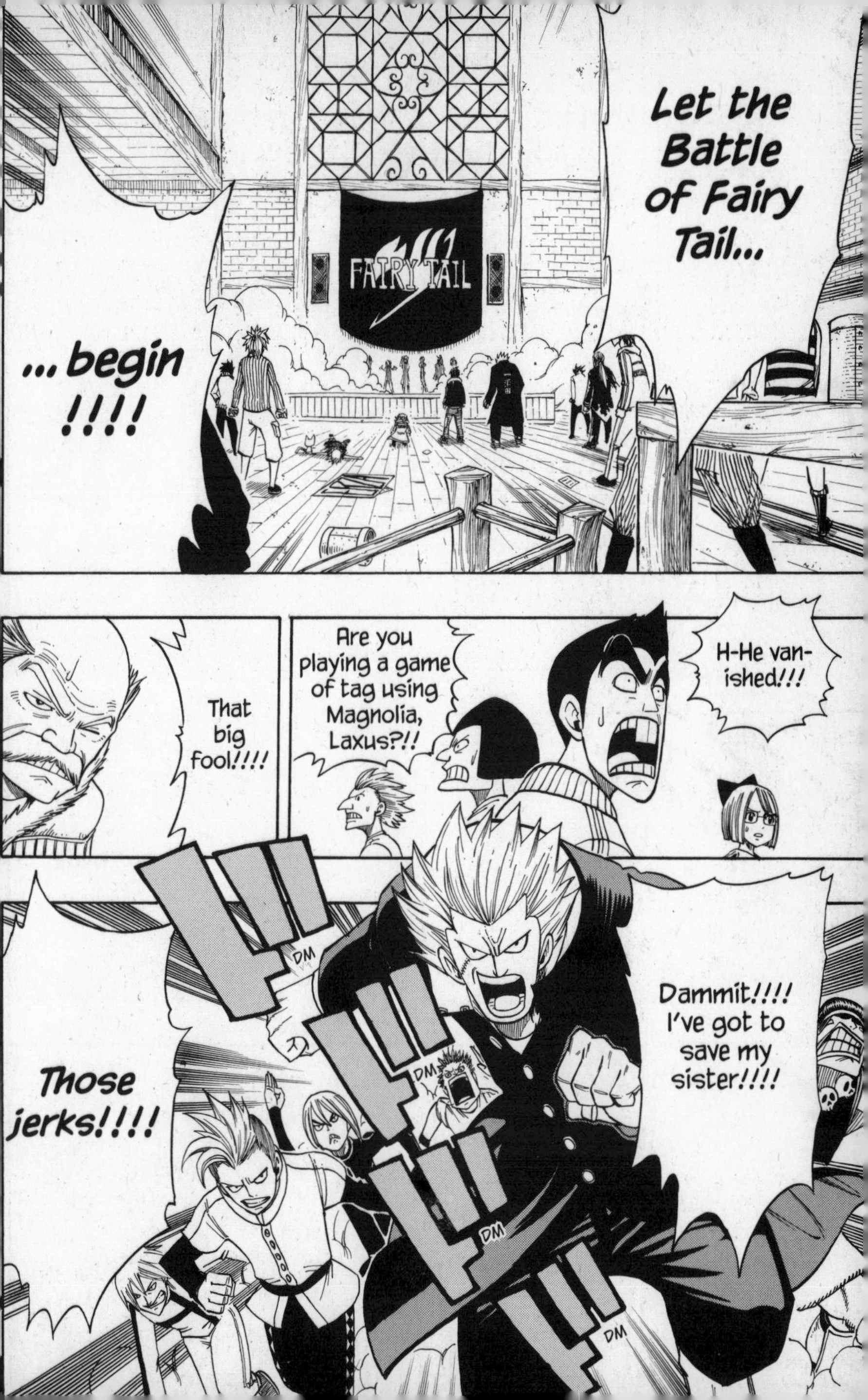
Let the Battle of Fairy Tail...
FAIRY TAIL
...begin!!!!
H-He vanished!!!
Are you playing a game of tag using Magnolia, Laxus?!!
That big fool!!!!
Dammit!!!! I've got to save my sister!!!!
DM
DM
DM
DM
Those jerks!!!!

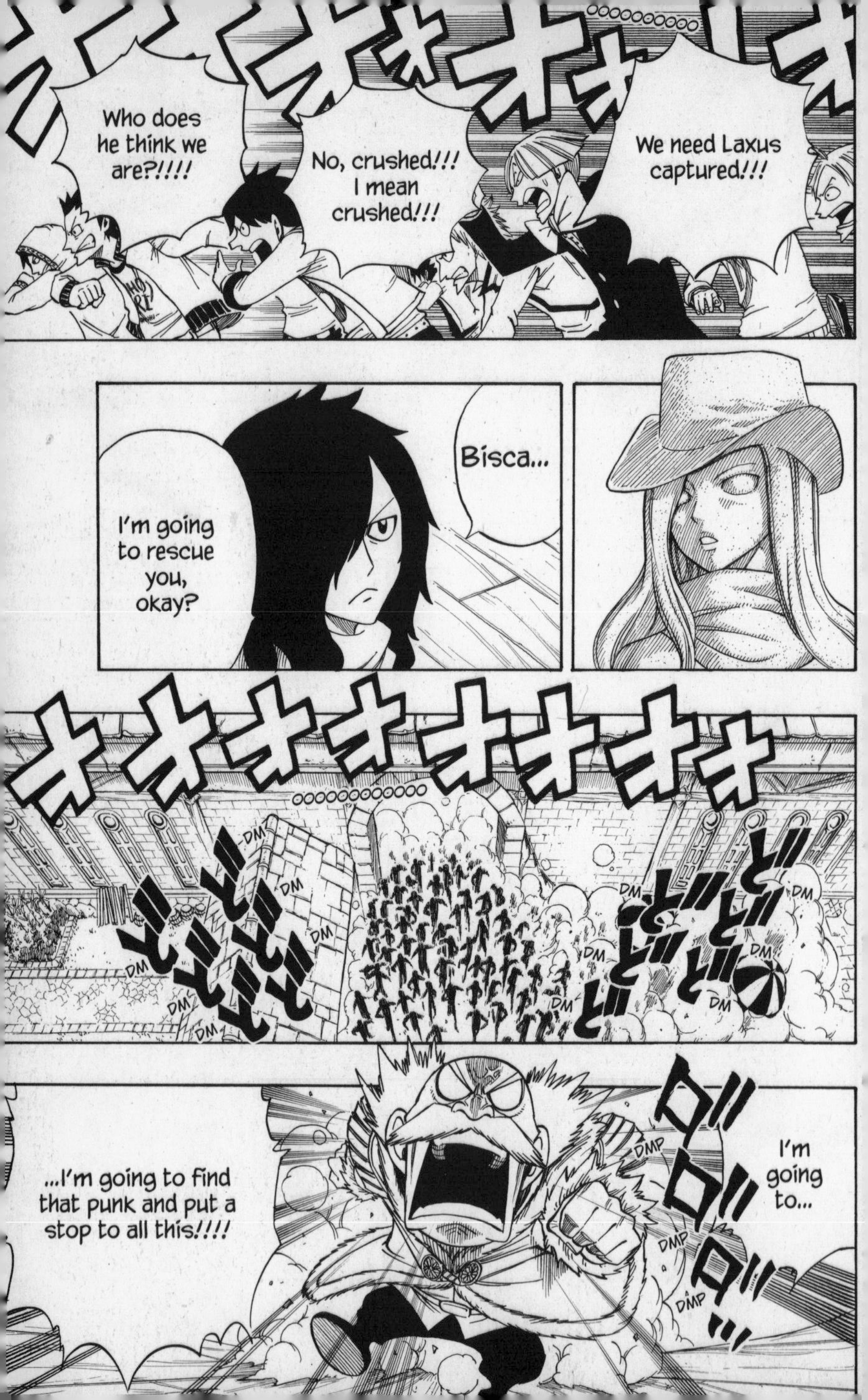

OOOOOOOOOO
We need Laxus captured!!!
No, crushed!!! I mean crushed!!!
Who does he think we are?!!!!
Bisca...
I'm going to rescue you, okay?
OOOOOOOOOOOO
DM
I'm going to...
...I'm going to find that punk and put a stop to all this!!!!
DMP

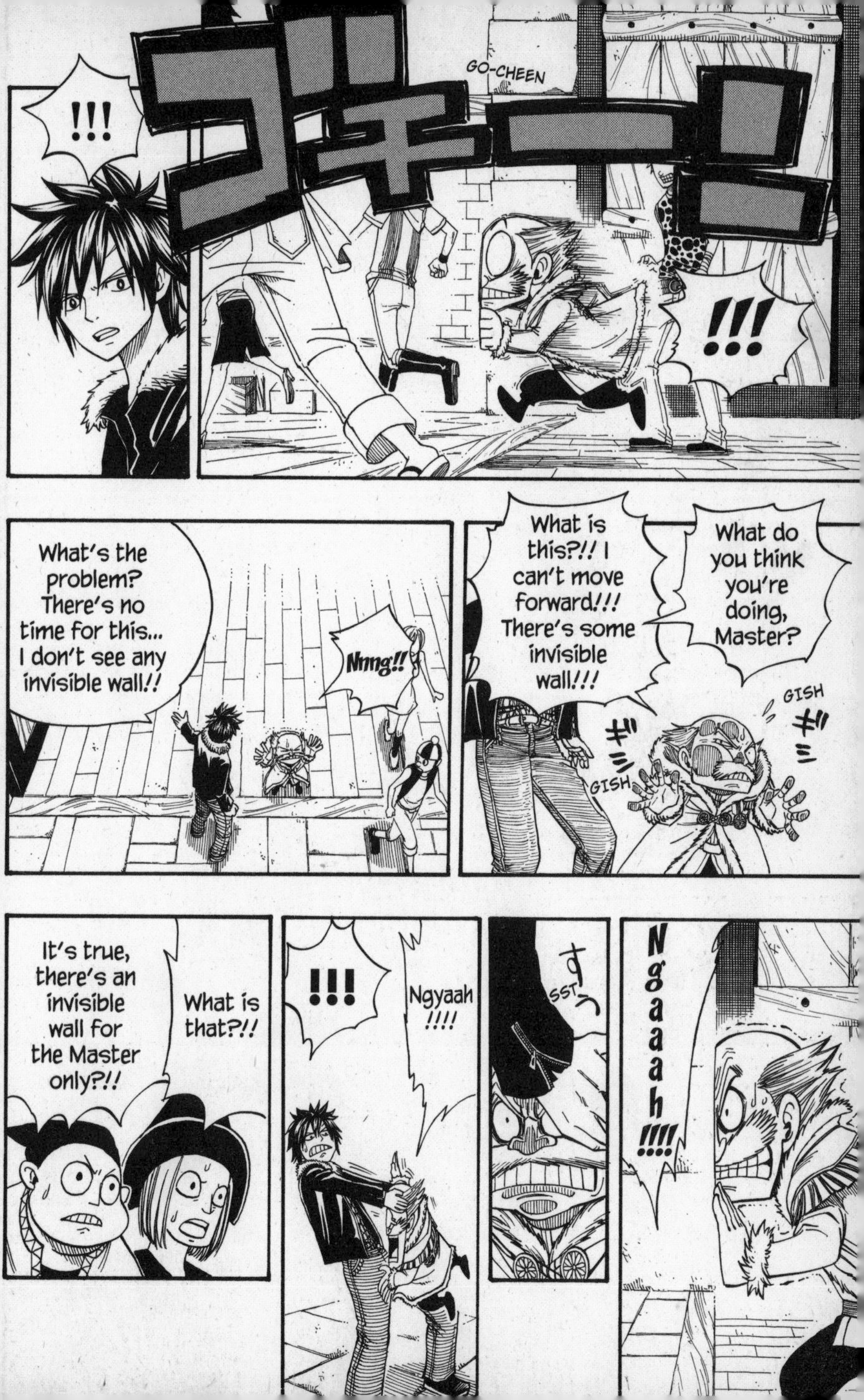

GO-CHEEN
!!!
!!!
What do you think you're doing, Master?
What is this?!! I can't move forward!!! There's some invisible wall!!!
GISH
GISH
What's the problem? There's no time for this... I don't see any invisible wall!!
Nnng!!
Ngaaah!!!!
SST
Ngyaah!!!!
!!!
What is that?!!
It's true, there's an invisible wall for the Master only?!!

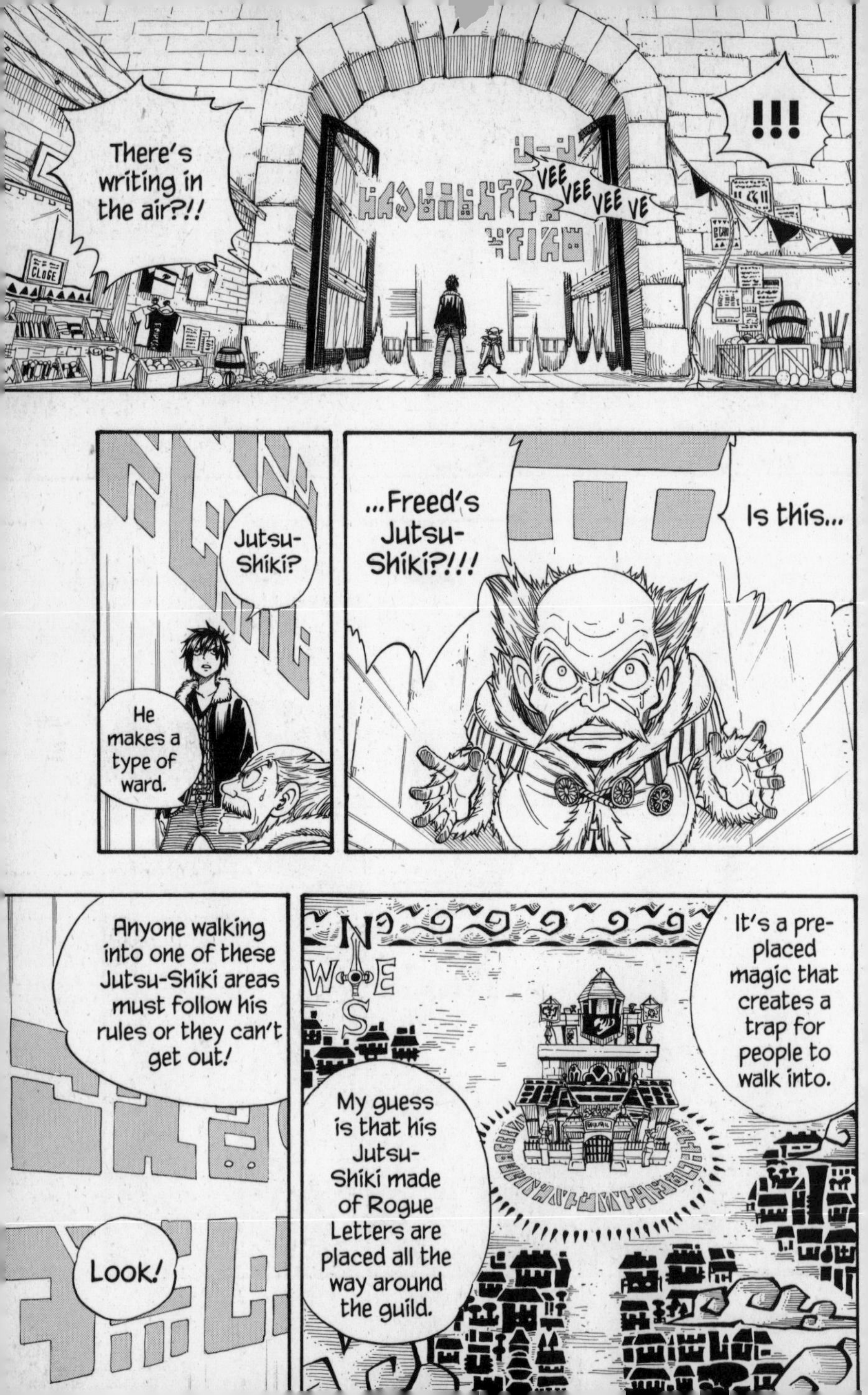
!!!
VEE VEE VEE VE
There's writing in the air?!!
Is this...
...Freed's Jutsu-Shiki?!!!
Jutsu-Shiki?
He makes a type of ward.
It's a pre-placed magic that creates a trap for people to walk into.
N
W E
S
My guess is that his Jutsu-Shiki made of Rogue Letters are placed all the way around the guild.
Anyone walking into one of these Jutsu-Shiki areas must follow his rules or they can't get out!
Look!

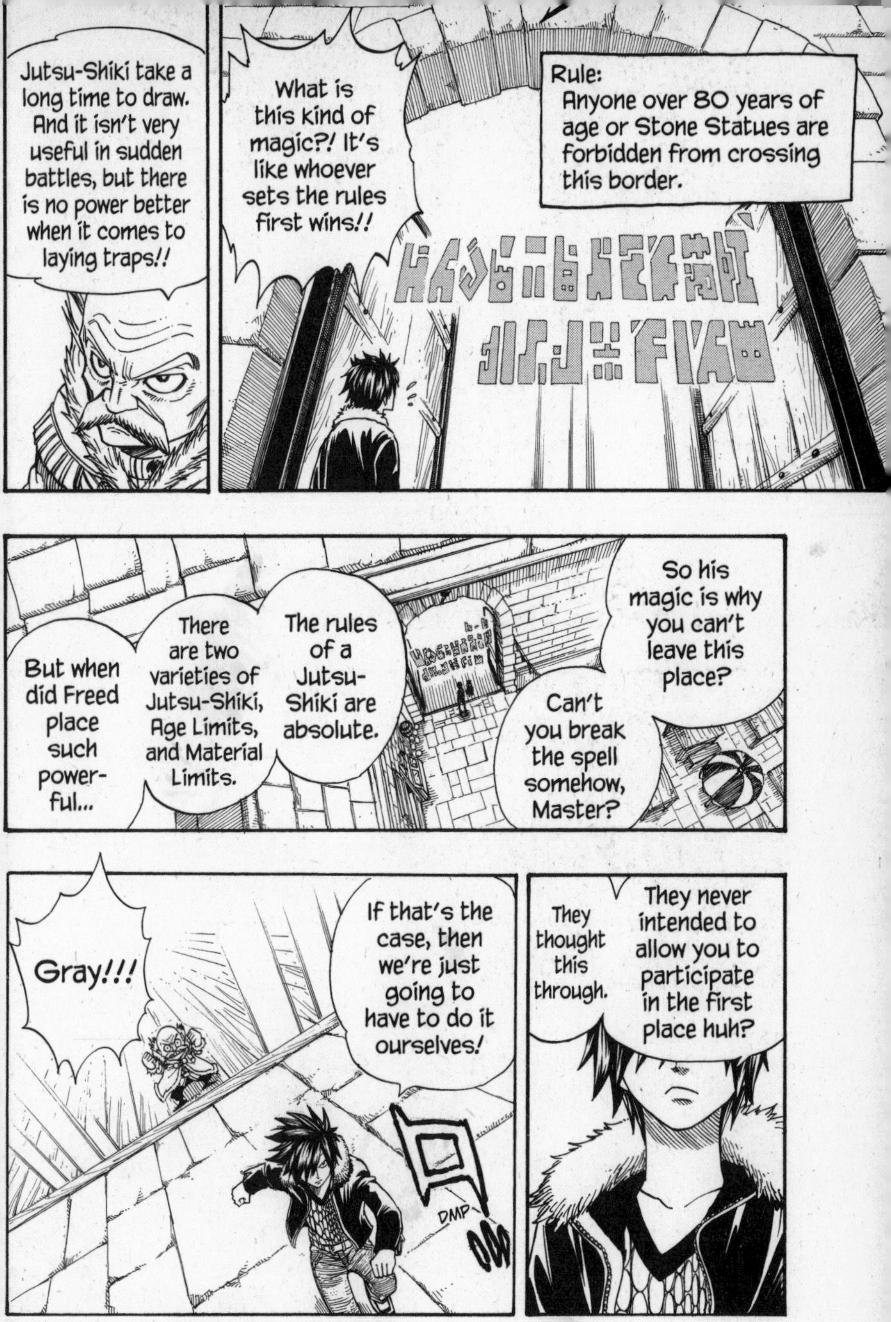
Rule:
Anyone over 80 years of age or Stone Statues are forbidden from crossing this border.
What is this kind of magic?! It's like whoever sets the rules first wins!!
Jutsu-Shiki take a long time to draw. And it isn't very useful in sudden battles, but there is no power better when it comes to laying traps!!
So his magic is why you can't leave this place?
Can't you break the spell somehow, Master?
The rules of a Jutsu-Shiki are absolute.
There are two varieties of Jutsu-Shiki, Age Limits, and Material Limits.
But when did Freed place such power-ful...
They never intended to allow you to participate in the first place huh?
They thought this through.
If that's the case, then we're just going to have to do it ourselves!
Gray!!!
DMP

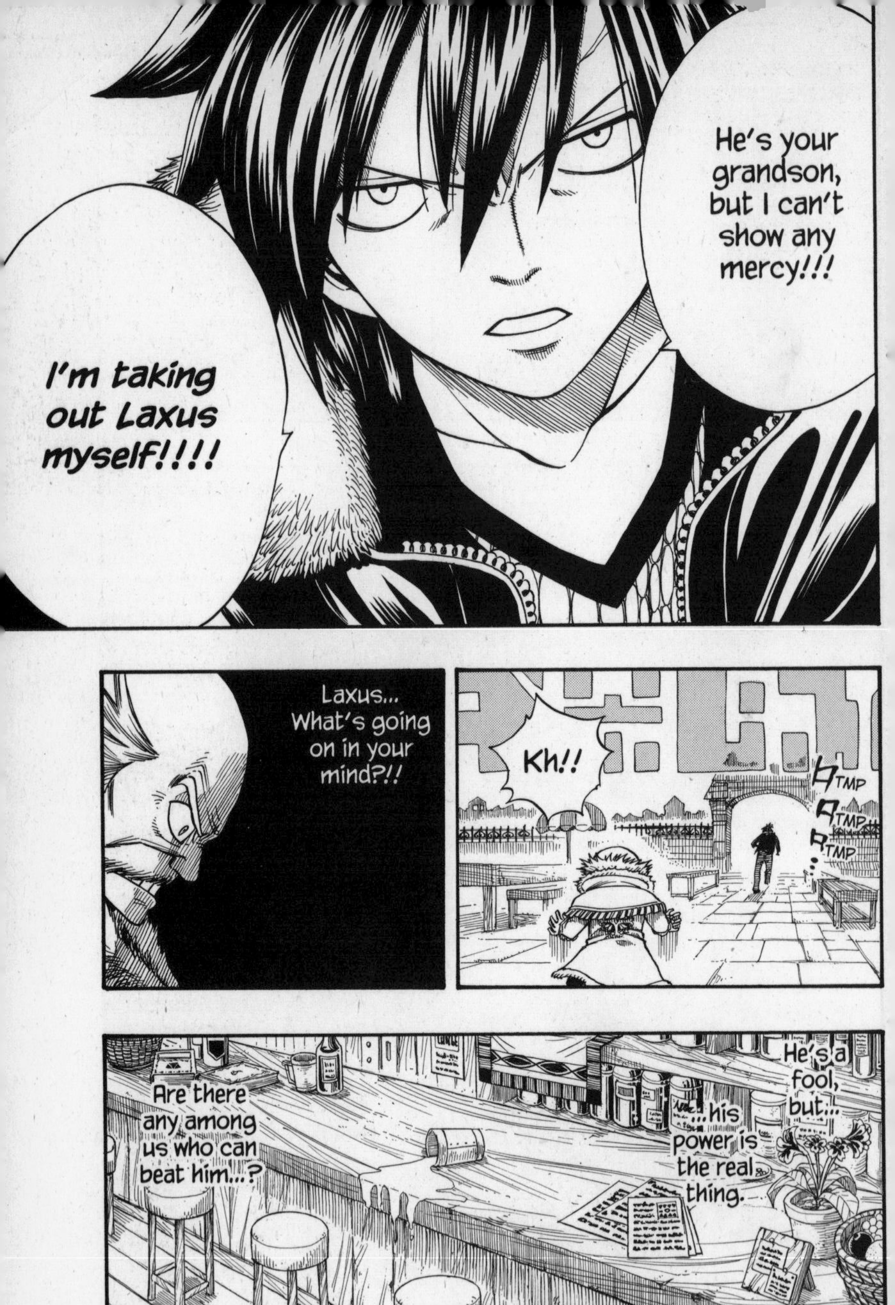
He's your grandson, but I can't show any mercy!!!
I'm taking out Laxus myself!!!!
Kh!!
TMP
TMP
TMP
Laxus... What's going on in your mind?!!
He's a fool, but...
...his power is the real thing.
Are there any among us who can beat him...?

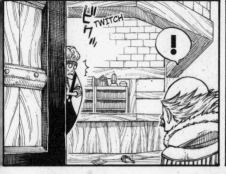

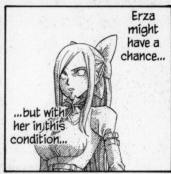

Erza might have a chance...
...but with her in this condition...
TWITCH
!
F-Forgive... I-I am... afraid...of Laxus...
It's you, Reedus!!
Good!
Now, do you know where in the East Forest Poluchka is?
Oui!
There should be some medicine that cures petrification!
Can you go get it?
Oui!!! That, I can do!!!

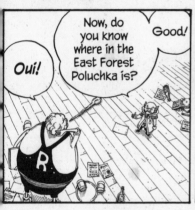

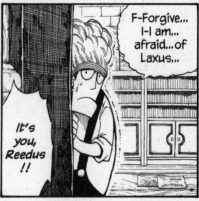

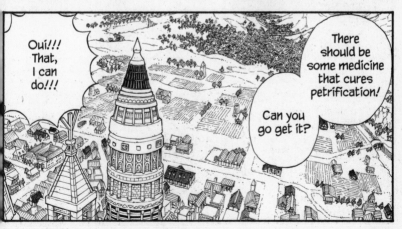

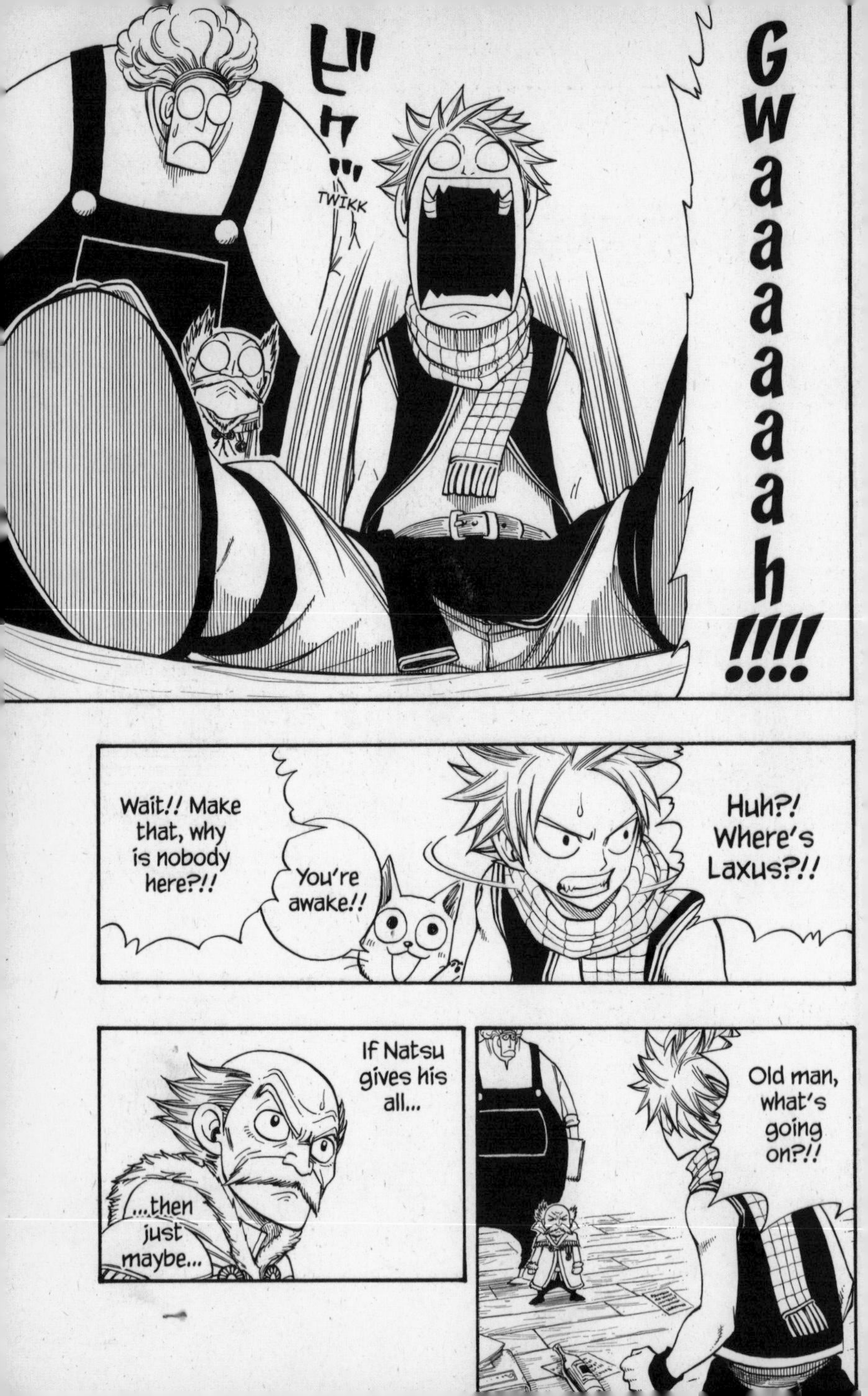
Gwaaaaaah!!!!
TWIKK
Huh?! Where's Laxus?!!
You're awake!!
Wait!! Make that, why is nobody here?!!
Old man, what's going on?!!
If Natsu gives his all...
...then just maybe...

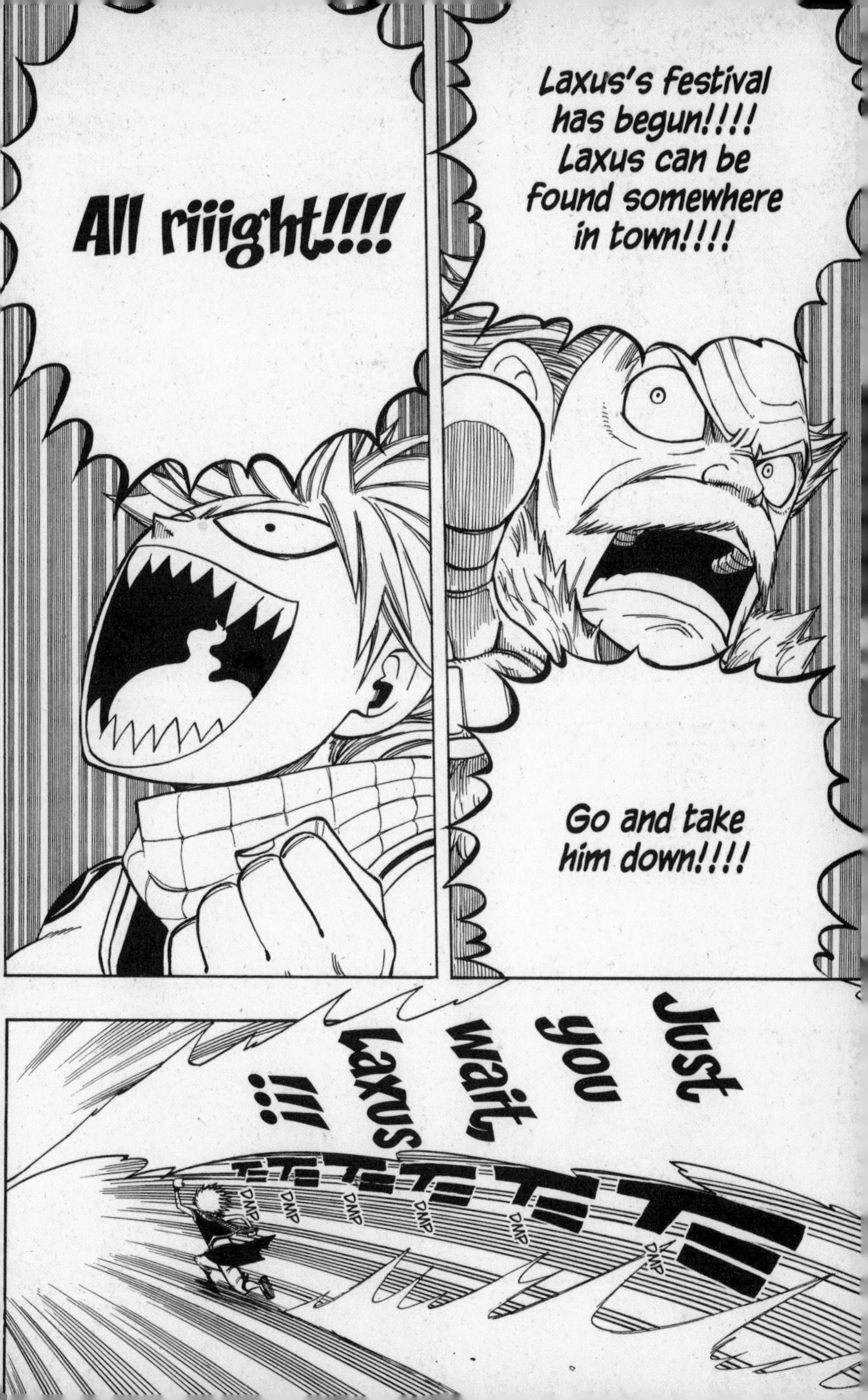
Laxus's festival has begun!!!! Laxus can be found somewhere in town!!!!
Go and take him down!!!!
All riiight!!!!
Just you wait, Laxus!!!
DMP
DMP
DMP
DMP
DMP
DMP

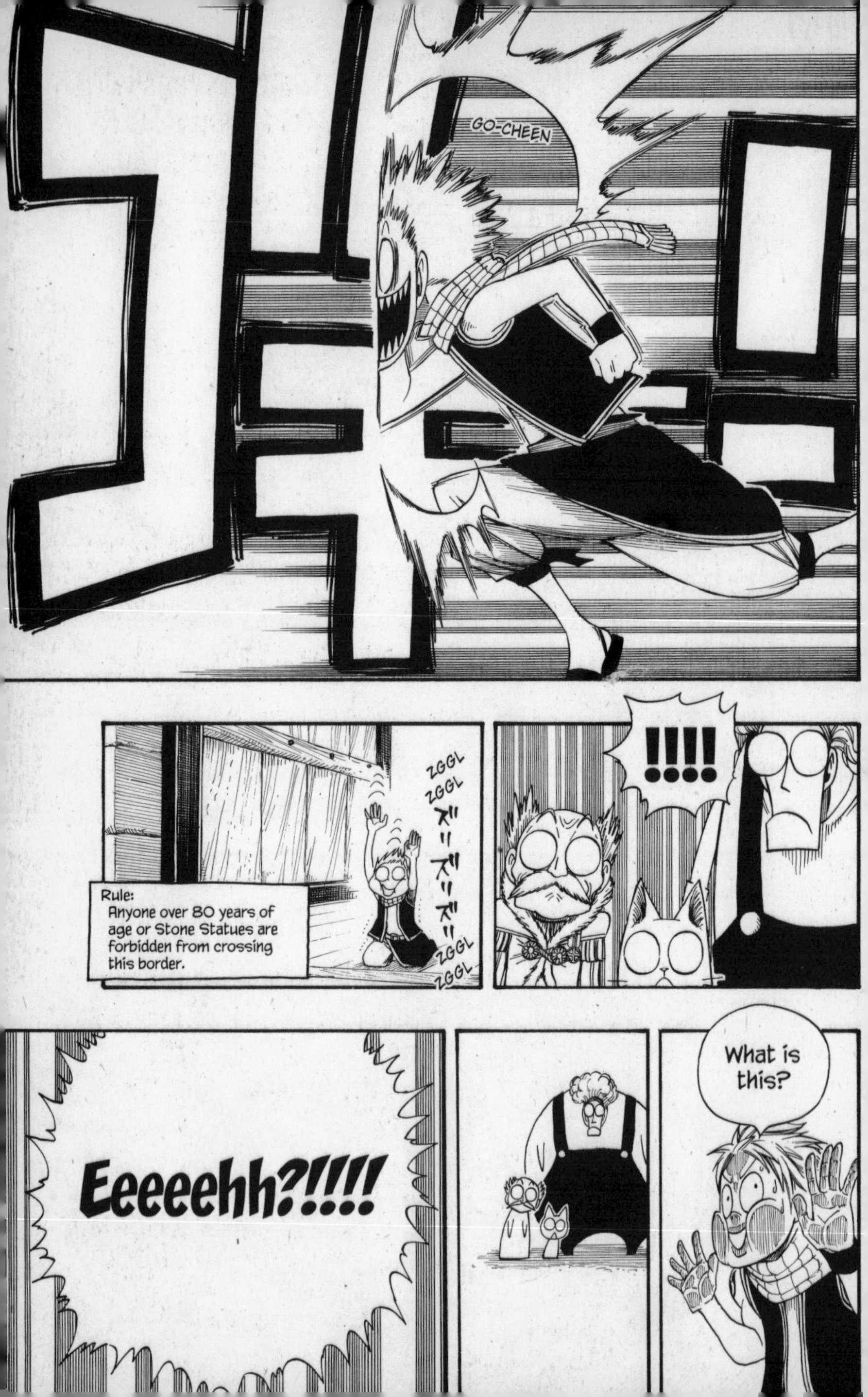
GO-CHEEN
!!!!
ZGGL
ZGGL
ZGGL
ZGGL
Rule:
Anyone over 80 years of age or Stone Statues are forbidden from crossing this border.
What is this?
Eeeeehh?!!!!

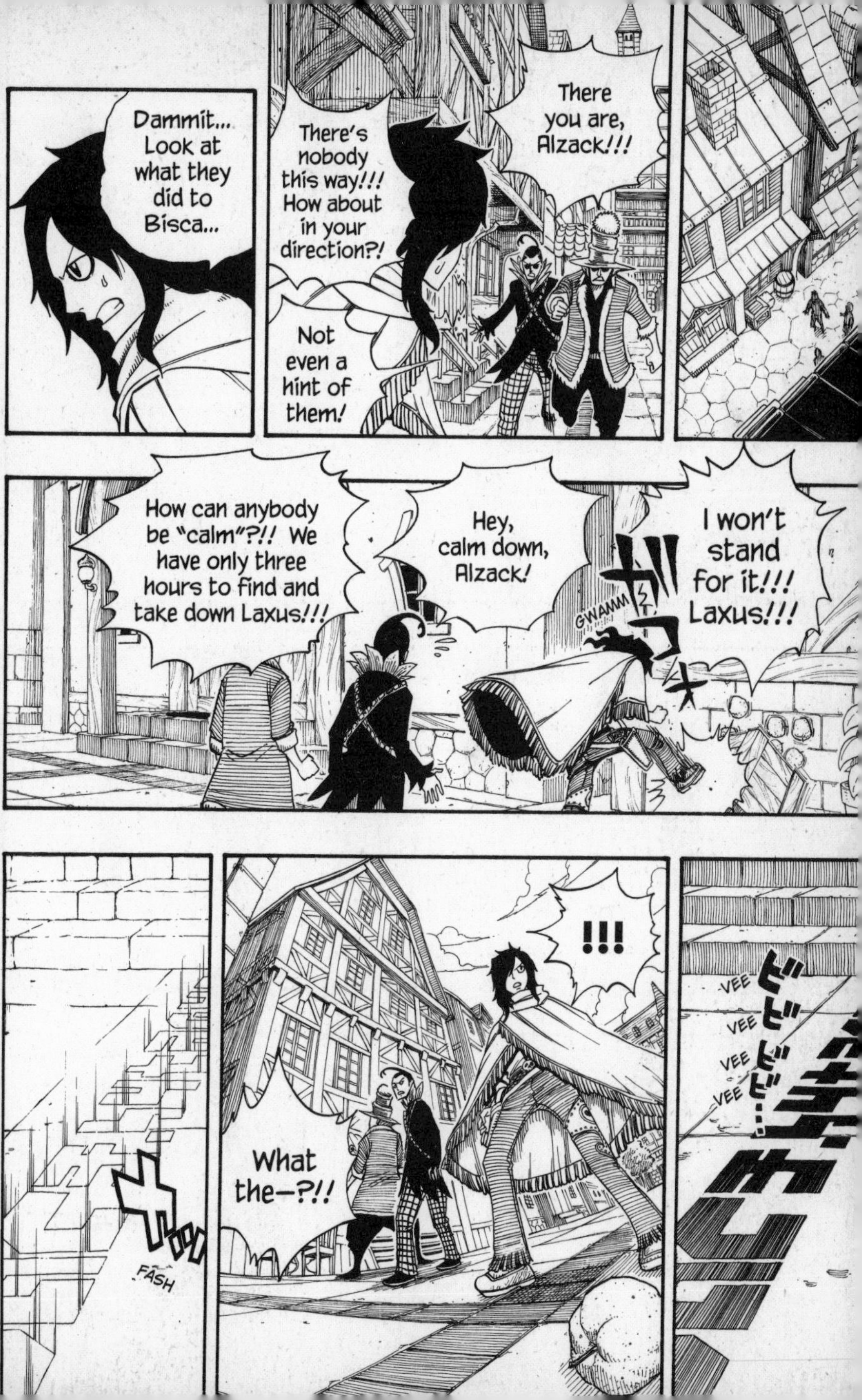
There you are, Alzack!!!
There's nobody this way!!! How about in your direction?!
Not even a hint of them!
Dammit... Look at what they did to Bisca...
I won't stand for it!!! Laxus!!!
GWAMM
Hey, calm down, Alzack!
How can anybody be "calm"?!! We have only three hours to find and take down Laxus!!!
VEE
VEE
VEE
VEE
!!!
What the—?!!
FASH

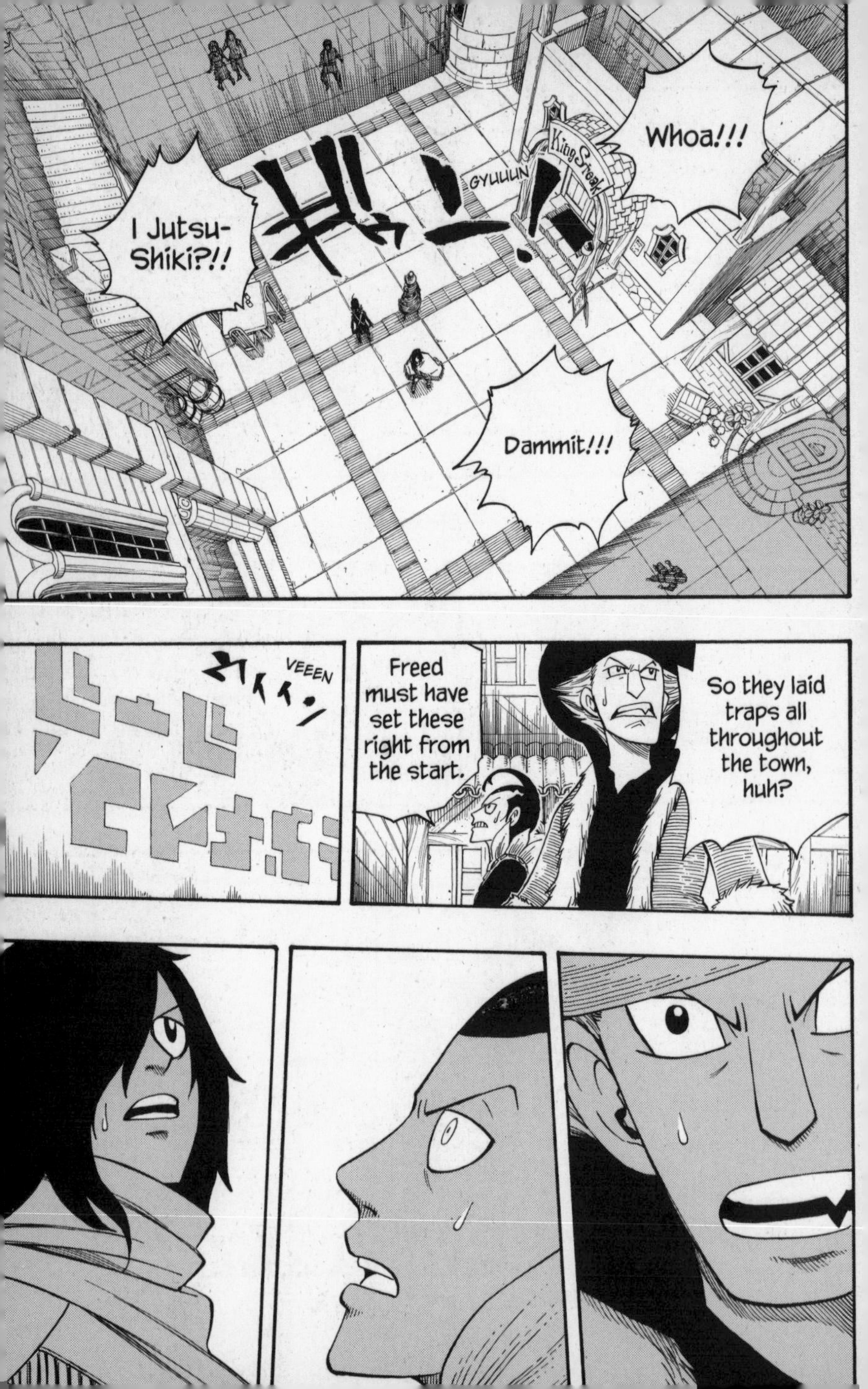
Whoa!!!
GYUUUN
I Jutsu-Shiki?!!
Dammit!!!
So they laid traps all throughout the town, huh?
Freed must have set these right from the start.
VEEEN

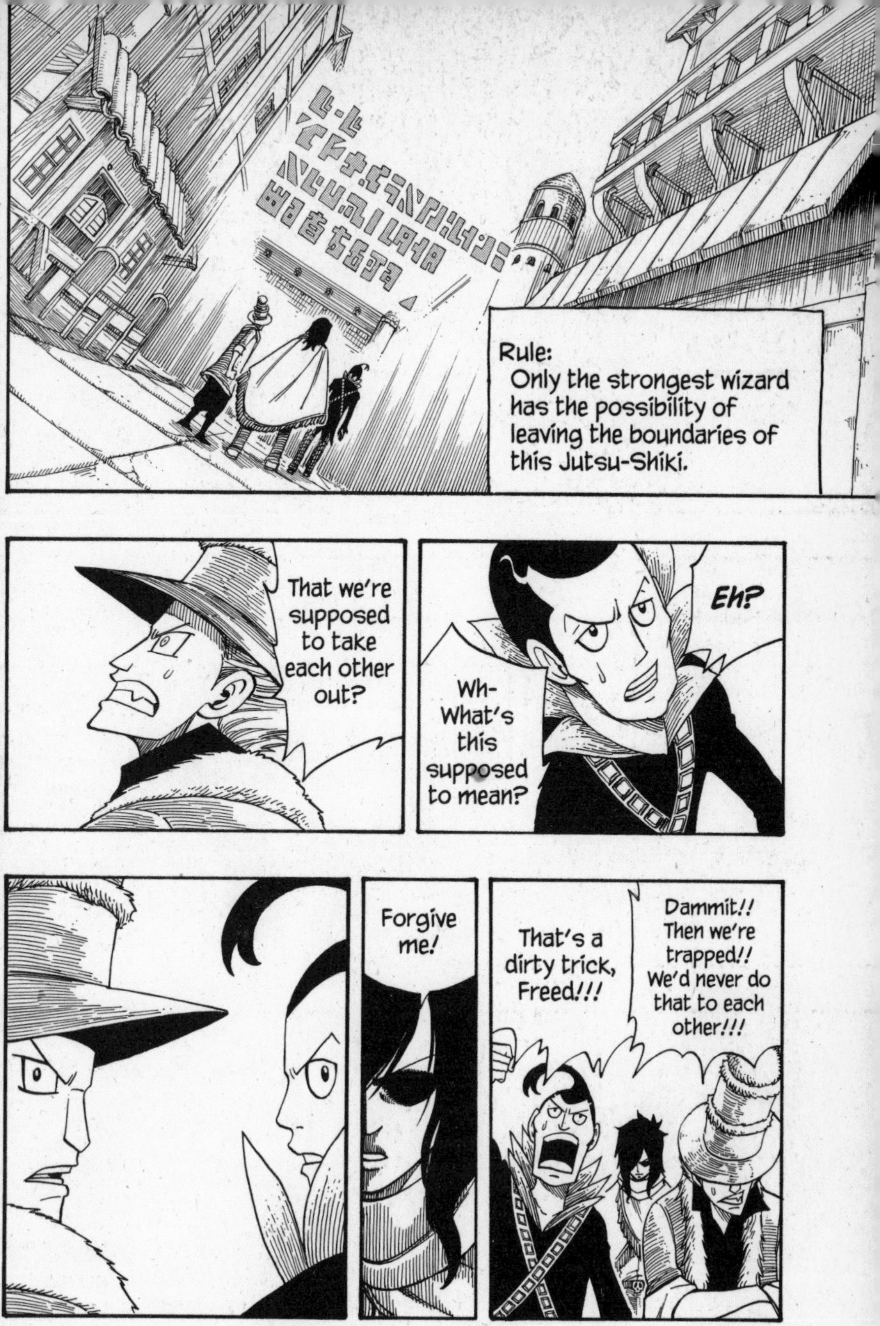
Rule:
Only the strongest wizard has the possibility of leaving the boundaries of this Jutsu-Shiki.
Eh?
Wh- What's this supposed to mean?
That we're supposed to take each other out?
Dammit!! Then we're trapped!! We'd never do that to each other!!!
That's a dirty trick, Freed!!!
Forgive me!

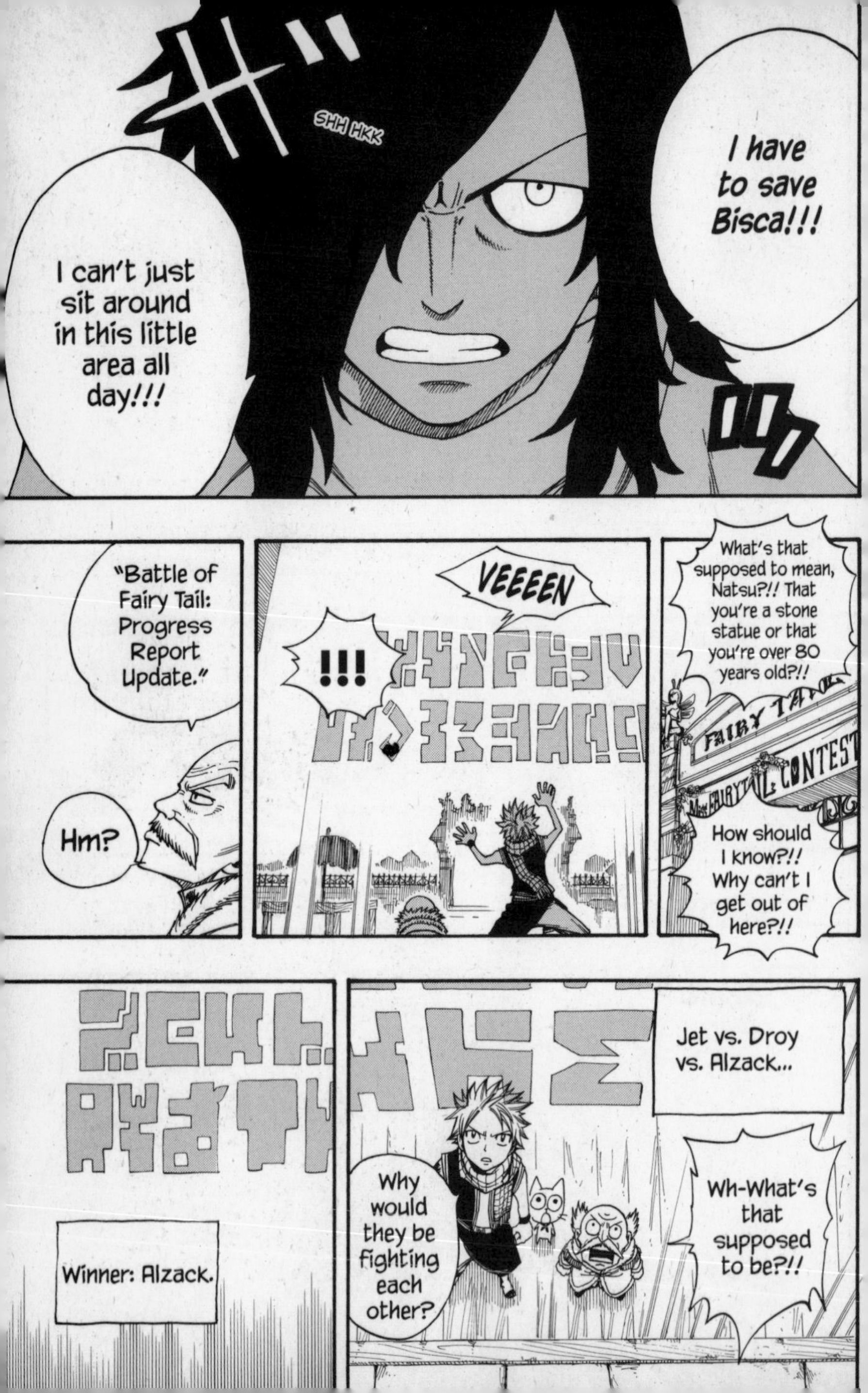
I have to save Bisca!!!
SHH HKK
I can't just sit around in this little area all day!!!
What's that supposed to mean, Natsu?!! That you're a stone statue or that you're over 80 years old?!!
How should I know?!! Why can't I get out of here?!!
VEEEEN
!!!
"Battle of Fairy Tail: Progress Report Update."
Hm?
Jet vs. Droy vs. Alzack...
Wh-What's that supposed to be?!!
Why would they be fighting each other?
Winner: Alzack.

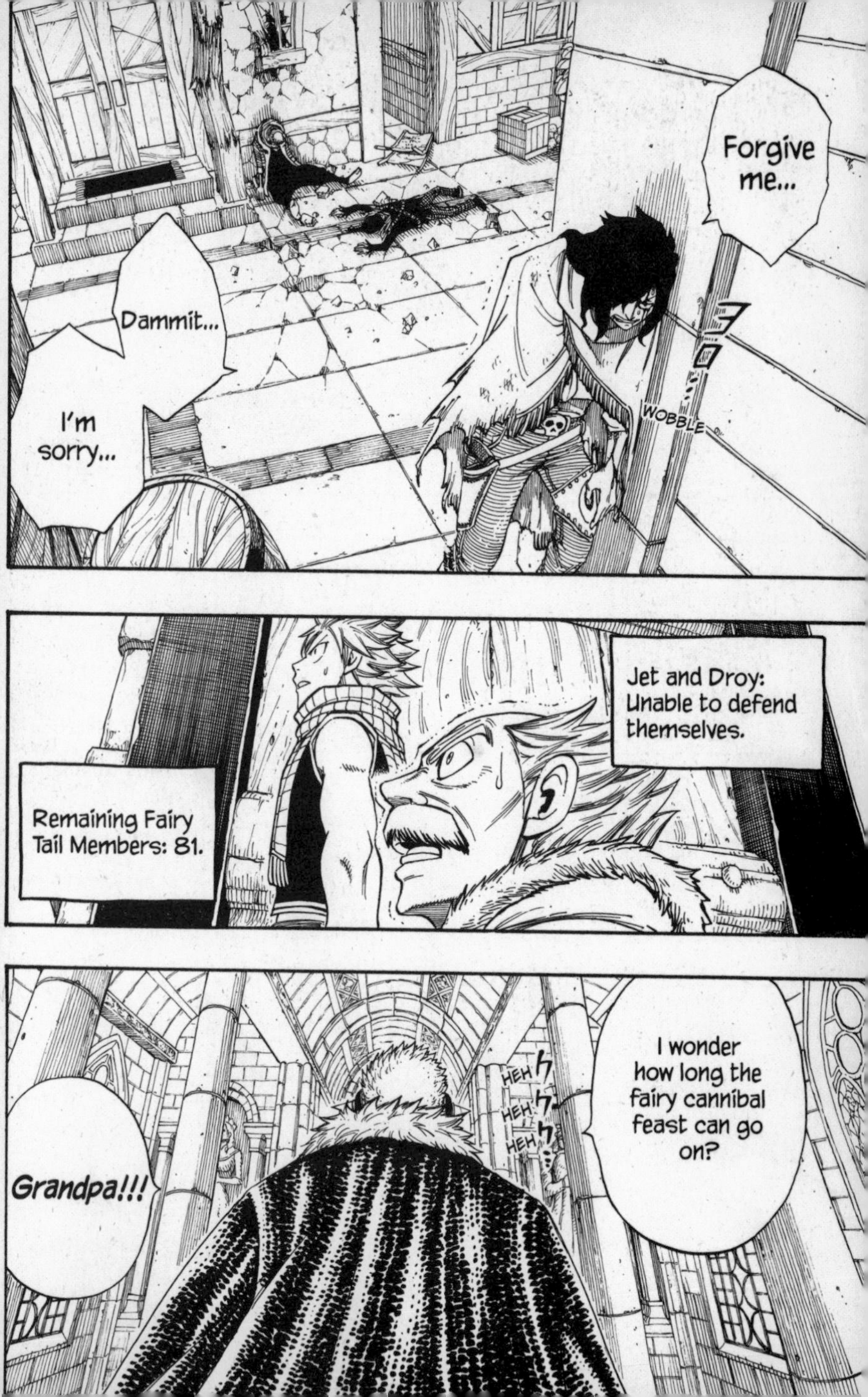
Forgive me...
WOBBLE
Dammit...
I'm sorry...
Jet and Droy: Unable to defend themselves.
Remaining Fairy Tail Members: 81.
I wonder how long the fairy cannibal feast can go on?
HEH HEH HEH
Grandpa!!!

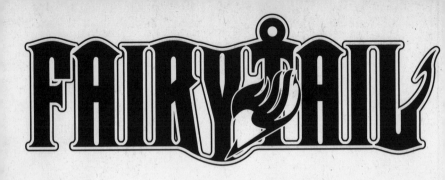

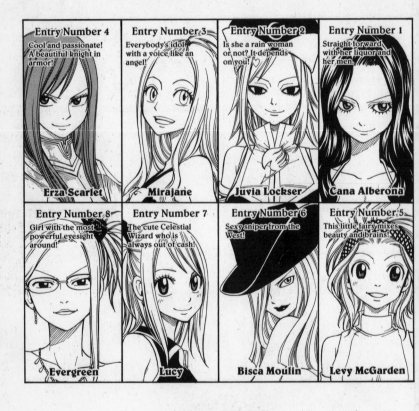

FAIRY TAIL

Entry Number 1
Straight forward with her liquor and her men.
Cana Alberona
Entry Number 2
Is she a rain woman or not? It depends on you! ♡
Juvia Lockser
Entry Number 3
Everybody's idol with a voice like an angel!
Mirajane
Entry Number 4
Cool and passionate! A beautiful knight in armor!
Erza Scarlet
Entry Number 5
This little fairy mixes beauty and brains!
Levy McGarden
Entry Number 6
Sexy sniper from the West!
Bisca Moulin
Entry Number 7
The cute Celestial Wizard who is always out of cash!
Lucy
Entry Number 8
Girl with the most powerful eyesight around!
Evergreen

Chapter 109: Friendly Fire for Friendship's Sake

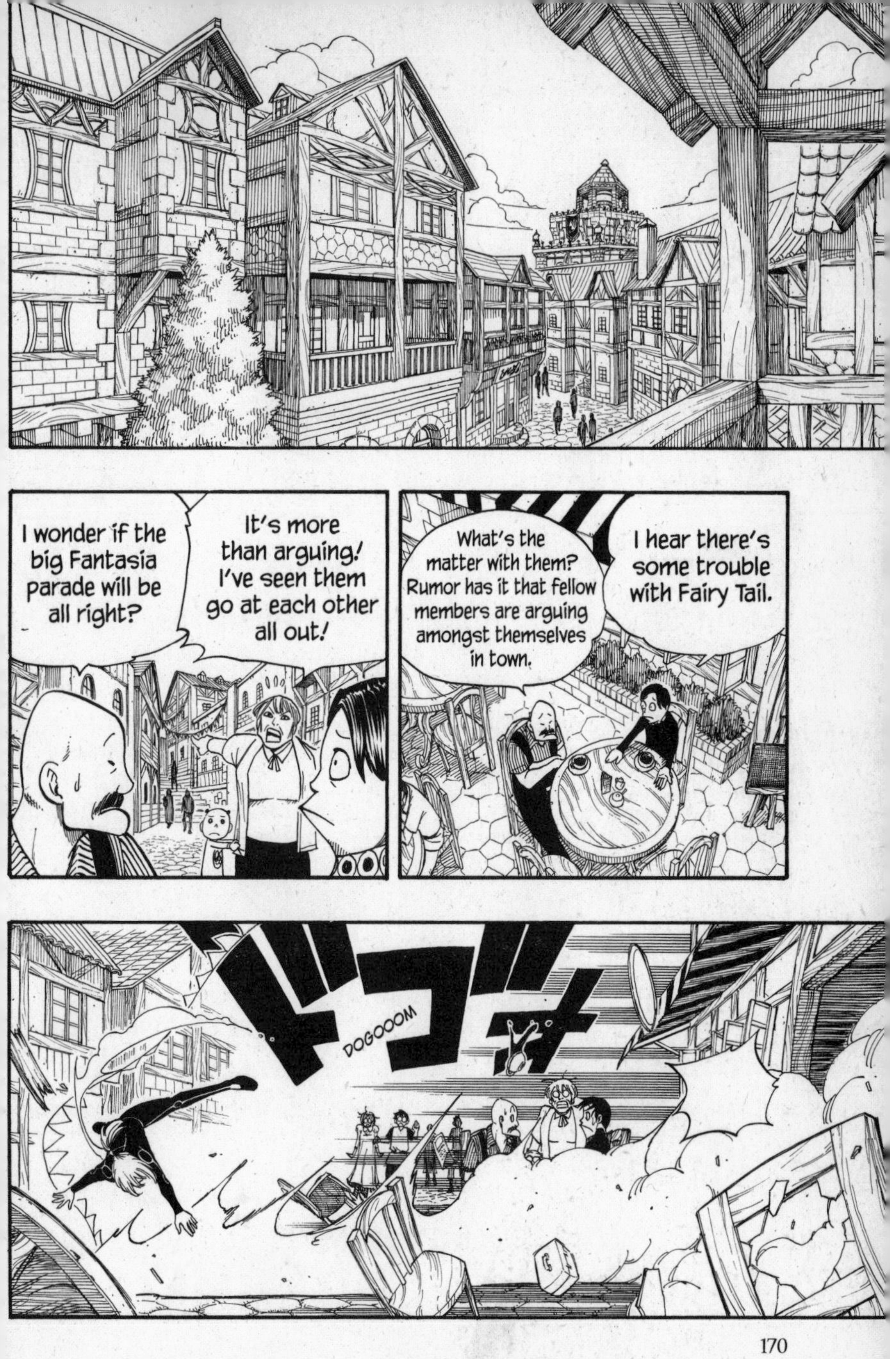
I hear there's some trouble with Fairy Tail.
What's the matter with them? Rumor has it that fellow members are arguing amongst themselves in town.
It's more than arguing! I've seen them go at each other all out!
I wonder if the big Fantasia parade will be all right?
DOGOOOM

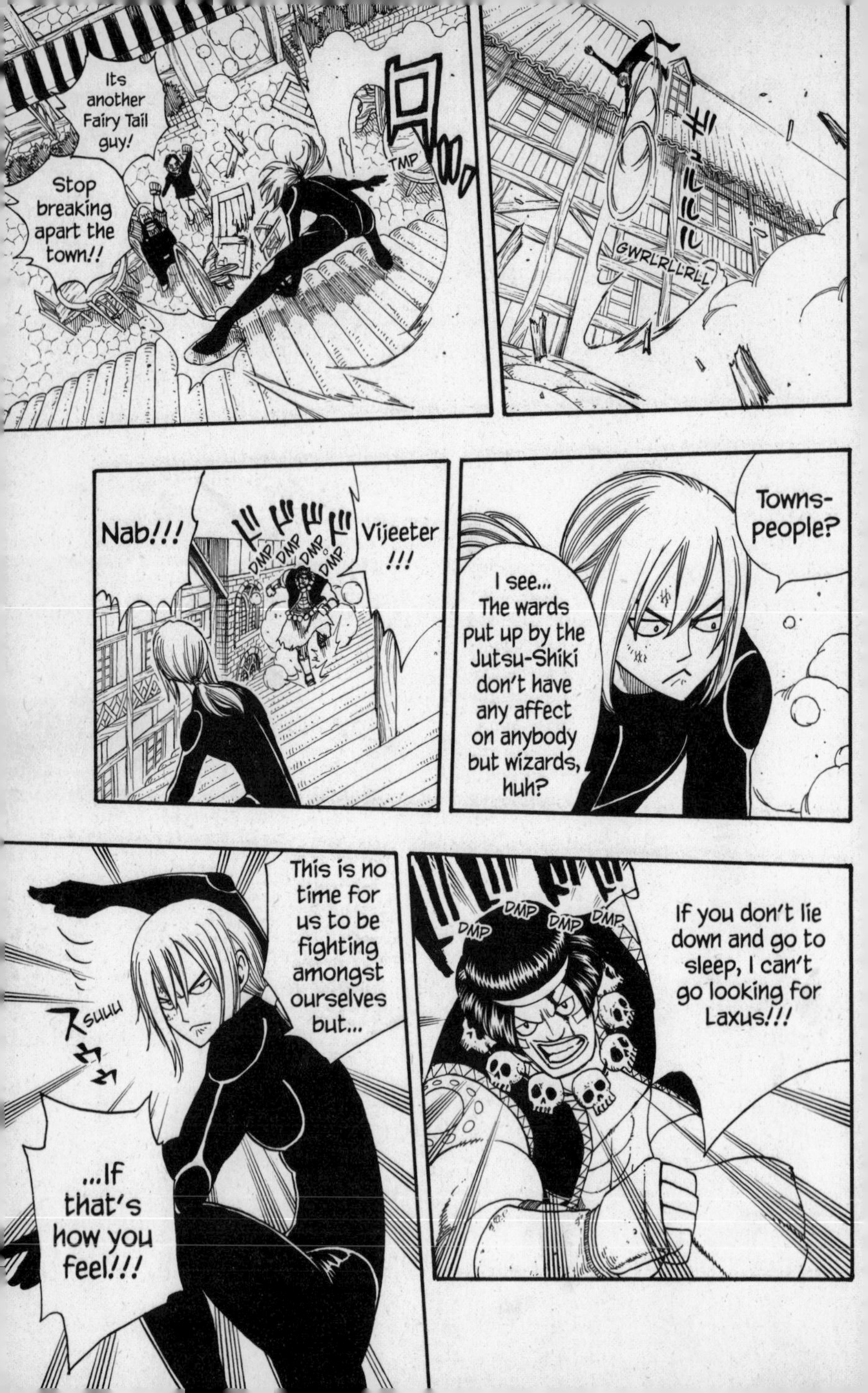
GWRL'RLL'RLL
Its another Fairy Tail guy!
Stop breaking apart the town!!
TMP
Towns-people?
I see... The wards put up by the Jutsu-Shiki don't have any affect on anybody but wizards, huh?
Vijeeter !!!
DMP DMP DMP DMP
Nab!!!
DMP DMP DMP DMP
If you don't lie down and go to sleep, I can't go looking for Laxus!!!
This is no time for us to be fighting amongst ourselves but...
SUUU
...If that's how you feel!!!

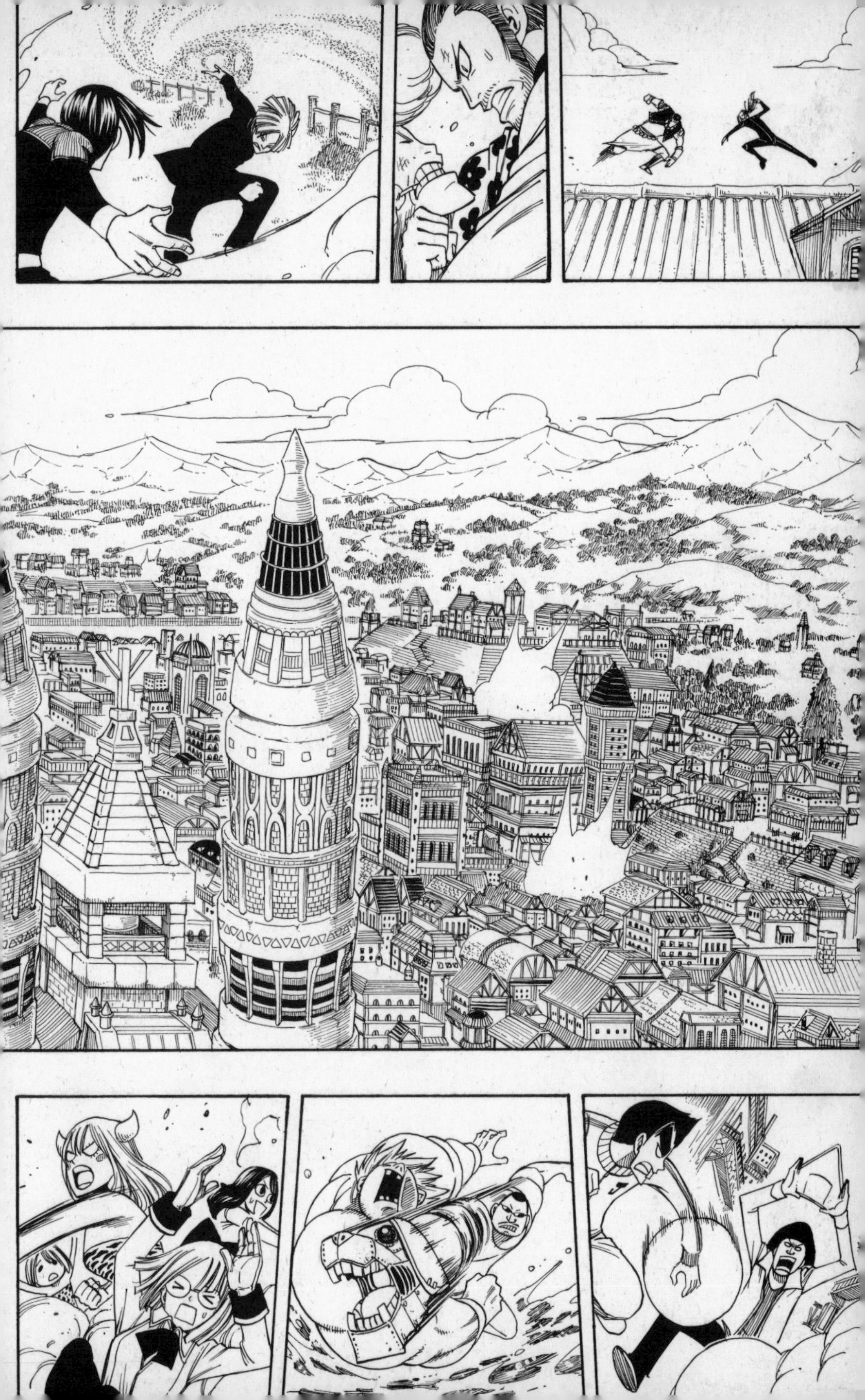

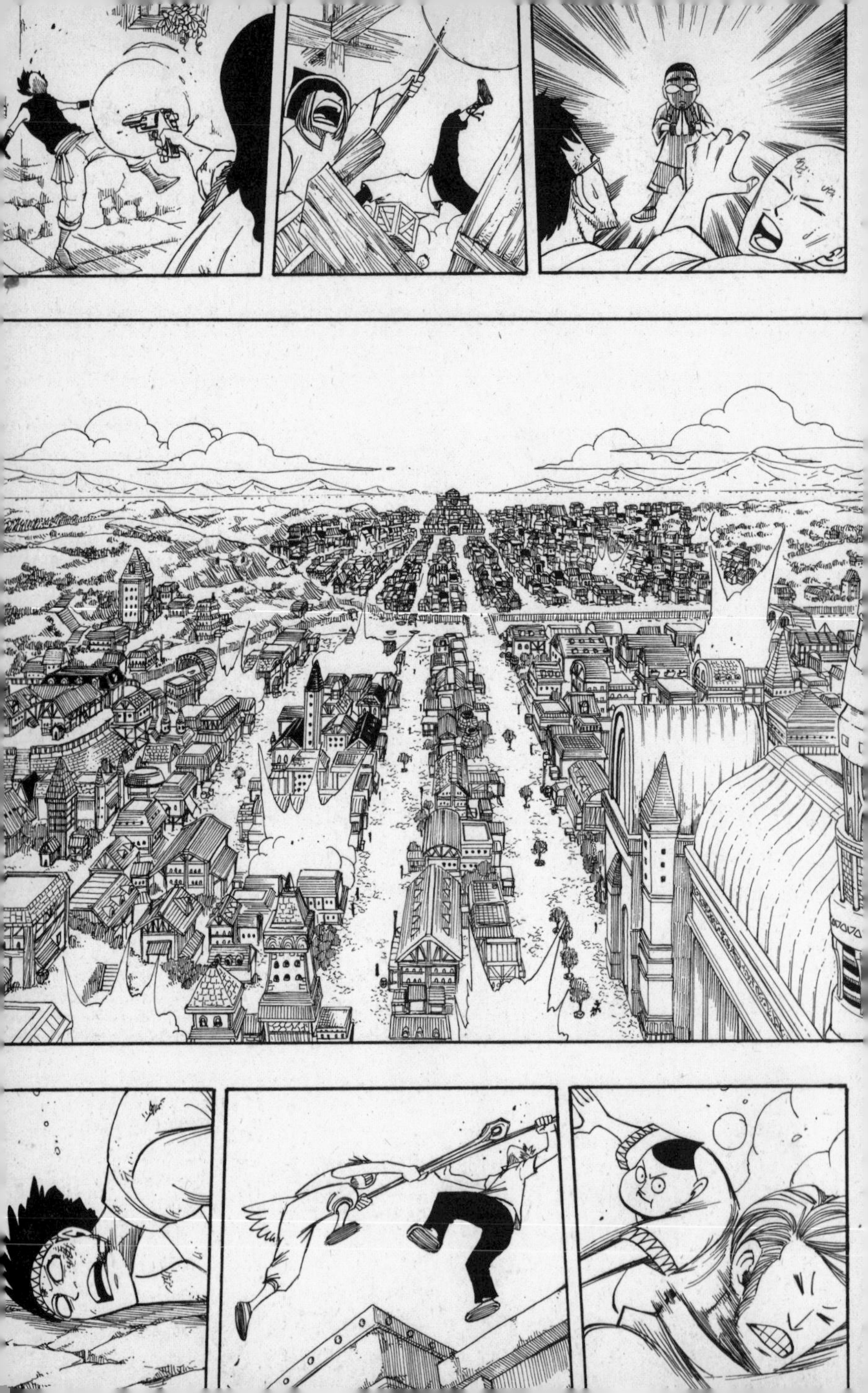

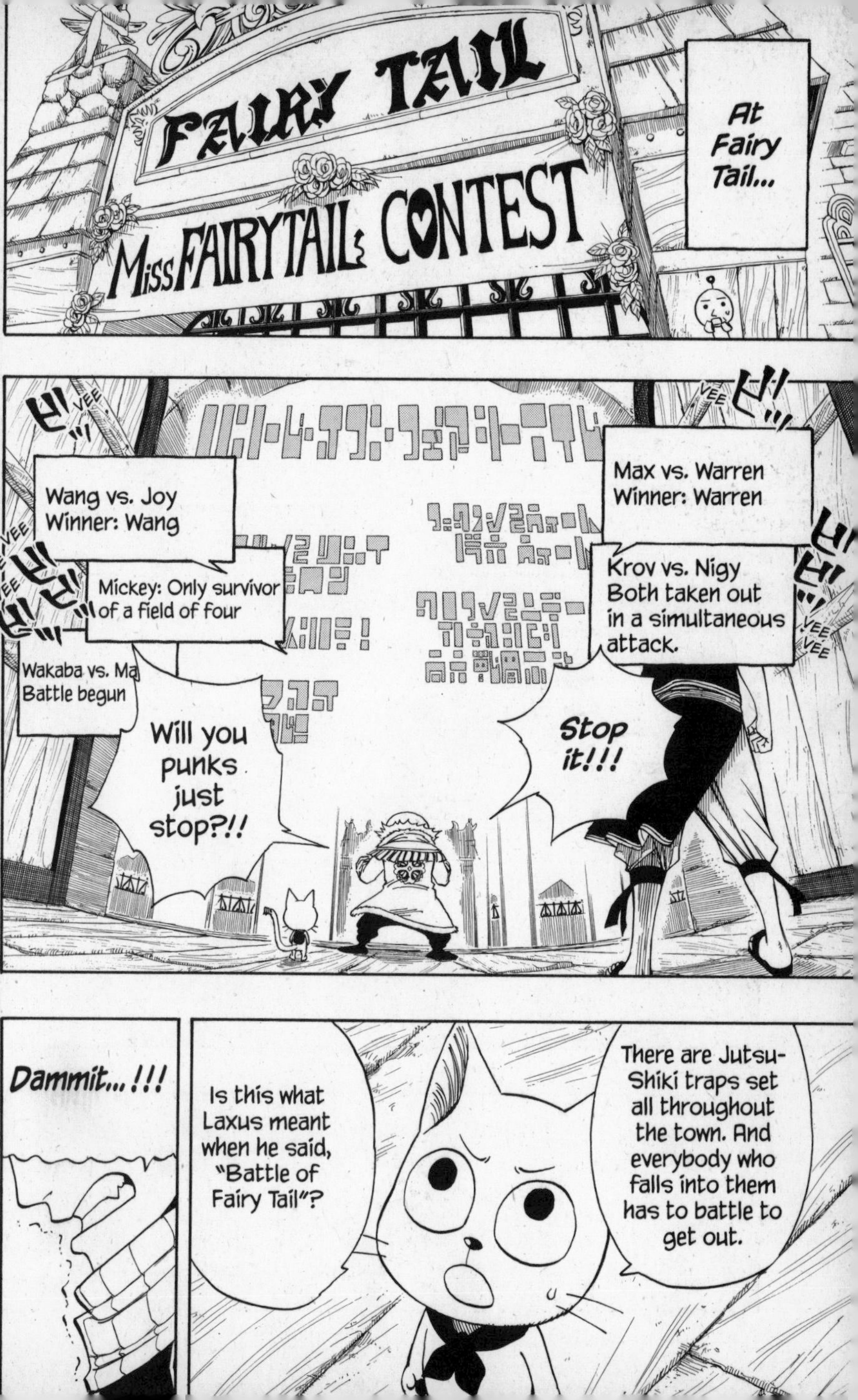
At Fairy Tail...
FAIRY TAIL
Miss FAIRYTAIL CONTEST
VEE
Max vs. Warren Winner: Warren
Krov vs. Nigy Both taken out in a simultaneous attack.
VEE VEE
VEE
Wang vs. Joy Winner: Wang
VEE VEE
Mickey: Only survivor of a field of four
Wakaba vs. Ma Battle begun
Stop it!!!
Will you punks just stop?!!
There are Jutsu-Shiki traps set all throughout the town. And everybody who falls into them has to battle to get out.
Is this what Laxus meant when he said, "Battle of Fairy Tail"?
Dammit...!!!

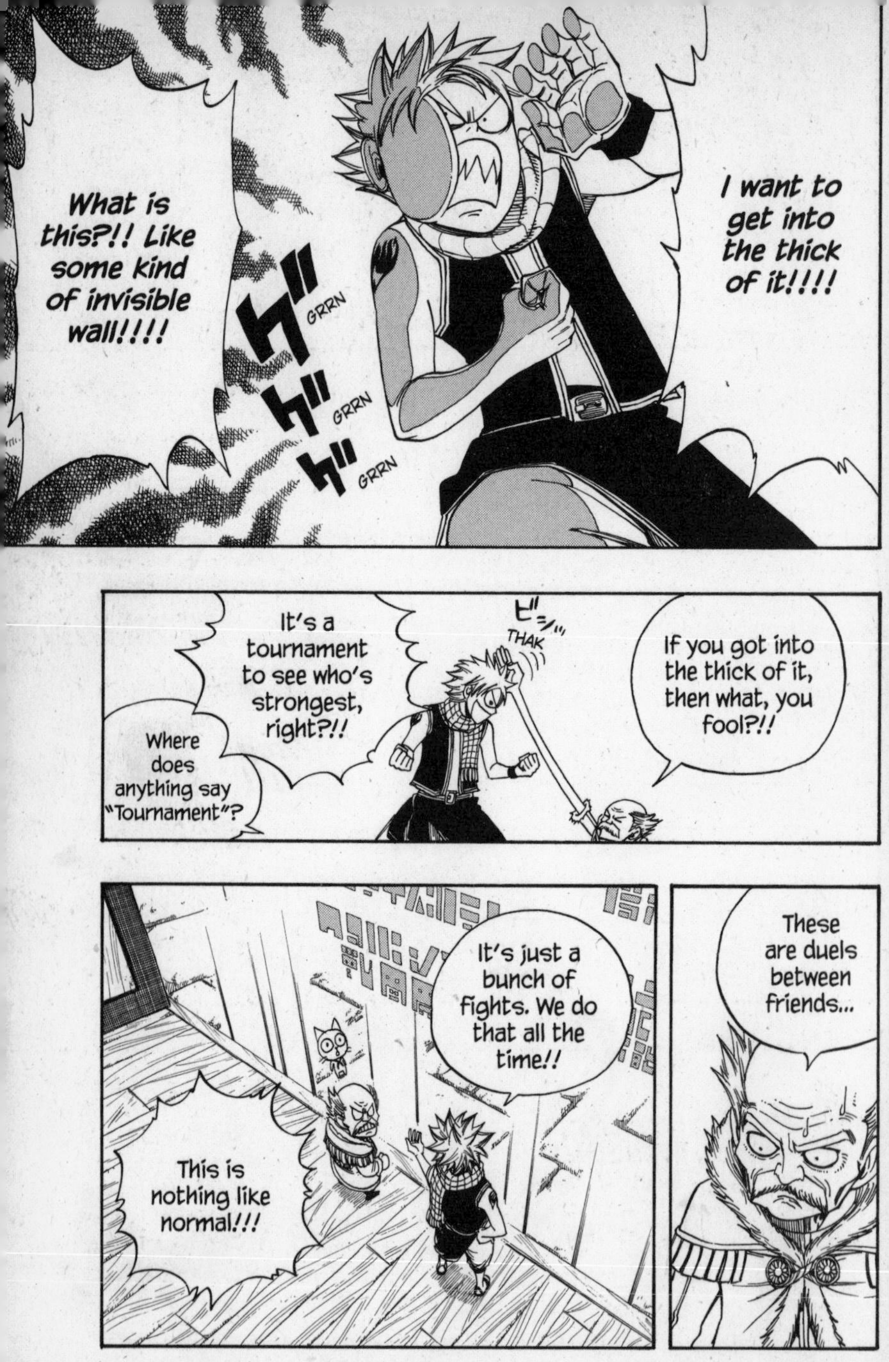
I want to get into the thick of it!!!!
What is this?!! Like some kind of invisible wall!!!!
GRRN
GRRN
GRRN
If you got into the thick of it, then what, you fool?!!
THAK
It's a tournament to see who's strongest, right?!!
Where does anything say "Tournament"?
These are duels between friends...
It's just a bunch of fights. We do that all the time!!
This is nothing like normal!!!

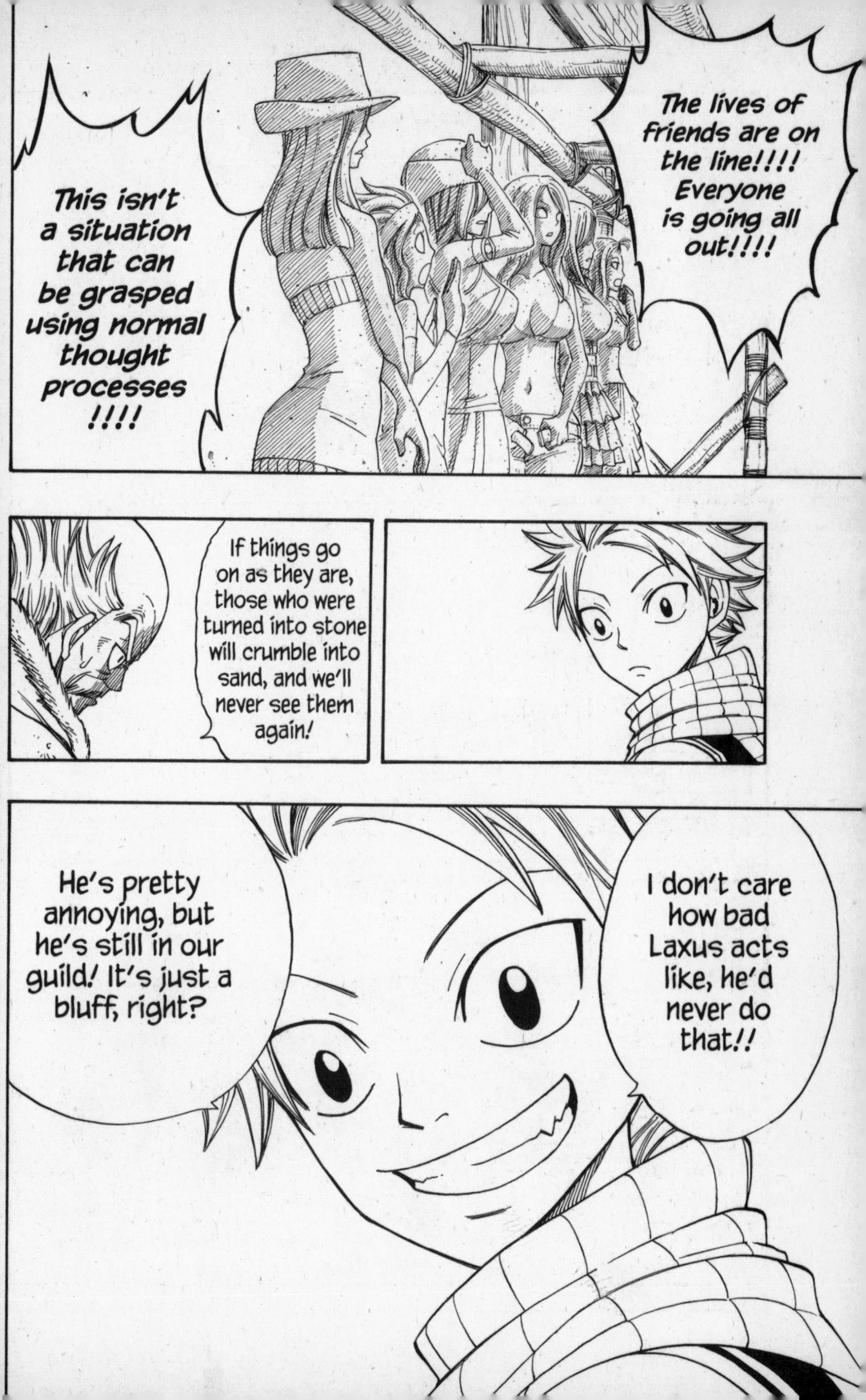
The lives of friends are on the line!!!! Everyone is going all out!!!!
This isn't a situation that can be grasped using normal thought processes !!!!
If things go on as they are, those who were turned into stone will crumble into sand, and we'll never see them again!
I don't care how bad Laxus acts like, he'd never do that!!
He's pretty annoying, but he's still in our guild! It's just a bluff, right?

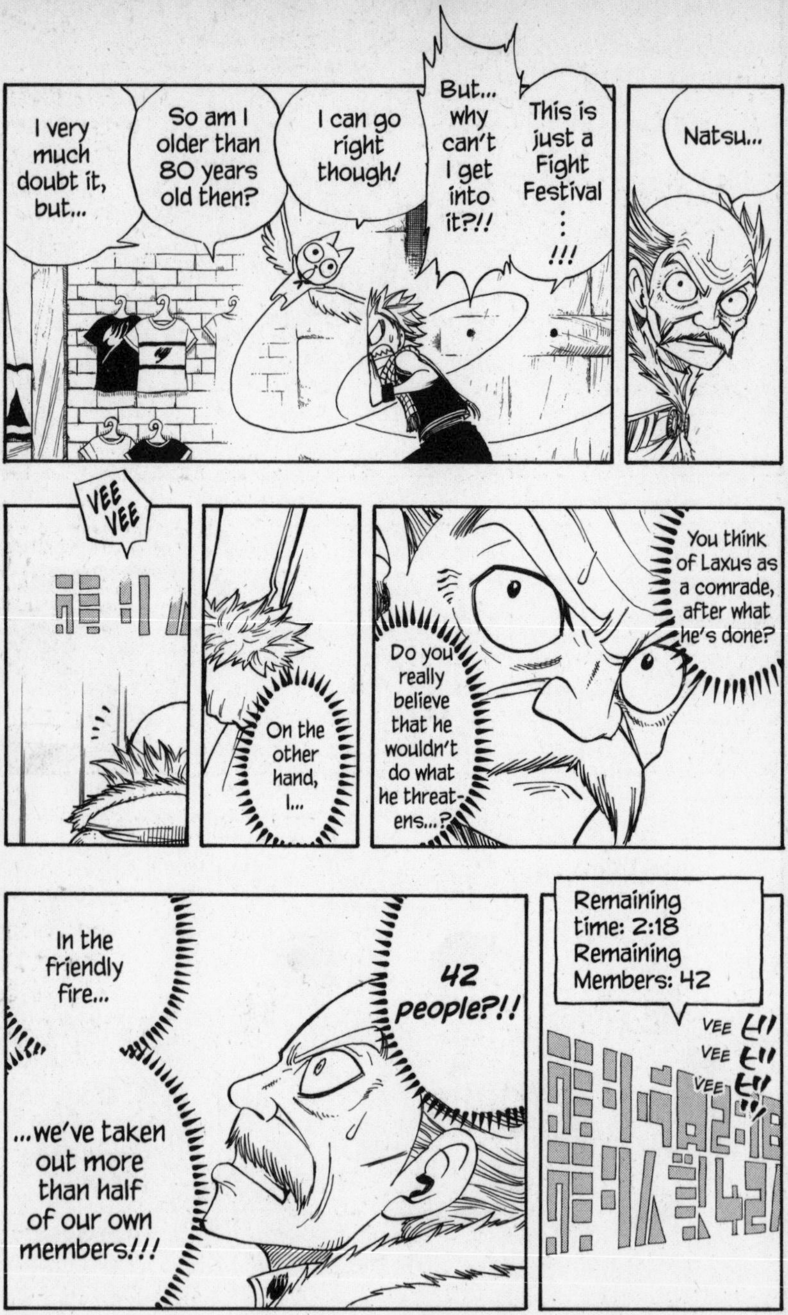
Natsu...
This is just a Fight Festival ... !!!
But... why can't I get into it?!!
I can go right though!
So am I older than 80 years old then?
I very much doubt it, but...
You think of Laxus as a comrade, after what he's done?
Do you really believe that he wouldn't do what he threatens...?
On the other hand, I...
VEE VEE
Remaining time: 2:18 Remaining Members: 42
VEE
VEE
VEE
42 people?!!
In the friendly fire...
...we've taken out more than half of our own members!!!

East Forest! East Forest!!
Poluchka-san's house!!
SKETCH
どっ どっ どっ
TMP TMP TMP
Must get out of town...
SKETCH BOOK
ゴチーン
GO-CHEEN
Eh?
I-It could not be!!! This town in its entirety is inside Jutsu-Shiki?!!!
ぞわっ
SHIVVER

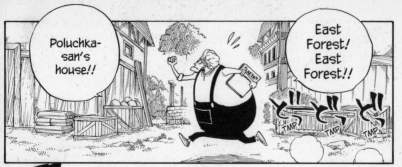

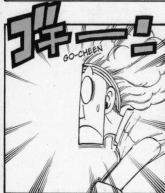

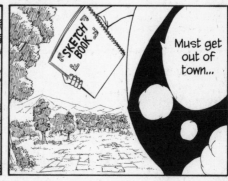

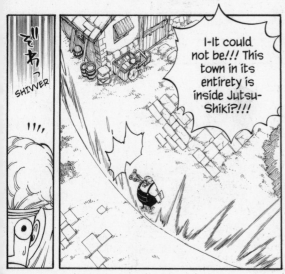

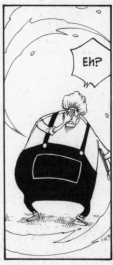

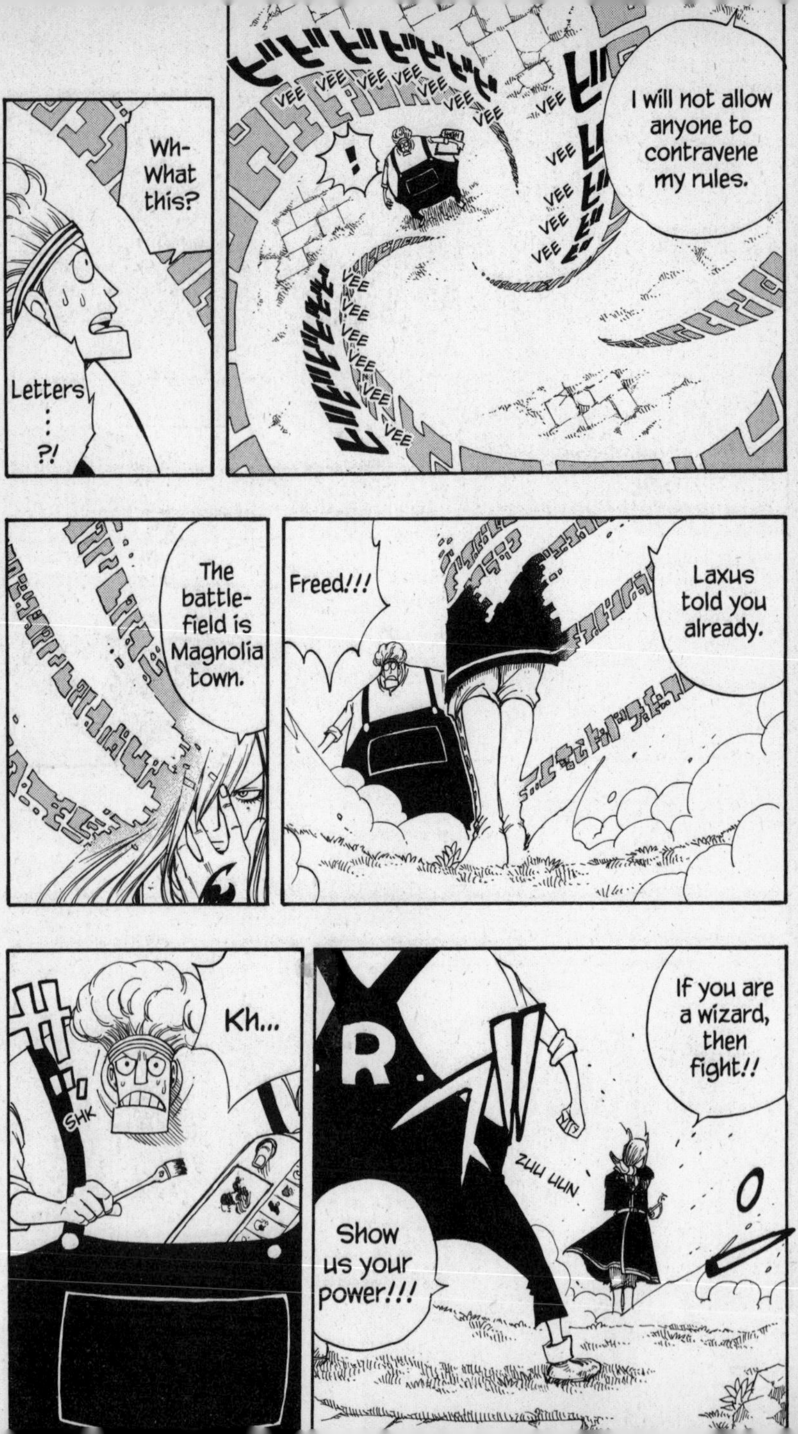

I will not allow anyone to contravene my rules.
VEE VEE VEE VEE VEE VEE VEE VEE
VEE VEE VEE VEE VEE
VEE VEE VEE VEE VEE VEE VEE VEE
Wh- What this?
Letters ... ?!
Laxus told you already.
Freed!!!
The battle-field is Magnolia town.
If you are a wizard, then fight!!
ZUU UUN
Show us your power!!!
Kh...
SHK

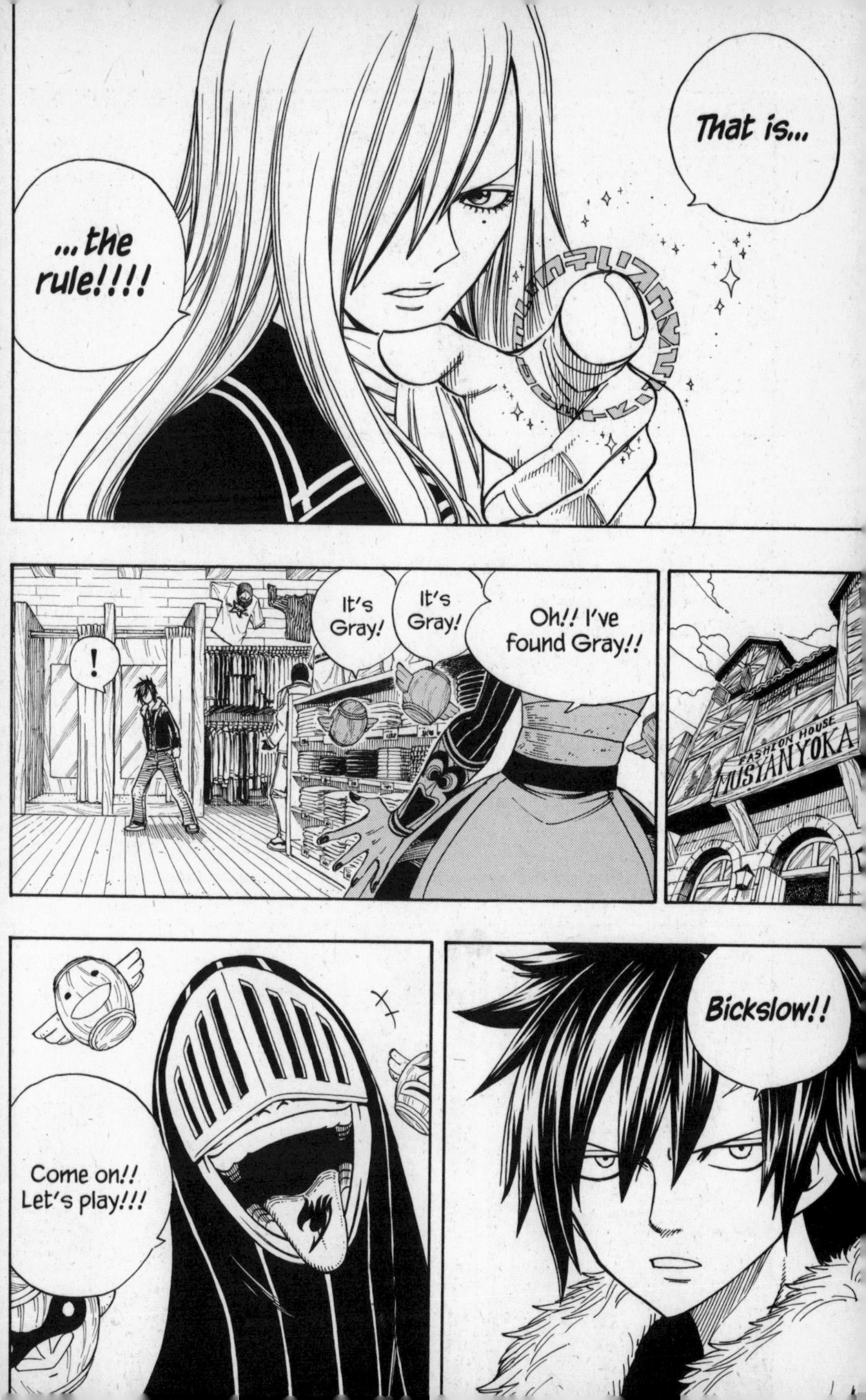
That is...
...the rule!!!!
FASHION HOUSE
MUSIANYOKA
Oh!! I've found Gray!!
It's Gray!
It's Gray!
!
Bickslow!!
Come on!! Let's play!!!

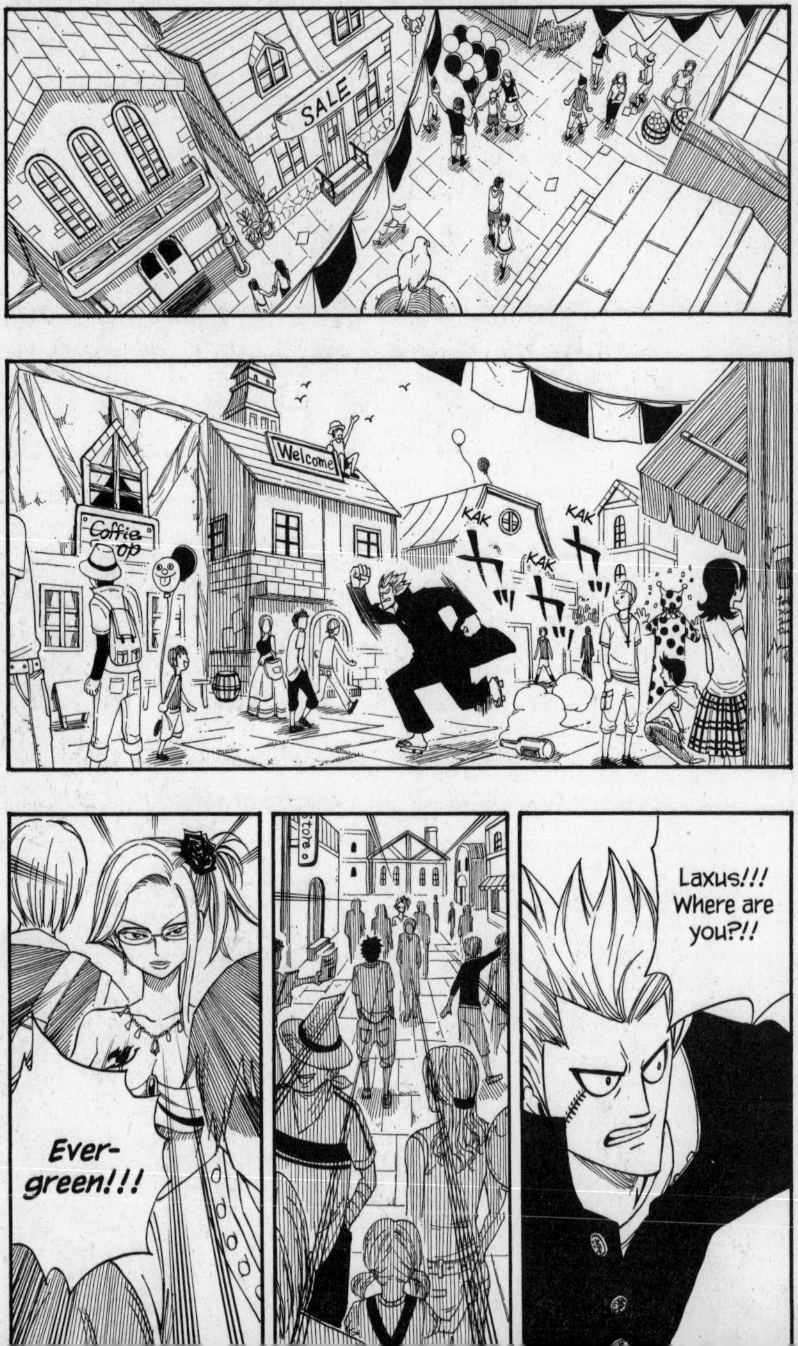
SALE
KAK
KAK
KAK
Welcome
Coffie
op
Laxus!!! Where are you?!!
Store
Ever-green!!!

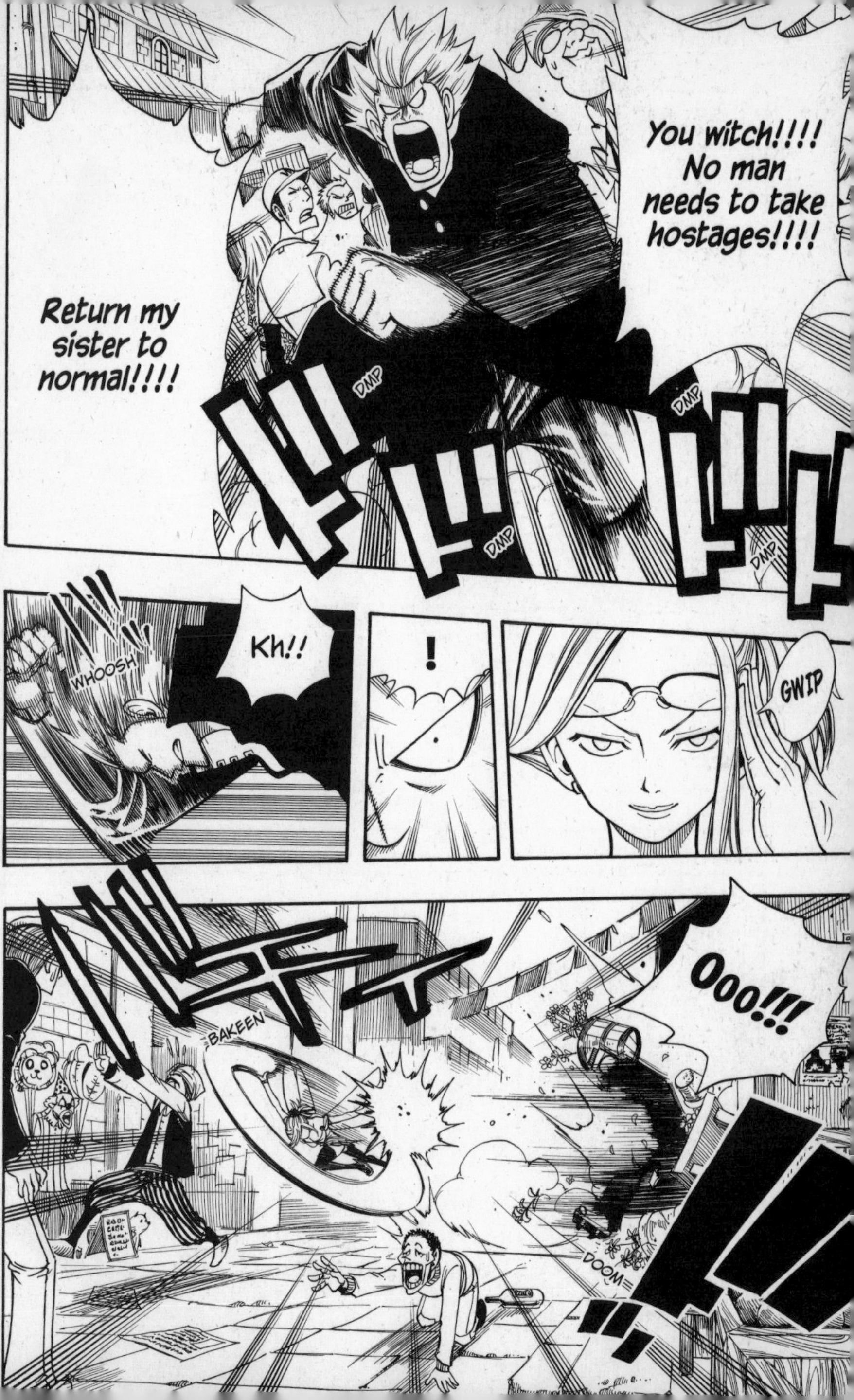
You witch!!!! No man needs to take hostages!!!!
Return my sister to normal!!!!
DMP
DMP
DMP
DMP
GWIP
!
Kh!!
WHOOSH
Ooo!!!
BAKEEN
DOOM

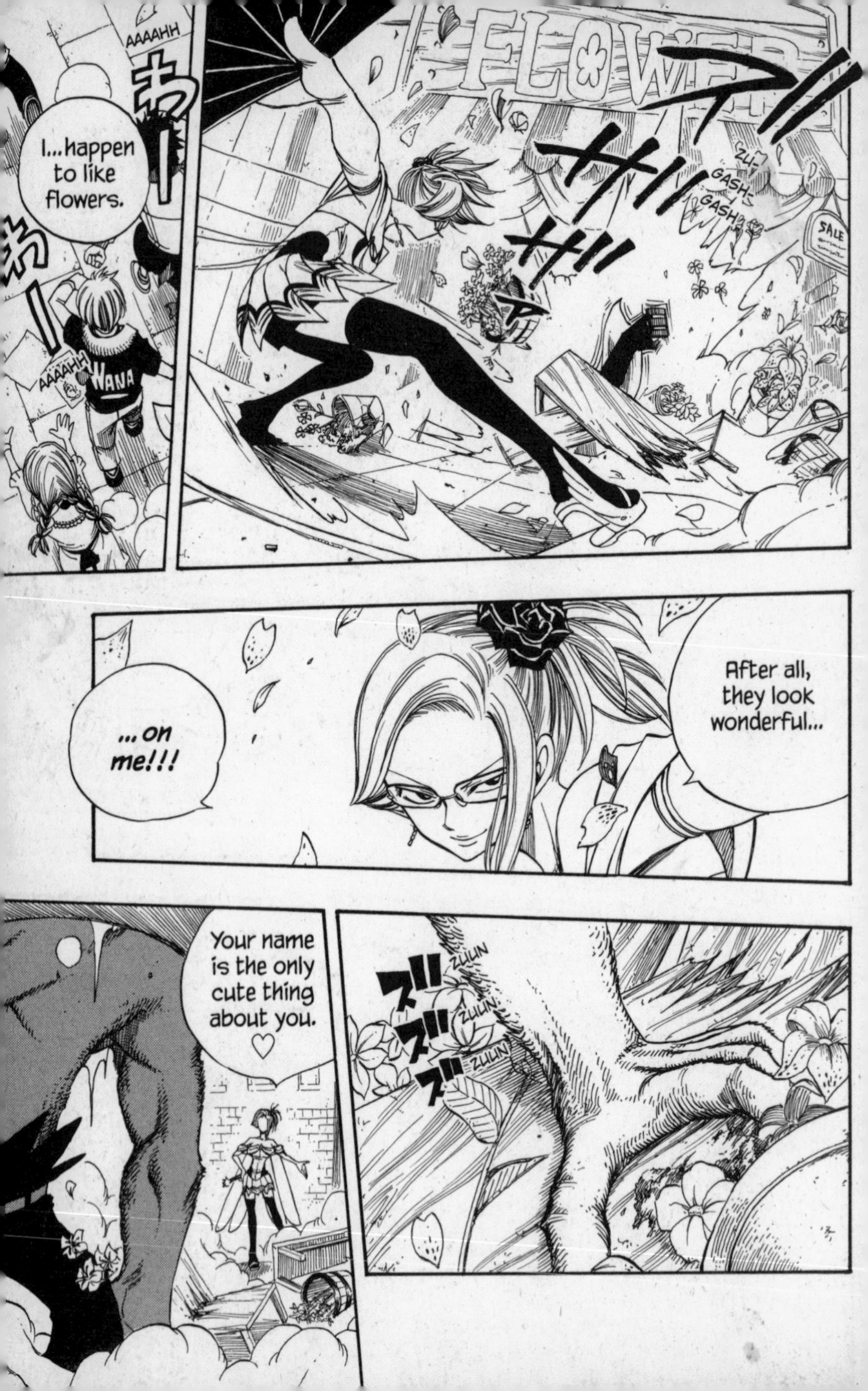
FLOW
ZU-GASH-GASH
SALE
AAAAHH
I...happen to like flowers.
AAAAHH
WANA
After all, they look wonderful...
...on me!!!
ZUUN
ZUUN
ZUUN
Your name is the only cute thing about you. ♡

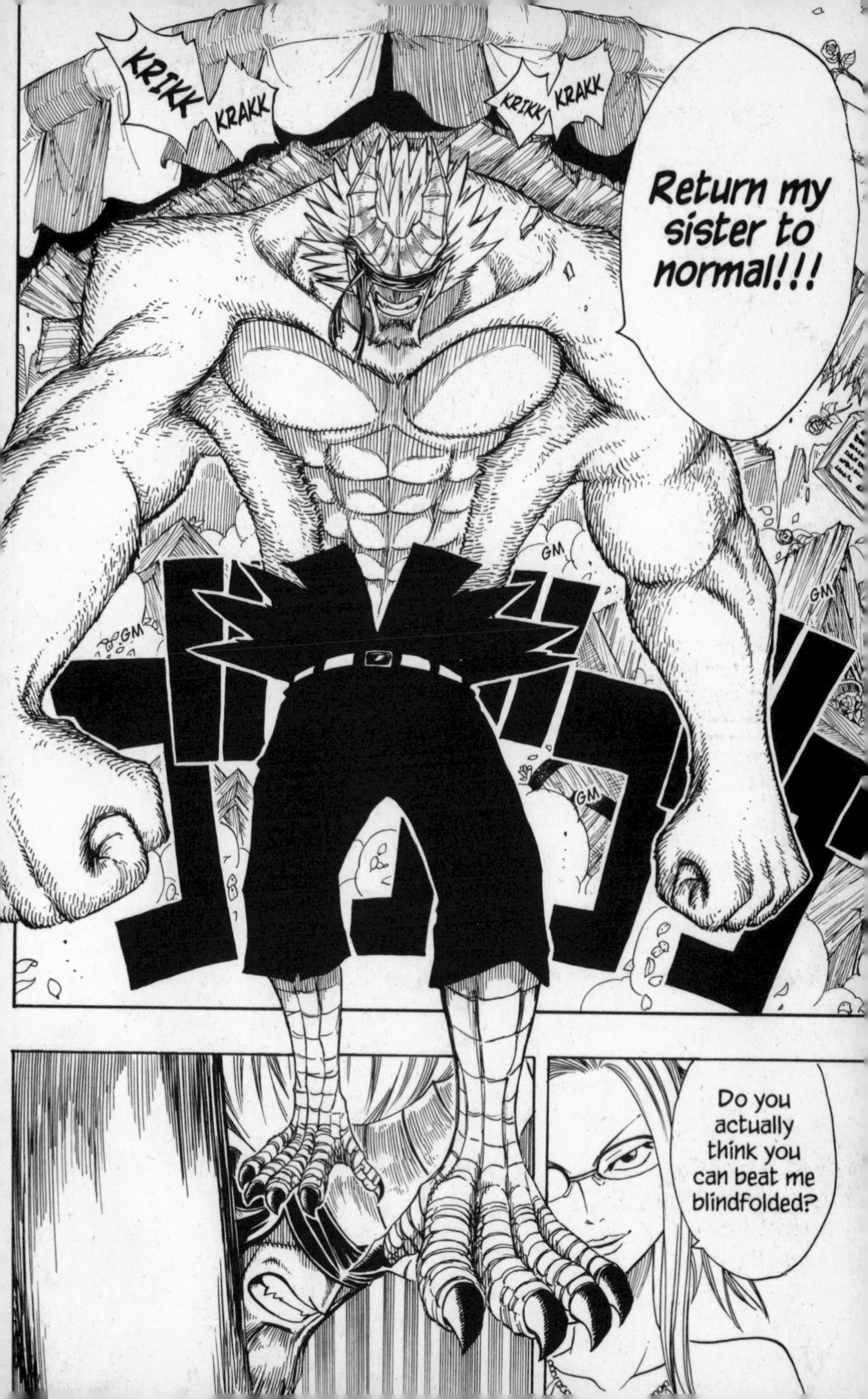
Return my sister to normal!!!
KRIKK KRAKK
KRIKK KRAKK
GM
GM
GM
GM
Do you actually think you can beat me blindfolded?

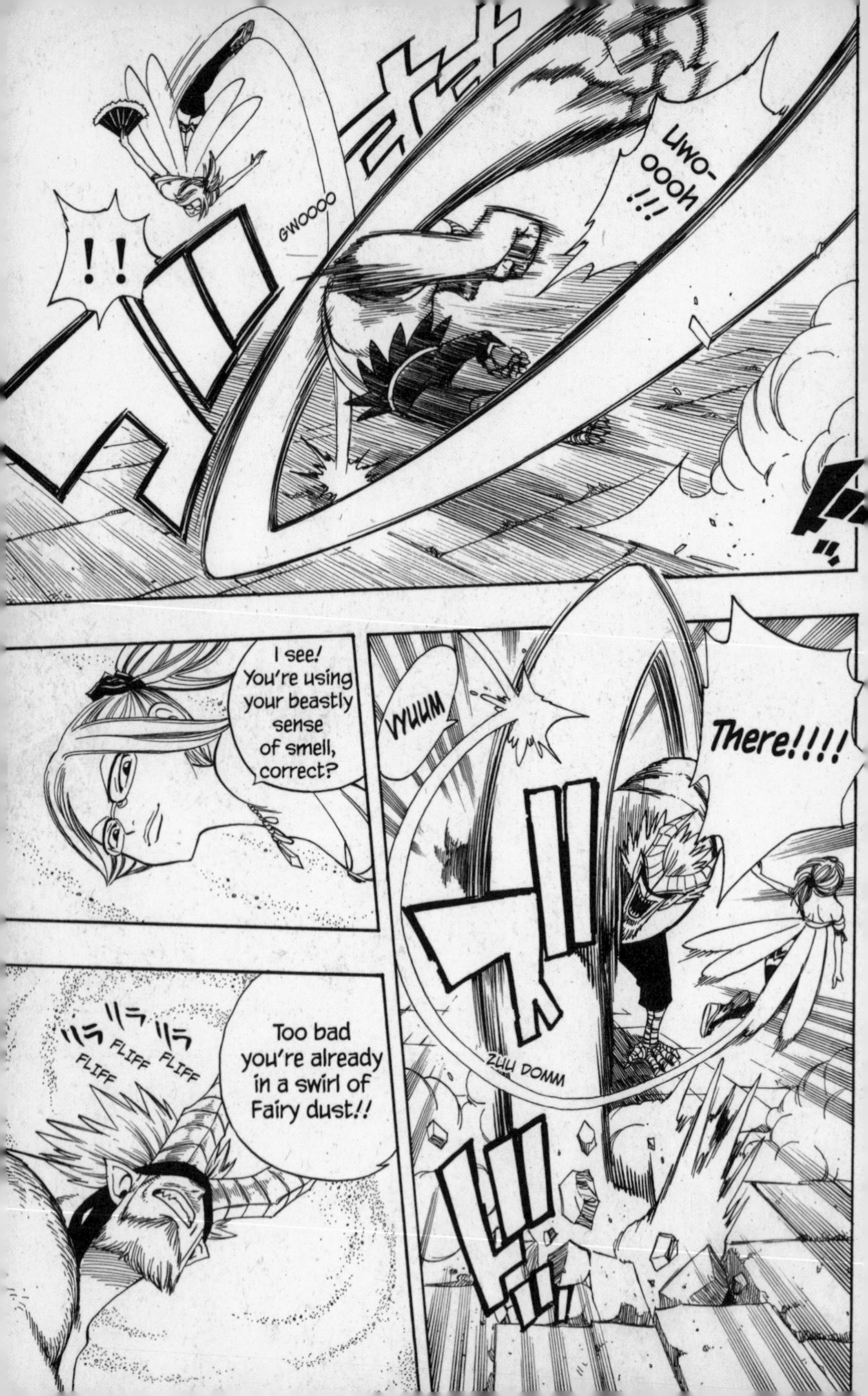
Uwo-oooh!!!
GWOOOO
!!
There!!!!
VYUUM
ZUU DOMM
I see! You're using your beastly sense of smell, correct?
Too bad you're already in a swirl of Fairy dust!!
FLIFF
FLIFF
FLIFF

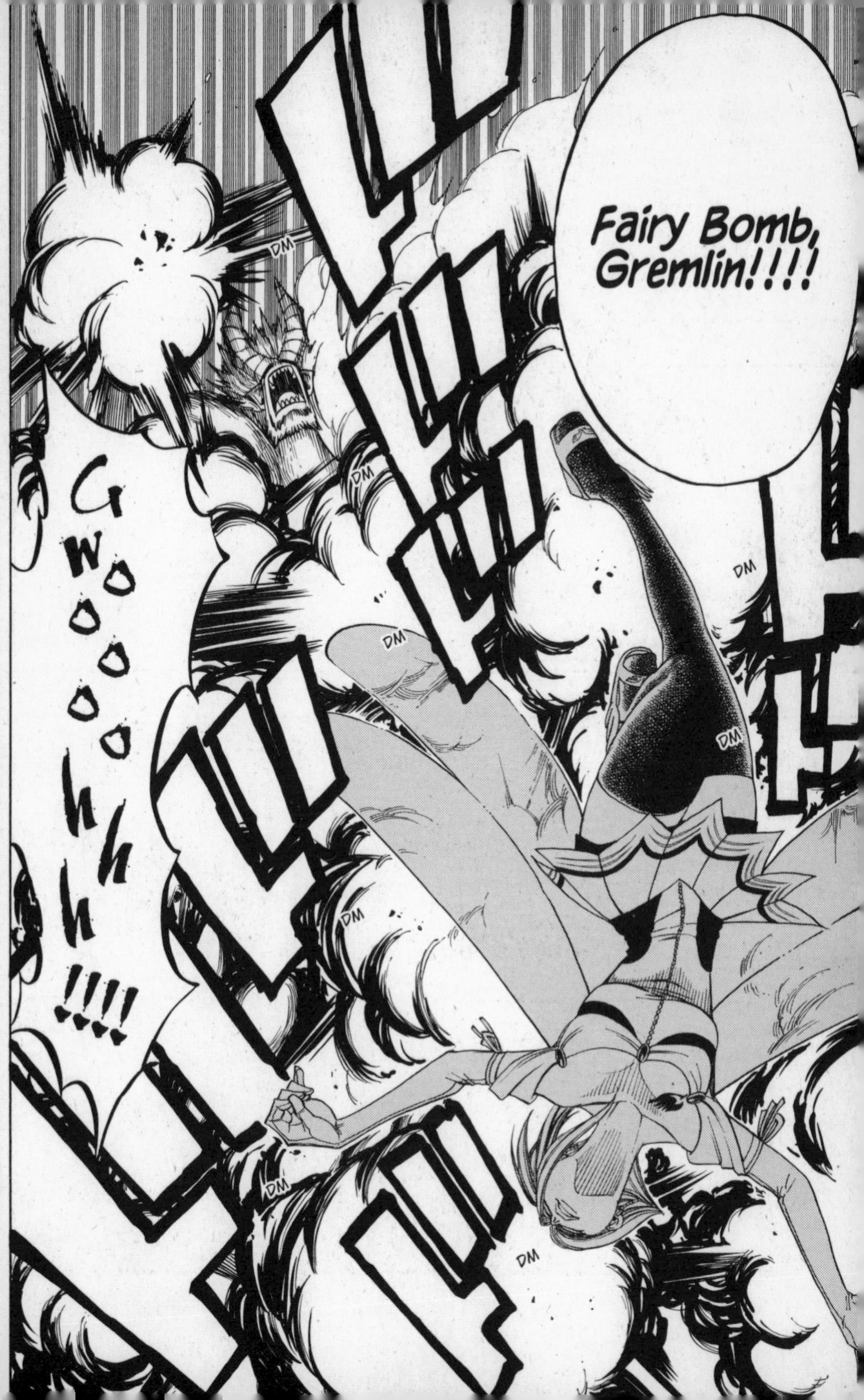
Fairy Bomb, Gremlin!!!!
Gwooooooohhhh!!!!

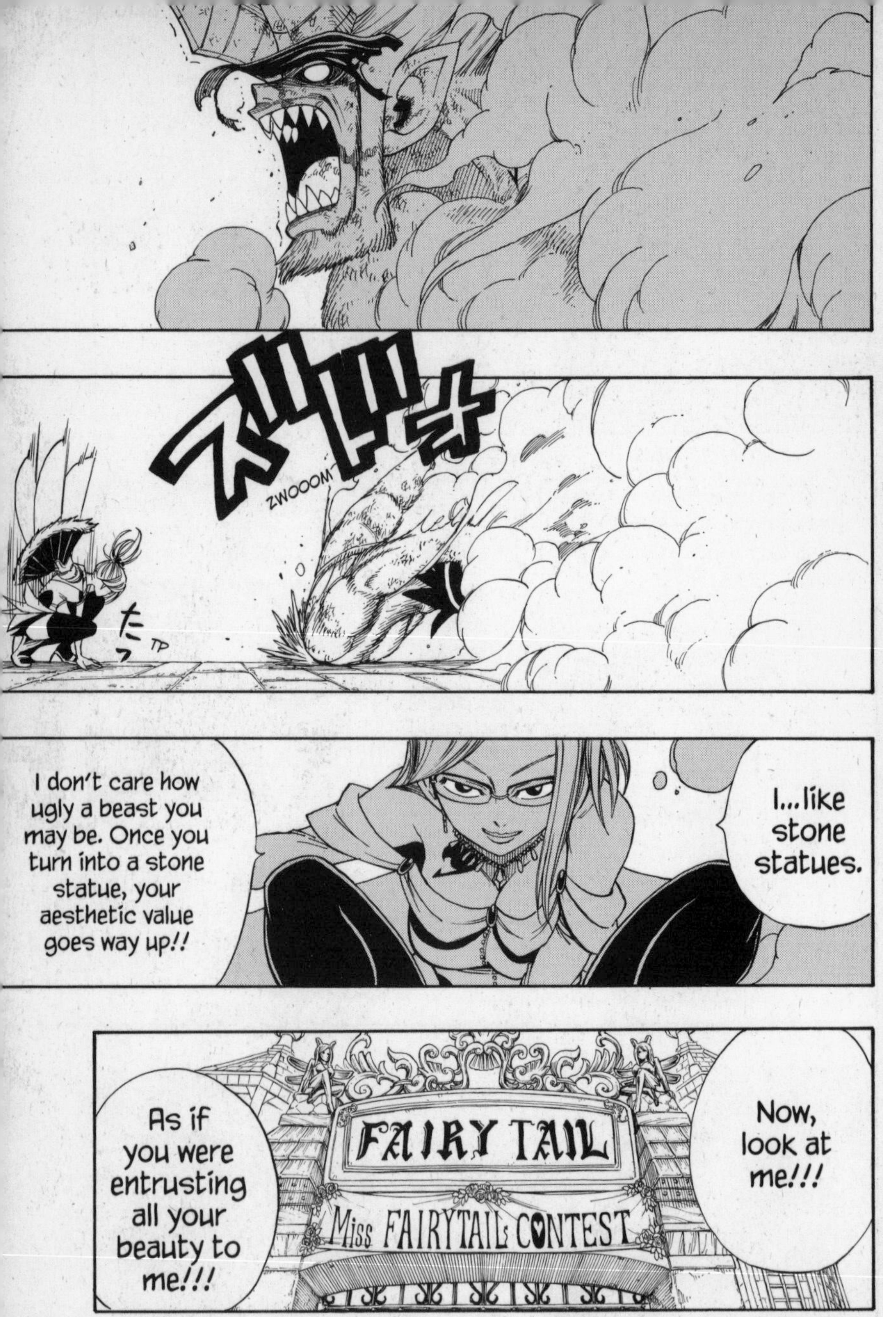
ズドォ
ZWOOOM
たっ
TP
I...like stone statues.
I don't care how ugly a beast you may be. Once you turn into a stone statue, your aesthetic value goes way up!!
Now, look at me!!!
FAIRY TAIL
Miss FAIRYTAIL CONTEST
As if you were entrusting all your beauty to me!!!

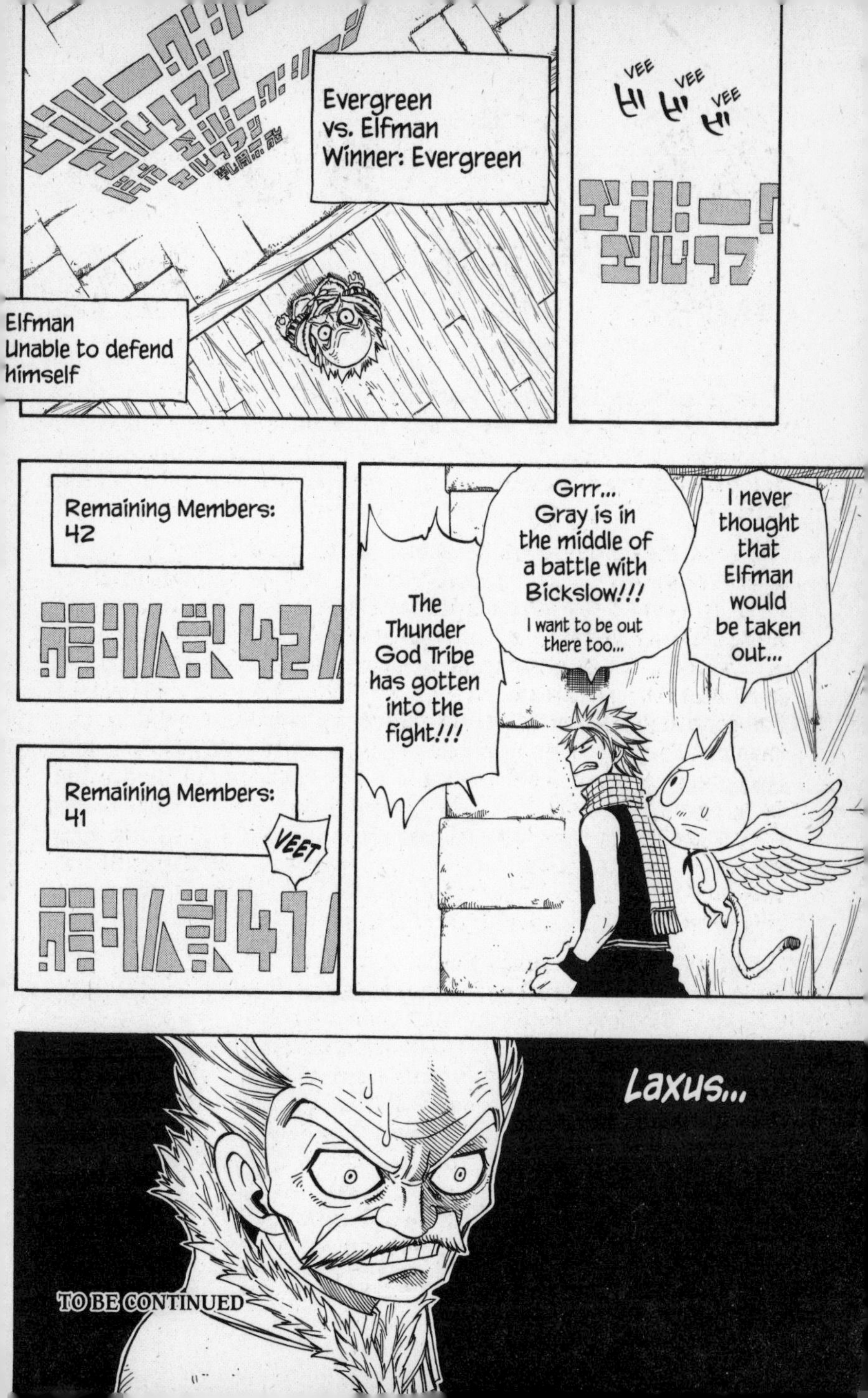
VEE VEE VEE
Evergreen vs. Elfman Winner: Evergreen
Elfman Unable to defend himself
I never thought that Elfman would be taken out...
Grrr... Gray is in the middle of a battle with Bickslow!!!
I want to be out there too...
The Thunder God Tribe has gotten into the fight!!!
Remaining Members: 42
Remaining Members: 41
VEET
Laxus...
TO BE CONTINUED

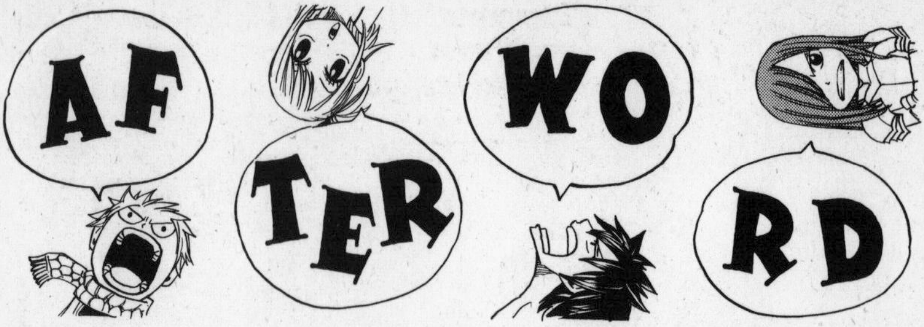
AF
TER
WO
RD

Last time, I wrote, "The Erza chapter is over!" But the real end was in this volume. (sweat sweat) I really liked the fireworks installment, if I do say so myself. Also, in that installment, I included somewhere in the crowd scenes, numbermen (people with numbers 1-8). Look for them when you have spare time!

Now the story enters the Laxus chapter, but this is another series that I just suddenly came up with. Actually, up to now, I was thinking of doing a completely different story arc, but just as I was doing the installment where Fairy Tail is featured in the magazine, I thought, hold on a second... If Laxus saw that article, wouldn't he get really angry at it? And little by little the present story line developed. And before I had gone much farther in my musings, bang!! I'm writing the Laxus chapter!! The plot twists were plot twists that just suddenly came to me (well, that's nothing new). The Harvest Festival and the Thunder God Tribe, they were all things I came up with during that installment. And the featured twist, how Natsu couldn't leave the Jutsu-Shiki-rule area!!! That was also decided as I was working on that one installment!! (I wonder if that's okay...?) And with everything else, there's the big plot twists coming in the next volume! (Look for them!)

Speaking of things I came up with, this volume also includes the new Fairy Tail, but I was working on those designs for weeks before that chapter. I had them down pat!! That is until it actually showed up, and then characters would appear and disappear from their places on a **whim,** and the **size** of the interiors would change bit by bit. (sweat sweat) Aww! Maybe I should say that I have corrected mistakes in the original designs, or even better, refined them to make them even better! When you look closely the size of the floorboards has changed as has the height of the ceiling little by little. Magic is certainly incredible, isn't it (let's just call it magic and leave it at that, huh?)! If you take off the slipcover of the Japanese version, you can see my guild designs!

B-But even so, the guild is a bit **big,** huh?

TAIL D'ART

The *Fairy Tail* Guild d'Art is an explosion of fan art! Please send in your black-and-white art on large postcard stock!! Those chosen to be published will get a signed mini poster!♪ Make sure you write your real name and address on the back of your postcard!

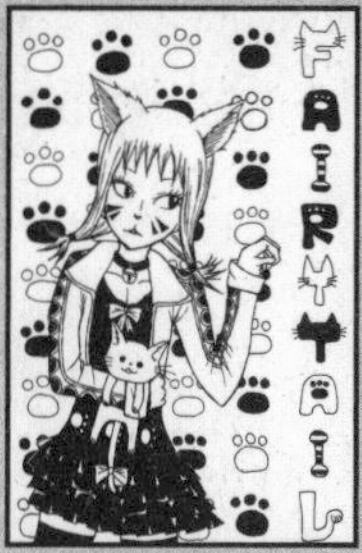

Gifu Prefecture, Nekôto-san

▼ Whoa! This has a lot of details in it! During the installment with the fireworks, I personally came to really like Millia.

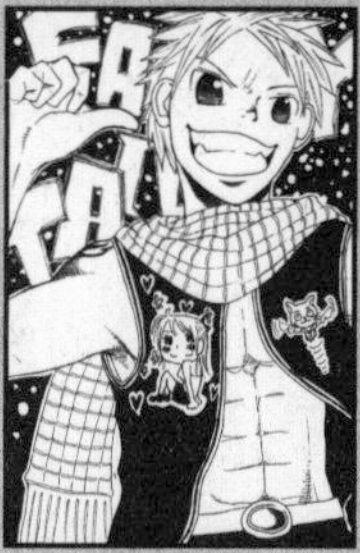

Yamagata Prefecture, Inumansee

▼ I really love these fun, high-energy pictures!!♥

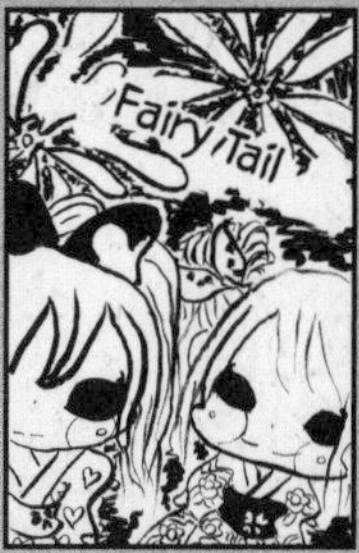
Fairy Tail

Kyoto, Ami Inoue

▼ Sort of "puny" versions of Lucy and Erza. It's really cute!

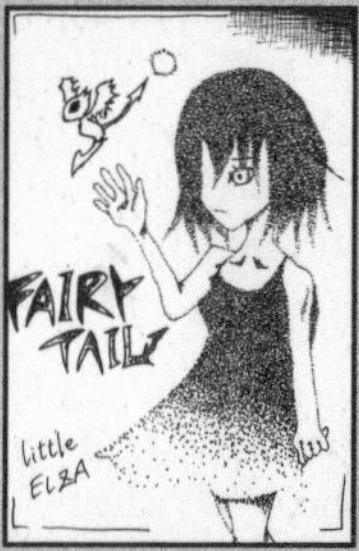
FAIRY TAIL
little ELZA

Saitama Prefecture, Lee

▼ Erza in pointillism! This kind of picture takes a lot of time to draw!!

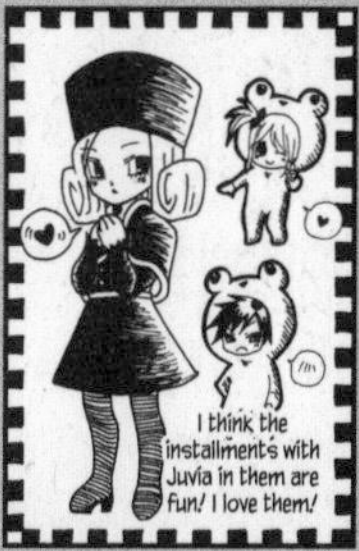
I think the installment's with Juvia in them are fun! I love them!

Hokaido, Helmet

▼ What a cute Juvia! Please continue to support her now that she's a FT member!

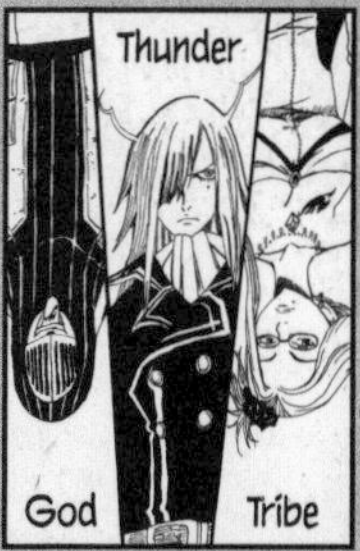
Thunder
God
Tribe

Tokyo, Reisuke Ogawa

▼ Very quickly, the first Thunder God Tribe image!! Which one will turn out to be the strongest?

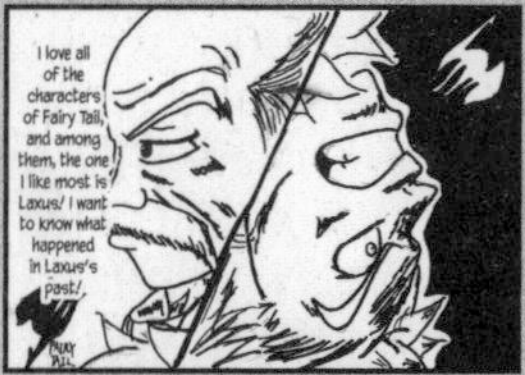
I love all of the characters of Fairy Tail, and among them, the one I like most is Laxus! I want to know what happened in Laxus's past!

Mie Prefecture, Yûsuke Kobayashi

▼ We've finally started the Laxus chapter! How will it play out?

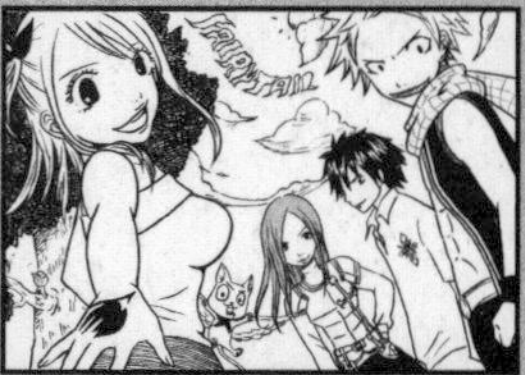

Hyogo Prefecture, Tomeo

▼ Now, here we go off on another job! Why don't you come along too? Everybody in one frame!

Send to DEL REY MANGA, Hiro Mashima, 1745 Broadway, New York, NY 10019, delreymanga@randomhouse.com*

*Del Rey Manga will make every effort to send your letters to Mashima, but cannot guarantee a response.

FAIRY GUILD

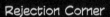

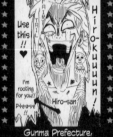

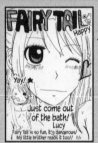

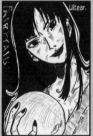

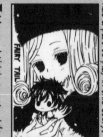

FAIRY TAIL

Tokushima Prefecture, Aoi Hyûga

▼ Recently Juvia's popularity has really taken off! I wonder if she has a part to play in this story?

FAIRY TAIL
Happy
Yay!
Just come out of the bath!
Lucy
Fairy Tail is so fun, it's dangerous! My little brother reads it too!!

Wakayama Prefecture, Ayana

▼ Mmm... I think somebody's figured out that I'm a sucker for sexy illustrations.

Rejection Corner

FAIRY TAIL
Use this!!
Hiro-kuuuuun!
I'm rooting for you!!
P-l-e-a-s-e!!
Hiro-san

Gunma Prefecture, Haruji Uchida

▲ S-Scary... I'm going to put it in because it scares me...

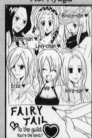

Bisca-san
Cana-san
Levy-chan
Erza
Me
Mira-san
FAIRY TAIL
To the guild. You're the best!!

Nagasaki Prefecture, Yumemi-zuki

▼ Miss Fairy Tail! Who won it anyway?

Ultear.
FAIRY TAIL

Aomori Prefecture, KID

▼ Now she's turned out to be a baddie, huh? I tend to like slightly twisted art like this.

Any letters and post cards you send means that your personal information such as your name, address, postal code, and other information you include will be handed over, as is, to the author. When you send mail, please keep that in mind.

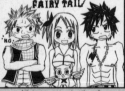

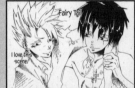

Fairy Tail
I love this scene!

Niigata Prefecture, Raiki

▼ A very old, nostalgic scene. Did everyone notice the one place in this volume where Lyon shows up?

FAIRY TAIL
NG

(Taiwan, Wu Yu-Tong)

▼ Art from a foreign country! Thanks to everybody sending art from across the seas!!

Translation Notes

Japanese is a tricky language for most Westerners, and translation is often more art than science. For your edification and reading pleasure, here are notes on some of the places where we could have gone in a different direction in our translation of the work, or where a Japanese cultural reference is used.

Names

Hiro Mashima has graciously agreed to provide official English spellings for just about all of the characters in Fairy Tail. Because this version of Fairy Tail is the first publication of most of these spellings, there will inevitably be differences between these spellings and some of the fan interpretations that may have spread throughout the web or in other fan circles. Rest assured that what is contained in this book are the spellings that Mashima-sensei wanted for *Fairy Tail*.

Wizard

In the original Japanese version of Fairy Tail, there are occasional images where the word "Wizard" is found. This translation has taken that as it's inspiration, and translated the word *madôshi* as wizard. But *madôshi*'s meaning is similar to certain Japanese words that have been borrowed into the English language such as judo (the soft way) and kendo (the way of the sword). *Madô* is the way of magic, and *madôshi* are those who follow the way of magic. So although the word "wizard" is used, the Japanese would think less of traditional western wizards such as Merlin or Gandalf, and more of martial artists.

Night Festivals, page 23

A Japanese Summer tradition are night markets and night festivals. These are usually a bunch of small stalls set up on the grounds of a local temple, shrine, park, or other public place, that sell foods, souvenirs, or chances to play midway-style games. The markets/festivals are usually in connection with some local or religious celebration, but they can also take place without any special connection to outside events. Often women go to these markets or festivals in elaborately decorated light cotton kimono called *yukata*. Men can also go in more subdued *yukata*, however western dress is more common for male attendees.

Welcome back, page 46

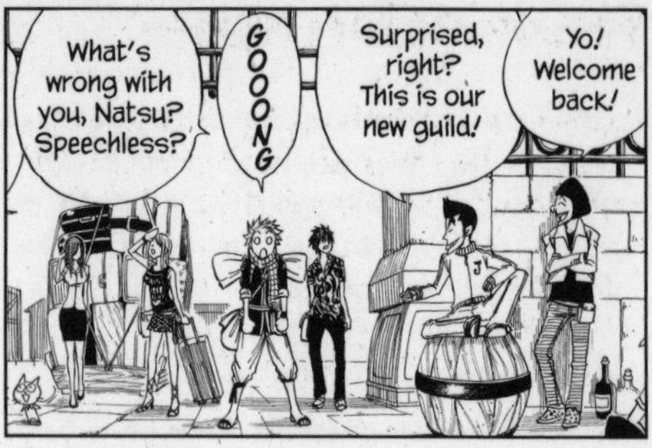
Yo! Welcome back!
Surprised, right? This is our new guild!
GOOOONG
What's wrong with you, Natsu? Speechless?

There are a number of standard Japanese phrases, and *okaeri-nasai* (or *okaeri* for short) is one of the most used. It means "welcome back" to a home, place of business, or any place that a person can feel he/she belongs. A guild is one such place, so when Natsu, Lucy and the others return to Fairy Tail, all of their guildmates start by saying "welcome back." The traditional response to this is *tadaima* meaning "just now" but is a shortened version of *tadaima kaerimashita*, "I have just now returned."

Cast-off figure, page 47

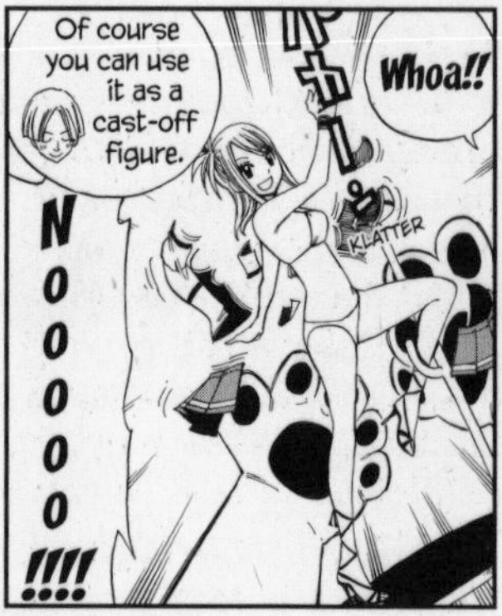
Whoa!!
Of course you can use it as a cast-off figure.
NOOOOOO!!!!
KLATTER

Leave it to the hardcore culture of Akihabara otaku to create (or at least embrace) any trend that makes it possible to undress their favorite female anime characters. Cast-off is a pun referring not only to the fact that the figure's plastic clothing can be cast off the figure, but since PVC figures are injection molded (or "cast") some of the "castings" can come off the figure.

Jason, page 69

Jason is based on the author of Manga the Complete Guide, Jason Thompson. Jason interviewed Mashima-sensei when he came to the San Diego Comic-Con in 2008, and Mashima-sensei was so impressed by Jason's energy and enthusiasm that directly after the interview, he decided to put Jason's character into Fairy Tail. Of course, the Fairy Tail version Jason is somewhat more animated than the real person, but...

Moe, page 77

Moe is a Japanese word that comes from the verb *moeru* which means "to bud" as in a flowerbud. It refers to young girls who display a naive innocence, but also a certain eagerness for new experiences (too-old or too-mature characters are not considered *moe*). The *moe* idea has been adopted by idols, maid cafes, certain types of manga and anime, and other cute-girl otaku-oriented goods and services to indicate a very energetic and cute attitude. In the middle 2000s, it was estimated that *moe* goods and services accounted for a third of all the overall otaku market, but that number has been reported to be declining as the fad wears off.

Dallas, page 87

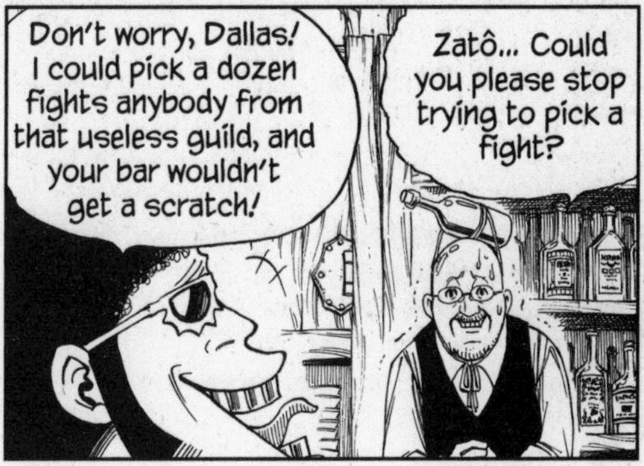
Zatô... Could you please stop trying to pick a fight?
Don't worry, Dallas! I could pick a dozen fights anybody from that useless guild, and your bar wouldn't get a scratch!

The hapless bartender, Dallas, is based on Random House's chief manga man, Dallas Middaugh, who became friends with Mashima-sensei during the 2008 San Diego Comic-Con. Just so you know, I have known Dallas for quite some time, and I have never seen him wear a liquor bottle on his head in real life. (But one can always hope!)

Nosebleed, page 134

A nosebleed is a standard manga/anime trope that indicates a sexually immature brain that is subject to a huge rise in blood pressure at the mere sight of a beautiful or sexy woman.

Goth-loli, page 138

The Gothic Lolita style of dress mixes the feminine frills of the Victorian or Rococo styles (Lolita style) with the heavy makeup and dark, macabre blacks and crimsons of the Gothic style. It was popularized by Mana, formerly of the popular band Malice Miser. The goth-loli style can be most frequently seen among the cosplayers who congregate in the Harajuku section of Tokyo on Sunday afternoons.

Cheer Dance, page 139

A cheer dance is what one sees in cheerleading competitions as popularized in the 2000 film Bring It On. Although cheerleading as a sport began in the U.S., and most of its practitioners are American, teams from Japan have come to the U.S. to win major competitions at both the high-school and college level.

Jutsu-Shiki, page 157

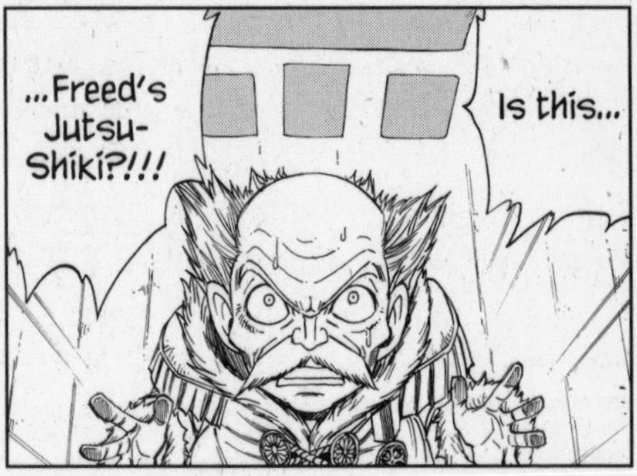
Is this...
...Freed's Jutsu-Shiki?!!!

The *kanji* that make up Freed's magic are *jutsu*, which means "technique" as in a martial art's technique, and *shiki* which is a *kanji* used for both to mean "ceremony" or "style." *Jutsu-Shiki* seems to be based on the Japanese Buddhist and Shinto practices of hanging paper with written incantations (such as sutras) on doorways or other objects to ward-off disasters, evil spirits, etc. However, unlike present Buddhist and Shinto wards which are made of paper, the *Jutsu-Shiki* wards are made of nothing more than magical techniques.

Names of Fan Artists, page 190-191

A little-known fact about the Japanese language is, if people's names are listed only in *kanji* (as they are in Guild de Art), no one but a person who is acquainted with the owner of the name knows with absolute certainty how the name is pronounced. Unlike in most other Asian languages, *kanji* in Japanese have multiple pronunciations. As an example, the *kanji* meaning "down" can be pronounced ka, ge, shimo, shita, moto, shi, ji, kuda, and ori (and probably a few more beyond that). Very commonly used names are relatively easy to make a correct guess as to the pronunciation, but unusual names or pennames can become very problematic. To avoid this confusion, Japanese official forms all have a location where one must write in a pronunciation guide to tell those processing the paperwork how one's name is pronounced. So, keeping this in mind, please remember that we do our best to make accurate representations of the names in the fan-art section, but a good many are best guesses, and some may turn out to be inaccurate.

About the Creator

HIRO MASHIMA was born May 3, 1977, in the Nagano prefecture. His series *Rave Master* has made him one of the most popular manga artists in America. *Fairy Tail*, currently being serialized in *Weekly Shōnen Magazine*, is his latest creation.

Preview of Volume 14

We're pleased to present you with a preview from volume 14. Please check our website (www.delreymanga.com) to see when this volume will be available in English. For now you'll have to make do with Japanese!

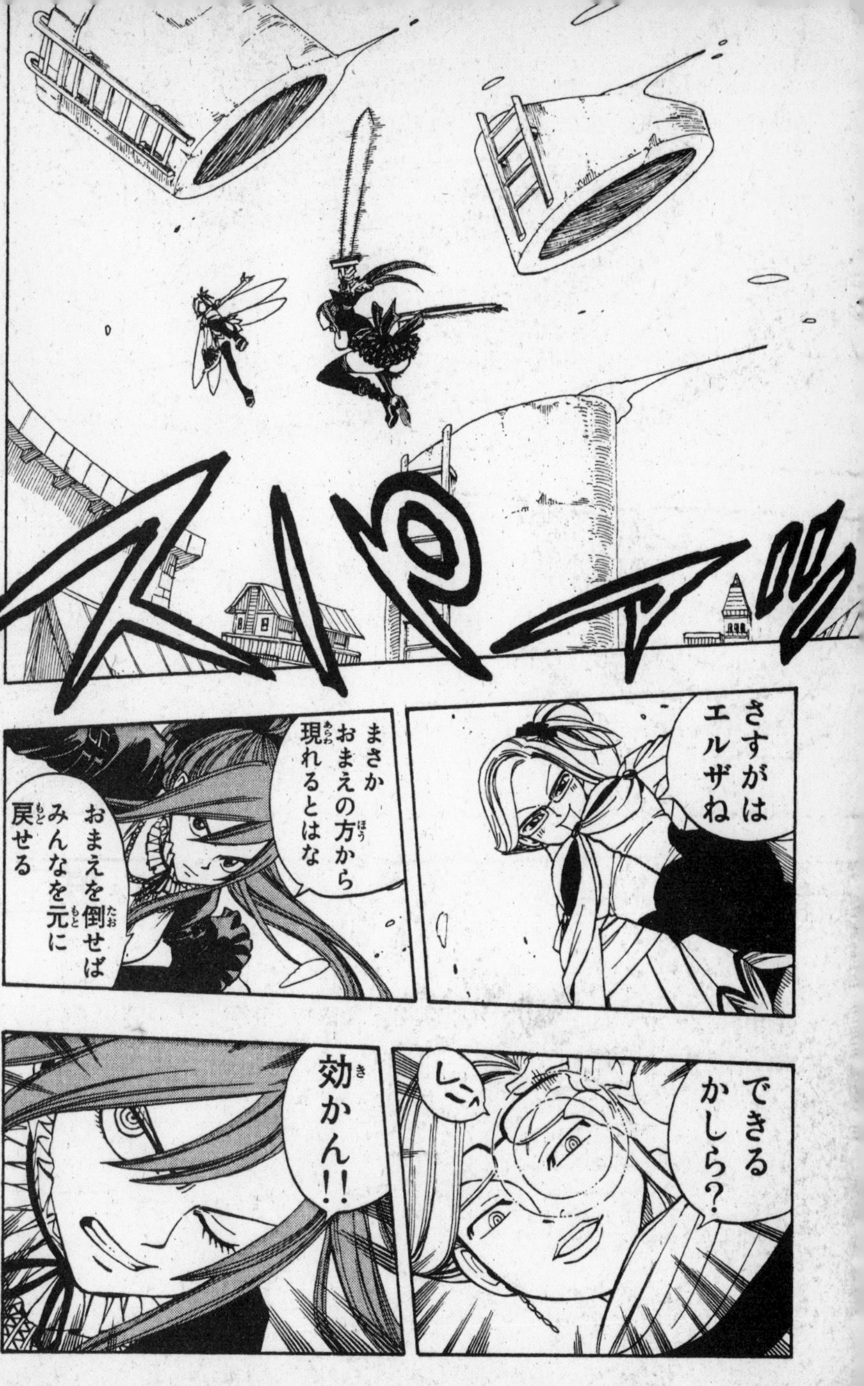
スパァッ
さすがは エルザね
まさか おまえの方から 現れるとはな
おまえを倒せば みんなを元に 戻せる
できる かしら?
効かん!!

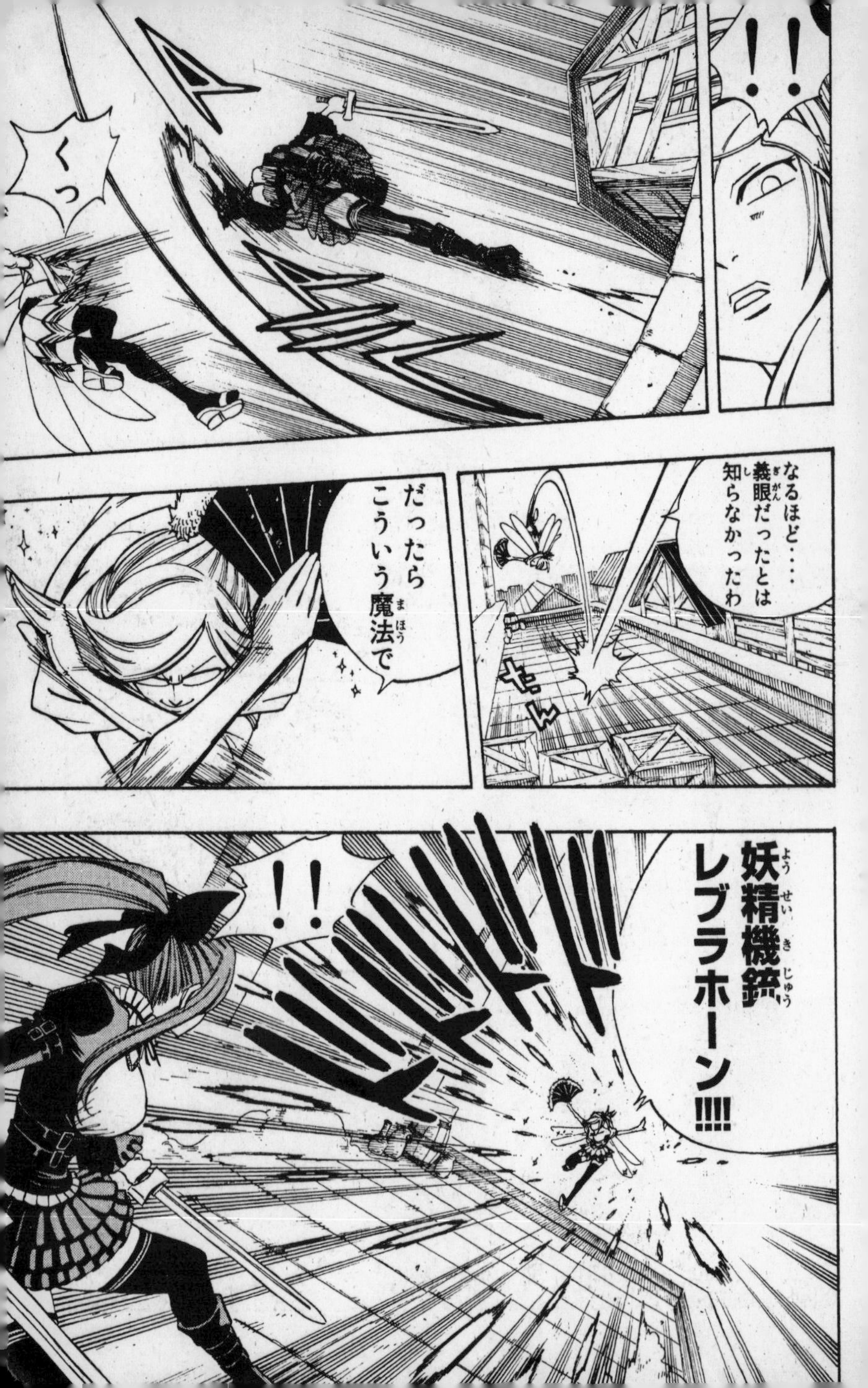
!!
くっ
なるほど…義眼だったとは知らなかったわ
だったらこういう魔法で
妖精機銃レプラホーン!!!!
!!

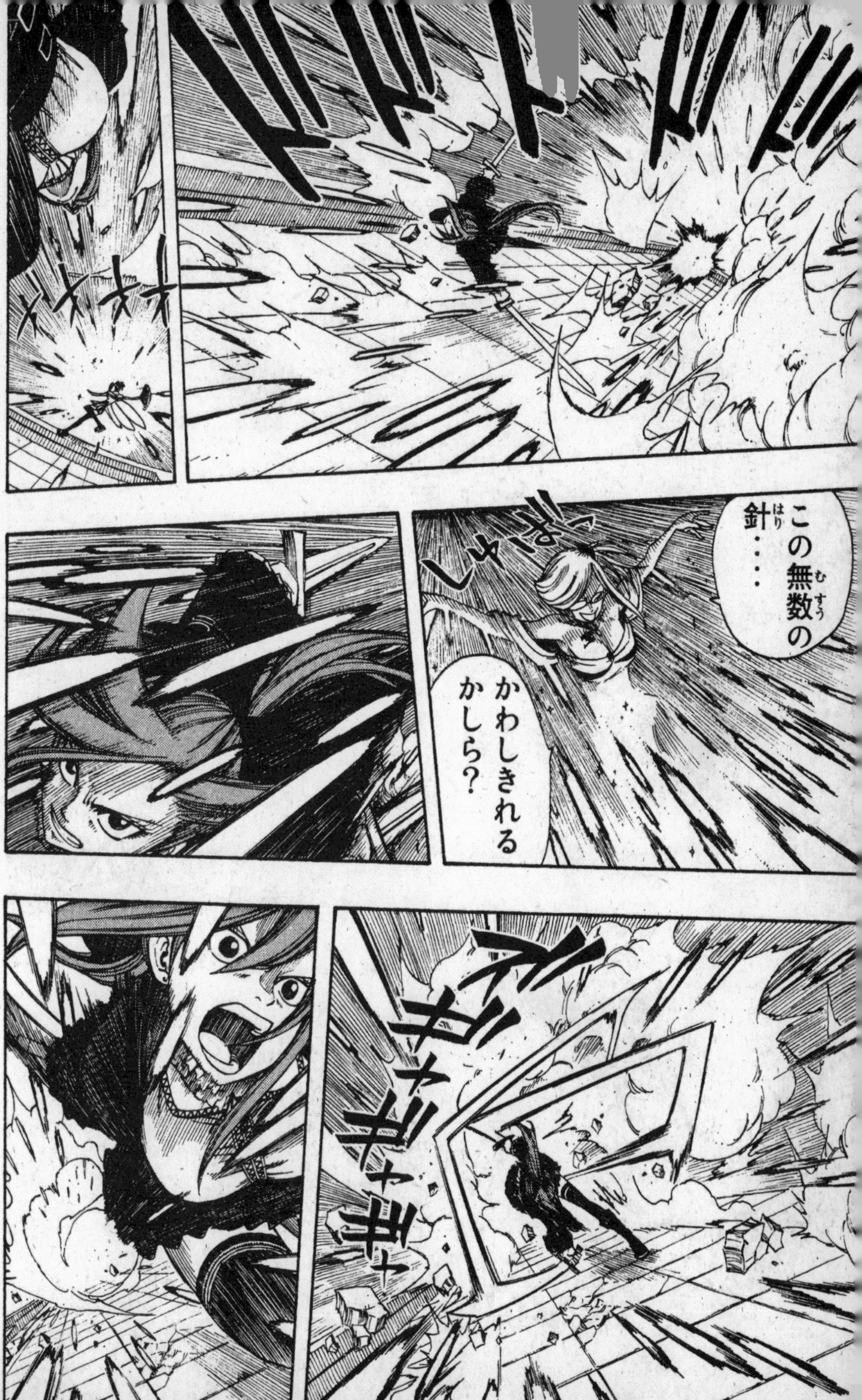
この無数の針・・・・
かわしきれるかしら?

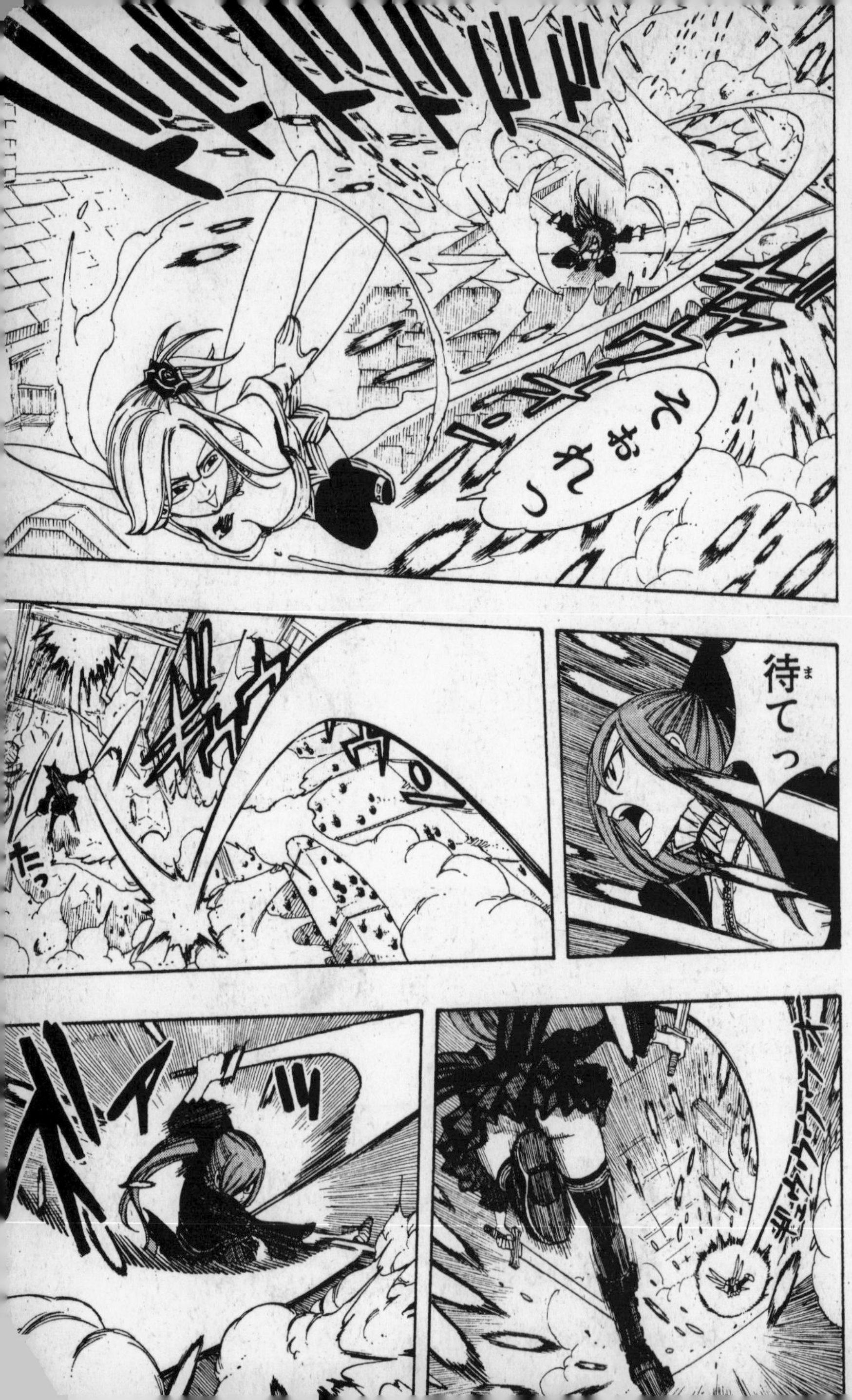
そおれっ
待てっ
たっ

TOMARE! 止まれ

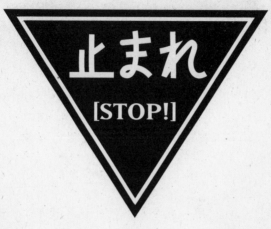

止まれ

[STOP!]

You're going the wrong way!

Manga is a completely different type of reading experience.

To start at the *beginning*, go to the *end*!

That's right! Authentic manga is read the traditional Japanese way—from right to left, exactly the *opposite* of how American books are read. It's easy to follow: Just go to the other end of the book and read each page—and each panel—from right side to left side, starting at the top right. Now you're experiencing manga as it was meant to be!